D1265751

Human Resource Management in Sport and Recreation

Packianathan Chelladurai, PhD

School of Physical Activity and Educational Services

The Ohio State University

Human Kinetics

Library of Congress Cataloging-in-Publication Data

Chelladurai, P.
   Human resource management in sport and recreation / Packianathan
Chelladurai.
      p.   cm.
   Includes bibliographical references (p.) and index.
   ISBN 0-87322-973-8
   1. Sport administration.   2. Personnel management.   I. Title.
   GV713.C5   1999
   796'.06'93--DC21   98-37051
                                                                    CIP

ISBN: 0-87322-973-8

Copyright © 1999 by Packianathan Chelladurai

Permission notices for material reprinted in this book from other sources can be found on page xii.

Developmental Editor: Julie A. Marx; **Assistant Editors:** Laura Ward Majersky, Bob Replinger, and Kim Thoren; **Copyeditor:** Elizabeth Harbison; **Indexer:** Craig Brown; **Graphic Designer:** Nancy Rasmus; **Graphic Artist:** Tara Welsch; **Cover Designer:** Jack Davis; **Illustrator:** Terry N. Hayden; **Printer:** Edwards Brothers

Printed in the United States of America   10 9 8 7 6 5 4 3 2 1

Human Kinetics
Web site: http://www.humankinetics.com/

United States: Human Kinetics
P.O. Box 5076
Champaign, IL 61825-5076
1-800-747-4457
e-mail: humank@hkusa.com

Canada: Human Kinetics
475 Devonshire Road Unit 100
Windsor, ON N8Y 2L5
1-800-465-7301 (in Canada only)
e-mail: humank@hkcanada.com

Europe: Human Kinetics
P.O. Box IW14
Leeds LS16 6TR, United Kingdom
(44) 1132 781708
e-mail: humank@hkeurope.com

Australia: Human Kinetics
57A Price Avenue
Lower Mitcham, South Australia 5062
(088) 277 1555
e-mail: humank@hkaustralia.com

New Zealand: Human Kinetics
P.O. Box 105-231
Auckland 1
(09) 523 3462
e-mail: humank@hknewz.com

To Ponnu, the manager who has made the best
use of the available human resources and has knit
them into a fine family

Contents

Preface

Sport organizations and their managers are concerned with several issues relating to their operations. Of these issues, the management of human resources takes a center stage for several reasons. First, as emphasized in total quality management, the source of all quality is the human resource engaged in the production of goods and services. This view is particularly true in the case of services in which the production and consumption occur at the interface of the clients and employees, who are the human resources of the organization. Because most sport organizations produce services, management of human resources is a critical concern of sport managers. An understanding of the dynamics of human resources and their management is necessary to be an effective manager.

I have been teaching management of human resources in sport and recreation for more than two decades. In these years, I have been assigning a set of readings for the courses because of the lack of a comprehensive text to cover the subject. Because these readings were drawn from several disparate sources, such as texts and journal articles from the diverse fields of business administration, sport psychology, and sport sociology, they did not present a coherent picture of the concepts studied. In this text, I attempt to present a clear and concise treatise on the critical aspects of management of human resources within sport and recreation organizations.

The systemic theme of the book is to bring into focus the three divergent groups of people who constitute the human resources in sport and recreation organizations (i.e., the paid professional workers, the volunteer workers, and the clients themselves) and to match managerial processes with individual differences among the three types of human resources. I have limited the selection and treatment of individual difference and organizational process variables to those that impinge on individual motivation and performance within the context of sport and recreation organizations.

I have organized the book into four parts and have included an introduction and conclusion. In the introduction, I describe consumer, professional, and human services and emphasize the importance of volunteer workers and the clients themselves as human resources. I also provide a model of human resource management to highlight the organization of the book.

Part I outlines the unique and common characteristics of the three sets of human resources: the volunteer workers, the paid professional workers, and the clients. In chapter 1, I discuss volunteerism, volunteers, and volunteer organizations and give an explanation of the concepts of altruism and volunteer incentives. In chapter 2, I describe the attributes of professions and professionals and emphasize that the concept of professionalism is applicable to any occupation irrespective of its status as a profession. Chapter 3 emphasizes the clients and customers as one set of human resources because their participation and involvement is necessary for the production of sport services.

Part II focuses on differences among people and how they affect behavior in sport organizations. In chapter 4, I describe the nature of cognitive and psychomotor abilities and their relevance to sport and recreation management. Chapter 5 covers personality traits and their impact on behavior in sport and recreation organizations. I discuss the nature of personal values and their influence on attitudes and behaviors in chapter 6. The processes of individual motivation and their implications are the focus of chapter 7.

In part III, I describe significant organizational processes in the management of human resources. In chapter 8, I describe attributes of a job and their effects on motivation, the concept of job enrichment, and methods of coordination among jobs. In chapter 9 I discuss job analysis, job description, and job specification as preliminary steps in recruitment, hiring, and training. This chapter also includes a discussion of the concept of career from the perspectives of the individual and the organization. The importance of leadership that sport managers provide is the focus of chapter 10, which also includes a description of relevant theories of leadership. Chapter 11 covers the purposes and processes of evaluating individual performances and the pitfalls associated with performance appraisal. I discuss the types and bases of reward systems that can be instituted in sport and recreation organizations in chapter 12. In chapter 13, I describe the concepts of organizational justice and its components of distributive, procedural, and interactional justice, and I describe the methods of enhancing these in sport organizations.

Part IV covers two significant outcomes expected of human resource practices. Chapter 14 describes significant theories of satisfaction and discusses components of satisfaction of paid and volunteer workers and of clients. The importance of commitment to both the organization and the occupation are the focus of chapter 15.

Finally, as a synthesis of the information from the previous chapters, I present a set of founding and guiding themes. These themes focus on the products and the people in our field, the purposes of human resource management, empowerment, organizational justice, and reward systems.

Each chapter begins with a listing of the learning objectives for the chapter to help the reader. I also have included elements "In a Nutshell" to summarize the material covered up to that point. The chapters are interspersed with sections entitled "In Their View" to highlight significant statements from scholars and experts related to the topic at hand. Some of these statements present viewpoints that are opposed to the one stressed in the text and that facilitate a healthy discussion on the topic. At the end of each chapter, I have listed key terms that readers may use to review their understanding of the chapter's content. I have also provided several

questions at the end of each chapter under the heading "Your Perspectives." In a classroom setting, discussion of the questions will help students understand the content of the chapter. It also permits the teacher to present other perspectives on the topic of the chapter.

The most obvious audience of this text comprises the students in sport and recreation management, which encompasses physical education, athletics, campus recreation, and community recreation. Further, teachers of coaching courses also may find most of the content of the book relevant to their courses. These management areas face the same, or similar, contingencies and have to work with the three types of human resources. Readers will find the content of the book straightforward. Teachers will have the flexibility to choose or emphasize specific chapters and to introduce their own material to supplement the book.

Finally, the content and organization of this book are born out of my insights and experiences from two decades of teaching the subject. My own training in both physical education and management science coupled with feedback from the vast number of undergraduate and graduate students have contributed to the distillation of the content. Obviously, the theories presented, the references cited, and the position taken are a reflection of my own preferences and biases. This orientation provides the opportunity for the teachers to bring up views and theories that run counter to those expressed in this text. That kind of discourse is vital for the advancement of the field.

Acknowledgments

The publication of this text is the culmination of long and arduous work sprinkled with moments of joy as well as frustration. However, several individuals and institutions who have been instrumental to my growth and development have reinforced the effort and success.

I am forever indebted to Earle Zeigler and Garth Paton for introducing me to the field of sport management, expressing confidence in my abilities, and providing continued support for all of my academic efforts. I am also grateful to Bert Carron who taught me the "ropes" of research.

The University of Western Ontario and The Ohio State University have provided the institutional base and support to facilitate my academic endeavor. I am particularly grateful to Dorothy Zakrajsek, who recruited me to The Ohio State University.

Over the years, a countless number of undergraduate and graduate students have critiqued my teaching and writing and, thus, have helped in the design of this text. I am particularly thankful to Jeff James of the University of Illinois and Galen Trail of the Iowa State University who read the first draft of this text and offered very useful comments and suggestions.

Rainer Martens, president; Becky Lane, acquisitions editor; and Julie Marx, developmental editor of Human Kinetics deserve special mention for their support of my work and their patience with my habits. Julie provided an extensive review of the text and great insights that have resulted in a fine text.

Finally, my family has provided the motivation and support for all my efforts. Ponnu, Ruban, Karen, Chandran, Sally, Jason, Daniel, Shane, Andrew, and Michelle are constant sources of energy and excitement. I hope that this book will make them proud of me.

Credits

Figure 2.1 Forsyth, P., & Danisiewicz, T.J., *Work and Occupations 12*(1), pp. 59-76, copyright ©1985 by Sage Publications, Inc. Reprinted by Permission of Sage Publications, Inc.

Appendix, chapter 2 Reprinted, by permission, from the North American Society for Sport Management (NASSM) Executive Council. Code of Ethics (1992).

Table 4.1 Adapted, by permission, from Peterson, N.G., & Bownas, D.A. (1982). Skill, task structure, and performance acquisition. In M.D. Dunnette & E.A. Fleishman (Eds.), *Human performance and productivity.* Hillsdale, NJ: Erlbaum.

Table 4.3 Reproduced, by permission, from G.O. Klemp, Jr., and D.C. McClelland, 1986, What characterizes intelligent functioning among senior managers? In *Practical intelligence: Nature and origins of competence in the everyday world,* edited by R.J. Sternberg and R.K. Wagner (New York: Cambridge University Press), 31-50.

Table 5.4 Adapted, by permission, from L.V. Gordon, 1970, "Measurement of Bureaucratic orientation," *Personnel Psychology* 23: 1-11.

Figure 6.4 Adapted, by permission, from S.H. Schwartz, 1992, Universals in the content and structure of values. In M. Zanna (Ed.), *Advances in experimental social psychology* (Vol. 25, pp. 1-65). New York: Academic Press.

Herzberg's Motivation-Hygiene (Two-Factor) Theory, p. 103 Adapted by permission of *Harvard Business Review* [Exhibit I. Factors affecting job attitudes]. From "One more time: How do you motivate people?" by F. Herzberg, Sept-Oct 1987, p. 57. Copyright ©1987 by the President and Fellows of Harvard College; all rights reserved.

Table 8.1 Reprinted by permission of *Harvard Business Review* [Exhibit III. Principles of vertical loading]. From "One more time: How do you motivate people?" by F. Herzberg, Sept-Oct 1987, p. 59. Copyright ©1987 by the President and Fellows of Harvard College; all rights reserved.

Fiedler's Contingency Model of Leadership, p. 168 Adapted, by permission, from F.E. Fiedler, 1967, *A theory of leadership effectiveness* (New York: McGraw-Hill Book Company).

Figure 11.3 Adapted, by permission, from J.C. MacLean and P. Chelladurai, 1995, Dimensions of coaching performance: Development of a scale, *Journal of Sport Management* 9: 194-207.

Conclusion table 1 Adapted, by permission, from G.M. Spreitzer, 1995, "Psychological empowerment in the workplace: Dimensions, measurement, and validation," *Academy of Management Journal* 38: 1442-1465.

Introduction: Services and Human Resources in Sport and Recreation

Learning Objectives

After reading this chapter you will be able to

- define and describe human resources in sport and recreation;
- describe a service and its unique attributes;
- distinguish between consumer and human services;
- describe and distinguish between participant, spectator, and sponsorship services; and
- explain the importance of clients as human resources.

Every organization can function effectively only if it has at its disposal the necessary resources. These resources are grouped conveniently into material resources in the form of capital, facilities and equipment, and human resources. The **human resources** comprise employees and their managers. While sufficient importance needs to be placed on the material resources, it is equally, if not more, important that the organization gives attention to the human resources because the human resources put the material resources into use and convert them into wealth (i.e., products). This is the central argument of this book, which focuses on the management of human resources within sport and recreation organizations.

This introduction is devoted to

- clarification of the products of sport and recreation organizations as consumer, professional, and human services;
- identification of the types of human resources in sport and recreation, i.e., paid workers, volunteer workers, and clients themselves; and

- specification of a model for the management of human resources in sport and recreation.

In essence, defining and describing the types of products and the types of human resources in sport and recreation would facilitate greatly the management of human resources in sport and recreation. Fortunately, two features of sport and recreation organizations help us clarify and define the human resources with which management has to contend.

First, sport and recreation organizations are involved in the production of services rather than of goods. This distinction identifies a new set of human resources: the clients or customers of these organizations. Further, most of the sport and recreation organizations are engaged in human services, i.e., the focal organizations work for people by changing them in specific ways. Thus, the client or customer is the input, as well as the output, of the organizational processes.

Second, both volunteer and paid workers staff several sport and recreation organizations. These two sets of workers bring different attitudes, beliefs, and biases. They also differ in their knowledge and expertise and in the rewards that they seek through participation in organizational activities. Managing the interplay of these two divergent sets of workers is complex and difficult.

These two features (i.e., sport organizations producing services and relying on volunteer, as well as paid, workers) define and describe the human resources in sport and recreation. They are elaborated in the following sections.

Service Operations

Many authors have documented the distinction between service producing organizations and goods producing organizations and the concomitant dif-

In Their View

Byars and Rue (1994) emphasized the importance of human resources by stating that

Human resource management encompasses those activities designed to provide for and coordinate the human resources of an organization. The human resources of an organization represent one of its largest investments. In fact, government reports show that approximately 73 percent of national income is used to compensate employees. (p. 6)

ferences in managerial practices (Grönroos 1990; Lovelock 1996; Mills and Margulies 1980; Sasser, Olsen, and Wyckoff 1978). Grönroos (1990) defined a **service** as

an activity or series of activities of a more or less intangible nature that normally, but not necessarily, take place in the interactions between the customer and service employees and/or physical resources or goods and/or systems of the service provider, which are provided as solutions to customer problems. (p. 27)

In contrast to a good that is a tangible physical object or product that can be created and used later, a service is an intangible and perishable occurrence that is created and used simultaneously (Sasser, Olsen, and Wyckoff 1978). Note that some goods can be involved in the production of services. For example, the expensive testing equipment that an exercise physiologist uses facilitates his or her services of fitness assessment and exercise prescription. Similarly, the services of renting a tennis court requires the existence of the facility. As a final example, the services that a retailer offers in assembling and displaying sporting goods involves the goods themselves. The price paid for a basketball includes the manufacturer's cost and profit for the basketball, the good, and the cost and profit of the retailer's services. Thus, in many service transactions, facilitating goods or facilities are likely to be involved to varying degrees. However, our discussion focuses on the service component because of its greater relevance to management of human resources.

Characteristics of Service

Many writers have emphasized the four basic characteristics of a service: intangibility, perishability, heterogeneity, and simultaneity. (Lovelock 1991; Sasser, Olsen, and Wyckoff 1978; Schmenner 1995)

- **Intangibility**—The notion of intangibility arises because the client or customer cannot judge the quality of the product before actually obtaining it. Sasser, Olsen, and Wyckoff (1978) pointed out that because the sensual and psychological benefits (i.e., feelings, such as comfort, status, and a sense of well-being) that customers derive are individualistic, the services offered will remain intangible.

- **Perishability**—This concept means that a service cannot be produced and stored for future use. A fitness consultant cannot continue to produce his or her services without the customers and store them for future use when customers arrive. In contrast, a manufacturer can continue to produce fitness equipment and inventory it for future sales.

• **Heterogeneity**—Services are likely to be heterogenous (variable) because of various influences. As noted earlier, customers' varying perceptions of a service contribute to the intangible nature of a service. First, two different clients may perceive differently the quality of the same service (e.g., the service of a fitness instructor) that the same employee provides because of the variations in their psyche. Further, the same client may perceive the service differently at two different points in time because of changes in one's frame of mind or mood. From the employees' view, two fitness instructors may not provide the same quality of service because of differences in their experience, expertise, or leadership style. Similarly, the same instructor may not provide the same quality services at different times. Just as the client is subject to changes in mood, instructors also are subject to them, which, in turn, affects the quality of the service offered.

• **Simultaneity**—As noted earlier, a service is perishable and cannot be stored. Therefore, it has to be consumed as it is produced. Because the production and consumption of a service are simultaneous, the interface between the employee (the producer of a service) and the client (the consumer of that service) becomes extremely important. In contrast, a tennis racket is produced at one point and time and sold to a customer at another point and time. Thus, no interface occurs between the producer and consumer of a good.

In a Nutshell

Services as products are experiences that are intangible, perishable, and variable over time and across different service providers. Because services are produced and consumed simultaneously, the interface between the service employee and the client becomes a critical element for the organization.

Professional Versus Consumer Services

As noted, the interface between the employee and the client or customer is critical to service operations. In fact, what transpires in the **employee-client interface** actually defines the nature of the service. The extent to which the service is complex and tailored to the needs of individual clients and the extent to which knowledge and expertise are involved have been used as critical criteria for the classification of services into professional services and consumer services (Sasser, Olsen, and Wyckoff 1978).

Professional services are "individualized for each customer and delivered by a relatively high-skill workforce" (Sasser, Olsen, and Wyckoff 1978, 400). Schools, colleges, and universities that hire expert coaches to train their athletes are offering professional services to their clients. Similarly, a fitness consulting firm that employs highly trained exercise physiologists falls into this category. The services of these organizations largely are based on employees' knowledge and expertise. Such services are nonstandardized in the sense that the needs of each customer determine them. Thus, these professional employees need to be allowed considerable freedom in their operations. Managers must recognize that traditional bureaucratic control mechanisms are neither relevant nor adequate.

Sasser, Olsen, and Wyckoff (1978) defined **consumer services** as "a limited range of services delivered by a relatively low-skill workforce to a large aggregate market" (p. 400). For instance, a city recreation department builds and operates an arena for the use of all the citizens of the city. The basic service provided is the use of the facility and scheduling of various activities in the arena. Similarly, a reservation clerk in that arena serves a large number of people in the community, and the operations are limited to simple acts, such as checking whether the applicants are entitled to reserve the arena and entering the date and time of such reservations. Thus, the operations of the reservation clerk largely are standardized and routinized.

These differing characteristics of the professional and consumer service employees entail different approaches to making decisions, organizing work, and motivating the employees in the respective services. Elaborating further on this distinction between professional services and consumer services, Mills and Margulies' (1980) scheme identifies seven variables associated with the employee-customer interface that differ among different service organizations.

1. **Information**—Services differ in the extent and type of information processed in delivering a service. For example, a professional coach in a tennis club processes many bits of information for training and instructing players, but a reservation clerk only needs to know the client's preferred schedule and whether the client is entitled to reserve a court.

2. **Decisions**—Services also can be distinguished on the basis of the relative complexity of decisions made during employee-customer interface. The reservation clerk's decisions are relatively simple; however, the tennis professional's decisions are more complex.

3. **Time**—With increasing information processing and complexity of decisions, professional services involve more time than the consumer services. The tennis professional spends more time with players than the reservation clerk spends with clients.

4. **Problem**—Another important distinction between the two operations is the extent to which the client is aware of the problem and its solution. In reserving a tennis court, the client knows exactly what he or she wants and informs the reservation clerk accordingly. In the case of tennis lessons, however, the coach knows more about the weaknesses of the client and the remedies.

5. **Transferability**—Another feature that distinguishes between the forms of services is the ease with which employees can be replaced. Because consumer services involve simple and routine decisions, training a newcomer or replacing the current employee is relatively easy. On the other hand, replacing a professional employee is relatively more difficult and disruptive of current service levels.

6. **Power**—In the earlier example, the professional coach is presumed to have more knowledge and expertise than the clients have and is more aware of their problems than the clients themselves are. These features bestow on the coach the power over his or her clients. This is not the case with the reservation clerk. Note that the power of the service provider stems from the knowledge and expertise that he or she has relative to the client. That is, the client is dependent on the professional to solve the problems. By the same token, an organization that specializes in knowledge-based services becomes dependent on its own professional employees. For example, a university athletic department is dependent on coaches to recruit outstanding athletes and to mold them into winning teams. To that extent, coaches have some power over the department.

7. **Attachment**—Because of the close association between the employee (e.g., the coach) and the client in a professional service operation, the employee is likely to be more attached to his or her clients (e.g., the athletes) than to the employing organization. In contrast, the consumer service employee (e.g., the reservation clerk) is likely to be more attached to the organization than to the clients.

Mills and Margulies (1980) pointed out that the discussed variables "are closely interrelated to each

Table 1   Consumer and Professional Service Operations

Dimensions	Consumer service (e.g., retailing of sporting goods)	Professional service (e.g., fitness consulting)
Information base	Weak	Strong
Decision type	Simple	Complex
Interface duration	Brief	Lengthy
Client's knowledge	High	Low
Type of product	Standard with low knowledge or skill	Nonstandard with high knowledge or skill
Substitutability of employees	High	Low
Perceived power of employee	Low	High
Type of employee	Low unskilled operators	Professionally trained, self-motivated individuals
Type of organizational structure	Rigid hierarchy Standard procedures Strict control	Unstructured hierarchy Loose control

Source: Mills and Margulies (1980) and Sasser, Olsen, and Wyckoff (1978).

Reproduced with permission from Chelladurai (1985), p. 39.

other and are linked to the need for information, the raw material of service organizations" (p. 262). The distinctions between consumer and professional services are based largely on the amount of information exchanged between the service employee and the customer and on the extent to which the employees must possess the expertise and knowledge to solve customer problems. Table 1 summarizes the differences between a consumer service and a professional service that Sasser, Olsen, and Wyckoff (1978) and Mills and Margulies (1980) suggested.

Human Services

While sport and recreation organizations provide consumer, as well as professional, services, note that professional services themselves comprise two major types. For instance, lawyers, architects, accountants, and stock brokers provide complex professional services to their clients or customers. By the same token, teachers, guidance counselors, physicians, and clergy also provide professional services. However, a distinction between the two sets of services exists; the former set involves knowledge and guidelines regarding something in which the clients are interested (e.g., a legal issue, a building, or an investment), and the latter set transforms, in some way, the clients themselves (e.g., educating the child, guiding the students, treating the patient, or enhancing the spiritual life). The latter set of services is called **human services** (as opposed to nonhuman professional services) in which

> (a) [the] input of raw material are human beings with specific attributes, and their production output are persons processed or changed in a predetermined manner, and (b) [the] general mandate is that of "service," that is, to maintain and improve the general well-being and functioning of people. (Hasenfeld and English 1974, 1)

Many of the services that sport and recreation organizations provide possess these features. Many of these organizations are involved in cultivating a healthy lifestyle among their clients, educating them about the benefits of physical activity, changing their attitude toward physical activity and recreation programs, and providing opportunities for health, fitness or skill enhancement, and overall fun and enjoyment.

The following three-level classification of human services elaborates further on the nature of human services in sport and recreation organizations (Hasenfeld 1983):

- People-processing functions
- People-sustaining functions
- People-changing functions

• **People-processing function**—This function refers to testing or screening people and designating them as belonging to a particular class based on some classification scheme. Normally, another agency uses such information or labeling. Juvenile courts, credit-rating bureaus, or testing and diagnosing units often are cited as examples of this kind of human service organization. Guidance counselors are also people processors when they test their wards on specific aptitude or attitude scales. Fitness testing laboratories perform this function when they rate their customers on a scale of relative fitness. Testing of athletes for drugs also is a people-processing service.

• **People-sustaining function**—Another function of human service organizations is sustaining people (i.e., preventing or delaying the decline in the welfare or status of the clients). This function is the major function of welfare departments, nursing homes, or chronic wards in hospitals. In our context, cardiac rehabilitation programs and athletic injury clinics provide people-sustaining services.

• **People-changing function**—This function is most characteristic of sport and recreation organizations. They are engaged in changing people in terms of one or more of the biophysical, psychological, or social attributes. For example, physical education degree programs change their clients into more knowledgeable persons in the field, fitness programs make people fitter and healthier, recreation programs make their clients more relaxed and energized, and coaching programs make their clients better performers.

In summary, sport, physical activity, and recreation organizations provide services. Further, while some of these organizations can provide consumer services, most of them provide professional services. A final distinguishing characteristic of sport

In a Nutshell

Human services are distinct from other forms of services because clients are the inputs and outputs of human services. They are concerned with processing and classifying people, preventing or delaying the decline in the welfare of people, and altering specific attributes of people (e.g., health, skills, and knowledge).

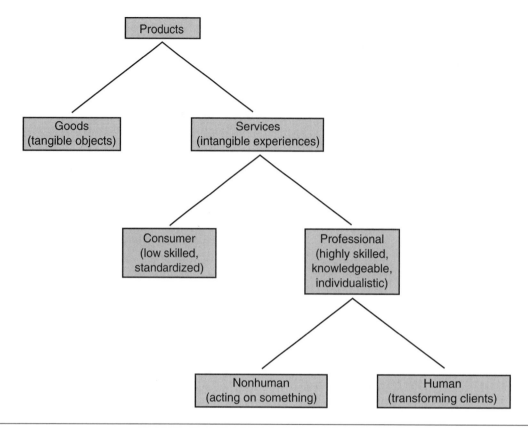

Figure 1　Classification of organizational products.

and recreation organizations is that some of them are engaged primarily in human services (i.e., in people-processing, people-sustaining, or people-changing services). The three types of services and their interrelationships are illustrated in figure 1.

Sport and Recreation Services

Based on the foregoing description of services, Chelladurai (1994) classified the services that sport and recreation organizations offer into three major classes: participant services, spectator services, and sponsorship services (see figure 2).

Participant Services

Participant services can be broken down into smaller categories.

• **Consumer-pleasure or consumer-health services**—Consumer services involve the scheduling reservations of facilities or equipment as clients request and organizing and conducting tournaments to enhance the pleasure in physical activity. Clients may use these services either for pleasure or for health reasons. Bowling alleys and weight rooms are prime examples of this service.

• **Human-skills or human-excellence services**—These services require expert application of teaching technology and leadership in developing the skills of the clients in various forms of sport and physical activity. When the clients want to become excellent in an activity, expert guidance and coaching (including techniques and strategies) need to be provided.

• **Human-sustenance or human-curative services**—These services entail organizing and conducting exercise and fitness programs on a regular basis under the guidance and supervision of expert leaders for the benefit of healthy clients (sustenance) or for the benefit of clients who are considered deficient in fitness, health, or physical appearance (curative). Exercise-based cardiac rehabilitation, relaxation and stress reduction, and weight-loss programs belong to this class.

Spectator Services

Spectator services are fundamentally an offshoot of pursuit of excellence, which was a participant service described earlier, and they are oriented toward providing entertainment for the direct (e.g., spectators at a competition) and indirect (e.g., television audiences) consumers of the sport.

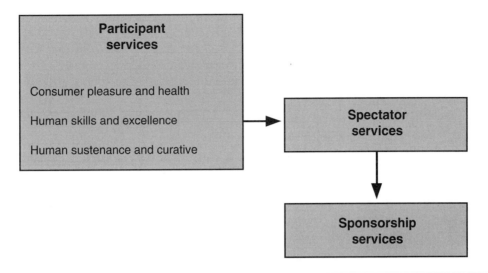

Figure 2   A classification of sport and recreation services.

Reprinted from P. Chelladurai, 1996, Sport management: Its scope and career opportunities. In *The management of sport: Its foundation and application*, edited by B.L. Parkhouse (St. Louis, MO: Mosby). Reproduced with permission of The McGraw-Hill Companies.

Sponsorship Services

Sponsorship refers to individuals or corporations offering some monetary or nonmonetary support in return for one or more of the three possible elements that a sport organization may offer: market access (e.g., sponsoring the Olympic games), association with excellence (e.g., sponsoring Michael Jordan), and social responsibility (e.g., sponsoring local sporting events).

A clear understanding of the products of a sport or recreation organization is essential for instituting human resource practices. For instance, the type of employees hired, their training, and their performance evaluation in a consumer services operation are different from those in a human services operation. Similarly, these human resource management practices would perforce be different for those who produce excellence than for those who market that excellence. Thus, a sport organization must define its own business (i.e., its products) before instituting specific human resource management programs.

In a Nutshell

The type of services that the organization produces has an impact on human resource management practices. These services can be classified broadly as participant services, spectator services, and sponsorship services. Spectator and sponsorship services are offshoots of human-excellence services that are one form of participant services.

Sport and Recreation Organizations

Note that while the sport and recreation services are many and varied, the organizations that provide these services also are quite diverse. Some of these organizations are created and run to make a profit for the owners, and others are not profit-oriented. For example, a private commercial fitness club is a profit organization; however, a university recreational sport department offering the same fitness services is not profit-oriented. Similarly, a Division I athletic department may provide the same type of entertainment services as a professional sport franchise, but the two differ in their profit orientation.

Another distinction that can be made among sport and recreation organizations is whether they belong to the public sector (i.e., government) or private sector. The fundamental distinction between public and private sector organizations is that the public organizations derive their funding through taxation of the public, and private organizations get their funding through contributions from private donors or investors. For example, a city recreation organization that city taxes fund can offer consumer-pleasure services in a golf course just as a private golf club can do.

Sport and recreation organizations also can differ in their size. Some universities are larger than others, and, therefore, their athletic and recreational sport departments also differ in their size. Similarly, city recreation departments differ in their size. Some of the sport governing bodies are larger than others

In Their View

From the literature, Amis and Slack (1996) identified four measures of size: physical capacity, volume of inputs and outputs, available discretionary resources, and number of personnel. However, they used the measures of total number of organization members and total organization income as the measures of size in their study of voluntary sport organizations.

---

based on the popularity of the sport and membership. These variations among sport and recreation organizations can impose certain demands and constraints on the management of human resources, and these will be discussed in subsequent chapters.

I have used the terms "sport" and "recreation" as adjectives to the term "organizations" because some confusion exists over the use of sport as the sole term. The constitution of the North American Society for Sport Management defines the field as "the theoretical and applied aspects of management theory and practice specially related to *sport, exercise, dance and play* [emphasis added] as these enterprises are pursued by all sectors of the population." Because this definition covers all of the services described earlier, it is legitimate to call all of these services sport services and all organizations providing these services sport organizations. However, some distinctions are made between sport and recreation in that the term "sport" is used to refer to elite sport (e.g., intercollegiate and professional athletics) and the term "recreation" is used to refer to other forms of participant sport (e.g., university or city recreational sports). Because this text is designed to cover management of human resources in organizations providing all forms of the services described, I have used both sport and recreation to refer to the services as well as to the organizations that provide those services.

Volunteer Workers

The foregoing discussions identified two sets of human resources, or employees: the human service workers and consumer service workers. However, both sets of workers were assumed to be remunerated for the work performed in some material form (e.g., usually salary or wages). Organizations and their managers can use such monetary rewards as a mechanism for controlling employee behavior. For example, the amount of salary or wages offered

facilitates the recruitment of an employee; increasing salaries or wages based on work done, experience, or cost of living indices fosters continued employee participation; and providing incentives, such as merit pay and bonuses, enhances employee motivation.

However, such practices do not have relevance in the case of a **volunteer** who is

> an individual engaging in behavior that is not bio-socially determined (e.g., eating, sleeping), nor economically necessitated (e.g., paid work, house work, home repair), nor sociopolitically compelled (e.g., paying one's taxes, clothing oneself before appearing in public), but rather that is essentially (primarily) motivated by the expectation of psychic benefits of some kind. (Smith 1981, 22-23)

Accordingly, participation of the volunteers and their contributions are not based on any material rewards; therefore, those rewards cannot be used as incentives. Instead, management of this set of human resources (i.e., recruiting them and, more importantly, retaining them) in sport and recreation organizations requires different approaches. The incentives behind volunteerism are discussed in chapter 1.

Many of the sport and recreation organizations depend on volunteers for carrying out their operations. For example, volunteers organize many of the youth leagues in various sports and coach the teams. As another example, intercollegiate athletic programs use volunteer workers on game days to manage the entrances to the stadiums and arenas. Further, volunteers have founded or have managed several sport governing bodies. However, the most common form of volunteer participation is as frontline workers delivering the services whether they are consumer or human services. It is inconceivable that sport and recreation can exist without the services of the volunteers. Thus, volunteers constitute a valuable set of human resources without the associated cost of material rewards.

A further issue related to volunteers is that a sport or recreation organization can consist of both volunteer and **paid professional workers**. This composition brings in a different kind of problem: the conflicts between the two groups. For instance, authors have suggested that a persisting problem facing the Canadian sport governing organizations is the conflict between paid professional administrators and volunteer administrators (Canadian Olympic Association, 1986). Such conflicts can emanate from perceived expertise on the part of the paid professional workers and perceived altruism on the part of volunteers. Inglis (1997) noted that the tension between volunteers and professionals was due to "differing opinions among the professional staff and board volunteers as to the degree of technical expertise, policy development or advice that constituted an appropriate relationship" (p. 161). Amis and Slack (1996) pointed out that the conflict between volunteer board members and professional staff in volunteer sport organizations in Canada may be attributed to the struggle for control.

> Despite efforts by government [Canadian] to make the process of decision-making in these organizations "more business like" by standardizing procedures and placing operational decisions in the hands of professional staff, many volunteers resisted this type of change.
> . . . The culture of informal control is thus retained as volunteers see any efforts to increase standardization as a possible erosion of their power base. (p. 83)

The potential for such conflicts poses a threat and challenge to the management of human resources.

The essential point to remember is that both paid employees and volunteer workers staff most sport and recreation organizations. Equally important is the fact that both of these types of workers can provide a consumer service, a human service, or both (see table 2).

In a Nutshell

Sport and recreation organizations rely heavily on volunteer contributions. While the economic value of volunteer participation in sport and recreation is quite significant, sport and recreation managers also must capitalize on the social benefits of volunteer involvement.

Clients or Customers

The two types of human resources (volunteer and paid workers) that can provide consumer or human services in sport and recreation are not the end of the story. Another form of human resources that is unique to services in general, and to sport and recreation in particular, exists: the clients of our services. While a more elaborate description of clients is provided in chapter 3, the issue of simultaneity of production and consumption highlights the importance of **clients as human resources** at this point.

As noted earlier, because a service has to be consumed as it is produced, the interface between the employee (the producer) and the customer (the consumer) become extremely critical. This feature of simultaneity of production and consumption brings the customers into the organizational domain as one set of human resources. In fact, Mills and Morris (1986) suggested that the customer should be considered as a partial employee of the organization. According to these authors,

> Clients or customers of service organizations are indispensable to the production activities of these organizations. . . . in complex services where customer performance is crucial to service production, boundaries of the service organization have to be expanded to incorporate the consumers as temporary members or participants. (p. 726)

Inclusion of the client in the service production process can be seen as a cost-saving effort on the part of the organization. This view largely is true in the case of profit-oriented organizations, such as the commercial banks or grocery stores, that may require the customer to perform certain activities that the service employee traditionally carried out (e.g., filling in the deposit slips or bagging your own groceries). However, such a limited utilitarian view

Table 2　Types of Workers and Services

	Workers	
Service or worker type	Paid	Volunteer
Consumer service	Locker-room attendant	Gymnasium supervisor
Human service	Exercise leader	High school coach

of customer involvement is inappropriate in the case of sport and recreation organizations that provide human services: people-processing, people-sustaining, and people-changing services. These types of services cannot be completed without the active participation of the clients in the production process. Thus, management of human resources entails specific processes to entice the clients to be active and compliant of directions. The participation of clients in our service operations affects management in two significant ways. The first effect is the obvious face-to-face interactions of the service employee and the client. The second concern is the need for, and the difficulty of, securing client compliance to the requirements of the production of a service.

A Model of Human Resource Management

The foregoing classification of human resources (paid professional workers, volunteers, and clients or customers) within sport and recreation organizations is only the first step in managing those human resources. A more comprehensive approach to managing human resources includes

- the individual differences among the three broad categories of human assets;
- the managerial processes appropriate to the recruitment, retention, and growth and development of the human assets; and
- the fundamental outcomes of organizational efforts (see figure 3).

While the three types of human assets (i.e., resources) are listed in box 1, box 2 demonstrates the importance of individual differences. People within each category may differ in abilities, personality, values, and motivation. Effective human resource management practices (box 3) consider not only the differences between classes of human resources but also the individual differences within each class

In a Nutshell

We need to view our clients as our human resources because they have to be involved actively in the production of our services. From this perspective, clients are part of the organization; they are its partial employees.

when approaching job design, staffing, leadership, performance evaluation, reward systems, and organizational justice.

Productivity of individuals, groups, and the organization as a whole can be enhanced if management strives to secure the commitment of both the workers and the clients and to secure their collaborative effort in achieving the organizational goals. That commitment and effort constitutes a significant outcome in the model (box 4). The second, and equally important, concern is with employee satisfaction (box 4). In other words, management should ensure that the workers and clients grow in their competence and performance capabilities. Further, opportunities should be available to meet their personal needs. Meeting these needs, in turn, enhances their satisfaction with their involvement in organizational activities. The congruence among the characteristics of the three types of human resources, individual differences, and human resource management practices leads to the desired outcomes of commitment and satisfaction.

This book is organized according to the framework of figure 3. A more elaborate description of the human resources in sport and recreation is presented in part I, individual differences among the organizational participants are addressed in part II, the processes of managing human resources are discussed in part III, and the desired outcome of employee and client satisfaction and the certain underlying themes of human resource management are presented in part IV.

Summary

In summary, people implement the organizational policies and procedures and help the organization achieve its goals. Therefore, management of human resources is as critical as any other process of management. Facilities and equipment that an organization possesses are resources only when people use them. Sport and recreation organizations are concerned largely with the production of services, so I described the concept of a service and its attributes in detail.

In addition, this introduction emphasized the distinctions among consumer, professional, and human services. The broad category of human services can be subdivided into people-processing, people-sustaining, and people-changing services. Further, because services within sport and recreation require the physical involvement of the clients (i.e., our services cannot be produced without their

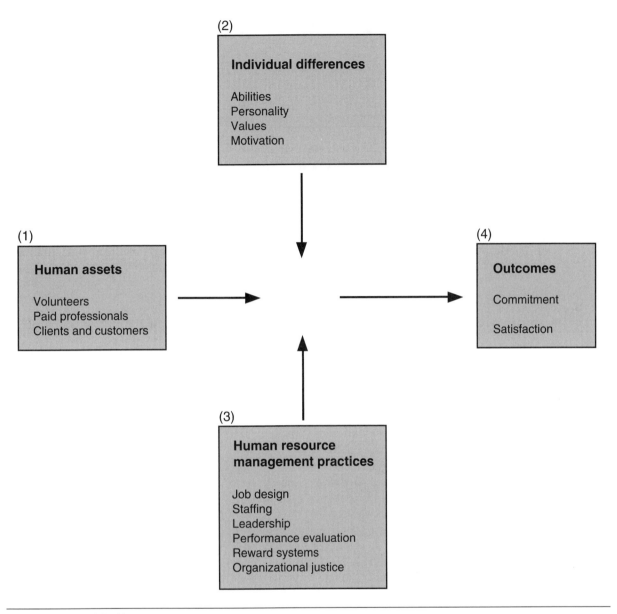

Figure 3   A model of human resource management.

participation), the clients constitute one set of human resources that need managing. Several sport and recreation organizations rely heavily on volunteer workers, and thus, the volunteers are another category of human resources within sport and recreation. The needs of paid workers themselves, particularly the professional workers, also are addressed in human resource management practices.

Finally, the framework presented in the introduction suggests that human resource management practices of job design, staffing, leadership, performance evaluation, reward systems, and organiza-

tional justice should address the concerns of the three types of human resources (i.e., volunteers, professionals, and clients) and should be consonant with selected individual difference variables (i.e., abilities, traits, values, and motivation). Effective human resource management practices should result in satisfaction of volunteer and paid workers and in their commitment to the organization. By the same token, effective human resource management practices ensures that clients' adherence to sport and recreation and their commitment to the organization is enhanced.

Key Terms

human resources, services, employee-client interface, professional services, consumer services, human services, volunteer, paid professional workers, clients as human resources

Your Perspectives

- Compare and contrast the employee-client interface in sport and recreation organizations with such interface in other service organizations (e.g., a bank).

- The chapter proposed three kinds of human resources at the disposal of sport and recreation organizations. Discuss the relative importance of these types of human resources in different kinds of sport and recreation organizations.

- In your experience as a volunteer or a paid worker, have you found any conflict between volunteers and paid staff? Discuss the reasons and solutions for such conflicts.

- Human services may involve processing people, sustaining people, or changing people. Focusing on various sport and recreation organizations, discuss the extent to which these organizations are engaged in the three forms of human services.

Part 1

Human Resources in Sport and Recreation

The definitions of organizations and management (Certo 1992) generally include the three distinct entities of (1) specific goals to be achieved within (2) limited resources through coordinating the efforts of (3) people.

Of these three, it is the entity of "people" that is most perplexing and problematic and most demanding of managerial attention. Many authors contend that, for a manager to be effective, he or she must be a good manager of people because it is the people who make up an organization and because it is they who make everything work (Tosi, Rizzo, and Carroll 1986).

In fact, the "people" can be seen as the most important element in management or organizations because it has an impact on the other two elements. That is, it is people in the form of different constituents (e.g., managers, employees, and clients or customers) of the focal organization who argue, discuss, and influence the decisions on the goals of the organization and the distribution of available resources in pursuing these goals.

From another perspective, it is people who make money and materials meaningful as resources and turn them into wealth. For instance, a stadium becomes a resource only when athletes perform in the stadium and spectators flock to the stadium to see the contest. The most modern electronic scoreboard becomes a resource only when knowledgeable technicians are available to operate it and people are present to watch it. These two examples show that a material resource is a resource only when people with the "know-how" (e.g., athletes or technicians) use it to serve the needs of other people (spectators).

It is trite to say that human resources are much different from material resources. However, it is useful to look at some of the unique characteristics of human resources that affect managerial practices. Management of human resources is of greater importance than management of other resources and requires a totally different type of attention because the organization has to recruit it individually. Each targeted individual has the option not to participate in the organization, and the return on the investment in human resource is not predictable, i.e., one cannot be too certain how individuals will perform in the organizational context (Killian 1976).

Thus, it is not surprising that the field of study known as "human resource management" has gained greater significance. Several textbooks and scholarly journals have been and continue to be published, and almost every school of business administration has one or more specialized courses in this field. Human resource management is defined as

> a distinctive approach to employment management which seeks to achieve a competitive advantage through the strategic deployment of a highly committed and capable workforce, using an integrated array of cultural, structural and personnel techniques. (Storey 1995, 5)

The definition emphasizes that organizations can be effective if they engage in appropriate techniques and practices to create a committed and capable workforce. Management of human resources has been placed in a central position in general management mainly because of the pressures that slumping employee productivity and growing international competitions have created. However, this approach is rather narrow because the focus is on productivity and profit for the organization and because the employees are viewed as cost. Theorists emphasize that for long-term benefits of all concerned (i.e., the organization, the employees, and society in general) organizations would do well to consider the employees as capital and attempt to enhance their growth and potential, which, in turn, will contribute to performance and productivity (Beer and Spector 1985, Odiorne 1984). Legge (1995) called these two perspectives (i.e., employees as cost and employees as capital) hard and soft models of human resource management. The hard model views the employees as a factor of production just as land and capital are. The soft model treats "employees as valued assets, a source of competitive advantage through their commitment, adaptability and high quality of (skills, performance and so on)" (p. 35). She also refers to the two approaches as utilitarian instrumentalism and developmental humanism, respectively. The hard and instrumental approach cannot be dismissed easily; however, this text takes the orientation of the soft, developmental approach.

The emphasis on human resources as capital is much more pronounced in the case of service organizations because

- their products are intangible,
- customer involvement is necessary for the production of services, and
- the production and consumption of a service occur simultaneously.

Theorists and practitioners note that quality in services ultimately resides in the service providers, which is called human resources in this text (Becker and Gerhart 1996; Bitner 1990; Chelladurai 1995a; Goetsch 1994; Parasuraman, Zeithaml, and Berry 1990; Schneider and Bowen 1995). Because service providers are in contact with both the clients and the organizations that they symbolize, they project the image of the organization (Schneider and Bowen 1995). Thus, it is critical that greater emphasis be placed on management of human resources in sport and recreation.

Three imperatives drive the concern with human resource management (Chelladurai 1995b). The first imperative is profitability. That is, profit-oriented organizations can enhance productivity and, thus, their profitability by instituting effective human resource practices to enable the human resources to function optimally. The second driving force is the changes in the values and awareness of the workforce and customer base. Their altered conceptions of good human resource practices and their expectations for enhancing these processes coupled with their influence constitute the second imperative. Finally, organizations as agencies of society are beholden to society, which includes the human resources of the organizations. Thus, when an organization institutes effective human resource practices to enhance the quality of life for their human resources, they also are contributing to the society as a whole. Therefore, the imperative of social responsibility is the third significant force.

The process of managing human resources should begin with an insight into the broad categories of human resources that the organization addresses. Based on this logic, each of the first three chapters is devoted to the description of one of these three forms of human resources: volunteers, paid professionals, and clients. Chapter 1 begins with a description of voluntary organizations and concludes with a discussion of volunteer motivation. Chapter 2 describes the nature of professions and the concept of professionalism. The chapter concludes with a comparison of professionalism and volunteerism that suggests that these two processes are quite similar. Chapter 3 addresses clients of sport operations and includes a greater focus on their motivation to participate.

1 Volunteers and Volunteerism

Learning Objectives

After reading this chapter you will be able to

- gain some insight into the economic significance of volunteer organizations,
- identify differences among various forms of voluntary organizations,
- understand why people volunteer their time and energy, and
- explain the role of altruism in volunteering.

As noted in the introduction, **volunteers** constitute an important set of human resources for many sport and recreation organizations. Volunteers run youth sport leagues in small cities and towns and serve as managers, coordinators, registration clerks, coaches, referees, and locker-room attendants. Charitable organizations, such as the Young Men's Christian Association (YMCA), recruit volunteers to manage their ongoing sport and recreation programs. The Special Olympics is a great success not only because of the great leadership that its administrators provide but also because of the time, energy, and effort of thousands of volunteers. Volunteers also serve on the governing boards of national sport organizations. Many university athletic departments capitalize on the services of volunteer ushers during game days.

The foregoing are just a few examples of how volunteers serve in sport and recreation. As Stephens (1991) noted from his study of several volunteers, two underlying dimensions exist for volunteering: leadership and nurturance. Leadership is the tendency of some volunteers to hold offices and to manage organizations, and nurturance is the inclination to serve the needy on a one-on-one basis. Thus, some of the volunteers in sport may be interested in serving as leaders and managers of organizations or programs. Inglis (1997) referred to the volunteers on the boards of directors of sport governing bodies in Canada as the policy volunteers because they are involved in setting policy, which is a leadership function. In contrast, some sport and recreation volunteers may prefer to be involved directly with the clients, such as coaches, teachers, and counselors. Irrespective of the specific roles of volunteers in sport and recreation, it is critical that the organization manage them and their contributions effectively. While the specific managerial concerns and practices associated with volunteering will be identified and discussed in subsequent chapters, this chapter addresses

- the history of volunteerism in America,
- the economic significance of volunteer action with special reference to volunteers in sport and recreation,
- the types of volunteer organizations,
- the demographics of volunteers,
- the motivation and incentives in volunteering, and
- altruism as related to volunteerism.

The Need for Volunteerism

One distinguishing characteristic of North American society is the enormous contributions that volunteer workers make to the national economies and social welfare (Moyer 1985). Historically, the tradition of **volunteerism** and community service in the United States began with the early settlers (Ellis and Noyes 1990). They found that their survival depended on their banding together and helping each other in various affairs, such as defense of their settlement, the procurement of the resources, and the building of individual houses as well as common facilities.

> It was a new kind of society: a culture of cooperation. It was a culture comprised of people who believed in self-help, in hard work, and in voluntarily going out of their way to reach out and help those whose need required their strength. In bustling coastal cities and on the isolated frontier, they had to cooperate voluntarily in order to survive. As they moved beyond survival and into prosperity, they held on to their ethic of cooperative voluntary action. (Mason 1984, 1)

The significance of joining associations for the common good began to diminish as all levels of governments took over several of the functions of these voluntary associations through various social programs. In recent years, however, voluntary action has made an upsurge due to several sets of factors. First, citizens believe that big governments and big businesses do not act in the best interests of the common person, so concerted pressure must be brought to bear on them. Such pressure can be generated only if people band to together as action groups (Carter 1983). These views have resulted in

the birth of a number of associations, such as the consumer groups that sometimes are labeled third-sector organizations (Etzioni 1973, Levitt 1973).

The second factor stems from the government budgetary actions funneling fewer and fewer dollars to those social programs that the governments usurped from the associations in the first place. Beginning with President Ronald Reagan, a constant push toward trimming the "big" government and its budget has led to reductions in support for social programs. Recognizing the need for these social programs, leaders in both Canada and the United States have begun to emphasize the role of voluntary action. For instance, Pierre Elliott Trudeau (cited in Morrison 1986), while prime minister of Canada, suggested that

> The not-for-profit and voluntary sectors of our societies could be made to flourish. . . . Their decline has been inevitably reflected in the growth of government and commercial services. It has resulted in a loss of a sense of community. Surely we need this sector. We need to develop alternate styles of work and leisure and we need to demonstrate that there are other ways of doing the community's work. On a broad second front we must give encouragement and sustenance to these efforts. (p. 17)

In the United States, leaders have expressed similar, often more emphatic, views. For instance, President George Bush's theme of "a thousand points of light" was advocacy of self-help and volunteerism. President Bill Clinton reiterated this theme in April 1997 in Philadelphia when he organized the Presidents' Summit for America's Future. Former Presidents Bush, Jimmy Carter, and Gerald Ford along with former First Lady Nancy Reagan and former Chief of Staff Colin Powell joined President Clinton to call people to service and citizenship. Clinton stated: "The era of big government may be over, but the era of big challenges in our country is not. And so we need an era of big citizenship. That is why we are here" (*Columbus Dispatch*, 29 April 1997, 1A).

More importantly, the enactment of the Volunteer Services Act and the formation of ACTION, which is the governmental program for volunteer services, illustrates the governments' enthusiasm for volunteer action (Ilsley 1990). Similar efforts in support of volunteer services may be found at the state and local government levels. As noted earlier, departments of recreation or sports in many cities rely heavily on the volunteers to run their programs (e.g., youth soccer leagues and men's and women's softball leagues).

In Their View

Former President Bush at the eve of the Philadelphia Summit said that

> Volunteerism isn't an excuse for government to be completely rolled back. But the public sector can't do it all—the old view was that if a federal program didn't work, double the spending and see if it will work then. That's not the way to do things. When I was in the White House, some critics used to charge that our emphasis on "a thousand points of light" was just a dodge, a way of saying that encouraging volunteerism could justify spending cuts. That wasn't the case at all: our thinking then, and the philosophy behind the Philadelphia Summit, is that fixing the country requires our time, not just our tax dollars. It takes both. Somewhere in this country at this very minute the problems that plague us nationally are being solved at a local level through volunteers. (*Newsweek*, 28 April 1997, 32)

Another factor that makes volunteering significant is the changes that have taken place and are taking place in the workplace. In the past, technological innovations and advances were expected to exert two different types of influence on the volunteer sector (Smith 1986). First, a large segment of the society was expected to have more time to spare because of shorter work hours, weeks, and years. That time would need to be spent effectively in the pursuit of health and happiness. Volunteering would be one of the avenues in which individuals could seek personal growth and comfort. Thus, more human resources would be available for the voluntary sector. This promise of more free time as a function of technological innovations has not been fulfilled necessarily. To the contrary, technological innovations coupled with fierce foreign competition have resulted in many business and industrial organizations downsizing their workforce and paying the remaining workers less money. This practice, in turn, has led many employees to work longer hours and at more than one job. The average citizen has less time and energy to volunteer. *USA Today* reported that the number of people volunteering has declined progressively from 1960 to 1995 (*USA Today*, 28 April 1997, 11A). This decline is due to lack of time. The number of Americans working has increased from 55% in 1970 to about 66% in 1996, and they work one hour more per week on the job. The

implications of these trends is that sport and recreation organizations that depend on volunteers have to work harder at recruiting and retaining volunteers.

According to Smith (1986), a second influence is that the demand for human services in the future would be greater and that neither the private nor the public sectors could meet all of this demand. Therefore, greater pressure would be placed on the voluntary sector to provide these services. The 1997 Presidents' Summit for America's Future stressed this point to urge citizens to help the youth at risk.

The foregoing review indicates that the need for voluntary action will continue to grow. It is going to be a strong determinant of how well society can handle itself and can assure the welfare of its members. Thus, management of volunteers needs as much emphasis as management of paid workers.

In a Nutshell

The recent emphasis on voluntary action is brought about by a recognition that such action is needed to force both big business and big government to fulfill their mandates to serve the people, make up for the decreasing financial support to social programs, and provide more programs for those people who may have increased leisure time.

Economic Significance of Volunteers

National economies generally consist of the products of businesses and government agencies. However, as Beamish (1985) pointed out,

> The economy is much larger and far more pervasive than the work world of wage labor, capital, and public bureaucracies or corporations; a highly significant and ever present part of the economy is the production and distribution of resources based upon private, nonremunerated work. (p. 218)

Consider the nonremunerated work to which Beamish referred. According to the *1996 Statistical Abstract of the United States* (U.S. Bureau of the Census 1996), the estimated rate of volunteering for 1996 was nearly 45% for men and 52% for women. Further, the average volunteer spent 4.2 hours each week in volunteer work. These figures add up to a large number of hours of nonremunerated labor (see page 18).

The need for and the significance of voluntary action is no more pronounced than in sport and recreation. In fact, a vast network of voluntary associations or volunteers largely organize and deliver sport services at the amateur level (Government of Canada 1992; McPherson 1975; Slack 1985; Tedrick and Henderson 1989). Volunteer involvement in sport and recreation takes many forms. In many of the national sport governing bodies in both the United States and Canada, the governing boards comprise volunteers who help make policy for their respective organizations. Volunteers also head the state-level (or provincial-level) organizations. At the grass-roots level of any sport, the volunteers sustain the activities. As noted before, volunteers help with many projects that government agencies or for-profit enterprises initiate and run.

According to the *1996 Statistical Abstract of the United States*, 5.4% of all people who volunteered did so in the area of adult recreation; 11.7%, in youth development; and 10.8%, in health-related activities. The abstract does not provide a breakdown of those who volunteered in sport, recreation, or fitness; however, Tedrick and Henderson (1989) in 1985 estimated that 21% of all who volunteered did so in sport and recreation. If this estimate was valid in 1996, then the total value of volunteering in sport and recreation was one-fifth of the more than $118 billion value of volunteering, or more than $15 billion, that year. That is an impressive figure indeed!

Three caveats must be noted in relation to the earlier calculations. First, the respondents to the surveys self-report the rates on which volunteering is based. Second, the time spent volunteering may not equate to work done. For example, the person in charge of the nets and corner posts for a soccer game needs to be present about 30 minutes before and about 30 minutes after the game. As an estimate, the person spends about three hours in volunteering. However, the time spent doing any work is less than one hour. Third, the earlier calculation was based on minimum hourly wages. However, some volunteer work may be worth more (in economic terms) than other volunteer work.

Noneconomic Significance of Volunteers

Apart from the economic significance of their contributions, volunteers also bring certain intangible and nonquantifiable assets to the situation. As Tedrick and Henderson (1989) suggested, clients perceive that volunteers are more credible, legitimate, and sincere because of their free service in an activity of their liking. Because they are free from considerations of financial benefits to themselves, they can be objective and critical in their evaluation of organizational processes. Such unbridled and constructive feedback helps keep the organization on the right track.

Another advantage is that volunteers compared with full-time paid employees have greater control over the pressures associated with the performance of the service. Because volunteers choose the type of service that they perform and the times during which they offer their time and skills, they can tailor their volunteering to be consistent with their tolerance level for stress and pressures. This tailoring proves beneficial both to the volunteers and their clients. Further, organizations can expect volunteers to try out new and innovative approaches to

---

To estimate the total value of all the volunteering in the United States (based on 1995 volunteer statistics), use the minimum wage at that time ($4.25) as the value of each hour spent on volunteering. The calculations are as follows:

45% of men (n=128,314,000)	57,741,300
	+
52% of women (n=134,441,000)	69,909,320
	127,650,620 (total number of volunteers)
	× 4.2 (average volunteer hours per week)
	536,132,604 (volunteer hours per week)
	× 52 (numbers of weeks per year)
	27,878,895,408 volunteer hours per year
	× 4.25 (minimum wage)
Total Value of Volunteering	$118,485,305,484

delivering their services because they are less concerned with organizational constraints or reprisals.

On a broader perspective, volunteers can serve the public relations and fundraising functions more effectively and unobtrusively because they are drawn from the community in which the organization operates. These benefits are equally, if not more, important than the economic value of their contributions. Managers of sport and recreation organizations should make every effort to capitalize on the availability of volunteers and their enormous tangible and intangible contributions.

In a Nutshell

Volunteering is a significant economic activity when placing a dollar value on the time, energy, and expertise that people provide in their volunteer work. Equally important is the non-economic or social significance of volunteering. Volunteers are a source of credibility and legitimacy for their organizations, they provide objective and constructive evaluation of organizational processes, and they serve the public relations functions admirably.

Volunteer Organizations

The foregoing discussion addressed volunteer action in general. However, such volunteer action takes place in different organizational contexts, for different purposes, and with different motives. Therefore, considering the basic types of volunteer organizations is useful.

Sills (1972) defined a voluntary organization as

> an organized group of persons (1) that is formed in order to further some common interest of its members; (2) in which membership is voluntary in the sense that it is neither mandatory nor acquired through birth; and (3) that exists independently of the state. (p. 363)

Sills' definition is similar to Knoke's (1986) definition of an association: "A formally organized named group, most of whose members—whether persons or organizations—are not financially recompensed for their participation" (p. 2). These definitions are broad enough to include a variety of organizations ranging from the local sport clubs to nationally organized groups that promote the interests of a group of persons or organizations (e.g., National Collegiate Athletic Associations [NCAA]) or a particular ideology (e.g., National Association for Girls and Women in Sport). However, these voluntary associations differ among themselves in several ways, so they can be subdivided into specific categories. While several classifications of voluntary organizations exist, the classification that Palisi and Jacobson (1977) proposed seems to best fit our purposes. These authors based their scheme on earlier efforts of Gordon and Babchuk (1959) and Warriner and Prather (1965). Their scheme consists of five classes of voluntary organizations: **instrumental-productive for members, instrumental-productive for others, expressive-pleasure in performance, expressive-sociability,** and **expressive-ideological** (see figure 1.1).

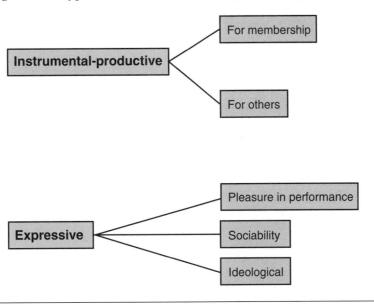

Figure 1.1 Palisi and Jacobson's typology of voluntary organizations.

• **Instrumental-productive for members**—Some volunteer organizations have been created and maintained for the benefit of the members. For instance, labor unions formed to ensure the rights, privileges, and benefits of its members (i.e., the workers). In the context of this discussion, the players' associations (e.g., National Football League [NFL] Players Association) and referees' guilds (e.g., Baseball Umpires Association) are examples of this class of volunteer organization that is instrumental in enhancing the welfare of its members.

• **Instrumental-productive for others**—Instrumental-productive volunteer organizations (e.g., Humane Society, American Red Cross, Goodwill Industries) exist for the primary purpose of producing goods or services for the benefit of the community or one of its deprived segments. Their critical activities are carried out with the intent of changing or improving something or somebody outside the membership, and such activities do not create specific benefits for the membership itself. Some of the charitable organizations, such as the Rotary Club, are engaged in providing sport and recreation services for the youth of the community. The major purpose of a national sport governing body (e.g., Basketball Canada), which is a volunteer organization, is to govern and regulate its activities for the benefit of participants in the sport.

• **Expressive-pleasure in performance**—The expressive-pleasure in performance organizations offer activities in which their members can participate exclusively. The activities of the organization (e.g., square dancing, bowling, and curling) can provide pleasure in the performance itself without any intention to produce goods or services. An intramural coed volleyball team and a community bowling league belong to this type of organization. Rules that external agencies, such as a national association or a professional group (e.g., American Bowling Congress and Curling Canada), set generally govern the activities around which the associations are formed.

• **Expressive-sociability**—Some volunteer organizations focus on satisfying the sociability needs of their members. The activities of such an organization can serve as a means for people to get together and satisfy their social needs (e.g., the Happy Hour Club and the Birthday Club). The activities of these clubs vary to a great extent: "In each case, however, it is clear that these activities are solely a vehicle for communion among the members, and it is incidental that the member [of a sewing club] may get her husband's socks darned" (Warriner and Prather 1965, 143).

• **Expressive-ideological**—When the organization's activities are carried out to evoke and reaffirm a valued belief system (e.g., communion in the Christian church), the association performs a symbolic function. These associations are formed on the basis of a sacred belief or doctrine that standardized or ritualized activities symbolize. Certain lodges and churches are examples of this class of associations.

The classification scheme of voluntary organizations has some relevance for sport and recreation organizations. Many of the sport clubs, such as intramural teams, provide the pleasure of participation in physical activity. Similarly, many other clubs (e.g., recreational soccer or volleyball clubs) serve the sociability function in addition to pleasure of participation. Several of the service clubs, such as the Lions, Kiwanis, and Knights of Columbus, exhibit the production function when they organize sport teams and competitions for the youngsters in their community. Organizations such as Little League are exclusively production-oriented; adults manage the organization and carry out its activities for the benefit of the youth (i.e., instrumental-productive for others).

It is hard to think of sport and recreation organizations that are organized around the symbolic function. However, one may argue that a group of body builders or joggers who do their activity with a religious fervor and create routines and symbolic rituals of their own may be considered as belonging to this type of association. Athletes in Action is an example of a sport organization that uses sport as a means to propagate the Christian ideology.

Note that individual participants may perceive that a volunteer organization or its activities gives pleasure either in a performance or in a sociability function. For example, a participant in a city recreational volleyball league may engage in that activity for the pleasure of performance, while another may participate in it for the social aspects.

The contrast among volunteer associations in their orientation toward benefits for their members compared with benefits for outsiders has implications for management. For instance, the recruiting practices need to vary according to the respective orientations. Organizations that are instrumental-productive for members recruit volunteer *members*. Organizations that are instrumental-productive for others recruit volunteer *workers*.

Obviously, recruiting a member is not as difficult as recruiting a worker without pay. This issue will be discussed in greater detail in chapter 9.

In a Nutshell

Volunteer organizations can be distinguished on the basis of instrumentality (whether they are formed to create benefits for their members or for other external target groups) and expressiveness (whether they offer opportunities for the members to engage in specific forms of activities, to satisfy their sociability needs, or to express an ideological perspective). Each type of volunteer organization imposes certain demands and constraints on management.

In addition to the described distinctions, volunteer organizations also differ in the degree of accessibility and status-conferring capacity (Gordon and Babchuk 1959). Volunteer organizations may be so open that persons with different social, economic, and demographic backgrounds can become members of that organization or participate in its programs. For instance, the YMCA sets membership criteria and allows everybody in the community to participate in its programs. On the other hand, some organizations restrict their membership to specified classes of people who possess some valued attributes. For example, a club comprising former athletes of a particular university restricts its membership on the basis of achievement. Similarly, some clubs restrict their membership based on sex, which once was an ascription. However, such restrictive membership based on factors such as sex or race have been challenged successfully in the courts, so they are becoming obsolete.

Volunteer organizations also differ in their capacity to bestow prestige on their members. That is, belonging to an association like the New York Athletic Club may bring status to a member without reference to the activities of the organization or the member's participation in those activities. Organizations also may confer status and prestige on their members because of the inherent worth of their programs or because of the significance that the community attaches to those activities. For instance, consider the various sport governing bodies. Members of all of these organizations enjoy a degree of status and prestige because they are engaged in developing elite athletes in their respective sports. However, because some of these sports are more popular and have great fan and media support, members of those organizations enjoy even greater status and prestige.

Who Volunteers?

The foregoing description of volunteer organizations provides a framework for analysis and prescription of managerial activities. However, it is also important that we gain some understanding of the people who compose those organizations. After all, those who manage or carry out the activities of an organization considerably influence the character and operational procedures of it. Further, volunteering need not be confined to volunteer organizations. It is becoming increasingly common for other forms of organizations including government organizations to use the services of volunteers. Therefore, the discussion of volunteers and volunteering should not be confined to just volunteer organizations. We need to understand the dynamics of volunteering without reference to organizational context.

Volunteer Demographics

One enduring line of research in this regard focuses on the social correlates of joining voluntary associations. Background variables, such as age, sex, education, income, marital status, and race, have been studied in cross-sectional surveys. Table 1.1 lists the rates of volunteering in 1996 among groups that sex, race, educational level, age, and income level define. A major advantage of this line of research is the identification of the target groups whose members are likely to volunteer. Unfortunately, however, the research results have not provided a clear pattern of relationships between these background variables and the rates of volunteering. While several studies have shown a relationship between selected variables and volunteering, such relationships have not been significant when considered simultaneously. For instance, Edwards and White (1980) found that several of the variables were moderately related to participation when considered individually, but none of them had a unique influence on participation when considered along with other variables. They concluded that "no definitive statement can be made regarding the seemingly ineffectual nature of the correlates [background variables, such as age, education, sex, and race] in predicting social involvement" (p. 71).

Along similar lines, Williams and Ortega (1986) found that only education and race were related to

Table 1.1   Rates of Volunteering by Sex, Race, Education, Age Group, and Income

Group	Volunteer rate (%)
Sex	
Men	45
Women	52
Race	
Whites	52
Non-whites	36
Education	
High school or less	36
Trade school	54
College	71
Age group (years)	
18-24	38
25-34	51
35-54	55
55-64	48
65-74	45
75 or more	34
Income ($)	
Less than 10,000	35
10,000-19,999	34
20,000-29,999	45
30,000-39,999	46
40,000-49,999	53
50,000-74,999	60
75,000-99,999	65
100,000 or more	69

Source: Giving and Volunteering in the United States. V.A. Hodgkinson and M.S. Weitzman, et al. 1996. Independent Sector.

volunteering in five different kinds of voluntary associations: church-related, job-related, recreation, fraternal or service, and civic or political. They concluded that "affiliation is not a unidimensional process and memberships in different types of associations are not interchangeable" (p. 35). Thus, the best judgment to make is that different background variables may be related to volunteering in different kinds of associations.

Regarding the background factors of volunteers in sport and recreation, a study of the volunteer and professional administrators of Canadian national sport organizations (Canadian Olympic Associa-

tion 1986) found that 77% of the volunteers were men and 23% were women, 58% were in the age range of 35 to 49 years, 83% were married, 75% had children, 77% had some or had completed university education, 81% worked full time with 42% in professional field and 27% in executive or administrative positions, and 57% had an income of more than $50 000. These figures are similar to the figures reported in the literature about volunteers in general.

Traditionally, women volunteered more often than men presumably because they had more leisure time. However, abundance of leisure time cannot be advanced anymore as a reason for this differential rate of volunteering because most women are in the workforce and an increasing number of women are single parents. Yet, even as late as 1996, more women (52%) than men (45%) continued to volunteer (see table 1.1).

Through their research, McPherson and Smith-Lovin (1986) highlighted another aspect of gender-related volunteering. They reported that segregation within voluntary organizations is considerable. Their results showed that almost 50% of the membership of the voluntary organizations that they surveyed comprised exclusively women and 20% comprised exclusively men. They also reported that the instrumental organizations were most heterogenous and that expressive groups were most likely homogenous. It is not clear if such differences exist in sport and recreation organizations. While gender-based segregation could exist among sport teams because of the rules surrounding the sport, cross-gender participation is becoming increasingly popular. The ever-changing views on gender-based roles and recent court rulings could further nudge sport and recreation organizations toward more heterogenous membership.

Corporate Employee Volunteering

A modern trend is for business and industrial enterprises to help the community by giving their own employees time off to volunteer their time and effort to community-oriented programs (Ilsley 1990; Steckel and Simons 1992; Tedrick and Henderson 1989). A significant thrust of the 1997 Presidents' Summit for America's Future was to encourage corporations to give their employees time off for volunteer work. Several corporate enterprises, including some nonprofit organizations such as Big Brothers/Big Sisters and the NFL Players Association, have committed to help in this regard.

This practice of corporations volunteering their employees is not restricted to North America. Consider corporate volunteering in sport and recreation in Japan. Universities in Japan do not support collegiate sports as well as universities in North America. Often the athletes have to find coaches for their teams. Many of the former members of the team volunteer to coach their former teams. It is not uncommon for their employing corporations to give time off to these volunteer coaches. The contributions of such corporate employees are not voluntary in the conventional sense because their corporations pay them for their time. However, those sport and recreation organizations that use their services may view them as volunteer workers and manage them accordingly. Managers of sport and recreation organizations may well consider corporations as the source of volunteers. While such corporate volunteering is one form of sponsorship, it may not cost the sponsoring organization as much in actual dollars because co-workers may share the workload of those corporate volunteers or the corporation may be over-staffed at the time.

In a Nutshell

While some differences exist in the rates of volunteering due to gender, race, age, education, and income, it is not clear if volunteering for a particular sport and recreation organization or a program is related to any of the demographic characteristics. Sport and recreation managers may request business and industrial enterprises to give time off to their employees for volunteering.

Why Do People Volunteer?

Although identifying the types of people who are likely to volunteer is useful in itself, it is also equally necessary to understand why people volunteer. That is, the psychological and motivational patterns of those who volunteer are as important as their socioeconomic background. In fact, one could argue that the question of why people volunteer is more critical than the question of who volunteers.

People differ in many respects: attitudes, beliefs, and personality. All of these differences underlie their motivation to engage and persevere in an activity and, therefore, have a bearing on management of human resources. These individual differences are operative in any context, e.g., in the family, in friendship groups, or in organizational contexts, whether the individuals are paid or volunteer workers. Concerns with individual differences are addressed in chapters 7 through 10. However, a fundamental question that needs to be addressed at this stage is, Why do people volunteer? That is, Why do people choose to act out their beliefs, attitudes, and personality in volunteer activity? What do individuals seek through their participation in voluntary work?

The question of volunteer motivation can best be answered by outlining and clarifying the possible benefits (i.e., personal rewards) that can accrue through participation in voluntary organizations. Smith (1981) and Knoke and Prensky (1984) emphasized the significance of a three-mode incentive scheme for analysis and understanding of volunteer participation. Knoke and Prensky labeled these incentives as

- utilitarian,
- affective, and
- normative.

Utilitarian Incentives

By definition, voluntary action precludes direct payment of salary or material benefits to volunteers. The reimbursement of the expenses incurred on behalf of the organization is not considered a utilitarian benefit for our purposes. However, it is conceivable that individuals may gain some benefits indirectly from their volunteering experience. For example, a sport management student may volunteer to help in the organization and conduction of a Special Olympics event. In the process, the student may gain experience in such an event and may gain an understanding of the philosophy and ideals of the Special Olympics. By the same token, a parent of one of the participants also may volunteer to assist in the event and, in the process, help his or her own child. In these two examples, the same event provides two different bases for volunteer incentives: experience and child care. Such utilitarian benefits may be the motivating force for many people to volunteer. Sport and recreation managers need to recognize that different incentives motivate different individuals to volunteer for any given project. According to Vaillancourt and Payette (1986), these **utilitarian incentives** can be explained by two models from economic theory: the household production model and the human capital model.

Household production comprises domestic chores, child-rearing activities, and child-minding activities. According to Vaillancourt and Payette (1986), people may volunteer as an extension of their child-rearing and child-minding activities. For example, a parent may volunteer to coach a youth soccer team in which his or her child is a member. Such volunteering is based on the utilitarian incentives associated with child-rearing and child-minding. The value of these benefits to a household increases with the number of children in the household. Therefore, it is not surprising that one of the more often cited reasons for volunteering in youth sports programs is that one's own children participate in those programs. However, note that these benefits can accrue only if several households cooperate through volunteering to provide the necessary services. That is, several other children need to bring their parents to the playground to coach other teams, to referee the game, or to serve in another function.

Human capital is knowledge and skill that, in turn, are determinants of wages or salaries. To increase future monetary rewards, individuals generally attempt to improve their human capital through education and work. Volunteering also can be a source of such enhancement of human capital. That is, individuals may learn as many new skills and gain as much new knowledge through volunteer work as through paid work. Such opportunities are more welcome to people who are excluded from regular paid work, such as people who are unemployed, people who are too young or too old to work, or people who are taking time off to rear their children. Even the well-placed employees and professionals may use volunteering for human capital purposes not only for learning (e.g., joining professional associations) but also for making contacts (e.g., joining Rotary Clubs). Such learning and networking is profitable to those for whom goodwill and personal contacts are important (e.g., lawyers and salespersons). People have cited developing teaching, leadership, or administrative skills and knowledge in sport and recreation as a reason for volunteering (e.g., Henderson 1981; Mitchelson and Slack 1983; Tedrick and Henderson 1989).

Affective Incentives

The affective incentives are a function of interpersonal relationships that result in fellowship, friendship, prestige, and similar outcomes. Thus, the affective incentives play a greater role in the three forms of expressive organizations (see figure 1.1), particularly those organizations that emphasize the sociability function. Because all organizations are composed of people, these outcomes are theoretically possible in various organizations. However, the particular composition of the membership of an organization and the purposes and processes that the organization adopts may affect the degree to which these benefits accrue to an individual volunteer. Again, people have cited these social incentives as reasons for volunteering in sport and recreation (e.g., Henderson 1981; Mitchelson and Slack 1983; Tedrick and Henderson 1989).

Normative Incentives

Volunteer organizations may pursue the goals of helping others by enhancing their happiness, health, and welfare. Individuals may share these organizational goals and join these organizations because of their genuine concern for the welfare of others. The normative incentives are the satisfactions derived from having done something good as reflected in the organizational purposes. This particular set of incentives is more relevant to the instrumental-productive for others and expressive-ideological voluntary organizations than to any other type of volunteer organizations (see figure 1.1).

Note the similarities between the classifications of volunteer organizations and volunteer incentives (or motives). For instance, the expressive-sociability function of a volunteer organization is consistent with the affective incentives. Similarly, the expressive-ideological function subsumes the normative incentives. However, the distinction between the two schemes is that one is described from the organizational perspective and the other is based on individuals' perspective.

In a Nutshell

People may volunteer for utilitarian reasons (i.e., either as part of their household functions or as an enhancement of their human capital in terms of skills, knowledge, and experience), affective reasons (i.e., to satisfy their needs for friendship, fellowship, and status), and normative reasons (i.e., the need to do something good).

Altruism and Volunteerism

The previous sections have clarified to some extent the incentives and motives for volunteering. However, one issue that makes the discussion more complex and perplexing relates to the notion of altruism in volunteering. A clear understanding of the issue is critical to management of volunteers in sport and recreation organizations.

The most often cited reason for volunteering, and the reason often imbedded in the definitions of volunteerism, is **altruism** (Anderson and Moore 1978, Schindler-Rainman and Lippit 1975). *Webster's Ninth New Collegiate Dictionary* (1986) defined altruism as "unselfish concern for the welfare of others: opposed to egoism." In turn, it defined egoism as "the tendency to be self-centered, or to consider only oneself or one's own interests; selfishness."

In Their View

Psychologists studied the mechanism behind "helping" behavior (Batson 1991, Cialdini et al. 1987, Dovidio 1995). One view, the egoistic view, holds that people help others only to relieve their own stress or to improve their own moods (Cialdini et al. 1987). In the other view, the altruistic view, people also can be motivated to help only to improve the welfare of others without reference to personal stress or mood (Batson 1991, Dovidio 1995). Most of the research on this ongoing egoism-altruism debate addresses helping in a single incident of some form of emergency. However, when extended, these concepts suggest that volunteering in sport and recreation can be egoistically or altruistically based.

Scholars and practitioners debate the traditional view that altruism underlies volunteering. Smith (1981) pointed out that the debate about the relationship between altruism and volunteerism tends to be muddled with differing definitions, and the "arguments tend to be endless and heat tends to far exceed light in these debates" (p. 21). In his view, altruism is

an aspect of human motivation that is present to the degree that the individual derives intrinsic satisfaction or psychic rewards from attempting to optimize the intrinsic satisfaction of one or more other persons without the conscious expectation of participating in an exchange relationship whereby those "others" would be obligated to make similar/related satisfaction optimization efforts in return. (p. 23)

Smith's definition envisaged two kinds of outcomes emanating from the same action: egoistic outcomes (i.e., one's own intrinsic satisfaction or psychic rewards) and altruistic outcomes (i.e., the satisfaction and rewards of others). Smith further suggested that absolute altruism is not a necessary condition for volunteerism and that concern for some kind of personal rewards underlies all volunteering.

The essence of volunteerism is *not* altruism, but rather the contribution of services, goods, or money to help accomplish some desired end, without substantial coercion or remuneration. It is the voluntariness and nonremunerated character of volunteerism that is distinctive. . . . Volunteers are not angelic humanitarians in any sense. They are human beings, engaging in unpaid, uncoerced activities for various kinds of tangible and intangible incentives, with psychic or intangible incentives being especially important. Nor are volunteer organizations paragons of organizational virtue in any sense. Some do very positive things for the general welfare; others are harmful, and selfish in the extreme. (Smith 1981, 33)

In contrast, other authors hold that "altruism is a central, and potentially *the* central, impetus for volunteer activity" (Flashman and Quick 1985, 156). Miller (1982) stated that

Altruism does exist. Obviously it is sometimes hopelessly entangled with, and sometimes swamped by, other sorts of motives. There is not as much of it as many of us would wish; but it does exist, and it isn't even particularly rare. . . . Most of us fairly frequently, and probably almost all of us sometimes, act for the good of others. (p. 50)

While acknowledging that one's altruistic involvement in volunteering might yield psychic benefits to the participant, Miller argued that such personal rewards do not negate one's original altruistic motives.

The foregoing discussion leads to the conclusion that altruistic motivation and self-rewards (or self-reinforcements) can operate concurrently. That is, volunteer motivation simultaneously can be other-oriented and self-oriented. This view is analogous to the distinction that Sills (1972) made between the satisfaction derived from the purposes of the organization (other-orientation) and the activities themselves (self-orientation). To illustrate, consider two different sport associations (e.g., soccer and tennis) espousing the same altruistic goal of enriching the lives of youth. Assume that this altruistic goal attracts you and that you want to help the local youth by joining one of the two associations. Suppose also that the two associations choose different sets of activities to achieve the specified goal and adopt different organizational structures and processes and that the associations have recruited different sets of volunteers with different personal dispositions, abilities, and skills. Now your choice of one association over another is most likely to be based on your liking and preferences for the activities, organizational processes, and the people of the two associations. That is, your choice is based on self-orientation although the altruistic purpose of helping the youth (i.e., the goal of both associations) was the original reason for volunteering. These relationships are illustrated in figure 1.2.

From a different perspective, the initial entry into volunteering may indeed be altruistic, but subsequent continued participation is contingent upon the satisfaction of individual needs (Phillips 1982, Wolensky 1980). Henderson (1981, 1985) provided another view subscribing to the notion of simultaneity of other- and self-orientation in volunteering. The author suggested that volunteering, in fact, might be a form of leisure for those participants. In this case, leisure participation, which is personally oriented, could be coupled with altruistic intentions of helping others.

Yet another perspective holds that self-orientation in specific ways may indeed be necessary for carrying out other-oriented activities. Flashman and Quick (1985) introduced the notion of self-care (i.e., "keeping oneself in an optimal state of physical, mental,

and spiritual well-being") as opposed to self-neglect (i.e., "failure to properly care for one's basic needs"). Altruism, of course, is based on the degree of selflessness as opposed to selfishness. Flashman and Quick argued that selflessness and self-care were mutually reinforcing components of altruism.

Intelligent self-care enables an individual to be at his or her best, to function at a high level of well-being. When an individual is functioning at a high level of well-being, he or she is in optimal position to be aware of and contribute to the welfare of others. Similarly, as a person intelligently and selflessly contributes to the well-being of others, that person tends to enhance his or her own well-being in that he or she feels a sense of satisfaction and others tend to care for him or her (p. 159).

In a Nutshell

The essence of altruism defined as "unselfish concern for the welfare of others" is not minimized because a person gains some benefits, such as an increase in one's skills and experience, as by-products of volunteering. Personal growth of a volunteer actually ensures better service to the clients.

Summary

In summary, this chapter described and discussed the types of volunteer organizations, types of people who volunteer, and the reasons why they volunteer. The classification schemes of voluntary organizations, particularly that of Palisi and Jacobson (1977),

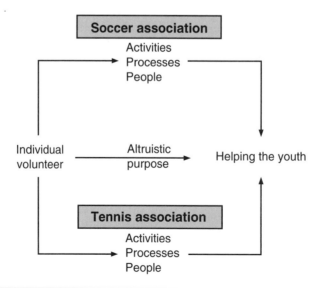

Figure 1.2   Organizational purpose and activities as sources of attraction.

clarify the organizational purposes of various associations. Whether they are managers or front-line workers, members need to understand these purposes because they are the basis for all organizational activities and processes. The literature on the types of people who volunteer does not show a consistent pattern and, therefore, is not much help to the practicing manager. Organizations have no clear indication of what groups, which various socio-economic factors define, they should target when recruiting volunteers. In addition, no indication exists regarding whether volunteers from a particular socio-economic background are more effective than other volunteers. Therefore, recruiters of volunteers should keep an open mind and should approach all segments of the population for volunteers.

The literature on the reasons for volunteering (i.e., volunteer motivation) is more promising and, thus, helpful to the manager. Self-orientation can be a significant motivational factor, and it does not minimize serving others (if the purpose of the organization is serving others). The literature reviewed shows that self-orientation of volunteers can be reflected in the indirect utilitarian benefits (i.e.,

household production, enhancement of human capital, or both); the solidary (social) benefits of participation; and the satisfaction derived from doing something good for others. The satisfaction of doing something well can be added to this list. Herzberg (1968) and other motivational theorists pointed out that the sense of achievement and gaining competence in that activity strengthens one's motivation to engage in an activity. These satisfactions are intrinsic to the activity and are attained only after the completion of the activity. In contrast, before volunteer work, individuals consciously seek other self-oriented benefits. Based on this information, managers may find the following guideline profitable:

> The clear implication of all of the foregoing is that volunteer organizations should never depend solely on appeals to altruism and other purposive incentives. . . . Material and solidary incentives, appropriate to the particular volunteer group or program, should be provided as the major elements of the reward system if volunteerism is to be maximized. (Smith 1981, 31-32)

Key Terms

volunteers, volunteerism, instrumental-productive for members, instrumental-productive for others, expressive-pleasure in performance, expressive-sociability, expressive-ideological, utilitarian incentives, household production, human capital, altruism

Your Perspectives

- Almost every student has had some experience in volunteering. What is your overall perspective on your volunteering experience?

- Consider only one of the organizations for which you volunteered. For what type of organization did you volunteer? Describe its purposes, its processes, and its membership. What did you like about the organization?

- What kind of work were you asked to do? What did you gain from your volunteering experience in that organization?

- Considering that experience, how would you rate yourself on altruism on the one hand and self-interest on the other hand? How did these two orientations (i.e., altruism and self-interest) affect your volunteer work? How did they affect your sense of self-worth?

2

Professionals and Professionalism

Learning Objectives

After reading this chapter you will be able to

- describe a profession and its attributes,
- explain how an occupation may gain a professional status,
- identify the forces of deprofessionalization,
- explain the professional status of sport and recreation management, and
- compare the similarities and dissimilarities between professionalism and volunteerism.

The introduction noted that most sport and recreation organizations comprise both volunteer and paid workers. The management of these two sets of workers with divergent orientations is a challenge. The introduction also noted that the professionals who form one group of paid workers need to be managed in a special way.

Who are the professionals in sport and recreation? Obviously, the paid managers themselves are a significant group of professionals. Intercollegiate athletic directors and their marketing directors are example of professionals. The NCAA and professional leagues in various sports hire managers with high professional qualifications. In addition, these agencies also hire lawyers to handle their legal matters. Similarly many athletic teams (collegiate as well as professional teams) hire qualified athletic trainers and other medical professionals. The coaches themselves constitute a professional group.

An understanding of the distinctions between what we call professional workers and nonprofessional workers would indicate the ways in which the professional workers should be managed. In this chapter, I review the concepts of professionals and professionalism. I also highlight the extent to which sport management itself can be considered a profession. More important, I show that professionalism and volunteerism are largely consonant with each other.

Characteristics of a Profession

The most common attributes of a profession include

- a systematic body of knowledge,
- professional authority,
- community sanction, and
- a code of ethics (Goode 1969, Jackson 1970, Ulrich 1997).

Systematic Body of Knowledge

A distinguishing characteristic of a profession is that it is founded on a **body of knowledge**. By basing the practice of a profession on a systematic body of knowledge, an occupation makes a conscious effort to

- generate more knowledge by carrying out research as well as compiling and distilling the experiences of successful members,
- transmit the specialized knowledge to the new entrants, and
- develop the special skills and competencies of the members through a prolonged and arduous period of training.

Training in the specialized body of knowledge consists of both intellectual and practical experiences. It is not surprising, therefore, that the status of the established professions largely is associated with the number of years of training for entry into that profession. Length of training is a surrogate measure of the quantity and quality of the knowledge to be absorbed.

Professional Authority

The members of the profession have the authority to decide on what, how, and when a service should be provided to a client. This professional authority stems from, and is limited to, the knowledge base of the profession referred to earlier. More specifically, it is the knowledge differential between the client and the professional that determines the extent of **professional authority** (Mills and Margulies 1980; Sasser, Olsen, and Wyckoff 1978). Obviously, the client must first recognize and accept this knowledge differential before authority can exist. The authority of a profession also is related to the extent to which the profession can claim monopoly over knowledge.

Community Sanction

A profession has the sanction of the community (i.e., society through its various levels of government) to control the training and admittance of members to its field of practice, to monitor and evaluate the activities of its members, and to reward members for good performance or punish them for deviations from the technical and ethical standards that the profession sets. In general, the control over the profession is vested in the national associations of the professional members. For example, the American Medical Association and the Canadian Medical Association regulate the activities of the medical profession and its members in their respective countries. Further, the governments restrain nonmembers from engaging in the activities of the profession, thereby creating a monopoly. For instance, nobody can practice medicine in the United States if he or she is not a member of the American Medical Association.

Regulative Code of Ethics

To enhance the legitimation of itself, a profession formulates a set of ideologies including its mission and values. Professions emphasize the values of service, impartiality, and rationality. Goode (1969) claimed that the ideal of service is critical to the concepts of a profession and professionalism. To ensure that the service orientation is maintained, a profession prescribes a code of ethics, which is a set of standards of behavior for members in their professional practice.

A cursory analysis of occupations would show that a large number of them fail to meet this criteria. The two occupations that have been recognized as true professions are the medical and legal professions. Other occupations can be placed at different points in a continuum ranging from crafts to full professions. For example, Etzioni (1969) designated occupations such as teaching and nursing as semi-professions because

> Their training is shorter, their status is less legitimated . . . there is less of a specialized body of knowledge, and they have less autonomy from supervision or societal control than "the" [e.g., legal and medical] professions. (p. v)

Process of Professionalization

Forsyth and Danisiewicz (1985) proposed a model of **professionalization** depicting the process through

In a Nutshell

An occupation is a profession when its services are based in an extensive body of knowledge, the knowledge differential between the service provider and the client is large enough, the community recognizes the importance of the occupation and sanctions its approval to monitor and control itself, and the occupation institutes a strict code of ethics.

which occupations strive to become true professions. The model shown in figure 2.1 includes both the nature of the service that an occupation provides and the efforts it takes to project its image.

As these authors noted,

> The nature of the service-task performed by the occupation predisposes that service-task to the profession phenomenon if it is *essential* (of serious importance to clients), *exclusive* (the occupational practitioners have a monopoly on the service-task), and *complex* (the service-task is not routine and typically involves the individual and discretionary application of a specialized body of knowledge). (p. 62) (emphasis added)

The following sections detail the process of professionalization by describing the concepts of **essentiality**, **exclusivity**, and **complexity**. As indi-

cated in figure 2.1, these three elements are critical for an occupation to attain the professional status.

Essentiality

Some services are deemed more essential than others. The professional rights and privileges referred to earlier are sanctioned only if an occupation addresses some universal social concerns and problems of living (Jackson 1970). According to Forsyth and Danisiewicz (1985), a hierarchy of essential needs of the society or its serious problems can be identified, and occupations can be rated on the dimension of essentiality based on which of the needs or problems they address. Thus, occupations addressing life and death problems are considered more essential than leisure services. The same kind of logic may be extended to members within a single occupation. For example, within the teaching occupation, society accords greater status to teachers of certain subjects because they deem those subjects more essential than the other subjects. As another example, people may consider the services of an exercise physiologist in a fitness club to be more essential than the services of the receptionist because the exercise physiologist engages in fitness assessment and exercise prescription. Similarly, some people may consider a sport psychologist's services to be more essential to an athletic team than the services of the team manager. In general, the contrasts between human services and consumer services discussed in the introduction suggest that

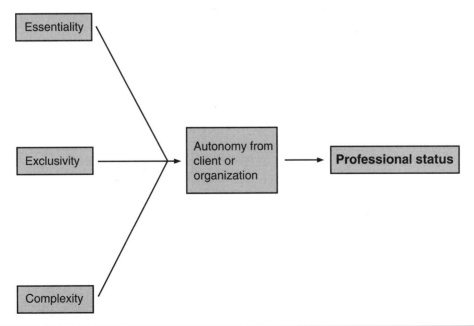

Figure 2.1   Model of professionalization.

Adapted from Forsyth and Danisiewicz 1985.

human services are relatively more essential from the perspective of society than the consumer services.

Exclusivity

Exclusiveness of a service refers to the occupation's monopoly over its services. Such a monopoly can arise because nonmembers of the occupation lack the knowledge or the special skills needed to perform those services. An occupation legally can forbid nonmembers from providing specific services only if it can prove that nobody else outside of that occupation has the knowledge and competencies necessary to perform such services. For example, being a brain surgeon requires much knowledge and training. As Friedson (1973) noted, professionalization is

> a process by which an organized occupation, usually but not always by virtue of making a claim to special esoteric competence and to concern for the quality of its work and its benefits to society, *obtains the exclusive right to perform a particular kind of work, control training for and access to it, and control the right of determining and evaluating the way the work is performed.* (p. 22) (emphasis added)

Exclusivity is suggestive of political maneuvering in competition against other occupations. Historically, forming associations and engaging in political activity were necessary conditions for occupations to gain professional status (Wilensky 1964).

Complexity

The complexity of the services refers to the application of a variety of techniques to conclude a service. It also implies that services themselves vary depending on the specific client or problem that the service provider addresses. Thus, because the problems that the physical therapists face are varied and

the treatment of each problem may involve different pieces of information and techniques, their services are more complex than those of the locker-room attendant. This idea of complexity underlies the distinction made in the introduction between consumer services and professional services. In accordance with this explanation, several of the sport and recreation services can be graded along the dimension of complexity.

Image Building

In addition to possessing the attributes of essentiality, exclusivity, and complexity, the occupation also must engage in image building, which refers to an occupation's efforts to convince society that its services are indeed essential, exclusive, and complex. The ultimate aim of such efforts is to gain society's recognition and sanctions to control its own activities. Such control is manifested in the power that the service providers have. In turn, the service providers make operational the power of their autonomy from both their clients and their employing organizations.

In a Nutshell

The community sanctions the professional status to an occupation and allows it to monitor itself only when the services of the occupation are considered complex and essential to the community and when only the members of the occupation, who have been extensively trained, can provide it. Occupations engage in image-building activities to convince the community that its services are essential, complex, and exclusive to their occupations so that they can obtain this sanction.

While the foregoing attributes of an occupation make it a profession, occupations vary in the extent to which they possess those attributes. By the same

An example of a fitness club can illustrate the idea that several jobs in an organizational context can be graded on the dimension of complexity. The chief accountant's job is more complex than that of a bookkeeping clerk because the accountant manages the complexities associated with city, state, and federal laws. The manager of the fitness club has a more complex job than an exercise leader because the manager addresses larger concerns, such as market trends, personnel decisions, legal issues, and public relations.

We can also place several jobs in a university athletic department on the continuum of complexity. The athletic director manages matters of greater complexity than a facility manager, whose job is more complex than that of a caretaker. The football coach's job is more complex than that of the equipment manager.

token, occupations also differ in the degree to which they can control the entry of individuals into the occupation and restrict nonmembers from engaging in the occupational activities. For instance, anyone who wants to be an athletic trainer needs to be certified by the Board of Certification of the National Athletic Trainers' Association. However, the occupation of athletic trainers does not enjoy the same professional status as medicine because it only partially meets other requirements to be a profession. For instance, the training period is much longer in medicine than in athletic training. Further, medicine is based on a much broader base of knowledge than athletic training. Finally, medical practitioners are permitted to carry out the functions of athletic trainers whereas the athletic trainers are prohibited from performing many of the functions of the medical professional. In a similar manner, many other occupations in sport and recreation may meet some but not all criteria of a profession. The designation for such occupations are described.

Professions, Semi-Professions, and Mimic Professions

Forsyth and Danisiewicz (1985) suggested that, based on the true nature of the services that occupations provide (whether they are essential, exclusive, and complex) and their promotional activities, society grants varying degrees of professional status, prestige, and power to these occupations. As noted earlier, the extent to which the practitioners are autonomous with reference to both their clients and their employing organizations exemplifies power. For instance, a client's perception of his or her own needs does not guide a medical practitioner as much as it would a salesperson. Similarly, the organization is likely to have greater control over the sales-

person than over the medical practitioner. Thus, some occupations, such as medicine and law, gain the true professional status because they have both kinds of autonomy; some occupations, such as education and nursing, can be considered semi-professions because they enjoy autonomy only from one source—their clients.

In the context of human resource management, the knowledge of the field and his or her assessment of the fitness level of clients guides an exercise physiologist at a large fitness club in prescribing an exercise program for the clients. Although the exercise physiologist may consider a client's personal preference for one form of physical activity over another, the clients are not likely to influence the duration, intensity, and frequency of the exercise program. Thus, the exercise physiologist can be considered to be autonomous of the clients. However, the exercise physiologist is not likely to experience such autonomy from the organization insofar as the organization decides his or her employment status and work assignment. Thus, exercise physiology may be considered a semi-profession.

Forsyth and Danisiewicz (1985) called those occupations that claimed professional status, but were not granted the same, mimic professions.

> Principles of natural selection may explain the evolution of one animal species to *look* like another species having some vital advantage. Analogously, mimic professions may have a code of ethics and other trappings of professions, but they have no power. They have taken on the coloration but not the substance of profession. . . . Thus, there are limitations on the role of image building in the professionalization process. Mimic professions have built an image that exceeds credibility. (pp. 64-65)

The Board of Certification of the National Athletic Trainers' Association conducts a three-part examination before certifying a prospective athletic trainer. The three parts are written examination, written simulation of an athletic injury and treatment, and oral or practical examination. A candidate is eligible to take the examination if he or she meets specific criteria including

- graduation from an accredited undergraduate athletic training program or
- successful completion of 1,500 hours of athletic training experience under a certified athletic trainer who has at least 1,000 hours in interscholastic, intercollegiate, or professional sports; at least one credit course in health, human anatomy, kinesiology or biomechanics, human physiology, physiology of exercise, basic athletic training, and advanced athletic training; and a bachelor's degree.

From: Brochure of the National Athletic Trainers' Association, 1997.

Finally, nonprofessional occupations that do not make any claim to be professional also exist.

Based on these factors, Hasenfeld (1983) classified human service workers as professionals, semiprofessionals, and paraprofessionals.

> Human service occupations vary in their degree of professionalization; they range from physicians, who enjoy the highest degree of professional power, to social workers, teachers, and nurses (who are classified as *semiprofessionals*), to hospital attendants, eligibility workers, and prison guards (who are classified as *paraprofessionals*). (p. 163)

For example, consider the medical staff attached to a high-level athletic team. The medical doctors, as noted before, are the professionals, while the athletic trainers are the semi-professionals. People who assist the doctors and athletic trainers in carrying equipment or injured athletes are the paraprofessionals.

Deprofessionalization

While occupations may continue to strive to gain the status of professions, counteracting forces work against such efforts; these forces deprofessionalize the occupations. Based on the works of Haug (1975) and Toren (1975), Lawson (1979) enunciated the bases of such **deprofessionalization** as

- the increasing educational level of the citizenry that, in turn, redefines the professional-client relationships;
- the reliance of occupations on experience and on experiential skills and knowledge that the lay public easily masters; and
- the advances in computer and media technology that facilitate the routinizing and packaging of the operations for persons who have minimal professional training to use.

The last factor simply implies that all one needs to know is where and how to get the routinized and computerized packages when one wants them (Lawson 1979).

Even the established professions, such as medicine and law, are losing some of their power over people for several reasons. First, the occupations that traditionally provided the support services to the professions have gained enough knowledge and competence to claim professional status for themselves. For instance, hospital nurses are sufficiently knowledgeable and competent that they can perform many of the services that only doctors traditionally provided. Secondly, the explosion of knowledge in every field has made mastering all of the knowledge in a field impossible for an individual, so specialists have emerged. With increasing specialization comes the dispersion of authority and consequent decrease in professional status. For instance, gone are the days when an athletic director of a Division I undergraduate school was able to handle all of the managerial functions and, thus, enjoy a greater degree of authority. Presently, specialists in areas such as marketing, public relations, and sport law know more about their specialties than a typical athletic director. Thus, the athletic director shares professional authority with these specialists.

Professional Status of Sport Management and Sport and Recreation Services

Jurkus (1978) noted that management (i.e., management in general) itself cannot yet be deemed a profession for two main reasons. First, no central professional association governs the activities of all managers. Since then, some strong associations, such as the Academy of Management, the North American Society for Sport Management, and the National Intramural and Recreational Sport Association, have emerged. These associations have formulated a code of ethics for their members. However, no mechanism equivalent to disbarment in the legal profession or defrocking in the clerical profession exists by which managers, including sport and recreation managers, could be forced to abide by a code of ethics.

The second factor that restrains management, including sport management, is that the extent of knowledge about management is less solid than in other recognized professions. As Jurkus (1978) noted,

> the knowledge of human behavior and organizational processes will never advance to such a stage that one can be as confident about the outcome of adding a new sales manager and six salespeople to a territory to increase market share as one can be about the effects of administering a dosage of penicillin to counteract a bacterial infection. (p. 984)

Raelin (1987) confirmed the view that management has progressed much toward being a profession, but it is not yet a profession. For instance, managers are being trained in accredited professional schools in a prolonged specialized education and have autonomy, at least at the top levels, as other established professions. However, in his view, management lags behind in two significant aspects. First, as Jurkus also stated, the professional associations in management are not strong enough to police the conduct of its members. Second, although service to society is part of the ethical code of management, managers typically are committed to the organization and its owners. Sometimes these two orientations conflict, and the orientation toward the common good is not guaranteed to prevail. Therefore, Raelin believes that management is not as professional as medicine or law. For instance, an athletic director may be committed to the development of athletes and to equity in athletics. However, the preferences and dictates of university authorities may run counter to these professional commitments. To the extent that the athletic director is beholden to the university, his or her professional commitments have to take a backseat.

However, the status accorded to specialized management fields may vary with the type of products with which the field is concerned and with the size of the operations. For example, hospital management is accorded greater status than restaurant management because the former is managing services that address life and death. Similarly, industrial management is more critical to society than parks management because of the greater economic impact associated with the former. Therefore, it is only appropriate to discuss the status of the services under the jurisdiction of sport management and not sport management itself.

How do sport and recreation services rate on the dimension of essentiality? Do they address universal social problems or problems of living? From this perspective, how would society view sport and recreation services compared with occupations such as medicine and law. While all address people per se, sport and recreation services differ from the other two in significant ways. First, most people view sport and recreation services as addressing diversionary, leisure-time activities. This perspective contrasts the views of professionals in the field who hold that sport and recreation services are essential to the quality of life. However, all would agree that some sport and recreation services are relatively more essential (e.g., therapeutic exercise and cardiac rehabilitation programs). Thus, the content of most sport and recreation services is not likely to be perceived to be as serious as life in medicine or justice in law. Just as dentistry is accorded less status than medicine because life can go on without the teeth, our services also are accorded much less status than other occupations because life can go on without leisure activities.

Second, the established professions address problems such as disease and disorder, whereas sport and recreation services largely are concerned with growth and learning. Society tends to favor occupations that solve immediate problems; they take other occupations for granted. Thus, a physiotherapist is likely to be respected more than a playground instructor.

What is the status of sport and recreation services in terms of knowledge and competency? These services are not likely to gain respect from outsiders for their knowledge base for several reasons. The field is not focused around a clearly defined subject matter and is not fully founded upon scientific knowledge. This statement does not deny the great progress that managers have made in generating and synthesizing a body of knowledge unique to our field. However, these advances cannot yet match the status of other established professions.

The introduction described the various sport and recreation services. How do these services and the people who provide these services rate on professional status? From our discussion of professional status, consumer services (i.e., consumer-pleasure and consumer-health services) have lower professional status than human services have (i.e., human-excellence, human-sustenance, and human-curative services). Considering the attributes of a profession, human-curative services and the people who provide those services have high professional status because they address life and quality of life.

Note the difference between professional status and economic significance. Consider the coaching ranks in Division I. Coaches of all sports are performing a human service because they help the athletes achieve excellence. Thus, they are rated the same on the professional status. Yet, administrators, media, and the public accord greater status to coaches of football and basketball teams because those sports are more popular than other sports and because they generate more fan support as well as revenue. The focus in this chapter is on the professional status.

If an occupation can claim power through knowledge, it must have a monopoly over that knowledge—i.e., the attribute of exclusivity (Jackson 1970). Sport and recreation services face a problem in this regard because their knowledge base is multidisciplinary. For instance, management, including sport and recreation management, is founded upon the knowledge generated in fields such as psychology and sociology. Take the case of marketing a sport or recreation service. The notion of market segmentation based on social and economic factors is derived from sociology, but attempts to "sell" the sport product are based on the knowledge of the dynamics of persuasion, which is a research thrust in psychology. To the extent that the knowledge base of management is anchored in other disciplines, those other disciplines are not likely to yield their "ownership" of the knowledge.

Insofar as the competencies and skills in sport and recreation services are based more on practical experience than on a body of knowledge (Morford 1972), many outsiders can claim the same expertise on the basis of having participated and having been involved in sport and recreation. This is particularly true of sports and recreation for the young. To use Jackson's (1970) comment on primary schools, it is where "everyone goes to learn what everyone knows." Along similar lines, Morford (1972) noted: "Few of the public are lay physicists or mathematicians. But lay coaches? They are dime a dozen. Their number is legion, far in excess of those with professional credentials" (p. 90). What Morford refers to is the common phenomenon of "Monday morning quarterbacks." A careful analysis of the numerous commentators' views expressed during a sport broadcast on the how, when, and why of coaching reveals how fragmented coaching knowledge is and the extent to which such knowledge is based on personal experiences and insights rather than on science.

Sport and recreation service workers in general do not enjoy the professional authority as defined earlier. The authority or power is a function of the knowledge differential between the professional and the client. Thus, to the extent that the physician has more knowledge about a patient's illness and the remedies thereof than the patients themselves, the physician possesses authority and power. In the absence of any extraordinary knowledge, as is the case in sport management, the practitioners do not possess as much professional authority as a physician.

Sport and recreation services do engage in image-building activities through their national associations. However, the way society perceives our services (i.e., they are not perceived to be that essential, exclusive, or complex) and the lack of a strong and unified voice representing all of our interests limits the effectiveness of these efforts.

In Their View

In pointing out the relationships between sport management and sport sociology, Professor James E. Bryant (1993) stated that

> Sport management is interdependent with sport sociology as specialization areas, and that in order for researchers in sport management to understand the social product of sport it is critical that they recognize a positive theoretical relationship between sport management and sport sociology. . . . Sport organizations and management are generic social phenomena that require a sociological analysis, and that analysis enables organizations and management to understand and address service related to the community and economic development. (p. 194)

Professor Andrew Yiannakis (1989) expressed similar views.

> Managing a sport or leisure organization in today's highly competitive world requires the application of highly developed multidisciplinary skills. It is imperative, therefore, to provide for the education and training of sport managers by employing, initially, a broad liberal arts perspective—a perspective that focuses on those most relevant analytic and conceptual skills from the social behavioral sciences. . . . To this end, the contributions of sport sociology to sport and leisure management, and in particular sport marketing, suggest that the field can make significant contributions both as an area of study and in providing solutions to a variety of marketing problems and concerns. (p. 113)

Professionalism in Sport Management and Sport and Recreation Services

Although management of sport and recreation services cannot be deemed a profession, its status

In a Nutshell

Given that general management itself cannot claim professional status, the community is unlikely to accord professional status to sport and recreation management. Because they are in a newer field of study, sport managers have not built up a body of knowledge that they can call their own. That is, many others outside of sport management can carry out their activities, albeit with less efficiency and effectiveness. Further, because sport managers are concerned with management of sport and recreation services, their efforts may not be considered essential.

should not be viewed as lessening the significance of the field. As noted earlier, the concept of a profession itself is outmoded and does not serve any useful purpose at the moment. However, the notions inherent in the ideal of a profession should guide all occupational efforts. The emphasis here is on being professional and not on being a profession. That is, occupations may be characterized by a high degree of professionalism without being a profession in the classical sense. The concepts of professionalism and being a professional has significance for all human services including sport and recreation services.

In order to be better equipped to serve the public, sport and recreation management needs to strengthen the following characteristics of **professionalism** as Morrow and Goetz (1988) outlined. By the same token, sport and recreation managers can facilitate the development of these characteristics in the occupations within sport and recreation services.

(1) application of skills based on technical knowledge,

(2) requirements of advanced education and training,

(3) some formal testing of competence and control of admission to profession,

(4) the existence of professional associations,

(5) the existence of codes of conducts or ethics, and

(6) the existence of an accepted commitment or calling, or sense of responsibility for serving the public. (p. 94)

On an individual basis, the members of our field would ideally

(1) use the profession and fellow professionals as a major referent,

(2) believe that the profession provides an important service to society,

(3) believe in the regulation of the profession by its members,

(4) believe that practitioners of the profession feel a life-long sense of calling, and

(5) believe that individuals should have the right to make decisions in their work without the approval of others. (Morrow and Goetz 1988, 94)

In recent years, the field of sport management has taken great strides toward professionalism. The formation of the North American Society for Sport Management (NASSM) has provided the impetus toward professionalism, particularly in setting curricular standards for university degree programs, creating a code of ethics for the field, and offering the means of communication of knowledge pertaining to the field. In collaboration with the National Association for Sport and Physical Education (NASPE), NASSM has drawn up a set of minimal standards for curriculum and faculty complement

The discussion here compares the professional status of sport management with the status of other established professions, such as medicine and law. This discussion does not deny that many occupational categories within sport management do possess extraordinary knowledge and competencies that are valuable and not easily replicated. Take the case of basketball coach and manager Rick Pitino, who in 1997 signed a contract worth $70 million over a 10-year period with the Boston Celtics. Other coaches in the National Basketball Association (NBA) are said to receive salaries of $5 million each year. Some sport agents enjoy a great amount of prestige and wealth based on their uncanny abilities. Remember, however, that these special competencies and insights are unique to individual coaches and agents and are not general characteristics of the occupations that they represent. For example, is there a body of knowledge in the coaching occupation that another coach can absorb?

for the university training of sport managers at the bachelor's, master's, and doctoral levels (NASPE-NASSM Joint Task Force 1993). These organizations also set up a mechanism to accredit interested universities in terms of these standards. As of June 1997, more than 20 sport management degree programs had been accredited. Finally, the annual conferences of NASSM provide a forum for theorists and practitioners to exchange their expertise and experiences in furthering the knowledge base of the field. As equally important, NASSM was also instrumental in creating the *Journal of Sport Management*. With the introduction of another journal—the *Sport Marketing Quarterly*—the field boasts two journals dedicated exclusively to promotion of sport management.

In a Nutshell

The important point for sport managers and service providers in sport and recreation to remember is to be professional in all of their activities. Being professional implies that they honestly believe in their cause and calling, constantly strive to improve their knowledge and skills, follow the guidelines of their professional associations, and are ethical in all of their actions.

Professionalism and Volunteerism

As noted in the introduction, one characteristic of many sport and recreation organizations is that they employ both paid professional and volunteer workers. The challenging task of managing these two sets of workers will be discussed in detail in part III. For the moment, consider some of the significant similarities and differences between professionalism and volunteerism.

Management of workers with a professional orientation can be both challenging and satisfying. A particular point to remember is that these professional workers cherish and seek autonomy from the employing organizations and their managers. The effectiveness of managing these workers lies in creating a climate in which their autonomous inclinations will not be stifled and at the same time facilitating their efforts in the service of their clients.

Earlier, I alluded to the presence of both professional and volunteer workers within one organization potentially creating problems for management. While researchers have documented many conflicts between volunteer and professional workers (Chelladurai 1987, Hinings and Slack 1987, Inglis 1997), a careful analysis of the bases of professionalism and volunteerism shows that, at least on a

NASSM's Ethical Creed

With the guidance from the eminent scholar-philosopher Dr. Zeigler, NASSM drew up a set of standards for ethical behavior in sport management (Zeigler 1989, 4). The following are excerpts from the version modified and accepted in June 1992:

Members of the NORTH AMERICAN SOCIETY FOR SPORT MANAGEMENT live in free, democratic societies within North American culture. As practitioners and scholars within a broad profession, we honor the preservation and protection of fundamental human rights. We are committed to a high level of professional practice and service. Our professional conduct shall be based on the application of sound management theory developed through a broadly based humanities and social scientific body of knowledge about the role of developmental physical activity in sport, exercise, and related expressive activities in the lives of all people. Such professional knowledge and service shall be made available to clients of all ages and conditions, whether such people are classified as accelerated, normal, or special insofar as their status or condition is concerned.

As NASSM members pursuing our subdisciplinary and professional service, we will make every effort to protect the welfare of those who seek our assistance. We will use our professional skills only for purposes which are consistent with the values, norms and laws of our respective countries. Although we, as professional practitioners, demand for ourselves maximum freedom of inquiry and communication consistent with societal values, we fully understand that such freedom requires us to be responsible, competent, and objective in the application of our skills. We should always show concern for the best interests of our clients, our colleagues, and the public at large.

Following these general statements, the NASSM also has a Code of Ethics that contains principles to cover the conduct of sport managers; ethical obligations to students and clients; and ethical responsibility to employers, colleagues, and society. These principles are presented in the appendix to this chapter.

theoretical level, no inherent conflict exists between the two concepts. To elaborate on this issue, the following section restates the most salient features of both professionalism and volunteerism.

Merton (1982) summarized the essence of professionalism as the triad of values in the professions. The first value is knowing; that is, the development of a body of knowledge unique to the field and the training of members in that unique body of knowledge. The second dominant professional value is doing; that is, the skilled application of the theoretical knowledge to the problems of life. Third, the acquired knowledge and skill are used in helping others.

How do these three processes of knowing, doing, and helping relate to volunteerism? The analysis of volunteerism in chapter 1 showed that volunteers' altruistic motivations (i.e., helping) and their concerns for self-development (i.e., learning) need not be inconsistent with each other, and in fact, they may complement each other. Thus, both professionalism and volunteerism are founded on the notion of learning (i.e., knowing) and acting effectively (i.e., doing) to serve (i.e., help) others. Both are striving toward the same ideal (see figure 2.2).

However, while the direction is the same for both sets of workers, the extent to which they have advanced in that direction obviously differs. On a theoretical basis, due to their relatively more extensive training, the paid professional workers are more knowledgeable in their chosen field than the volunteers in the same field. By the same token, the paid professionals also are more skilled in performance of the required activities. On the other hand, professional actions are relatively less altruistic because those actions are recompensed formally in some tangible ways.

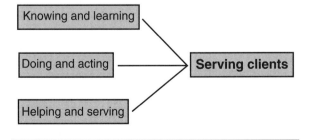

Figure 2.2 Triad of values for professionals and volunteers.

The boundary between the professionals and volunteers is blurred further because of the existence of the volunteering professionals and the professional volunteers. The volunteering professionals are professionals who volunteer their time and effort toward a particular cause without any remuneration. For example a medical professional may volunteer to work in a third-world country. In our context, a coach of a university team may volunteer to coach a team in the local community youth league. Such efforts would be as altruistic as another layperson's volunteering.

The professional volunteers are volunteers who make a profession of volunteering. As Pincus and Hermann-Keeling (1982) noted, they are the individuals

> who give their time, and have an extensive experience in a field. They make a profession of their volunteering, and are quite different from short term volunteers. They are committed, as deeply or more deeply, than many of their paid colleagues. (p. 87)

Because their services are focused on a particular cause over a period of time, these professional volunteers develop sufficient knowledge and expertise about that particular operation. For instance, a

In Their View

Ilsley (1990) believed that the trend toward professionalism has many causes including partnerships between volunteer organizations and government or big business and the need to be accountable in order to secure funds. While this is a healthy trend, the down side is that

> professionalism tends to produce an increased rigidity, an organizational "hardening of the arteries," that alienates volunteers. Rather than simply welcomed as people who have a desire to serve, entering volunteers are screened, trained, supervised, and fitted into predetermined slots. They are treated like interchangeable objects rather than like people with individual interests and abilities. (Ilsley 1990, 87)

volunteer administrator of a sport club may become as proficient in the sport and the management of such a club as a paid counterpart.

Thus, on a theoretical basis, the presence of both volunteers and professionals need not be a source of concern for management of human resources in sport and recreation. However, Hasenfeld's (1983) caution about the "dominant professional caste system" may be extrapolated to the professional-volunteer dichotomy.

> In their efforts to gain professional status and recognition, semiprofessionals attempt to delegate downward what they consider dirty work, resulting in the emergence of a paraprofessional cadre of workers such as nurse's aides, teacher aides, social work technicians, and the like. . . . In addition, some evidence suggests that aspiring professionals tend to increase their social distance from the poor and other "less-desirable" clients. (p.165)

If such tendencies on the part of professionals and semi-professionals exist, volunteers may be allocated all of the so-called dirty work, and the professionals and semi-professionals may abrogate to themselves the prestigious work. Unfortunately, these differences that are of degree and not of kind are allowed to dominate and create interpersonal conflicts between the two sets of workers. The challenge to management is to highlight the underlying and unifying forces of both volunteerism and professionalism: service and self-development (Ilsley 1990). As Pincus and Hermann-Keeling (1982) noted,

> The blurring of lines between professional and volunteer can be a healthy, humanizing process—one in which everyone gains something. Professionals, immersed in their own specialties, are exposed to new perspectives and greater spontaneity in working with individuals with other experiences. (p. 94)

Although the notions of volunteerism and professionalism are congruent theoretically, some characteristics of professionalism negate the central thrust of volunteerism. Ilsley (1990) cautioned that professionalization of volunteer organizations may negatively affect the volunteer experience. Table 2.1 presents the signs of professionalism, as Ilsley noted, in a volunteer organization. Table 2.2 lists the negative consequences of professionalism for volunteers. In Ilsley's view, the rigidity associated with professionalism tends to alienate volunteers.

Table 2.1   Signs of Professionalism in Volunteer Organizations

- Increased complexity of procedures and division of labor
- Management by hierarchy
- Fixed jurisdictional areas
- Emphasis on accountability and "putting things in writing"
- Elaborate training procedures (for volunteers)
- Appearance of ancillary materials (e.g., journals and newsletters), programs (e.g., workshops and conventions), and organizations (e.g., associations)
- Excessive use of scientific methods (reliance on statistics and jargon)
- Excessive standardization
- Unquestioning acceptance of assumptions

Source: Ilsley (1990).

Table 2.2   Negative Consequences of Professionalism in Volunteer Organizations

- Diminished comprehension of policies and procedures
- Managers' reluctance to permit volunteer participation in decision making
- Requirement to adhere to strict rationalized rules
- Limited public access to organization
- Increased respect and reward for expertise in management methods
- Increase in the budget for management including recruiting, training, and retention of volunteers
- Alienation of volunteers from paid staff
- Perception that the system is degrading
- Decreased allowance for diversity and innovation
- Increased totalitarian tactics and consequent disenchantment among volunteers and clients
- Tendency to solve problems rather than to satisfy clients' or volunteers' needs

Source: Ilsley (1990).

Managing professionalism in a way that allows organizations to reap its benefits without having the spontaneity and life choked out of them by its rigidifying force is likely to be one of the greatest challenges that volunteer managers [and professional managers as well] will face in the coming years. (p. 89)

In a Nutshell

Professionalism and volunteerism have very strong ties in their orientations toward increasing one's knowledge and skills and being dedicated to helping and serving the clients. The challenge to management is to harness these common attributes of the professional and volunteer workers and to minimize the effects of any divergence in less relevant characteristics.

Thibault, Slack, and Hinings (1991) found similar rigidifying tendencies among provincial-level sport governing bodies in Canada. These authors found that the introduction of professional staff resulted in greater centralization of decision making, specialization, and standardization. They also noted that the increases in standardization (i.e., formalization) and specialization were more pronounced in those subsystems of the organization concerned with the technical aspects of the sport (e.g., coaching, officiating, and training of athletes).

Summary

In summary, occupations can be distinguished on the basis of the extent to which they are based on a systematic body of knowledge, enjoy professional authority in relation to the clients, gain the sanction of the community to monitor and control the activities of their members, and institute a code of ethics. The sanction of the community is a function of the extent to which the services that an occupation offers are perceived to be essential to the community, can be provided exclusively by the occupation, and are complex in nature. The forces of deprofessionalization include increasing levels of education, easier mastery of skills and knowledge required of some occupations, and the advances in computer and media technology. While sport and recreation management and similar occupations cannot claim professional status, the idea and practice of professionalism is more critical than the attainment of professional status itself. Finally, the essential elements of professionalism and volunteerism have similarities, and both converge in their focus on serving the clients.

The challenge to sport and recreation managers is to understand the dynamics of the motivational patterns of volunteers and professionals and to recognize the parallel thrusts in these patterns that bind them together as well as the divergent forces that may set them apart. These insights help the manager harness the two valuable sources of significant contributions toward organizational survival and growth. Part III further elaborates these issues.

Key Terms

body of knowledge, professional authority, professionalization, essentiality, exclusivity, complexity, deprofessionalization, professionalism

Your Perspectives

- Considering the occupations with which you are familiar, identify those that rank higher on social status and discuss the reasons for the higher rank.

- Focusing only on the occupations within sport and recreation, can you identify those that enjoy greater recognition and status than others? How do you explain such differential status among the sport-related occupations?

- Many occupations strive to attain professional status. What is the significance of the professional status? That is, why should an occupation try to become a profession?

- The chapter concludes with the idea that professionalism and volunteerism are similar in their orientations toward serving their clients. Can you identify other similarities between professionalism and volunteerism? What attributes set them apart? How would such differences affect the management of the sets of workers?

Appendix

THE CODE OF ETHICS of the North American Society for Sport Management (accepted June 1992)

Canons or Principles

The following canons or principles, arranged according to category or dimension, shall be considered by the sport manager in the performance of professional duties:

Category I: The Professional's Conduct as a Sport Manager

A. **Individual Welfare.** The sport manager should hold paramount the safety, health, and welfare of the individual in the performance of professional duties.

B. **Service where Competent.** The sport manager should perform services only in his/her areas of competence.

C. **Public Statements.** The sport manager should issue public statements in an objective and truthful manner, and shall make every effort to explain where statements are personal opinions.

D. **Solicitation of Employment.** The sport manager should seek employment only where a need for service exists.

E. **Propriety.** The sport manager should maintain high standards of personal conduct in the capacity or identity of the physical and health educator.

F. **Competence and Professional Development.** The sport manager should strive to become and remain proficient in professional practice and the performance of professional functions.

G. **Integrity.** The sport manager should act in accordance with the highest standards of professional integrity.

Category II: The Professional's Ethical Obligations to Students/Clients

H. **Primacy of Students'/Clients' Interests.** The sport manager's primary responsibility is to students/clients.

I. **Service as Agent or Trustee.** The sport manager, when acting in professional matters for employer or student/client, should be a faithful agent or trustee.

J. **Rights and Prerogatives of Clients.** The sport manager should, in considering the nature of the relationship with the student/client, make every effort to foster maximum self-determination on the part of the students/clients.

K. **Confidentiality and Privacy.** The sport manager should respect the privacy of students/clients and hold in confidence all information obtained in the course of professional service.

L. **Fees.** When setting fees for service in private or commercial settings, the sport manager should ensure that they are fair, reasonable, considerate, and commensurate with the service performed and with due respect to the students'/clients' ability to pay.

Category III: The Professional's Ethical Responsibility to Employers/Employing Organizations

M. **Commitments to Employers/Employing Organizations.** The sport manager should adhere to any and all commitments made to the employing organization. The relationship should be characterized by fairness, non-maleficence, and truthfulness.

Category IV: The Professional's Ethical Responsibility to Colleagues/Peers and to the Profession

N. **Respect, Fairness, and Courtesy.** The sport manager should treat colleagues with respect, courtesy, fairness, and good faith.

O. **Dealing with Colleagues' Students/Clients.** The sport manager has the responsibility to relate to the students/clients of colleagues with full professional consideration.

P. **Maintaining the Integrity of the Profession.** The sport manager should uphold and advance the values and ethical standards, the knowledge, and the mission of the profession.

Q. **Development of Knowledge.** The sport manager should take responsibility for identifying, developing, and fully utilizing knowledge for professional practice.

R. **Approach to Scholarship and Research.** The sport manager engaged in study and/or research should be guided by the accepted convention of scholarly inquiry.

Category V: The Professional's Ethical Responsibility to Society

S. **Promoting the General Welfare.** The sport manager should promote the general welfare of society.

T. **Community Service.** The sport manager should regard as primary his/her professional service to others. He/she should assist the profession in making information and services relating to desirable physical activity and health practices available to the general public.

U. **Reporting Code Infractions.** The sport manager has an ethical responsibility to society in that minor and major infractions by colleagues should be reported to the appropriate committee of the professional society (when and where such mechanism exists).

3

Clients as Human Resources

Learning Objectives

After reading this chapter you will be able to

- explain the significance of including clients as one set of human resources in sport and recreation management;

- describe the various motives of individuals who participate in sport and physical activity and classify them into pursuit of pleasure, pursuit of skill, pursuit of excellence, and pursuit of health and fitness; and

- understand the significance of the broader classification of motives for the programming of sport and recreation services.

Some recent catchwords in management are **quality** and **total quality management**. These catchwords represent a new approach to management that focuses on consumers. All gurus of quality management suggest that every operation of an enterprise must be tuned to satisfying or delighting the customer (Goetsch 1994; Zeithaml, Parasuraman, and Berry 1990). This emphasis on customer (i.e., client) orientation is particularly critical to organizations that provide a service. (Please note that the terms "customer" and "client" are used interchangeably in this text.)

As noted in the introduction, one of the significant attributes of a service is the simultaneity of production and consumption of that service. Emphasized also was that customer participation in the production might be more critical in some forms of service. Most sport and recreation organizations are engaged in the provision of services that require the active participation of the client or customer. Even spectators at a sporting event are expected to conform to regulations and expectations regarding seating arrangements and orderly behavior. When spectators abide by these behavioral expectations, they themselves contribute to the quality of the service provided. The essential argument is that there is a need to secure compliance and cooperation of the customers or clients to ensure the production of the services and their quality. Hence, organizations need to include the customers or clients as part of their human resources.

A distinction exists between our customers or clients and the market that they represent. A market refers to a collection of potential customers. Almost every organization attempts to enroll these potential customers as its actual customers or clients. These efforts usually are labeled as marketing or promotional campaigns or programs. However, only when some of those potential customers opt for the products that an organization offers do they become customers or **clients** of that organization. Only then are they part of the organization's human resources. With this caveat in mind, the chapter describes

- the role of customers in the production and consumption of a sport or recreation service from a systems perspective,
- the uniqueness of customer participation in sport and recreation services, and
- customer motives for participation in sport and recreation.

Customer as Input, Throughput, and Output

As noted, customers in many of the sport and recreation services are both the inputs and outputs of the service operations. As Hasenfeld (1983) noted, this view is particularly pertinent to human service operations. Recently, Lengnick-Hall (1995, 1996) elaborated on this perspective to provide a systems view of customer participation in the production and consumption of a service. In her view, the customer is simultaneously a resource, a co-producer, a buyer, a user, and the product. This view of the customer is illustrated in figure 3.1 wherein the three significant roles of the customer (i.e., the resource, the co-producer, and the product) are superimposed on the input-throughput-output conceptualization of a system.

To the extent that the clients bring with them their personal physical and psychological attributes and to the extent that they provide the necessary information, they form a resource for the organization. As noted earlier, because human services aim at transforming the clients in specific ways, each client is a resource, as well as the product, of the service

enterprise. As noted also, clients of most sport and recreation services need to engage in vigorous physical activity for the service to be produced and for them to be transformed. Thus, they become co-producers of the service (Chelladurai 1996). From a systems perspective, Lengnick-Hall's (1996) customer role of resource relates to the input stage; the co-producer role, to the throughput stage; and the product role, to the output stage.

Customer Participation in Sport and Recreation Services

The notion of consumer involvement is generic to the production of many services. For instance, a hairdresser effectively can perform his or her services only if the customer is present in the chair while he or she provides the service. After expressing personal preferences for a specific hairstyle, the customer's involvement in the production of the service is restricted to his or her presence in the chair. This involvement is passive participation (or involvement) in the production of the service. In contrast, the service of an aerobic instructor cannot be completed unless clients actively engage in aerobics. This active involvement is necessary for the production of that service. Further, in some of the services, as in the case of aerobics class, the active involvement also could be agonistic, meaning that the **client's physical exertion** could be painful. The slogan "No pain, no gain" is illustrative of those sport and recreation services that require active and agonistic involvement of the customer in the production of that service. In so far as client participation is painful, getting the clients to participate in the physical activity programs becomes problematic for the service providers. Hasenfeld (1983) noted this issue with reference to human services in general:

Patients may refuse to comply with a physician's orders; students may ignore their teachers; and clients may resist discussing

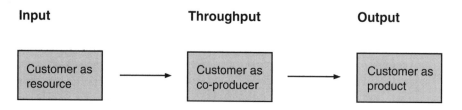

Input **Throughput** **Output**

Customer as resource → Customer as co-producer → Customer as product

Figure 3.1   Customer's roles in the input-throughput-output cycle of a system.
Source: Lengnick-Hall (1996).

their interpersonal problems. The need for client compliance and cooperation is particularly heightened when the method aims at some major changes in the client's behavior, and when it necessitates active client participation and involvement.... Consequently, the control of the client and the need to elicit conformity are critical issues in human service organizations and consume much of the efforts of their practitioners. (pp. 122-123)

Given the nature of client involvement in sport and recreation services, it is not surprising that many clients are not willing to engage in such agonistic endeavors. It is not uncommon for clients to drop out of sport or exercise programs. In fact, exercise adherence is a major topic among many researchers (Dishman 1993). On the other hand, countless others do exert themselves in several forms of sport and recreation activities. Two racquetball players grunting and groaning while running around the court to retrieve or to "kill" a ball endure pain. Similarly, the client grimacing while lifting the weights in a fitness club is another example in which such a person seeks, and enjoys, agonistic involvement.

These two contrasting scenarios highlight a significant issue for the sport and recreation manager. The issue relates to the relative ease or difficulty of securing client compliance in the production of sport and recreation services. Several factors (e.g., lack of time, accessibility of facilities, low fitness level, lack of motivation, and poor leadership) lead to the two differing phenomena. In addition to paying attention to the factors that they can control or modify (e.g., facilities and leadership), sport and recreation managers also should be concerned with the programs that they offer to clients who differ in their ability, fitness, and motivation. They need to design the programs to meet the specific needs and motives of the clients. With this in mind, the following section outlines the various motives of individuals for participation in sport and recreation.

In a Nutshell

All service operations require a certain degree of client involvement in producing the respective services. Some of the sport and recreation services are participant-oriented, so they require greater involvement of clients in terms of intensity and physical exertion.

Client Motives for Participation

The psychological dynamics in the given examples are best understood when considering **client motives** for participation in physical activities. Several schemes classify attitudes toward physical activity (Schutz et al. 1985) and motives for participation in sport (Gill, Gross, and Huddleston 1983).

In Their View

While several scholars focused on client motives for participation, other scholars have investigated the functions of sport from a societal perspective. For instance, Grove and Dodder (1982) reported that university faculty and students perceived psychophysical well-being, self-expression, gender roles (enhancing masculinity in males and femininity in females), pride in place of residence, and social integration as the most salient functions of sport.

Schutz et al. (1985) carried out several studies to develop psychometrically sound instruments to measure seven dimensions of children's attitudes toward physical activity. Gill, Gross, and Huddleston (1983) identified eight factors of motivation for youth sport participation (see table 3.1). Although such classifications have focused on different aspects of sport and physical activity participation (motives or attitudes), all of them underlie the reasons for participation in sport and physical activity.

While the foregoing schemes were concerned with motives or attitudes of participants in youth sport, Chelladurai (1992) proposed a scheme relevant to all ages. His four-level classification of motives for participation in sport and physical activity includes

- **pursuit of pleasure,**
- **pursuit of skill,**
- **pursuit of excellence,** and
- **pursuit of health and fitness.**

Pursuit of Pleasure

People may participate in physical activity because they enjoy the kinesthetic sensations that they experience in a physical activity or the competition that certain activities pose (e.g., the two players in a game of racquetball). Only during participation can they enjoy the pleasures that they seek; that is, they are not seeking any other benefits outside of actual

Table 3.1   Participation Motivation in Youth Sports

Dimension	Description
Achievement and status	To win, feel important, be popular, gain status, do something one does well, and reap rewards
Team	To be a part of teamwork, team spirit, and a team
Fitness	To stay in shape, get exercise, and be physically fit
Energy release	To get rid of energy, release tension, have something to do, travel, and get out of the house
Skill development	To improve skills, learn new skills, and go on to a higher level
Affiliation	To be with friends and make new friends
Fun	To have fun, action, and excitement
Miscellaneous and situational	To be with parent, close friends, or coaches, or to use equipment and facilities

Source: Gill, Gross, and Huddleston (1983).

participation itself. With such pleasure-seeking, or "hedonistic," motives on the part of the clients, the manager more easily can motivate them and secure their compliance to the rules and regulations of the organization.

Pursuit of Skill

The desire to acquire physical skills is innate to the human species. This desire may impel people to participate in physical activity. That is, individuals may focus on perfecting their skills through continued vigorous physical activity. The organized physical activity classes, sports camps and clinics, and lessons from professionals aim at imparting the skills of various sports to the members of the community. The participation of people of all ages in these efforts gives evidence of the pervasiveness of the desire to learn skills.

Pursuit of Excellence

Pursuit of excellence is broadly defined as the effort to win in a contest against a standard. The standard may be one's own previous performance, somebody else's performance, or simply winning against an opponent. People may participate in some form of physical activity to excel in that activity or in another activity. Recall the example of a client grimacing while lifting weights. That client may be training to compete in a regional weight-lifting

competition or in a track meet. The intention to prepare for such contests (i.e., the motive of excellence) generates a willingness to comply with the instructions of the coach or teacher. The scenario of athletes going through painful exercises chanting the motto "No pain, no gain" best illustrates the correspondence between pursuit of excellence and compliance to coaching and guidance.

Pursuit of Health and Fitness

Other individuals may participate in vigorous physical activity mainly for the health-related benefits, such as fitness, stress reduction, and longevity, that accrue as a consequence of such participation. The benefits of such participation are extrinsic to the activity itself; that is, they reside outside the actual physical activity and are derived after prolonged physical activity.

In this regard, Hasenfeld's (1983) distinction between those functioning adequately and those functioning below an adequate level has relevance for us. That is, many individuals who are sufficiently fit and healthy want to maintain that level of fitness and health, so they continue to participate in physical activity. Such motives may be properly labeled sustenance motives. On the other hand, others may participate in physical activity to enhance their fitness and health, which has been judged inadequate. These motives may be properly labeled as curative.

In Their View

Greer and Stewart (1989) noted that attitudes toward or motives for participation are not generalized dispositions of individuals. Their study of 585 fourth- and fifth-grade students showed that the attitude toward participation varied with the context: neighborhood play, organized sport, and school recess activities. These authors noted that "winning was more important when playing organized sports than when playing with peers in the neighborhood. . . . The schoolyard context was generally perceived as similar to organized sports in that winning was valued and seen as significantly more important than it was in the neighborhood" (p. 341).

In the foregoing description of the motives for participation in physical activity, the assumption was that individuals participate on their own volition. However, it is not uncommon to find that individuals participate out of necessity or coercion. Consider the case of a basketball coach taking her squad for a five-mile run as part of the training program. While some of the players would run with enthusiasm others may be reluctant. Even though all players recognize the value of enhancing their endurance through such running, their compliance is hard to secure because such benefits are extrinsic to the activity of running.

Motives and Outcomes

Although these motives are distinct from each other, the activities that are selected to satisfy any one of these motives may result in other outcomes. For example, racquetball players in pursuit of pleasure also may gain in fitness and enhance their performance capabilities. Similarly people who jog for the sake of fitness may learn to enjoy the kinesthetic sensations and the sense of achievement in jogging

longer distances or at a faster pace. However, from a managerial perspective, establishing the primary purpose for participation in a program of physical activity is critical for its development and implementation to be smooth and coordinated. For instance, the concern for motivating the clients before and during participation varies with the purposes of such participation. Thus, in pursuit of pleasure, the activity itself is the reward; therefore, it acts as the motivator for the participants. However, in pursuit of excellence, skill, or fitness and health, the reward is not immediate, so the agency has to have a greater responsibility in motivating the participants.

In a Nutshell

Motives for participation can be classified broadly into pursuit of pleasure, pursuit of skill, pursuit of excellence, and pursuit of health and fitness. Although these classes are conceptually distinct, active involvement in sport and physical activity may satisfy more than one motive.

Client Motivation and Sport Management

As outlined in the introduction, the discussion of client motivation is most relevant to **participant services**. However, participant services are just one kind of many services in sport management. Therefore, participant motivation, as described earlier, may not be relevant to other forms of services. For example, a significant component of sport management is the provision of entertainment through sport (i.e., spectator services). Although participant motives may have relevance to the athletes and to the coaching of those athletes, they do not have

The terms "intrinsic" and "extrinsic" need some clarification. According to *Webster's Ninth New Collegiate Dictionary* (1986), intrinsic implies "belonging to the essential nature or constitution of a thing," and extrinsic means "not forming part of or belonging to a thing." In our context, the terms are used to refer to whether individuals participate in sport for the rewards or benefits inherent in the activity itself (i.e., **intrinsic benefits of participation**) or for the benefits that come later as an outcome of the activity (i.e., **extrinsic benefits of participation**). According to Cratty (1989), intrinsic motivation refers to "performance encouraged by an interest in performing the task itself," and extrinsic motivation refers to "effort molded by material and social rewards, which are external to the basic nature of and interest in the task itself" (p. 195).

applicability to the fans who are also customers. It is true that these fans need to be present to consume the entertainment, but their presence is removed from the activity itself. That is, their participation is not required for the production of the service itself. Their motivational patterns to consume spectator services may be quite different from those discussed earlier. In fact, researchers have done considerable work in the study of motives, such as the motivation to consume sport services, patterns of such consumption, segmentation of sport consumers, fan behavior, and loyalty to teams (e.g., Backman and Crompton 1991; Hansen and Gauthier 1989; Howard and Crompton 1995; Mullin, Hardy, and Sutton 1993; Murrell and Dietz 1992; Wann and Branscombe 1993). These issues are critical to marketing sports and recreation.

The emphasis on the dynamics of client motivation for participation in sport and recreation is based on the requirement that clients need to participate vigorously for services to be produced. Thus, the position taken in this text is that for a client to be considered a human resource, the client must engage himself or herself in the production of that service. Two caveats are in order here. The first caveat is the indirect involvement of the sport manager in client motives. The second one relates to programming.

Role of the Sport Manager

Note that the sport and recreation manager may not be linked directly to the client in the production of the participant services. In the previous two chapters, I described two sets of workers (paid and volunteer workers) who may be involved in the production of human or consumer services. Because these workers are in direct contact with our clients, they must be more attuned to client motives than the managers themselves. The managers are more concerned with the motivation of the service providers, i.e., the paid and volunteer workers. For example, the director of an intercollegiate athletic department may not be involved directly in training and motivating the athletes. Those tasks are left to the coaches, who are the service providers. Similarly, the manager of a city recreation department may be removed from the clients as they consume the services of the department. Figure 3.2 illustrates the linkages between sport managers, service providers, and the clients.

Programming for Client Motives

Because the linkage between the clients and sport managers is largely through the service providers and because the manager's greater task is with the supervision of the service providers, sport managers may appear as though they do not need to be concerned with client motivation. However, in so far as the manager is responsible for developing and managing the programs that the organization offers, he or she must be aware of the broad classes of client motives. Such an understanding facilitates programming to suit client motives.

In general, sport and recreation programs are instituted to serve a class of clients rather than individual clients. For example, sport and recreation

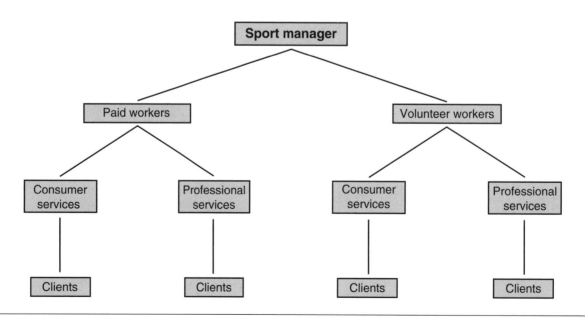

Figure 3.2   Linkages among sport managers, workers, and clients.

programs can be classified broadly as youth, adult, or senior programs. Youth programs may be divided into specific units based on age classification. Recreational sport programs also are conventionally separated from competitive sport programs. These programming aspects are discussed in part III.

Similarly, programming to meet client motives is generally on a group basis. That is, a sport manager may set up a program to cater to pursuit of pleasure, pursuit of skills, pursuit of excellence, or pursuit of fitness and health. Consider the programs that the Department of Recreational Sports of The Ohio State University offers (see table 3.2). An analysis of these various programs shows that, although not stated specifically in the descriptions of the programs, they cater to specific groups of people differentiated on the basis of abilities, interests, and motives. Note that the university controls entry into some programs, such as adapted recreational sports,

In a Nutshell

The client motives discussed earlier are not relevant to services other than participant services. Development of programs in sport and recreation may be based on age of participants (e.g., youth, adult, or senior programs), or on client motives (e.g., programs to enhance pleasure, skill, excellence, or health).

Table 3.2 Programs of the Department of Recreational Sports of The Ohio State University

Program	Description
Adapted recreational sports (ARS)	ARS comprises recreation and sport programs modified to meet the needs of an individual's disabilities to enhance the individual's mobility and socialization.
Family recreation instruction program (FRIP)	FRIP provides a variety of activities for parents and their children to participate in together or separately to have fun, stay in shape, and learn skills.
Fitness	BUCK-I-ROBICS provides a variety of activities to get or keep people in shape while they have a great time doing them.
Intramural sports	With more than 30 sports in which to participate, community members have many great choices for individual and team participation.
Sport clubs	More than 65 clubs offer different sport and recreational activities for participation at the intercollegiate competitive level or recreational level.
Informal recreation	Informal recreation provides an opportunity for a self-directed approach to participate in recreation and sports at the most convenient time.
Wellness	The Student Wellness Center, an integral component of the Student Health Center, implements multifaceted approaches to address the health-related needs and concerns of students through awareness, education, and prevention.
Outdoor recreation for the entire campus (O-REC)	O-REC provide adventurous activities for The Ohio State Community. These opportunities promote an awareness of the environment, leadership development, and teamwork.
Summer camps	The summer camp program offers educational, as well as recreational, experiences for children. The camps provide participants with a variety of sport-specific and life skills while helping them build self-confidence, and they enhance the development of talents and leadership abilities.

and leaves entry open to all into other programs, such as sport clubs or wellness programs. It is understood here that the clients of the department would choose a specific program and an activity in the program to satisfy their personal interests, needs, and motives.

Summary

In summary, this chapter discussed the significance of our clients as part of human resources. The relevance of clients to human resource management lies in the fact that the completion of most participant services under the purview of sport and recreation managers requires clients' vigorous participation. This participation requirement obviously excludes the customers enjoying spectator services because they do not participate in the production of those services. Such production is left to the athletes and their coaches. The critical issue for sport and recreation managers is to differentiate among the motives for client participation and to tailor their programs to satisfy those motives. One of the concerns for sport and recreation managers is the dropout rates among participants in sport and physical activity. This rate has an obvious implication for profit-oriented organizations. If clients do not continue to participate in the focal physical activity (e.g., tennis, golf, and weight-lifting fitness classes), these organizations face the uphill task of constantly recruiting new clients. The educational and community organizations that promote sport and physical activity also must be concerned with retaining their clients and encouraging them to continue participating in physical activity. Failure to do so would be tantamount to forsaking the organizational goals.

Key Terms

quality, total quality management, clients, client's physical exertion, client motives, pursuit of pleasure, pursuit of skills, pursuit of excellence, pursuit of health and fitness, intrinsic benefits of participation, extrinsic benefits of participation, participant services

Your Perspectives

- Considering your own participation in sport and physical activity, explain your reasons for such participation. Did these reasons change from your childhood to the present time?

- Discuss the utility of classifying client motives into pursuit of pleasure, pursuit of skill, pursuit of excellence, and pursuit of health and fitness. What are the managerial implications of such a classification?

- Can you think of other ways to classify the motives for participation in sport and physical activity?

- Discuss the various motives that may influence participation in each of the programs outlined in table 3.2.

Part II

Individual Differences in Human Resources

In the previous three chapters, I suggested that the human resources of sport organizations consist of volunteers, professionals, and clients. I also noted that these three groups of people differ in their motives for participation in the organizational efforts. The world would be much simpler and management would be much easier if we were content with these classifications. However, humans differ in an infinite number of ways along different dimensions. Therefore, a single classification, such as volunteers, professionals, and clients, cannot help us fully understand the members and motivate them toward organizational goals. The members within each classification can vary considerably in different characteristics. Thus, there is a need to understand individual differences and their influence on work performance.

Individual difference variables are those human attributes that set one individual apart from another. These individual differences can be classified broadly into

- abilities (i.e., cognitive and psychomotor abilities),
- personality,
- needs and values, and
- motivation.

Our interest in individual differences stems from the concept of person-task fit. That is, our major concern is in creating a fit between the task assigned to an individual and that person's profile on relevant individual differences. This notion of person-task fit begins with designing and describing jobs, specifying the necessary skills and competencies required to perform the job, and hiring the right people with those skills and competencies. While part III describes these critical managerial tasks, the chapters in part II outline the more salient individual difference variables.

The concept of person-task fit is critical from the perspectives of both the organization and the individual. The organization expects greater productivity if the members possess attributes required by the assigned tasks. On the other hand, the individual member also feels competent, confident, and satisfied if the assigned task matches his or her attributes.

The psychological literature abounds with several lists of individual difference characteristics. Some of these attributes, such as gender and height, can be measured accurately. Others are conceptually derived attributes that cannot be measured as accurately as the former kind. In fact, the latter attributes are inferred through values on some other indices, which are associated with the concept in question. For example, an individual's intelligence is inferred from his or her score on a series of tests that are supposed to measure some aspect of intelligence. Thus, individual difference variables differ in the extent to which they are tangible or abstract.

Keep in mind another aspect; some of the attributes may be relatively more stable over time than others. For instance, race is a permanent attribute, but skill in a sport is a transient attribute. That is, one's race does not change in a lifetime; however, skill in a sport can change with some training and practice. Thus, some individual difference variables are stable, and others are transient.

A distinction also exists between interindividual differences and intraindividual differences. For instance, employee A of a fitness club may be proficient in keeping the accounts of the firm, and employee B may be good in communicating with the clients of the firm. The differences between employees A and B in accounting and communication skills are the interindividual differences. From a different perspective, employee A is more proficient in accounting than in communicating. Similarly, employee B is better at communicating than accounting. Differing along different attributes is called intraindividual differences. Managers need to be aware of both types of individual differences. That is, interindividual differences imply that one cannot expect all individuals to perform a given task equally well. By the same token, intraindividual differences imply that one individual cannot be expected to be equally good in several different tasks.

As mentioned earlier, a myriad of differences distinguish one individual from another. Our interests, however, are restricted to those variables that contribute to or constrain performance in organizational contexts. While it appears to be a difficult task to identify the variables for our purposes, a well-known principle, that performance is a function of ability and motivation, facilitates the choice of variables discussed in this text. Another significant set of individual difference variables, which may affect interpersonal relations in the workplace and performance, includes needs, values, and personality.

While acknowledging that people differ in their capacities to carry out their tasks and in the manner of interactions with others, guard against making value judgments about people based on these individual differences. For example, how can anyone decide an individual's worth based on his or her height or score on the personality dimension of affiliation (i.e., the tendency to make friends and to enjoy association with people)? Thus, it is important to keep in mind that differences are not deficits.

If individual differences are not deficits, then management must take advantage and make best use of the variety of differences to further benefit both the organization and the members. For instance, while one's performance is a function of his or her abilities and motivation, management also has a responsibility to foster the abilities and raise the motivation and to channel them into task performance. In fact, many of the problems, such as lack of productivity and tardiness among U.S. workers, have been attributed to poor management practices.

Ability refers to the capacity of an individual to carry out the tasks assigned to him or her. These abilities, which can be either psychomotor or cognitive, are the subject of chapter 4. Chapter 5 focuses on personality, which is the relatively stable pattern of traits that define the uniqueness of a person. This pattern of traits predisposes people to behave in specific ways toward others and situations.

Chapter 6 discusses values. Values are the beliefs that individuals have about what is right and what is wrong and about what ought to be and what ought not to be. Such personal values have a great degree of influence in decision making in organizations. If these values are congruent with organizational goals and processes, the organization can expect greater performance from its employees. On the other hand, if those values conflict with organizational goals, the organization can expect inhibited performance from the employees.

Motivation in general refers to the inner force that drives people to act in specific ways. The driving force is the individual's desire to fulfill his or her needs. The individual scans his or her environment (i.e., the set of stimuli presented to the individual) and reacts in specific ways to satisfy those needs. I present and discuss several theories of motivation in chapter 7.

4

Abilities

Learning Objectives

After reading this chapter you will be able to

- define and describe the concept of abilities;
- understand the issues of inherent capacity compared with current capacity, heritability of ability, and generality of ability compared with specificity of ability;
- distinguish between abilities and skills or competence;
- identify and explain significant managerial competencies; and
- discuss the nature of psychomotor abilities and their relevance in sport management.

In any performance situation, ability related to the task at hand is critical. Certain abilities are required to be a good player in basketball and certain other abilities are required to be a good coach in basketball. Similarly, a leader of fitness classes needs to possess certain abilities, and the manager of the fitness club needs to possess certain other abilities. The specific abilities and skills can set apart the director of a city recreation department from the people who maintain the playing fields or from the people who organize and conduct competitions. That set of characteristics distinguishing an athletic director from some of his or her subordinates are the special abilities required of the athletic director. Referring to a discussion of the functioning of teams, McClelland (1996) stated that

> As would be expected, attention was first turned to such matters as being sure that there is a clear mission for the team, a proper assignment of tasks to different members of the team, good informational and organizational supports for the team, proper resources to work with, etc. All of these things are clearly needed—without them the team couldn't function—yet I kept feeling that you could have all these things like a well-designed Swiss watch—but the team might still not go. Why? Because fundamentally it is people with certain *competencies* that make teams go. (p. 17) (emphasis added)

In the final analysis, irrespective of the position in the organization, every worker needs to have specific abilities to perform effectively in his or her job. Defining and describing the abilities required of jobs in an organization is an important first step. Following this first step are other important steps of identifying people who have the required abilities and of placing them in the right jobs. This chapter presents a description of abilities in general terms. More specifically, after defining abilities in general, the chapter outlines cognitive abilities and psychomotor abilities as they relate to organizational contexts.

Definition of Abilities

Abilities refer to an individual's capacity to engage in a host of tasks, behaviors, or activities. In this context, ability is the same as aptitude (which is a term used to refer to an innate talent in individuals), and these terms (which are used interchangeably) refer to the innate potential for performance. The focus of this text, however, is on those tasks, behaviors, or activities that are relevant to the organizational context. Thus, a person's ability to cook is not of concern to an organization unless cooking itself is a task that the organization, such as a restaurant, undertakes. That is, a person's ability to participate in the organizational activities and to carry out the assigned tasks is the focus in this chapter.

The performance of organizational tasks requires two broad classes of abilities in varying degrees. **Cognitive abilities** (intellectual) include a person's capacity to comprehend what his or her task entails (i.e., to comprehend what is to be done, how, where, and why); an understanding of the relationships among one's own task, the tasks of others, and organizational goals; and the ability to make quality decisions. Although these abilities are cognitive in nature, some tasks may also require the person to possess some **psychomotor abilities** (physical capacities) to carry out the assigned task. A fitness instructor is expected to be physically fit and to be proficient in leading the class in some vigorous exercises. Obviously, the specific mix of cognitive

and psychomotor abilities required in a job varies from job to job. For instance, the task of a coach of a professional sport team requires relatively more cognitive abilities than psychomotor abilities. However, the task of a high school coach requires not only the cognitive abilities to demonstrate the skills of the sport but also the psychomotor abilities for the stamina to be involved in vigorous activity for prolonged periods of time.

Issues Over Ability

Controversies over the definition and measurement of the concept and the heritability of ability and over its generality have beset the study of ability. Generally, researchers accept that ability refers to one's potential capacity to carry out specified tasks (e.g., to learn in a school setting or to manage an organization). However, as Heneman et al. (1983) pointed out, measuring the potential is difficult. Early researchers defined intelligence as an individual's inherent capacity (i.e., potential) to learn (e.g., Guilford 1967). However, the existing tests of intelligence measure only "the individual's *current* capacity—whatever has been learned from whatever source" (Heneman et al. 1983, 70).

Regarding the **heritability** issue, one set of theorists (the behaviorists) hold that a person acquires ability through experience and learning and not because of any inherent factors. The opposing viewpoint (which biological determinists hold) is that ability is endowed genetically. According to the latter view, individuals are born with differing ability levels, and experience (i.e., learning) only accentuates these differences. However, most people subscribe to a compromising viewpoint (which interactionists hold) that ability is a function of both biology and environment. According to the interactionists, environmental influences can compensate the deficiencies in the biological component of ability to some extent. That is, practice and training can compensate for the lack of inherited capacity.

In this context, thinking of a continuum of abilities is useful. At one end lie those abilities that

While abilities are critical for performance in a task, they alone do not contribute to performance. Several other factors contribute to or detract from performance. For instance, an individual's motivation to perform well in a task is as critical as his or her abilities. By the same token, in addition to that individual's abilities, organizational practices that provide the opportunities for individuals to use their abilities, evaluate an individual's performance, and reward such performance all have an impact. That is, while abilities are necessary, they are not sufficient for performance.

cannot be trained easily (e.g., reaction time), and at the other end lie those abilities that are trained easily (e.g., muscular endurance). Researchers also generally accept that the influence of the environment is likely to be higher in the early stages of one's life than in adulthood (during which time it is minimal). This latter point has implications for management. That is, organizational members, in general, are adults; therefore, more or less permanent behavioral traits that define their ability are likely to characterize them.

In a Nutshell

While a distinction can be made between potential ability (i.e., potential capacity) and current ability (i.e., current capacity), any test of ability tends to measure only the current ability. Thinking of abilities as determined by both genetic (i.e., nature) and environmental (i.e., nurture) factors is useful. The relative influence of each set of factors may vary across different abilities.

Regarding the **generality** or **specificity** of ability, it was once believed that ability was a global factor. For instance, an individual scoring high in one intellectual task was expected to do well in other tasks also. Researchers subsequently have modified this view to allow for a general intellectual factor (a *g* factor) as well as a number of specific cognitive abilities (*s* factors) (Heneman et al. 1983).

Similar debates have occurred with reference to psychomotor ability. One belief was the concept of a "natural athlete" that included the notions of heritability of ability and generality of ability (Fleishman and Quaintance 1984). That is, the natural athlete is supposed to possess some innate and general capacity to perform in a number of sporting events. Now, considerable research evidence suggests that no one general ability factor exists (e.g., Henry 1960, Singer 1972). Instead, individuals possess varying degrees of different ability factors. Thus, an athlete can have a high ability in speed and a low ability in strength, and the reverse may be true of another individual.

A last point regarding abilities is that while comprehensive lists of abilities are available, not all of those abilities have relevance to all organizational contexts. Some of those abilities may be relevant to some organizational contexts and to some specific tasks. With this caveat in mind, consider, in the next section, the cognitive and psychomotor abilities that are relevant to organizational contexts.

Cognitive Abilities

As noted earlier, a number of specific abilities exist. However, differing conceptualizations of the type and number of specific abilities and their descriptions exist, and several schemes, each describing a varying number of cognitive abilities, exist. For instance, Guilford (1967) suggested that as many as 120 distinct cognitive aptitudes may be present. However, because such a scheme is too specific, most researchers are content with describing the cognitive domain in 10 to 20 dimensions. For instance, Peterson and Bownas (1982) collated 12 significant abilities included in several lists that other scholars offer. They believe that this list, which is shown in table 4.1, constitutes an adequate set capable of predicting performance in organizations.

The list of abilities that are shown in table 4.1 are fundamental to the execution of any type of task in any context. However, their theoretical origins and their jargon do not help the manager to a great extent. Therefore, managers need to look at this issue from the practitioner's point of view. Fortunately, some management scholars have identified several work-related competencies or skills that are more comprehensible and useful to the practicing managers.

As noted at the beginning of the chapter, the relevance of specific abilities or skills varies from management level to lower operating levels. For

Although the issue of potential versus current capacity is real, the distinction may not necessarily impede the process of hiring people. If a sport or recreation manager can be specific about what abilities the specific job requires, then the manager can verify whether an applicant to that job currently has those abilities. That is, the solution is to match current ability requirements of the job to current capacity of the applicant. For instance, if a sport management job requires problem-solving skills, then the manager can ask the candidate to solve a series of problems that may arise in the job and can evaluate him or her on the solutions. Previous experience and success in similar jobs also indicates a capacity to solve problems.

Table 4.1 Cognitive Abilities

Ability	Description
Flexibility and speed of closure	Ability to "hold in mind" a particular visual percept and find it embedded in distracting material and the ability to "take in" a perceptual field as a whole, to fill in unforeseen portions with potential material, and to coalesce somewhat disparate parts into a visual percept
Fluency	A combination of four different fluencies that include • associative—producing words from a restricted area of meaning; • expressional—supplying proper verbal expressions for ideas already stated or finding a suitable expression that would fit a given semantic frame of reference; • ideational—quickly producing ideas and exemplars of an idea about a stated condition or object; and • word—producing isolated words that contain one or more structural, essentially phonetic, restrictions without reference to the meaning of the words (Peterson and Bownas include Ekstrom, French, and Harman's figural fluency under this category, i.e., the ability to produce a response quickly by drawing a number of examples, to elaborate, or to restructure based on a given visual or descriptive stimulus.)
Inductive reasoning	Ability to form and test hypotheses directed at finding a relationship among elements and to apply the principle to identifying an element fitting the relationship
Associative (rote) memory	Ability to remember bits of unrelated material
Span memory	Ability to recall perfectly for immediate reproduction a series of items after only one presentation of the series
Number facility	Ability to manipulate numbers in arithmetical operations rapidly and facility in performing elementary arithmetical operations (typically under speeded conditions)
Perceptual speed	Speed in finding figures, making comparisons, and carrying out other very simple tasks involving visual perception
Deductive reasoning	Ability to reason from stated premises to their necessary conclusion and ability in formal reasoning from stated premises to rule out nonpermissible combinations and thus to arrive at necessary conclusions
Spatial orientation and visualization	Ability to perceive spatial patterns or to maintain orientation with respect to objects in space and ability to manipulate or transform the image of spatial patterns into other visual arrangements
Verbal comprehension	Knowledge of words and their meanings as well as the application of this knowledge in understanding connected discourse
Verbal closure	Ability to solve problems requiring the identification of words when some of the letters are missing, disarranged, or mixed with other letters
Visual memory	Ability to remember the configuration, location, and orientation of figural material

Adapted from Peterson and Bownas (1982).

instance, the skills and competencies that a university requires of the athletic department director are different from those it requires of a facility manager. While this perspective is generally true, also remember that the lower-level workers (e.g., supervisor of facilities and playing fields and of competitions) are managers in their own right. The person managing a stadium may supervise the work of 20 other workers who may possess different kinds of requisite skills.

> Management is best defined not as a limited number of "top" or "leading" positions, but as a set of competencies, attitudes, and qualities broadly distributed throughout the organization. Management skills are not the property of the few. Effective local authorities [sport managers] will recognize that many jobs which have not conventionally borne the tag "manager" rely none the less on that bundle of action—taking charge, securing an outcome, controlling affairs—which amounts to "managing." (Local Government Management Board 1993, 8)

From the quoted perspective, several of the managerial abilities and competencies described next may be relevant to successive levels of workers in an organization. As noted in the introduction, human services vigorously involve the control, direction, and motivation of the clients in some form of physical activity. In essence then, human service providers manage the people, the activity in which they engage, and the facilities and equipment, as necessary. Therefore, several of the **managerial competencies** outlined may be relevant to the human service providers even though they may not be designated as managers.

Korman (1977) suggested that a competent manager should be able to carry out the activities listed in table 4.2.

The activities listed in table 4.2 are not abilities in the strictest term. They are skills, some of which are derived from the abilities that Peterson and Bownas (1982) collated. For example, expressing ideas clearly and logically is a function of a combination of fluency and of inductive and deductive reasoning. Similarly, stating problems concisely and clearly is a function of verbal comprehension, fluency, and inductive and deductive reasoning.

The distinction made here between abilities and skills (or competencies) needs some clarification.

> An *ability* is a general trait of the individual that has been inferred from certain response

Table 4.2 Competencies of an Effective Manager

- Focus in on a fast-running conversation, redirect, sum up differences, and encourage a coordinated effort.
- Express ideas clearly and logically.
- Make a thorough analysis of alternate solutions to a problem and select the best.
- Pull together scattered information from various sources into a meaningful proposal.
- Give useful advice based on a sound grasp of current methods in his or her field.
- State problems concisely.
- Take the initiative in implementing a program.
- Grasp essential issues, make decisions, and delegate items for action.
- Expedite a complicated project and see it through to completion.
- Be adequately prepared before discussing problems.
- Establish a timetable and performance goals against which to measure success of a project.
- Look for ways to improve existing systems.

From Korman, A.K., *Organizational Behavior,* © 1977. Adapted by permission of Prentice-Hall, Inc., Upper Saddle River, NJ.

consistencies. . . . In contrast, a *skill* is defined as the level of proficiency on a specific task or group of tasks. The development of a given skill or proficiency on a given task is predicated in part on the possession of relevant basic abilities. (Fleishman and Quaintance 1984, 162-163)

Bass (1982) used the term "task-relevant proficiency" to refer to the skills or competencies required of a task. The advantage of focusing on skills (i.e., competencies or proficiencies) is that it allows organizations and their managers to capitalize on the notion of trainability of skills. Truly, as noted before, skills are partly a function of innate ability, but they also are trainable to some extent. Consider, for example, the managerial competencies listed in table 4.2. Each one of the listed behaviors evidently is based on one or more of the abilities listed in table 4.1. However, a person can enhance each one of the competencies through training and experience in a job.

In their study of what characterizes intelligent functioning among senior managers, Klemp and

---

In a Nutshell

Ability refers to a specific root talent for performance. Skill or competence refers to the learned application of one or more abilities to a particular task.

McClelland (1986) identified eight general competencies that underlie intelligence (see table 4.3). These authors group the eight competencies into three broad categories: intellectual competencies, influence competencies, and other. The intellectual competencies relate to gathering, analyzing, and evaluating information; understanding the whole system and its parts and how they interact with each

Table 4.3 Competencies of Intelligent Managers

Competency	Competency indicators
Intellectual competency	
Planning and causal thinking	Sees implications, consequences, alternatives, or if-then relationships.
	Analyzes causal relationships.
	Makes strategies and plans steps to reach a goal.
Diagnostic information seeking	Pushes for concrete information in an ambiguous situation.
	Seeks information from multiple sources to clarify a situation.
	Uses questions to identify the specifics of a problem or other situation.
Conceptualization and synthetic thinking	Understands how different parts, needs, or functions of the organization fit together.
	Identifies patterns and interprets a series of events.
	Identifies the most important issues in a complex situation.
	Uses unusual analogies to understand or explain the essence of a situation.
Influence competency	
Concern for influence (the need for power)	States a desire to persuade people.
	Anticipates the impact of actions on people.
Directive influence (personalized power)	Confronts people directly when problems occur.
	Tells people to do things the way he or she wants them done.
Collaborative influence (socialized power)	Operates effectively with groups to influence outcomes and get cooperation.
	Builds "ownership" of controversial decisions among key subordinates by involving them in decision making.
Symbolic influence	Sets a personal example for an intended impact.
	Uses symbols of group identity.
Other	
Self-confidence	Sees self as prime mover, leader, or energizer of the organization.
	Mentions being stimulated by crises and other difficult problems.
	Sees self as the most capable person to get the job done.

Reproduced from Klemp and McClelland 1986.

other; and visualizing the alternatives and the implications of selected actions. While these competencies are critical for managerial effectiveness, they by themselves do not make an intelligent manager. Because a manager's competencies in these areas have to be translated into action and because subordinate members of the organization typically carry out such actions, the manager has to be "intelligent" in influencing the members of the organization to carry out specified activities efficiently and effectively. Therefore, the manager needs to possess what Klemp and McClelland call the "influence competencies." These influence competencies include the capacity to exercise power in order to direct members' actions, to participate in and collaborate with groups, and to set a personal example (which includes only self-confidence).

In a Nutshell

The many and varied competencies in the workplace can be divided into intellectual capacities (i.e., capacity to gather and analyze information, see the whole picture, and make effective decisions) and influence competencies (i.e., capacity to cooperate, collaborate, and direct individuals and groups).

The concern with skills and competencies also has been a research thrust in sport management (Fielding, Pitts, and Miller 1991; Jamieson 1987). As discussed in chapter 2, the NASPE and NASSM jointly proposed curricular requirements for sport management degree programs. A careful analysis of those guidelines shows that they are aimed at developing specific skills or competencies in specific areas of sport and recreation management. In their survey of 73 sport management academics from 38 universities in the United States and Canada, Fielding, Pitts, and Miller (1991) found that the respondents rated management skills (37% of the respondents), communication skills (30%), math skills (15%), marketing skills (15%), accounting skills (14%), and thinking skills (12%) as the more significant competencies required for success in sport management jobs. Note that some of the skills identified parallel the functional areas of management. For example, management, marketing, and accounting skills relate to the functions of management, marketing, and accounting, respectively. In contrast, communication, math, and thinking skills are general in nature and transferable across functional areas.

In Their View

Peters (1987) and Klemp and McClelland (1986) argued that success in work and everyday life depends not only on the conventional academic intelligence but also on the other practical intelligence. Peters (1987) identified several components of "practical intelligence" that include

- self-understanding (to understand one's needs and abilities),
- social intelligence (to manage group processes through effective communication),
- body intelligence (to control the body and manipulate objects),
- spatial intelligence (to get, process, and use information about shapes, sizes, distances, and geometrical relationships),
- verbal intelligence (to have verbal comprehension, fluency, and vocabulary),
- logical-mathematical intelligence (to think systematically and abstractly using the concepts of logic and mathematics), and
- critical thinking (to think creatively, intuitively, and, above all, critically).

It is important to note that the above components of practical intelligence include cognitive abilities as well as psychomotor abilities as described in the text.

Psychomotor Abilities

Several jobs also require psychomotor abilities in addition to cognitive abilities. This is particularly true in sport management-related activities, such as fitness instructing and coaching. Not surprisingly, scholars and students of the sport and physical education field always have been interested in psychomotor abilities because performance in sports largely depends on these abilities. The management field also is concerned with psychomotor abilities in so far as they contribute to task accomplishment and to organizational performance. Thus, managers expect many of the "blue collar" workers (e.g., assembly line workers and carpenters) to possess some psychomotor abilities. Some schools of dentistry require that their incoming students pass tests involving the manipulation of tiny objects with fingers and the steadiness of positioning movements. Obviously, some of the tasks within sport, physical education, and recreation entail higher levels of specific psychomotor abilities. For instance, the success of a tennis coach, an aerobics instructor, and a basketball referee depends on them having the necessary physical capacities. From a different perspective, most of the services in our field are aimed at improving the psychomotor abilities of our clients.

In Their View

"Despite advances in technology, many jobs are still physically demanding. Successful performance of these jobs requires that individuals possess various types and levels of physical abilities. It is widely recognized that workers who are lacking in the requisite physical abilities incur an increased risk of physical injury to themselves and others" (Blakley et al. 1994, 248).

The most comprehensive and sustained research efforts regarding psychomotor and physical abilities have been that of Fleishman and his associates (e.g., Fleishman 1964, 1972, 1975, 1979, 1988, 1992; Fleishman and Hempel 1954; Fleishman and Quaintance 1984; Fleishman and Reilly 1992;

Fleishman and Rich 1963; Myers, Gebhardt, Crump, and Fleishman 1993). The main purpose of their research, which has spanned three decades, was to identify and describe a set of independent abilities that might contribute to performance in a wide variety of tasks. The nine psychomotor and nine physical abilities that Fleishman and associates identified are described in table 4.4.

Note that, without reference to any external cues, the individual initiates and controls performances in the strength and flexibility factors. The other abilities in the list are associated with performances that external cues and stimuli trigger (i.e., such performances occur in response to some stimulus). This view is analogous to the distinctions made between closed and open activities. In a closed activity, such as high jumping, the athlete executes the activity in a stable environment. That is, the position of the crossbar is established, and the approach to the crossbar remains the same. The athlete decides when to initiate the activity. In contrast, a rebounder in basketball does not know in advance the direction of the rebound and the actions of the opponents. External cues initiate and control his or her rebounding performance. Thus, he or she is executing an open skill. Both skills (i.e., high jump-

Table 4.4   Psychomotor Abilities

Ability	Description
Static strength	This strength is the capacity to apply maximal force against a maximal resistance. The intended movement may be pulling, pushing, or lifting.
Explosive strength	This strength is the ability to explode into a muscular activity as in sprint starting or in shot putting. Known also as muscular power, it is the mobilization of energy for a sudden burst of activity.
Dynamic strength	This strength is an individual's capacity to engage in repeated movements in which the body is supported or moved. Known also as muscular endurance, it is critical to successful performance in activities such as gymnastics.
Stamina	Known also as cardiorespiratory fitness, stamina is the capacity for physical exertion over an extended period of time. This capacity is highly trainable.
Extent flexibility	This ability is the capacity of muscle groups to extend or stretch in bending the body or parts of the body. The emphasis is on the extent of stretch and not the speed or repetitions of such stretching.
Dynamic flexibility	This flexibility is the ability to bend one's body or parts of the body with speed and flexibility. It reflects the capacity of the muscles to recover rapidly from the stretch.

Ability	Description
Gross body equilibrium	This equilibrium is the ability to maintain one's balance against upsetting forces or to regain balance. Thus, this ability pertains only to body balance and not to the balance of objects.
Response orientation	This ability is the selection of the correct response from among several options to the correct stimulus. The focus is on the selection and initiation of the correct response and not on the execution of that response.
Reaction time	In contrast to response orientation, this ability is the quickness of initiating a given response to a single stimulus (e.g., the sprinter leaving the block in response to the starter's gun). That is, there is no choice of responses or stimuli.
Speed of limb movement	This ability refers to moving the arms and legs with speed. The focus is on the speed of limb movement and not on the accuracy or coordination of these movements. Even the initiation of the movement is excluded from this ability.
Wrist-finger speed	This ability relates to the speed with which one can move the wrists, hands, and fingers. The accuracy of the movement is not of concern.
Gross body coordination	This ability is the coordination of the trunk and limbs while the entire body is in motion, such as in soccer dribbling.
Multilimb coordination	This ability also is the coordination of two or more limbs, but such coordination generally occurs while the body is at rest. Steering an automobile wheel while applying the brakes is an example of this ability.
Finger dexterity	This ability is the skillful and coordinated movement of the fingers. Manipulation of small objects, such as in repairing watches, may be involved.
Manual dexterity	This ability is the skillful and coordinated movements of a hand and arm. Manual dexterity is greatly involved in activities such as catching and throwing.
Arm-hand steadiness	This ability relates to positioning one's arm and hand and holding that position, such as in archery and shooting. The emphasis is on steadiness and not on strength or speed.
Rate control	This ability relates to making motor adjustments in relation to an object that has an unpredictable speed and direction. A badminton player's reaction to the opponent's smash involves this ability.
Control precision	This ability relates to adjusting or positioning a machine or equipment in a controlled manner in relation to a moving object that has a predictable speed and direction.

Source: Fleishman 1975, 1988, 1992; Fleishman and Quaintance 1984; Fleishman and Reilly 1992; Myers et al. 1993.

Adapted, by permission, from E.A. Fleishman and M.K. Quaintance, 1984, *Taxonomies of human performance: The description of human tasks* (Orlando, FL: Academic Press). © Edwin A. Fleishman.

ing and basketball rebounding) require explosive strength, speed of limb movement, and gross body coordination. However, success in basketball rebounding also requires response orientation and reaction time. This difference between closed and open skills underlies the relative emphasis that coaches place on consistency of performance in closed skills compared with quality decision making in open skills.

The given list of psychomotor abilities underlies all physical movements. In one sense, our whole field is built around the concept of psychomotor abilities. Obviously, all of our participant services are aimed at enhancing or maintaining

Sport and recreation managers need to address the question of what abilities are required in any given job. This necessitates a thorough analysis of the job in question to assess the specific abilities required in that job. The subject of job analysis is discussed at length in chapter 8. The Fleishman Job Analysis Survey (Fleishman 1992) includes behaviorally anchored scales for the cognitive, psychomotor, physical ability, and sensory-perceptual requirements of jobs and tasks. Also, Fleishman and Reilly's (1992) handbook on human abilities provides the test specifications and commercial tests available to measure each ability.

the psychomotor abilities of our clients. Even the spectator services are based largely on the psychomotor abilities of the professional athletes. The contribution that other elements, such as competition, the suspense regarding outcomes, and the spectacle of the event, make to spectator appeal is a given. However, they by themselves cannot create that entertainment value without the extraordinary physical skills of the athletes.

The practitioners in the field may use different terminology than that of Fleishman and Quaintance (1984). For example, quickness, agility, balance, strength, and explosion are familiar terms that coaches and athletes use. The practitioners also may be more interested in a combination of abilities rather than in specific individual abilities. For instance, take agility, which is "the rapid and accurate movement of the total body in response to perceived stimuli" (Chelladurai 1976, 37). The predictability of the onset of the stimuli, of the spatial location of the stimuli, or even of a combination of both time and location characterize the stimuli. Based on these two dimensions, Chelladurai (1976) classified agility into

- simple agility that involves no variation in the stimulus field, such as in high jumping;

- temporal agility that involves variation only in the timing of the appearance of the stimulus, such as in the start of sprinting events or the snap in football;

- spatial agility that involves only spatial variations, such as in receiving a tennis serve; and

- universal agility that involves a response to both temporal and spatial variations, such as in a squash competition.

From the foregoing, the different classes of agility performance may depend to varying degrees on Fleishman and Quaintance's (1984) abilities of explosive strength, dynamic flexibility, gross body equilibrium, response orientation, reaction time, and gross body coordination. Thus, agility is a practical composite index of several psychomotor abili-

ties, and its measurement is relatively easy. Therefore, not surprisingly, many teachers and coaches rely on agility and several other composite indices of psychomotor abilities (e.g., 40-yard run and bench press).

Blakley et al. (1994) and Hogan (1991) considered that all physical abilities underlying physical performance can be categorized into three broad dimensions: muscular strength (i.e., the ability to apply or resist force by muscular contraction), cardiovascular endurance (i.e., the capacity for repeated or sustained physical activity), and movement quality (i.e., the capacity for skilled performance, such as balance and coordination). According to Blakley et al. (1994), muscular strength is a more predominant dimension in physically demanding jobs than cardiovascular endurance or movement quality. Obviously, the type of physical abilities required vary from task to task. For example, the weight-training instructor in a fitness club requires muscular strength and muscular endurance, and the aerobics instructor requires high cardiovascular endurance.

In a Nutshell

Psychomotor abilities underlie most of the services produced in our field. Even spectator services are based on the psychomotor abilities of the athletes. These abilities can be grouped into muscular strength, cardiovascular endurance, and movement quality.

Summary

In summary, the chapter described a short list of cognitive and psychomotor abilities and included the issues of inherent capacity compared with current capacity, heritability of ability, and generality of ability compared with specificity of ability. Explained also were the competencies associated with effective managers. Not all of the abilities are relevant to all organizations or tasks. A prudent manager would view these abilities in juxtaposition with the contingencies that his or her organization poses.

These classification schemes of abilities provide the basis for analyzing the jobs in terms of what they require, classifying the jobs on the basis of similarity of ability requirements, setting performance standards for each set of jobs, hiring new employees who possess the necessary abilities, assessing the abilities of current employees, assigning employees to appropriate jobs, and instituting appropriate training programs to enhance those abilities in which they are deficient. In addition, services have to be tailored to the ability levels of the clients. In some cases, such as in recruiting athletes, the current status of the athletes on specified psychomotor abilities may be used as primary criteria. Subsequent chapters discuss the processes of recruiting, hiring, training, and assigning individuals to specific jobs and evaluating their performance.

Key Terms

cognitive abilities, psychomotor abilities, heritability, generality, specificity, managerial competencies

Your Perspectives

- Discuss the issue of heritability of ability. How much of your own abilities do you attribute to genetics and to contextual factors?

- What is your perspective on natural athletes? Do you think that you have or someone you know has some general ability that is transferable across different task requirements?

- Considering the competencies listed in table 4.3, discuss the relative importance of each competency in different managerial positions within sport and recreation management.

- In your opinion, which of the psychomotor abilities are important in which of the jobs in sport and recreation?

5 Personality

Learning Objectives

After reading this chapter you will be able to

- define and describe the terms personality and traits,
- explain the genetic and environmental factors on the formation of personality,
- distinguish between personality as a state and as a trait,
- understand Jackson's comprehensive list of personality traits and the big-five personality domains, and
- identify and describe the personality traits that are more relevant to organizations and management.

In chapter 4, I noted that ability is one of several factors that affect performance and that one's personality, values, and motivation also affect how one behaves and performs. Because personality predisposes an individual (i.e., manager as well as worker) to react in specific ways, an understanding of personality facilitates better management. For instance, the selection and placement of individuals in specific jobs, as well as promotions, can be based partly on the personality characteristics of an individual. Similarly, methods of supervision and motivation also may be modified to suit the personality of individual workers. Therefore, developing some insights into the dynamics of personality in the workplace and into how to make the best use of individual differences in personality to benefit both the individuals and the organization is important.

As with many psychological concepts, confusion and controversy over its definition characterize personality. Several theories address the development of personality and its description. The intention is not to delve into these issues but to discuss

- the modern view of development and manifestation of personality,
- the descriptions of personality, and
- the personality constructs relevant to organizations and their management.

Definitions of Personality

After collating the information from 50 different definitions, Allport (1937) offered his own definition of **personality**: "Personality is the dynamic organization within the individual of those psychophysical systems that determine his unique adjustments to his environment" (p. 48). One would expect that after such elaborate analysis and synthesis, researchers would come to a consensus on the concept of personality. Instead, differing views on personality and its definition still exist.

In Their View

Because personality characteristics create the parameters for people's behavior, they give us a framework for predicting behavior. For instance, individuals who are shy, introverted, and uncomfortable in social situations would probably be ill suited as salespeople. Individuals who are submissive and conforming might not be effective as advertising "idea" people. . . . Can we predict which people will be high performers in sales, research, or assembly-line work on the basis of their personality characteristics alone? The answer is NO. But a knowledge of an individual's personality can aid in reducing mismatches, which, in turn, can lead to greater job stability and higher job satisfaction. (Robbins 1997, 360-361)

Tosi, Rizzo, and Carroll (1986) defined personality as "the relatively stable organization of all of a person's characteristics, an enduring pattern of attributes that define the uniqueness of a person" (p. 130). According to Luthans (1985) personality means "how people affect others and how they understand and view themselves, as well as their pattern of inner and outer measurable traits, and the person-situation interaction" (p. 98). In Lefton's (1991) view, personality is "a set of relatively enduring behavioral characteristics and internal predispositions that describe how a person reacts to the environment" (p. 424). To Schermerhorn, Hunt, and Osborn (1997), "personality is the overall profile or combination of traits that characterize the unique nature of a person" (p. 47). Maddi (1980) defined personality as "a stable set of characteristics and tendencies that determine those commonalities and differences in the psychological behavior (thoughts, feelings, and actions) of people that have continuity in time" (p. 10).

These definitions suggest that people are alike (i.e., they have commonalities) and yet different (i.e., they have differences). They also refer to personality as being stable and having continuity in time. Much of the debate over personality centers around determinants of personality and the relative influence of personality and situation on behavior.

In a Nutshell

Many authors have defined personality in slightly different ways. The essence of these definitions refers to personality as an enduring pattern of psychophysical attributes that defines the uniqueness of a person and influences the person's thoughts, feelings, and behavior.

Determinants of Personality

The traditional view is that personality largely is determined genetically. However, Mischel (1973) argued that personality traits are learned characteristics and that personality development is both a cognitive and a social learning process. It is a cognitive process in the sense that individuals consciously process the information that they receive, and it is a social learning process in the sense that an individual learns from the social interactions and their consequences and reorients himself or herself to the environment. Bandura's (1986) social cognitive theory (formerly known as social learning theory) also suggests that cognitive processes revolving around personal experiences, as well as perceptions of others' experiences, also shape one's behavior.

These two views need not be viewed as exclusionary. The growing consensus among psychologists is that heredity plays a part in the development of personality (i.e., **genetic influences**) and that personality also is modified through one's exposure to culture, family, and referent groups (i.e., **environmental influences**).

Cultural Influences

If personality is a function of the developmental process, the culture in which the individual is reared has a significant impact on one's personality. Culture as a general influence determines the range of experiences and situations to which the individual is exposed and the values that he or she holds. All of this has a bearing on the personality of the individual. For instance, independence and competitiveness are values cherished and rewarded in the

North American culture, but they are not fostered in the Asian cultures. However, note that all individuals within a culture may not develop the same personality traits or may not develop them to the same extent.

Family and Social Groups

In line with the arguments for the influences of culture, one's immediate family and social groups also help define the personality dispositions of the individual. The family and social groups interpret and inculcate the values and norms derived from the culture. Thus, the members closely associated with the individual mediate culture's influence on personality development. Further, the family and social groups also define the roles for the individual and the appropriate behaviors for each role (e.g., parent, child, leader, and follower). Individuals performing different roles acquire those tendencies that are appropriate to their specific roles.

Personality, Situation, and Behavior

The second issue, which is related to the issue of heritability, is whether the personality of the individual or the demands of the situation determine a behavior in a given situation. If one holds the view that personality is inherited, then the logical conclusion is that, in any given situation, personality determines behavior. On the other hand, a person who believes in Mischel's (1973) position that personality is a learned characteristic also holds that the situational demands determine a behavior. Research and experience support neither of these views. Instead, the interactionist view that the characteristics of both the person and the situation interact with each other in influencing behavior is gaining acceptance. This view is consistent with Lewin's (1935) formula B = f (P,E) that suggests that behavior (B) is a function (f) of the person (P) and the environment or situation (E).

For example, when a basketball player constantly crashes the board for rebounds, the player is supposed to possess an "aggressive personality." According to earlier theories, the player should be aggressive in all situations. However, research has not supported such an assertion. Instead, the basketball player might be submissive in his or her dealings with the family or coach. What emerges from this example is the notion that the basketball situation calls for aggressive actions and that the player's aggressive personality manifests itself in

that situation. However, the family situation does not require such behavior, so the personality lies dormant in that situation. Thus, particular situations constrain an individual's behavior in specific ways.

In a Nutshell

One view holds that genetics largely determines personality; that is, personality is an inherited characteristic. A contrasting view is that personality is a learned characteristic; such learning occurs through personal experiences as well as perceptions of others' experiences. The most widely accepted perspective is the interactionist perspective that holds that both genetic and environmental factors determine personality.

Trait Versus State

The realization that personality manifests itself in some circumstances and not in others has led scholars to distinguish between **personality as a trait and as a state**. A trait is a general predisposition to specific experiences or behaviors; a state is the activation of the trait in specific situations. A good example is the distinction between trait and state anxiety. Some individuals are prone to be more anxious than others, implying that they are high on the anxiety trait. However, this implication does not mean that those who score higher on the trait will be more anxious in all situations than the low scorers. Anxiety manifests itself and sets apart the more anxious persons only in situations in which some element of threat, such as an evaluation or comparison by others, is present. For instance, a gymnast who has a high level of the anxiety trait may be perfectly normal and perform as well as those who have a low level of the anxiety trait during practice sessions. However, prior to and during competitions, the focal gymnast may become very anxious and nervous, which may lead to poor performance. This example shows the interaction of the anxiety trait with the threat imbedded in the competitive situation, i.e., the threat of being evaluated or being defeated.

The foregoing analyses have two implications for students of sport management. First, given the same situation for all members of the organization, those members who have differing personalities tend to behave in different ways. That is, if the situation does not exert a strong influence, then members behave differently based on their personality predispositions. The second implication is that if the situational influences are strong enough, then all members behave according to the dictates of the situation. For example, if a fire is in the stands, everyone reacts the same way; that is, they run for their lives! Bear these premises in mind when reading the next section, which reviews some of the personality traits, particularly those more relevant to the organizational context.

In a Nutshell

A general disposition to act in a specific way is a personality trait. However, that trait is exhibited only when strong situational cues activate it. The trait may lie dormant in the absence of such cues. When situational cues trigger a trait into action, it is a state.

Type Theories

In the early days of this century, psychologists commonly referred to types when describing a person in terms of personality. A good example from the sport and recreation management field is Sheldon's (1954) classification of temperaments derived from body types. He viewed that every individual is characterized by

- mesomorphy (i.e., muscular, strong body type),
- ectomorphy (i.e., tall, fragile body type), or
- endomorphy (i.e., round, soft body type).

While all individuals have more or less of each of the three components, only one is dominant in some people. Sheldon also viewed that each body type is associated with a particular temperament: mesomorphy with somatotonia, ectomorphy with cerebrotonia, and endomorphy with viscerotonia. Table 5.1 illustrates his three body types and associated temperaments. Sheldon developed his theory based on his clinical experiences with his psychiatric patients. The problem, however, is that his measurement of both body types and temperaments were not independent. Because he was the originator of the theory, he measured all the variables in his theory, and because all measurements were subjective, researchers have not given much credence to his theory of linking temperament to body type.

However, his model serves to illustrate the social learning process of personality development described earlier. Consider, for example, a group of boys or girls in a playing field. Those children endowed with a muscular body (mesomorphs) can perform some physical feats that are beyond the capacities of others. Others recognize and praise such performance capabilities. Such recognition may also engender some respect or fear on the part of the weaker members. Further, because of the positive feedback from others, the mesomorphs may persist in their adventurous, dominant, noisy, and aggressive behaviors. In short, one's body type may affect his or her perspective of the situation, the expectations of others for his or her behaviors, and others' reactions to the focal person's behaviors. These interactions, in turn, may impinge on personality development (Mussen 1963).

Table 5.1 Sheldon's Body Types and Temperaments

Body type	Temperament
Endomorphy	**Viscerotonia**
Is soft and spherical and has underdeveloped bone and muscle and an overdeveloped abdomen.	Has a love of comfort and food and is affectionate, tolerant, even-tempered, complacent, and a follower.
Mesomorphy	**Somatotonia**
Is hard, rectangular, and strong and has developed bone and muscle.	Prefers physical adventure and risk taking and is aggressive, insensitive, noisy, courageous, and dominant.
Ectomorphy	**Cerebrotonia**
Is linear, fragile, delicate, flat-chested, thin, and light-muscled.	Is restrained, inhibited, secretive, distrustful, anxious, ambitious, and dedicated.

Source: Sheldon (1954).

In a Nutshell

Sheldon's classification of body types into meso-morphy, endomorphy, and ectomorphy is based on muscularity and linearity of the body structure. Sheldon also classified individuals on the basis of their temperament (i.e., personality): somatotonia, cerebrotonia, and viscerotonia. While the concept of body types generally is accepted, its linkage with personality dispositions is discounted.

Trait Theories

Trait theories may be considered an extension of the type theories. That is, instead of placing individuals in one of a limited number of categories as type theories do, individuals are described in terms of several traits. Thus, trait theories acknowledge the complexity of personality and describe it in more elaborate terms than the type theories do.

Bear in mind that researchers have identified several hundred traits (Allport and Odbert 1936). Several scholars have attempted to reduce the multitude of traits into fewer, more meaningful categories. Usually, development of scales (or inventories) to measure the specified personality traits follow these attempts. Of these, Cattell's (1957) Sixteen Personality Factor Questionnaire, Hathaway and McKinley's (1967) Minnesota Multiphasic Personality Inventory, Gough's (1969) California Psychological Inventory, and Jackson's (1984) Personality Research Form are the more well-known instruments. The traits that the Personality Research Form measure are comprehensive enough and are applicable to any group of subjects. Because they are representative of many other schemes proposed, they are defined in table 5.2 for illustrative purposes.

More recently, a move to describe individuals in terms of the "big-five" personality domains has begun (Barrick and Mount 1991, Goldberg 1990, McCrae and Costa 1987):

- Surgency and extraversion
- Agreeableness
- Conscientiousness
- Neuroticism and emotional stability
- Intellect

The purpose here is to group several of the individual traits included in other schemes into meaningful domains. Researchers have found that these five domains, which are described in table 5.3, relate to several forms of behavior within organizations (e.g., Mount and Barrick 1995). For instance, Barrick and Mount (1991) found that the personality domain of conscientiousness was predictive of job performance measures among professional, police, managerial, sales, and skilled and semi-skilled workers. Surgency or extraversion was related to performance in those jobs that required social interactions (e.g., managerial and sales). Note that conscientiousness seems to be related meaningfully to all job contexts. As Barrick and Mount (1991) noted,

> This aspect of personality appears to tap traits which are important to the accomplishment of work tasks in all jobs. That is, those individuals who exhibit traits associated with a strong sense of purpose, obligation, and persistence generally perform better than those who do not. (p.18)

In a Nutshell

Researchers have proposed many lists of personality traits. The proposal of the big-five personality domains (surgency, agreeableness, conscientiousness, neuroticism, and intellect) may be sufficient to describe a person.

Personality and Organizational Behavior

The foregoing description of personality and dimensions of personality are general in nature and can be applied in any context. However, some of the personality traits are more relevant to organizations and their management (Morse and Young 1973; Robbins 1997; Schermerhorn, Hunt, and Osborn 1997; and Tosi, Rizzo, and Carroll 1986). The following sections describe the personality traits considered to be germane to management of human resources: authoritarian personality, bureaucratic personality, attitude toward authority, attitude toward individualism, tolerance for ambiguity, locus of control, positive and negative affectivity, **service orientation**, Machiavellianism, and problem-solving style. Note that these traits generally are included in the big-five personality domains described earlier. Some of the traits overlap each other.

Authoritarian Personality

Adorno et al. (1950) advanced the concept of **authoritarian personality**. In their view, a person whom

Table 5.2   Traits Measured by Jackson's Personality Research Form

Scale	Description of high scorer
Abasement	Shows a high degree of humility, accepts blame and criticism even when not deserved, exposes self to situations where he or she is in an inferior position, and tends to be self-effacing.
Achievement	Aspires to accomplish difficult tasks, maintains high standards and is willing to work toward distant goals, responds positively to competition, and is willing to put forth effort to attain excellence.
Affiliation	Enjoys being with friends and people in general, accepts people readily, and makes efforts to win friendships and to maintain associations with people.
Aggression	Enjoys combat and argument, is easily annoyed, sometimes is willing to hurt people to get his or her way, may seek to "get even" with people whom he or she perceives as having harmed him or her.
Autonomy	Tries to break away from restraints, confinements, or restrictions of any kind; enjoys being unattached, free, and not tied to people, places, or obligations; and may be rebellious when faced with restraints.
Change	Likes new and different experiences, dislikes routine and avoids it, may readily change opinions or values in different circumstances, and adapts readily to changes in environment.
Cognitive structure	Does not like ambiguity or uncertainty in information, wants all questions answered completely, and desires to make decisions based upon definite knowledge rather than upon guesses or probabilities.
Defendence	Readily suspects that people mean him or her harm or are against him or her, ready to defend self at all times, takes offense easily, and does not accept criticism readily.
Dominance	Attempts to control his or her environment and to influence or direct other people, expresses opinions forcefully, and enjoys the role of leader and may assume it spontaneously.
Endurance	Is willing to work long hours, does not give up quickly on a problem, is persevering even in the face of great difficulty, and is patient and unrelenting in his or her work habits.
Exhibition	Wants to be the center of attention, enjoys having an audience, engages in behavior that wins the notice of others, and may enjoy being dramatic or witty.
Harm avoidance	Does not enjoy exciting activities, especially if danger is involved; avoids risk of bodily harm; and seeks to maximize personal safety.
Impulsivity	Tends to act on the "spur of the moment" and without deliberation, gives vent readily to feelings and wishes, speaks freely, and may be volatile in emotional expression.
Nurturance	Gives sympathy and comfort; assists others whenever possible; interested in caring for children and for disabled or infirm people; offers a "helping hand" to those in need; and readily performs favors for others.
Order	Is concerned with keeping personal effects and surroundings neat and organized; dislikes clutter, confusion, and lack of organization; and is interested in developing methods for keeping materials methodically organized.
Play	Does many things "just for fun" and spends much time participating in games, sports, social activities, and other amusements; enjoys jokes and funny stories; and maintains a light-hearted, easy-going attitude toward life.
Sentience	Notices smells, sights, tastes, and the way things feel; remembers these sensations and believes that they are an important part of life; is sensitive to many forms of experience; and may maintain an essentially hedonistic or aesthetic view of life.

Scale	Description of high scorer
Social recognition	Desires acquaintances to hold him or her in high esteem, is concerned about reputation and what other people think of him or her, and works for the approval and recognition of others.
Succorance	Frequently seeks the sympathy, protection, love, advice, and reassurance of other people; may feel insecure or helpless without such support; and confides difficulties readily to a receptive person.
Understanding	Wants to understand many areas of knowledge and values synthesis of ideas, verifiable generalization, and logical thought, particularly when directed at satisfying intellectual curiosity.
Desirability	Describes self in terms judged as desirable and, in response to personality statements, presents favorable picture of self whether consciously or unconsciously or whether accurately or inaccurately.
Infrequency	Reponds in implausible or pseudorandom manner, possibly due to carelessness, and has poor comprehension, passive noncompliance, confusion, or gross deviation.

Jackson, D.N. (1984). Personality Research Form Manual, Port Huron, MI: Sigma Assessment Systems, Inc. © Sigma Assessment Systems, Inc., 1984, Port Huron, MI 48061-0984. Reproduced by Permission.

Table 5.3   The "Big-Five" Personality Domains

Domain	Defining terms
Surgency and extroversion	Enthusiastic, spirited, extroverted, expressive, playful, gregarious, sociable, active, energetic, dominant, assertive, ambitious, and courageous
Agreeableness	Cooperative, helpful, amiable, cordial, friendly, empathetic, understanding, considerate, courteous, generous, affectionate, easy-going, and honest
Conscientiousness	Organized, concise, efficient, self-disciplined, precise, cautious, punctual, deliberate, decisive, predictable, economical, and logical
Neuroticism and emotional stability	Defensive, fretful, insecure, emotionally instable, temperamental, excitable, envious, nervous, anxious, fearful, gullible, and intrusive
Intellect	Contemplative, intellectual, insightful, complex, perceptive, bright, smart, curious, inquisitive, creative, innovative, and sophisticated

Source: Goldberg (1990) cited in Lillibridge and Williams (1992).

Reprinted from J.R. Lillibridge and K.J. Williams, Another look at personality and managerial potential: Application of the five factor model. In *Issues, theory, and research in industrial organizational psychology,* edited by K. Kelley, Copyright 1992, pages 91-113, with permission from Elsevier Science.

this trait characterizes respects authority and order. This is reflected both in the person's adherence to rules and regulations and obedience to superiors' orders and in their expectations for others to abide by the rules and obey superiors' orders. Note that persons of authoritarian personality make good followers. They tend to put events and persons into categories and to behave consistently toward them based on such categorizations. They also are intolerant of uncertainties and weaknesses. They believe that some are born to lead; others, to follow.

People who have an authoritarian personality are likely to fit neatly into those organizations that a hierarchy of positions and extensive rules and regulations characterize. However, they may find it difficult to address the emerging organizational values of democracy, egalitarianism, and openness in various organizations. Their persistence in their innate preferences for a stable and ordered environment might disrupt the organizational change processes and might destroy their own health and well-being.

While considerable evidence suggests that personality is related to job performance and reactions to job and organizational characteristics, sport and recreation managers must be careful about making judgments about employees. Analyze a particular job in terms of the specific personality traits required for successful performance in that job. As noted in the chapter 4, the manager can use a general factor of ability (either cognitive ability or psychomotor ability) as a predictor of success in several jobs. Unfortunately, this is not the case with personality. As Tett, Jackson, and Rothstein (1991) noted: "There is no *g* factor for personality that would allow the relatively straightforward inference that what is required for one job is probably required for others. On the contrary, individual differences in personality pose a severe challenge to personnel decision makers, and meeting this challenge will require careful analysis of both the person and the job" (pp. 732-733).

In Their View

It would be wrong, however, for you to conclude from this discussion that managers or work groups should try to change or otherwise directly control employee personality. This is, of course, impossible and, even if it were possible, would be highly unethical. Rather, the challenge for managers and employees is to understand the crucial role played by personality in explaining some aspects of human behavior in work settings. (Hellriegel, Slocum, and Woodman 1992, 84)

Bureaucratic Orientation

Weber (1947) coined the term "bureaucracy" to refer to a form of organization that he considered to be efficient and rational. In his view, an efficient form of an organization has the characteristics of specialization and division of labor, a hierarchy of author-

ity structure (i.e., superiors and subordinates), an explicit set of rules and regulations to govern the activities of both superiors and subordinates, impersonality in managing customers or clients, technical competence as the basis for hiring and promotions of employees, and written documents attesting to the activities and decisions of the members of the organization.

Based on the notion that individuals' preferences to function in a bureaucratic organization may vary, Gordon (1970) developed a scale to measure the personality trait that he labeled **bureaucratic orientation**. Bureaucratic orientation consists of five subcategories as shown in table 5.4.

In summary, bureaucratic orientation refers to a preference for rules and regulations and for order as major means of managing organizations. People who have this orientation value discipline, compliance to rules, and impersonal relationships. They believe that those people in higher positions have the right to make decisions. They also emphasize organizational loyalty and commitment.

Table 5.4   Subcategories of Bureaucratic Orientation

Subcategory	Description
Self-subordination	A willingness to comply fully with the stated wishes of a superior and to have a higher authority make the decisions
Compartmentalization	Complete confidence in expert judgment and a need to restrict one's concern to one's own area of specialization
Impersonalization	A preference for impersonal or formal relationships with others on the job, particularly with individuals at different organizational levels
Rule conformity	A desire for the security that the following of rules, regulations, and standard operating procedures affords
Traditionalism	A need for the security that organizational conformity to the in-group norm provides

Adapted from Gordon 1970.

The three personality traits outlined so far (i.e., authoritarian personality, bureaucratic orientation, and attitude toward authority) are quite similar in shaping an individual's reactions to organizational factors. More specifically, people who have a high level of these traits are likely to feel at home and to be more productive in organizational settings that have the characteristics of a high degree of authority, structure, rules and regulations, and well-defined tasks. For instance, the recreation department of a large metropolitan city is likely to be highly bureaucratized with a number of levels of authority and extensive rules and regulations. Such bureaucratization is necessary to ensure consistency and uniformity of operations and to ensure efficiency in the delivery of services. However, individuals who have a low level of the earlier mentioned personality traits find themselves at odds with organizational requirements for compliance and submission. By the same token, individuals who have a high level of the traits are uncomfortable and less productive in those organizations (e.g., a small fitness club) or organizational units that do not have an extensive and rigid authority and rule structure.

Attitude Toward Authority

Attitude toward authority refers to "an individual's desire for freedom and autonomy as opposed to willingness to be controlled, and to be dependent on others for direction" (Morse and Young 1973, 312). People who have a positive attitude toward authority are likely to comply with superiors' orders and to obey all of the rules and regulations. This trait is very similar to Gordon's bureaucratic orientation.

Morse and Young (1973) suggested that the development of this trait is a function of one's experiences with authority relationships in the early years of development:

> The individual faces the autonomy dilemma when he [or she] realizes that he [or she] has the ability to submit to parental demands or withhold the behavior which will please his parents. If the individual derives pleasure from failure to submit to parental demands, the emerged tendency will be strong desire for autonomy and a need to defy authority figures and restrictions: this is a keystone in the development of the attitude toward authority. (p. 312)

In addition, the support that the parents and others provide for the individual's initiatives in the use of one's own cognitive abilities and skills fosters the development of preference for lower levels of control and direction from others.

Attitude Toward Individualism

Individuals differ in the degree to which they prefer to "work alone and be alone as opposed to working or spending time with others" (Morse and Young 1973, 311). This attitude is a reflection of an individual's willingness to share responsibilities and duties with others. That is, the person oriented toward individualism does not like to be responsible to or for others in work performance.

According to Morse and Young (1973), development of the **attitude toward individualism** (or group interaction) is a function of the individual's experiences involving trust and mistrust, optimism and pessimism, and frugality. If a person's early experiences lead to mistrust and pessimism about the environment and foster the need to be frugal, then that person probably will develop a preference to work alone. Such a person relies on his or her own efforts to complete the task and develops internal standards to judge the task performance. The individual also is reluctant to share the time, effort, or expertise with others. In contrast, the individual who had more positive experiences fostering trust and optimism probably prefers group interaction in the task environment and is willing to share in both the duties and responsibilities.

Individuals who have a high level of the individualism trait are likely to be happy and successful in those jobs that do not involve much interaction and coordination with other jobs. For example, a tennis professional in a racket club may operate by himself or herself without much dependence on other jobs in the club. The owner of the club may give considerable freedom to the professional in his or her activities. People who have a high level of the individualism trait would fit well into that job.

Tolerance for Ambiguity

The **tolerance for ambiguity** reflects a person's "desire for change and new and unusual activities or for a routine, structured existence" (Morse and Young 1973, 313). The development of this trait largely is based on the child's acceptance or otherwise of parents' values of cleanliness and orderliness.

> Incorporation of this parental value does not just influence physical orderliness but is generalized to all behavior. Thus, attributes are formed regarding orderliness in feelings, ideas and thoughts. These affect the ability to tolerate ambiguity and confusion and influence desires for a neat and tidy world and punctiliousness. Moreover, submission to parental desires for cleanliness can result in suppression of spontaneity, a doubting of impulses and the inhibition of creative and novel behavior (Morse and Young 1973, 313).

The implication for management is to place individuals with a low tolerance for ambiguity in well-defined and regulated tasks. For example, the job of a locker-room attendant is clearly specified and routinized, so it matches people with lower tolerance for ambiguity. In contrast, the marketing manager of an athletic department faces considerable ambiguity in his or her dealings with potential clients and sponsors. Such a person has to possess a high level of tolerance for ambiguity and must be able to enjoy such ambiguous tasks.

Locus of Control

Rotter (1966) noted that people differ in the extent to which they attributed personal outcomes to themselves or to external sources. Individuals who believe that events in their life are under their control and that what happens to them is a function of their own decisions and behaviors are called internals, i.e., those who believe in internal **locus of control**. On the other hand, individuals who believe in external locus of control, i.e., the externals, attribute what happens to them to luck, fate, or others.

Research has shown that the internals and externals have different reactions to organizational factors, particularly with regard to involvement in decision making (Robbins 1997a). Table 5.5 shows Schermerhorn, Hunt, and Osborn's (1997) summary of the research findings. A general conclusion that one can draw from the research findings is that internals do well in managerial and professional positions that involve information processing, initiative, and independent decision making (Robbins 1997a). The director of a university athletic department, the chief of a city recreation department, or a sports agent would do well if he or she has an internal locus of control. On the other hand, the externals do well in those positions that require strict adherence to rules, regulations, and directives from superiors (Robbins 1997a). The assistants in the ticketing department of an elite athletic program need to follow established protocol in the distribution of tickets; therefore, individuals with an external locus of control are likely to perform well and to be satisfied with this type of job.

Positive and Negative Affectivity

Two traits that have gained greater attention in recent years in organizational psychology are positive affectivity and negative affectivity (Watson and Clark 1984; Watson, Clark, and Tellegen 1988). **Positive affectivity** refers to the tendency to be active, self-efficacious, interpersonal, and achievement-oriented. Individuals who have a high level of the positive-affectivity trait tend to perceive things in such a manner as to experience positive emotional states and a sense of well-being. On the other hand, individuals who have a low level of the positive-affectivity trait tend to view things not as positively and tend to have a low self-efficacy and a low sense of well-being.

Negative affectivity refers to the inclination to view everything in a way that leads to negative emotional states. Individuals who have a high level of the negative-affectivity trait in general have a negative orientation toward themselves and their environment including other people. They view

The personality traits of attitude toward individualism, tolerance for ambiguity, and locus of control have some direct implications for management. Because these traits generally point to one's preferred ways of acting and doing things, they also suggest the types of jobs suited for individuals who have a high level of these traits. Individuals who have a high level of the individualism trait should be placed in jobs that require less interaction with other jobs (e.g., accountant in a fitness club), and those individuals who have a low level of the tolerance-for-ambiguity trait and a high level of the external-locus-of-control trait should be placed in well-defined and structured jobs (e.g., locker-room attendant).

Table 5.5   Effects of Locus of Control on Organizational Variables

Organizational variable	Locus of control (internals compared with externals)
Information processing	Internals make more attempts to acquire information, are less satisfied, with the amount of information they possess, and are better at using information.
Job satisfaction	Internals are generally more satisfied, less alienated, and less rootless, and there is a stronger job satisfaction and performance relationship for them.
Performance	Internals perform better on learning and problem-solving tasks when performance leads to valued rewards.
Self-control, risk, and anxiety	Internals exhibit greater self-control, are more cautious, engage in less risky behavior, and are less anxious.
Motivation, expectancies, and results	Internals display greater work motivation, see a stronger relationship between what they do and what happens to them, expect that working hard leads to good performance, and feel more control over their time.
Response to others	Internals are more independent, more reliant on own judgment, and more likely to accept information on its merit. They are less susceptible to the influence of others.

From J.R. Schermerhorn, J.G. Hunt, and R.N. Osborn, *Organizational behavior,* 6TH ed. Copyright © 1997 by John Wiley & Sons, Inc., New York. Reprinted by permission of John Wiley & Sons, Inc.

themselves as being in stressful and unpleasant circumstances. They also tend to experience negative feelings over time and across situations. Those who have a low level of the negative-affectivity trait tend not to view their situations as stressful or upsetting. They are less prone to experience negative emotional states. George (1992) found that both positive affectivity and negative affectivity influence attitudes and behavior in organizations, particularly, and in job satisfaction.

Service Orientation

Hogan, Hogan, and Busch (1984) identified service orientation as another trait that is relevant to service operations. They define service orientation as "a set of attitudes and behaviors that affect the quality of interaction between . . . the staff of any organization and its customers" (p. 167). Individuals who have a high level of service orientation have the characteristics of good adjustment, social skills, and willingness to follow rules. Service-oriented employees take an interest in their customers and are more courteous to them. Further, they try to find ways of satisfying customers' wishes within the boundaries that the organization sets. They also take extra efforts to correct any faults in the service provided

or to manage any unexpected events in the provision of their services.

Machiavellianism

Christie and Geis (1970) promoted the concept that individuals differ in their tendency to be manipulative in their interactions with others. They called this trait **Machiavellianism**. The name of the trait is derived from Niccolò Machiavelli, the Florentine statesman who wrote *The Prince* in 1513 (Buskirk 1974). The book is a compendium of recommendations to the prince on how to manipulate his subjects (including his immediate subordinates) in order to gain and hold power in ruling his state. Over the years, his writings have been interpreted to mean deceitfulness, dishonesty, and cunning in manipulating others for personal gain. In fact, *Webster's New Twentieth Century Dictionary* defines Machiavellianism as "the principles and methods of Machiavelli; political cunning and duplicity, intended to favor arbitrary power." However, Buskirk (1974) pointed out that such negative evaluation of Machiavellian principles does not do justice to Machiavelli's insightful comments on the art of managing people and institutions.

The descriptions of the traits of positive and negative affectivity and of service orientation suggest that those who interact with clients directly in the delivery of sport and recreation services need to have a high level of both positive affectivity and service orientation. These traits in the service provider contribute to warm and friendly interpersonal interactions in the service encounter. This type of interaction is critical because the quality of the service provided and the perceptions of such quality are enhanced during this encounter.

Many times Machiavelli says in essence, "if you must do such and such, then here is how you should do it." In such cases, he is not recommending an action—in fact, many times he strongly advises against an action, citing the probable adverse outcomes—but is merely accommodating the ruler in power by advising his conduct in action that is a foregone conclusion. (pp. xii-xiii)

Buskirk (1974) also argued that the merit of Machiavelli's book is reflected in its survival; most of the literary works of his time have perished. More importantly, he suggested that "Machiavelli's basic advice is not only applicable to the ruling of a state but is also germane to the problems of managing any organization" (p. xii). Despite Buskirk's arguments, the term "Machiavellianism" still has a negative connotation. Individuals who have a high level of this trait (called high Machs) tend to be cool and calculating in pursuit of their self-interests. They are likely to form coalitions with relevant others so that their power and profits will be maximized. They may resort to lies, deception, and flattery in exploiting others for personal gains. They also have high self-esteem and self-confidence. Sentiments, such as sense of loyalty, and friendship do not carry much weight with high Machs. They may break their promises without much guilt or regret. Christie and Geis' (1970) Mach scale, which contains items similar to those shown in figure 5.1, measure these tendencies. The higher the score on the Mach scale, the higher the Machiavellian tendencies. Note that some of the items are reverse scored.

While the foregoing description of high Machs is negative, such orientation does have a positive aspect. That is, high Machs do well in jobs that require face-to-face interactions and that rules and regulations govern less; these jobs, in turn, permit improvisation (Robbins 1997). For example, a marketing director seeking sponsorships or donations needs to be persuasive, flexible, and innovative. Thus, the positive aspects of the Machiavellian orientation benefits a person in that position. However, the danger is that the negative aspects of cunning and deceit may violate the principle of business and managerial ethics.

Problem-Solving Style

In solving problems, individuals differ in the way they go about gathering information, evaluating information, and making decisions (Myers 1987). In gathering information, one person may prefer de-

		Disagree			Agree	
Item		A lot	A little	Neutral	A little	A lot
1. The best way to manage people is to tell them what they want to hear.		1	2	3	4	5
2. When you ask someone to do something for you, it is best to give the real reason for wanting it rather than to give reasons that might carry more weight (reverse scored).		1	2	3	4	5
3. Anyone who completely trusts anyone else is asking for trouble.		1	2	3	4	5
4. It is hard to get ahead without cutting corners here and there.		1	2	3	4	5
5. Honesty is the policy in all cases (reverse scored).		1	2	3	4	5

Figure 5.1   Sample items from Mach scale (to measure Machiavellianism).

Adapted, by permission, from R. Christie and F. Geiss, 1970, *Studies in Machiavellianism*. (New York: Academic Press).

tailed, well-defined, and concrete pieces of information; however, another person may prefer the "big picture" and new problems to solve. The former individual belongs to the sensation type while the latter individual belongs to the intuitive type.

In evaluating the information, one may be concerned about other people and possible disagreements or conflicts with them and, therefore, may tend to conform to others' views and preferences. Such a person is the feeling type. In contrast, another person may base the judgments on reason and intellect and may exclude emotions in such judgments. This second person is the thinking type.

The combination of these two dimensions—sensation-intuitive and feeling-thinking—yields four **problem-solving styles**. In figure 5.2, a listing of some job areas that better fit a particular style follows the description of each of the four problem-solving styles. Some examples from the sport and recreation management also are provided.

Sensation-Thinkers

The sensation-thinkers tend to be decisive and make well-thought-out decisions. Further, they are persevering and committed and are realistic in their expectations. They prefer clearly specified rules and regulations. A negative characteristic is that they tend to be impatient and judgmental about people. They are preoccupied with data, and they conceive of and prepare for too many contingencies.

Intuitive-Thinkers

The intuitive thinkers take a global or gestalt perspective in analyzing their situation. They are intellectuals and focus on principles and abstract ideas. They tend to plan and design rather than to execute. By the same token, they are impersonal and, therefore, may engender or encounter interpersonal problems. They may feel restless and let their restlessness rub off on their associates.

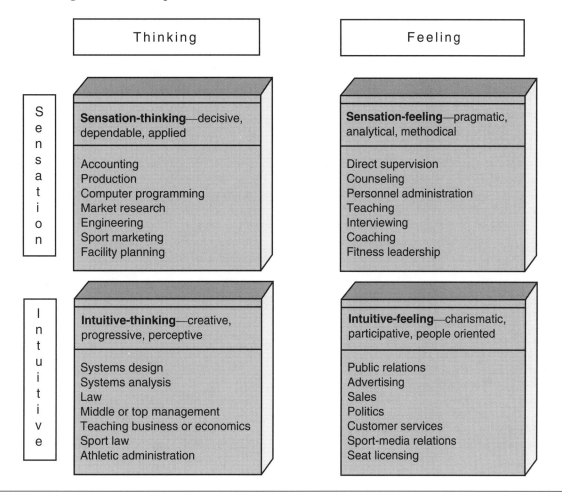

Figure 5.2 Four styles of problem solving and associated occupations.

Sensation-Feelers

The sensation-feeler type of individuals are pragmatic, and they manage concrete problems effectively. They tend to work within reality and make the best use of the opportunities that the situation offers. These individuals are oriented toward the present and attend to the demands of the immediate situation. However, they dislike new or abstract ideas. They may fail to be effective in the absence of rules and regulations.

Intuitive-Feelers

Intuitive feelers are articulate and communicate their positive feelings to associates. They are capable of seeing things in an abstract manner and managing unstructured and complicated situations. A negative characteristic is that they may make decisions based on their personal likes and dislikes. These individuals may try to please too many people. Insofar as they understand and appreciate the emotions of others, they tend to become slaves of others' emotions. They constantly seek recognition from others.

Managerial Potential

Researchers also have made attempts to identify the potential for management in terms of personality. The concern generally has been to identify a set of personality traits related to managerial effectiveness. For instance, Gough (1984) advanced the Managerial Potential Scale derived from the earlier-mentioned California Psychological Inventory. The researcher collated the 34 items in the scale after a series of studies relating the scores on personality variables to managerial effectiveness. Thus, these items do not reflect a particular trait or traits but represent what Gough called "**managerial potential.**" These 34 items require an individual to respond true or false to each item (see figure 5.3 for sample items). High scores (i.e., approximately more than 24) on this questionnaire correlated with managerial effectiveness. The scale is purported to recognize behavioral effectiveness, self-confidence, cognitive clarity, and goal orientation, which make managers more effective. Although the notion of managerial potential was advanced in the context of industrial and business organizations, it is equally relevant to management of sport and recreation organizations.

In a Nutshell

Several personality traits may be more relevant to organizations and their management. These traits include authoritarian personality, bureaucratic orientation, attitude toward authority, attitude toward individualism, tolerance for ambiguity, locus of control, positive and negative affectivity, service orientation, Machiavellianism, problem-solving style, and managerial potential.

Summary

In summary, I defined personality and described the factors associated with the formation of personality. Researchers suggest that an individual's behavior is a function of both his or her personality and the characteristics of the situation in which the behavior occurs. After discussing the trait and type theories, the chapter presented 12 personality traits

---

The following five items are drawn from Gough's (1984) Managerial Potential Scale. Those who take the test are required to respond **True** or **False** to each item.

1. I have no dread of going into a room by myself where other people have already gathered and are talking.	True	False
2. If given the chance, I would make a good leader of people.	True	False
3. I enjoy planning things, and deciding what each person should do.	True	False
4. Success is a matter of will power.	True	False
5. People naturally seem to turn to me when decisions have to be made.	True	False

Figure 5.3   Gough's managerial potential scale.

Source: Gough (1984)

that are associated with behavior in organizations and that include authoritarian personality, bureaucratic personality, attitude toward authority, attitude toward individualism, tolerance for ambiguity, locus of control, positive and negative affectivity, service orientation, Machiavellianism, problem-solving style, and managerial potential. Sport managers need to understand that despite clear-cut goals, policies, and procedures, members of an organization may react and behave differently partly because of the differences in their personality. By the same token, members' preferences for the way the manager acts toward them may vary as a function of their personality differences. Possession of specific traits is conducive for better performance and satisfaction in specific jobs. However, as Certo (1992) cautioned, "personality tests can be used advantageously if the personality characteristics needed to do well in a particular job are well defined and if individuals possessing those characteristics can be pinpointed and selected" (p. 326).

Thus, member personality is one more of the complex variables with which a manager has to contend and manage. Subsequent chapters address the issue of how these traits impinge on managerial practice.

Key Terms

personality, genetic influence, environmental influences, personality as a trait and as a state, service orientation, authoritarian personality, bureaucratic orientation, attitude toward authority, attitude toward individualism, tolerance for ambiguity, locus of control, positive affectivity, negative affectivity, Machiavellianism, problem-solving styles, managerial potential

Your Perspectives

- Discuss the terms "personality" and "traits."

- Give examples that illustrate the difference between personality as a trait and as a state.

- Discuss the personality differences between two individuals whom you know well.

- Which of the various personality traits described in the chapter would make a tennis professional, fitness instructor, facility manager, or ticket office clerk effective in his or her job? Why?

6 Values

Learning Objectives

After reading this chapter you will be able to

- define and describe values and distinguish them from attitudes and norms,
- distinguish between terminal and instrumental values,
- identify and discuss the sources and functions of values,
- understand how values of management and members may affect sport organizations, and
- relate the values in sport to societal values.

Previous chapters described some of the cognitive and psychomotor abilities and the personality traits that people bring to organizations. Some of the characteristics are transient (i.e., trainable) and some others are more or less permanent attributes of individuals. This chapter presents another set of attributes that have a bearing on the management of human resources; they are the values that members of an organization hold.

The term "value" has different meanings in different contexts. In general, value refers to the equivalence or worth of a thing or an act in terms of money or goods (e.g., the worth of one's athletic talent), something that is desirable (e.g., the value of sport participation), or a belief of what ought to be (e.g., there should be no emphasis on winning in sport). The concern here is with the last meaning, which this chapter explores in greater detail.

As Brunkan (1991) noted, values are probably the most nebulous area of individual difference variables including abilities and personality traits and are difficult to pin down. However,

> getting a handle on a person's values is important because it is frequently these values that influence long-term goals and decisions. Many people can tolerate almost anything for a short period of time. But when faced with the prospect of doing something distasteful as part of a long-term career with one company, they are less likely to be tolerant. In such situations, the individual's value system becomes much more important in decision-making. (Brunkan 1991, 244)

The idea that the performance of individuals, groups, and organizations is a function of, among other things, a congruence among the values that different members hold generally is accepted. In fact, the increasing diversity of the workforce in North America is seen as both an opportunity and a threat to organizational performance. The opportunity refers to the fact that different people bring different strengths to the workplace. By the same token, different people bring different values to the workplace. To the extent that these values are divergent from each other, conflict and confusion exist. Therefore, sport and recreation managers must understand the concept of values and their impact in the workplace.

Analyzing the comfort level of one's association with specific individuals or groups, one recognizes that part of the comfort (or discomfort) stems from the degree of congruence (or divergence) between one's beliefs and attitudes and those of others. You might also have experienced such convergence or divergence of values in your own jobs. Accordingly, you might have been more satisfied and more motivated in some jobs and not others. If you had felt the impact of values (including beliefs and attitudes) on work, then as a manager you should be concerned about hiring those people who share your organization's values and goals and about communicating to your employees those organizational values and goals.

Values, Beliefs, Attitudes, and Norms

While several definitions of **values** exist, the following definition by Rokeach (1973) is most often used in the context of organizations and management.

> A *value* is an enduring belief that a specific mode of conduct or end-state of existence is personally and socially preferable to an opposite or converse mode of conduct or end-state of existence. A *value system* is an enduring organization of beliefs concerning preferable modes of conduct or end states of existence along a continuum of relative importance. (p. 5)

Values and Beliefs

Sproull (1984) organized **beliefs** into three broad categories. Phenomenological beliefs relate to the nature of things or people. Thus, a student may believe that the athletic program spends more money

on one particular sport than on others. Causal beliefs refer to the causal relationships among observed phenomena. For example, the student also may believe that the athletic program spends so much money on one sport because of pressures from the alumni and media. Finally, normative beliefs describe one's preferred states of nature. The student may believe that the athletic program ought to budget the total dollars equitably among all sports.

Rokeach (1973) also noted that three kinds of beliefs exist: descriptive beliefs (which can be verified as true or false); evaluative beliefs (which are judged to be good or bad); and prescriptive, or proscriptive, beliefs (which refer to the desirability, or otherwise, of some means or ends).

Values as Rokeach defined belong to the prescriptive, or proscriptive, beliefs as well as to the normative beliefs of Sproull (1984). These sets of beliefs about "what ought to be" are the essence of values. Goldthwait (1996) noted that "every value-claiming proposition has the idea of ought at its very foundation" (p. 34).

A significant difference exists between values as normative beliefs and the other two forms of beliefs. One can prove both phenomenological and causal beliefs to be true or false. For instance, by verifying the budget and statement of expenses, one can determine whether the athletic program spends more money on one sport than another. Similarly, by interviewing the decision makers and perusing the records, one can verify the relative influence of the alumni and media over budget allocations. In contrast, one cannot prove values (i.e., the normative beliefs) to be right or wrong.

In a Nutshell

A value is a belief of what ought to be, what ought not to be, what is right, or what is wrong. Values are relatively enduring traits that influence our thoughts, feelings, and actions.

Values and Attitudes

Another term that is used in conjunction, and often synonymously, with values is **attitude**. Rokeach (1973) contrasted values and attitudes as follows:

> An attitude refers to an organization of several beliefs around a specific object or situation. . . . A value, on the other hand, refers to a single belief of a very specific kind. It concerns a

desirable mode of behavior or end-state that has transcendental quality to it, guiding actions, attitudes, judgments, and comparisons across specific objects and situations and beyond immediate goals to more ultimate goals. (p. 18)

Figure 6.1 shows the relationships between the three kinds of beliefs, values, and attitudes. Of the three kinds of beliefs, normative beliefs generate the values that the individual holds. The values that an individual holds lead to the formation of attitudes toward specific persons, objects, or events. Figure 6.1 also shows that one's behavior reflects his or her attitudes toward the person, thing, or event in question. Terminal and instrumental values shown in figure 6.1 are described later in this chapter.

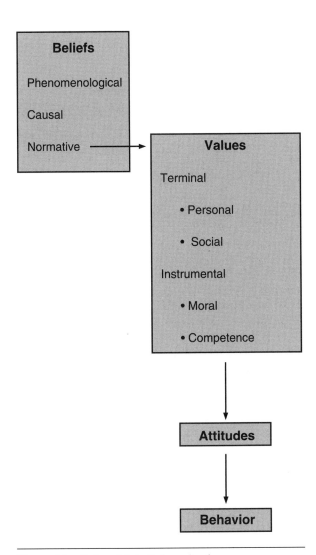

Figure 6.1 Rokeach's beliefs and values.

Rokeach (1973) further pointed out that "values occupy a more central position than attitudes within one's personality makeup and cognitive system, and they are therefore determinants of attitudes as well as of behavior" (p. 18). While a person's values are relatively fewer, the number of attitudes may be higher depending on the number of objects and situations to which one is exposed. In addition, values are much more deeply held and are more enduring over time than attitudes. Figure 6.2 illustrates the idea that an attitude toward a target is a manifestation of more than one value and that a single value may influence several attitudes.

In Their View

Everyone needs to be aware of their own personal values and value systems so that they may deal pragmatically with any situation that may arise. This awareness allows for any marked differences between individuals or between an individual and the demands of the organization to be taken into account before action of any sort is contemplated. Value conflicts often arise at places of work. It is necessary to recognize that this does occur, and to take action to formulate a management style that can accommodate it where necessary and reconcile divergent values. (Pettinger 1997, 82)

Values and Norms

This section distinguishes between values and **norms**. According to Rokeach (1973), a value refers to both the end-states and the means to them, and a norm refers only to the means, i.e., the modes of behavior. As noted earlier, a value is not limited to a specific situation, but a norm specifies a code of conduct to a specific situation. Finally, a value is something personal and internal to the individual. In contrast, a norm is a code of conduct reflecting a common understanding by the people involved in the situation; therefore, it is external to the individual. For example, although society values winning in competition, norms control the means to such winning. Take the case of a coach yelling, screaming, and throwing a chair. While society tolerates such behaviors somewhat at higher levels of competition, it frowns upon them in youth sports. The normative expectation is that the coach is gentle and caring in addressing his young wards.

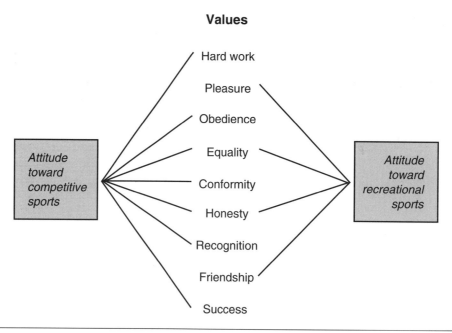

Figure 6.2 Hypothetical relationships between values and attitudes toward sports.

In a Nutshell

Although the terms "values," "beliefs," "attitudes," and "norms" are closely related, they refer to distinct concepts. The concept of value is broader in scope and subsumes the other three. Values are one set of beliefs (i.e., normative beliefs) that influence one's attitude to an entity. Norms, which are the accepted standards of behavior in a given situation, may reflect values that the group shares.

Sources of Values

As noted earlier, values are personal to the individual. This does not mean, however, that values are totally individualistic. From the early stages of life, sources (e.g., family, friends, school, church, the media, celebrities, and movie and sport idols) have bombarded all people with value statements; thus people tend to share several of the values with each other. For instance, most North Americans hold similar values regarding liberty, freedom, equality, democracy, activism, and optimism. In our context, society generally values pursuit of excellence in sport.

Yet, despite such convergence of values on some crucial issues, people also may differ on other equally important issues. Consider, for example, the issue of abortion. Society's divergent values on abortion are as divisive as its values on freedom of expression are binding. As another example, while most in society value pursuit of excellence, the values applied to distribution of resources to different teams are divergent. One group of people emphasizes the value of equality and suggests that the athletic budget be distributed equally between the men's and women's programs or across all sports. In contrast, another group holds the value of equity and prefers that the budget be distributed differentially in proportion to certain selected criteria (e.g., spectator appeal or tradition). When different individuals or groups offer differing, and often conflicting, values, the significance that people attach to these values is most likely to be the deciding factor between one set of values and a competing set.

Terminal and Instrumental Values

The reference to "mode of conduct or end-state of existence" in Rokeach's (1973) definition of values leads to the classification of values into two broad categories: **terminal values** (which relate to the ends or goals being sought or desired) and **instrumental values** (which refer to the desirability, or otherwise, of the means to the desired ends). Instrumental values refer to one's personal views on what means should be employed to achieve a given terminal value. If two means exist to achieve a terminal value, an individual may prefer one means over the other because of the instrumental values that he or she holds. For instance, many people hold the value of achievement, so they applaud the excellence achieved in athletics. However, some do not approve of the means of recruiting athletes (Trail 1997). Instead, they prefer that the best among those who report for tryouts are selected and trained to be excellent. This perspective reflects the instrumental value.

Note the contrast between instrumental values and norms described earlier. Instrumental values focus on the means to achieve an end, and norms are behavioral expectations that a group of people in a particular context hold. For example, the norms to which administrators, coaches, and educators subscribe are generally that the athletes should be treated as students first, with dignity and concern for their academic progress. This normative expectation holds irrespective of whether the school recruited the athletes or developed them internally (a function of instrumental values).

Terminal values can be broken down into personal (or self-centered) and social (or society-centered) values. For instance, peace of mind is a personal value, and world peace is a social value (Rokeach 1973). Similarly, an individual may not value personal achievements in sport but may share the value of national achievements in international sport.

Instrumental values are also of two kinds: moral and competence values. Moral values focus on the interpersonal aspects of one's mode of behavior. For instance, being honest and responsible is moral behavior. Failure to abide by this type of value leads to feelings of guilt and shame in most people. Competence values, on the other hand, are focused internally. That is, these values refer to one's abilities and capacities to perform adequately in a given context. Thus, one would value being logical and intelligent, and deficiencies in these aspects would lead to feelings of shame. A basketball player who tries to avoid flagrant fouls and, when committing one, acknowledges it and apologizes for it is expressing moral value. Competence is perhaps the primary value that all athletes share. Thus, when an athlete continuously tries to improve his or her performance, competence values may drive him or her.

Rokeach (1973) suggested that an average adult holds about 18 terminal values and from 60 to 70 instrumental values. Table 6.1 provides Rokeach's 18 terminal values and 18 of the more common instrumental values.

In a Nutshell

Terminal values refer to the beliefs about the ends that people seek. Instrumental values refer to the convictions about the means that people adopt in achieving the desired end states. That is, while an individual may prefer an end state that someone proposes, he or she may object to the means that the other person suggests to achieve that end state. Conversely, a person's values may be consistent with the proposed means but not with the end state.

Hierarchy of Values

As noted, individuals may have several values at any point in their life. The important point, however, is that not all of these values have equal force in any given situation. Rokeach argues that although people were taught certain values as absolute and unchanging, they learn through the course of their life to make a **hierarchy of values** according to the priority or importance of each.

> When we think about, talk about, or try to teach one of our values to others, we typically do so without remembering the other values, thus regarding them as absolutes. But when one value is actually activated along with others in a given situation, the behavioral outcome will be a result of the relative importance of all the competing values that situation has activated. (p. 6)

In essence, different situations evoke different values that people hold, and the intensity with which they uphold those values also vary with the situation. Consider, for example, an individual who holds the values of social recognition, pleasure, and equality. Suppose that the person is exposed to two situations: competitive sports and recreational sports. Conceivably, the value of social recognition would dominate the individual's orientation to the competitive situation. That is, the individual may strive to perform better and to be recognized for that performance. The situation also might activate the value of equality because the individual would prefer that every competitor be treated equally. However, the value of pleasure may lie dormant in that situation. In contrast, when the same individual is exposed to recreational sports, the situation might activate the values of pleasure and equality but might not activate the value of social recognition. Figure 6.3 illustrates these notions of hierarchy of values and situational cues.

Table 6.1 Rokeach's (1973) Terminal and Instrumental Values

Terminal values	Instrumental values
A comfortable life (prosperous life)	Ambitious (hard-working, aspiring)
An exciting life (stimulating and active life)	Broad-minded (open-minded)
A sense of accomplishment (lasting contribution)	Capable (competent, effective)
A world at peace (free of war and conflict)	Cheerful (lighthearted, joyful)
A world of beauty (beauty of nature and the arts)	Clean (neat, tidy)
Equality (brotherhood and sisterhood, equal opportunity for all)	Courageous (standing up for one's beliefs)
Family security (taking care of loved ones)	Forgiving (willing to pardon others)
Freedom (independence, free choice)	Helpful (working for the welfare of others)
Happiness (contentedness)	Honest (sincere, truthful)
Inner harmony (freedom from inner conflict)	Imaginative (daring, creative)
Mature love (sexual and spiritual intimacy)	Independent (self-reliant, self-sufficient)
National security (protection from attack)	Intellectual (intelligent, reflective)
Pleasure (enjoyable, leisurely life)	Logical (consistent, rational)
Salvation (saved, eternal life)	Loving (affectionate, tender)
Self-respect (self-esteem)	Obedient (dutiful, respectful)
Social recognition (respect, admiration)	Polite (courteous, well mannered)
True friendship (close companionship)	Responsible (dependable, reliable)
Wisdom (a mature understanding of life)	Self-controlled (restrained, self-disciplined)

Source: Rokeach (1973), p. 28.

Reprinted and modified with the permission of The Free Press, a Division of Simon & Schuster from UNDERSTANDING HUMAN VALUES: Individual and Societal by Milton Rokeach. Copyright © 1979 by The Free Press.

Individual's values

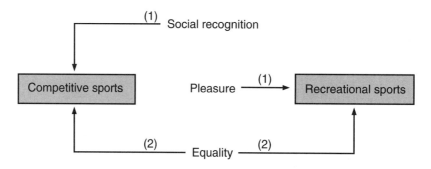

Figure 6.3 Hierarchy of values in different contexts.

The several values that an individual holds constitute his or her **value system.** A notable feature of these values or beliefs is that they most likely are consistent with each other in content, but the intensity of each one of them may vary. If an individual's values can vary in their intensity, then it follows that the individual can organize them into a hierarchy of values.

Value Types

As noted, a value system is a collection of values that individuals hold, and it also implies a hierarchy among the collection of values. An implicit point here is that the values that an individual holds are likely to be complementary, rather than contradictory, to each other. Schwartz (1992) empirically supported this idea and found that analyses of the relationships among 56 values, including those of Rokeach's (1973) terminal and instrumental values, yielded 10 clusters of values that he called value types (see table 6.2).

Further, Schwartz (1992) found that these 10 values tended to be arranged in a circular manner. According to Schwartz's circumplex model shown in figure 6.4, the value types adjacent to each other are more highly correlated to each other than to the ones on the opposite side of the circle. In other words, adjacent value types are compatible with each other, but the remote ones are incompatible. As an extension of this line of reasoning, Schwartz (1992) noted that the 10 value types form four quadrants that two dimensions define (see figure 6.4). The first dimension contrasts self-transcendence (which is a concern with people and things beyond the self that the value types of universalism and benevolence indicate) with self-enhancement (which is a concern with enhancing the self that the value

types of achievement and power indicate). The second dimension contrasts openness to change (which the value types of self-direction and stimulation characterize) with conservation (which the value types of conformity, tradition, and security characterize).

Schwartz (1992) also notes that one set of values (i.e., power, achievement, hedonism, stimulation, and self-direction) represent individual interests while another set (benevolence, tradition, and conformity) represent collective interests. The remaining values of universalism and security are mixed in nature. These groupings are indicated in the periphery of figure 6.4.

The implication for management is that persons who belong to adjacent value types (e.g., universalism and benevolence, self-direction and stimulation, or achievement and power) are likely to get along well, but people who have opposite value types (e.g., stimulation and conformity or universalism and power) are likely to be in conflict over critical issues. Individuals who hold the values of achievement and power may be comfortable in organizational settings, such as university athletics, that stress achievement and performance excellence. On the other hand, people with values such as universalism may be comfortable in recreation organizations that emphasize greater participation in sport by all segments of the population.

Table 6.2 Schwartz's Value Types

Value type	Description
Power	Control or dominance over people and resources
Achievement	Personal success through demonstrating competence
Hedonism	Pleasure and gratification for oneself
Stimulation	Excitement, novelty, and challenge in life
Self-direction	Independent thought and action
Universalism	Protection for the welfare of all people and for nature
Benevolence	Enhancement of the welfare of the people with whom one is in frequent contact
Tradition	Respect for and acceptance of time-honored customs
Conformity	Restraint of actions likely to upset others or violate norms
Security	Safety, harmony, and stability of society, of relationships, and of oneself

Adapted, by permission, from S.H. Schwartz, 1992, Universals in the content and structure of values. In M. Zanna (Ed.), *Advances in experimental social psychology* (Vol. 25, pp. 1-65). New York: Academic Press.

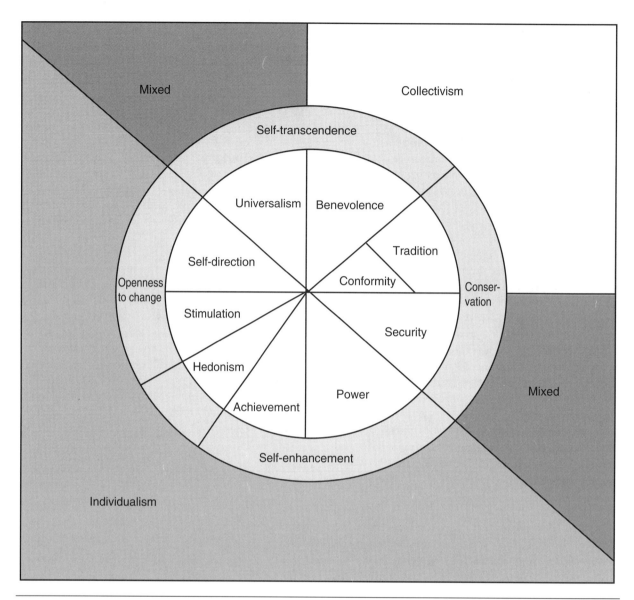

Figure 6.4 Schwartz's circumplex of value types.
Adapted from Schwartz 1992.

Functions of Values

The previous sections in the chapter alluded to how values can guide specific modes of behavior. For instance, Rokeach (1973) outlines values that would enable individuals to choose among a variety of terminal states as well as the means instrumental to achieve the end states. Similarly, Schwartz (1992) suggests that certain values would shape our orientation toward individualism or collectivism. Thus, values play a significant part in our lives through their many functions. Rokeach (1973) grouped the functions that values serve into three broad categories: standards guiding activities, plans for conflict resolution, and motivational functions.

Values as Standards

The function of values as standards that guide activities is exemplified by

- the position one takes on specific social issues (e.g., athletic scholarship),
- the tendency to favor a political or religious movement (e.g., the Republican or Democratic party),
- the presentation of oneself to others (e.g., some athletes project a high profile while others strike a low profile),
- the evaluation of oneself and others,
- the judgments about oneself being moral or competent,

- the attempts to persuade and influence others about what beliefs or attitudes are accepted or challenged, and
- the rationalization of one's actions that may be unpleasant or unacceptable to others ("an unkind remark made to a friend, for example, may be rationalized as an honest communication" [Rokeach 1973, 13]).

In essence, our values set the standards for our behavior. In our context, we may support drug testing or not, we may appreciate or deprecate the showboating after a touchdown in football, and we may try to influence the opinion of others on salaries to collegiate athletes. All these behaviors stem from our value systems. In other words, our values define the standards guiding our actions.

Values in Conflict Resolution and Decision Making

"A value system is a learned organization of principles and rules to help one choose between alternatives, resolve conflicts, and make decisions" (Rokeach 1973, 14). As noted earlier, different situations may evoke different values. A particular situation possibly may activate two contradictory values. For instance, the organization may ask a fitness instructor to evaluate a particular decision that the manager made. That situation may activate the values of behaving politely and behaving honestly. Because these two values call for contradictory behaviors, the choice between the two obviously is based on the relative importance that the individual attaches to each value. In other words, the individual can choose and abide by the value that is higher in the hierarchical system and, thereby, can resolve the conflict and make the appropriate decision. It should be apparent that the situation itself would elicit other values affecting the decision to behave one way or another. If the fitness instructor's response would affect his or her future in the club, the value of security may impel the person toward behaving politely rather than honestly.

Motivational Functions of Values

Rokeach (1973) argued that "values are in the final analysis the conceptual tools and weapons that we all employ in order to maintain and enhance self-esteem" (p. 14). Values contribute to this maintenance and enhancement of self-esteem by helping one to adjust to society, defend against threats to one's ego, and test one's own perceptions and competencies against reality in the process of self-actualizing.

Adjustive Function

The content of several values, such as desirability of obedience, civility, responsibility to others, and law and order, concerns the society as a whole. To the extent that one holds these values, the individual is adjusted to societal requirements. This adjustment is more evident in athletics in which obedience is valued highly. The obedience of all members of the team to the specifications of the coach is critical for the coordination of member activities and performance. Thus, each member needs to hold obedience high on the hierarchy of values. As another example, consider the thousands of spectators getting into and out of a stadium in an orderly fashion. The values of civility, responsibility to others, and law and order underlie the stadium behavior. Can you imagine the havoc created if the spectators did not share these values?

Ego-Defensive Function

When one's needs, feelings, and actions do not conform to social norms and expectations, individuals can protect their ego by relying on their values to justify their feelings or behavior. Thus, "values represent ready-made concepts provided by our culture to ensure that such justifications can proceed smoothly and effortlessly" (Rokeach 1973, 15-16). When a university football player quits a team and leaves it in disarray, he can justify his action by saying that he values education more than athletics. Society readily accepts and applauds such justification.

Self-Actualization Function

The content of some values focuses on personal competence, knowledge, accomplishments, and wisdom. An individual's desire to understand one's context and events therein and to be clear and consistent in one's own perceptions and beliefs reflects this function. To the extent that these values are rated highly, they make the individual strive toward self-actualization: "To become everything that one is capable of becoming" (Maslow 1943, 382). One's evaluation of personal competence, experiences, and situational requirements determines the choice of specific physical activity for participation and the level of competition at which one participates. Based on the evaluations, the individual chooses the appropriate activity and level of competition, which is a step in the process of self-actualization. According to Rokeach (1973), this testing of one's knowledge and competencies in relation to one's own values and against reality is fundamental to self-actualization.

In a Nutshell

The values that a person holds helps him or her because they provide a standard for the person's actions and decision-making, a rationale to maintain his or her self-esteem, a channel for his or her integration with the community and society, and a means for self-actualizing.

Values in Organizations

Although values as discussed earlier have a bearing on behavior in general, they also have an impact on organizational life. Given the fact that values underlie an individual's perceptions and behaviors (Gelfand, Kuhn, and Radhakrishnan 1996; Schwartz 1992), the values that the members of the organization hold logically affect organizational processes. On the one hand, the congruence of values of an organization's membership may lead to the development of an organizational culture with positive connotations, member commitment, and productivity (Chatman 1989; Connor and Becker 1975; Gelfand, Kuhn, and Radhakrishnan 1996; Graves 1970; Hughes and Flowers 1975). On the other hand, the divergence of values among the membership may lead to conflict and associated dysfunctional effects; the greater the divergence in values, the greater the negative consequences (Chatman 1989; Gelfand, Kuhn, and Radhakrishnan 1996; Meglino, Ravlin, and Adkins 1989, 1992).

In Their View

Raghuraman and Garud (1996) noted that members of an organization are interdependent with each other in two arenas: technical and institutional. The technical arena refers to the interdependencies in task-related knowledge and skills. The institutional arena is "where groups members are interdependent with one another on the basis of their work-related values. . . . The values become manifest in work rules and norms that dictate how productivity is measured, how rewards are disbursed, . . . and how people behave on the job. . . . In this arena, members focus on shaping value systems to enhance the effectiveness with which they as a group produce goods and services" (Raghuraman and Garud 1996, 160).

Values and Organizational Goals

Personal values affect organizational processes in many different ways. The first critical area is setting organizational goals and the choice of courses of action to achieve those goals. Expecting all of the employees and stakeholders to be involved in setting the goals for the organization is unreasonable. The senior administrators and more powerful stakeholders set goals. For instance, the senior administrators and the elected mayor and other representatives set goals for a city recreation department. Similarly, the athletic director, the president, and the board of governors of a university set the goals for the athletic department of that university. This powerful coalition also decides on the courses of action to achieve those goals. The critical point in the present context is that these goal choices are a function of the shared values among the coalition members. Another point is that most other people involved in these enterprises (e.g., employees or stakeholders) should endorse the selected goals and the values behind those goals for the organization to be successful. In the absence of such endorsements, the survival of the organization itself is doubtful.

Values and Communication

Apart from affecting the choice of goals and processes, values or, more specifically, value incongruities also affect the communication processes among the employees themselves. Generally, messages received are not identical to those sent; some distortions (e.g., additions, deletions, or modifications) to the original message always are present. A message sender encodes his or her ideas into either verbal or nonverbal symbolic form. The receiver of the message decodes the symbolic form to get the meaning of the message. Thus, errors possibly could occur at either the encoding or decoding phases of the message. The point is that such errors or distortions are accentuated among groups holding different values (Adler 1990). Citing Singer (1987), Gelfand, Kuhn, and Radhakrishnan (1996) suggested that values may affect the perceptions of the stimuli contained in a message:

> Thus, employees who have different values may select different information from the environment and have disparate interpretations of the same encounter. . . . Likewise in communicative encounters, we assert that the greater the differences in values between the sender and receiver, the greater the chance that

they will construe the situation differently and will attach different meanings to the same words and behaviors. (pp. 57-58)

Values and Attributional Confidence

Gelfand, Kuhn, and Radhakrishnan (1996) pointed out another process whereby value incongruity may affect group functioning. Society tends to attribute the behavior of others to certain reasons. By the same token, society also develops an expectation for others to behave in certain ways to a given set of stimuli based on previous experience: "The degree to which people are able to understand and predict how others will behave is referred to *attributional confidence*" (Gelfand, Kuhn, and Radhakrishnan 1996, 58). Note how critical this attributional confidence is in school as well as the workplace. According to Gelfand, Kuhn, and Radhakrishnan (1996): "Employees who share similar values (i.e., have value congruity) may be better able to recognize the behavior patterns of others and have the ability to predict their behavior in future situations (i.e., have greater attributional confidence)" (p. 59).

Values and Leadership

The foregoing line of reasoning can be extended to even the leadership process of coordinating and motivating group members. That is, insofar as members' personal values affect the communication and attributional processes, they also could affect perceptions of leadership. The perceptions of a leader's influence attempts and the reasons thereof can vary with the values one holds. James, Chen, and

Cropanzano (1996) found that Taiwanese and U.S. workers not only hold different cultural values but also endorse different leadership ideals. Even within one cultural context (e.g., the U.S. or Canadian context), leadership effectiveness is a function of the congruence of the values of leader and members.

Values of Managers and Employees

Value-based perspectives or conflicts are more pronounced between managers and their members. Brown (1976) suggested that the genesis of such manager-member conflicts is rooted in the differential exposure to organizational and **management values** (see figure 6.5). Society is the basic source of values for all members; however, involvement with organizations at the managerial level through the years exposes managers to an additional set of values that leads to divergent values and the resultant conflicts.

To be more specific, the notion of profit maximization is consistent with societal values that promote capitalism and private enterprise (Hay and Gray 1974). Therefore, not surprisingly, managers hold that value high in making decisions. Their background, training, and purpose is in profit maximization that, in turn, enhances organizational prosperity. In this sense, the notion of profit maximization is consistent with societal values. Yet, the same society also advances the notion of quality of life for all of its citizens. Different groups may emphasize one or the other of the two values (i.e., profit maximization and quality of life). For example, the owner and manager of a professional sport franchise (or a fitness club) emphasizes profit maximization, and

Concerns with managing diversity in the workplace recently have highlighted the significance of values in organizational life. With ever-increasing cultural differences in both the workplace and marketplace, management specialists have focused on the values that different groups hold as a significant factor (Cox 1991, 1993; Davis and Rasool 1988; Jackson 1992; James, Chen, and Cropanzano 1996; Meglino, Ravlin, and Adkins 1992). Such differences, however, are present even within one culture. For instance, the distinctions between the Democratic and Republican parties in the United States originate in the differences in values that members of those respective parties hold. The differences between the supporters and critics of intercollegiate athletics in the United States, to some extent, also are based on the values that each group holds (Trail 1997). Thus, the impact of values is everywhere, including on organizational processes, such as goal setting, decision making, communicating, and leading. Sport and recreation managers need to be attuned to the values that different members of the workgroup hold and need to attempt to create a degree of value congruence in the group.

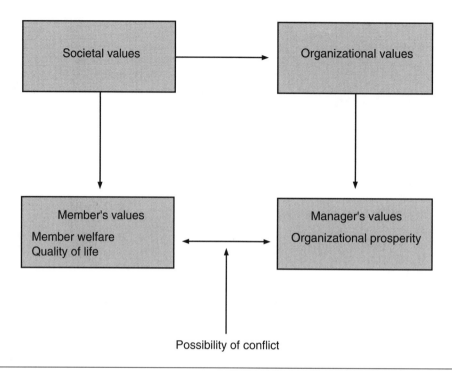

Figure 6.5   Genesis of value conflicts between managers and members.

Adapted, by permission, from M.A. Brown, 1976, "Values—A necessary but neglected ingredient of motivation on the job," *Academy of Management Review* 1 (4): 15-23.

the employees of the organization promote the quality of life. While both efforts are legitimate by themselves, they lead to the possibility of conflict between management and employees. For example, management wants to reduce the number of employees as a measure of cost reduction and, thus, profit maximization. However, the employees believe that such a move would increase the workload and associated stress for the remaining employees. In a similar manner, to increase profits, the managers of a fitness club attempts to enroll more members than are reasonable for their facilities. On the other hand, the fitness instructors and exercise leaders who provide the service favor quality service and, therefore, prefer fewer members so that they can provide better service.

Values of Loyalty and Duty

As indicated earlier, a congruence of the values of the organization and its members facilitates organizational functioning and effectiveness. Congruence of values may arise from three processes. The first process, as Wiener (1988) pointed out, involves individuals outside of an organization identifying themselves with the organizational value system. Such individuals may be willing to join the organization, and, by the same token, the organization

may recruit such individuals. The second process involves socializing new members into the value system of the organization. The third process through which organizational members begin to share the organizational value system involves the operation of the values of loyalty and duty. That is, some individuals may hold the value that "they have a moral obligation to engage in a mode of conduct reflecting loyalty and duty in all social situations in which they have a significant personal involvement" (Wiener 1988, 541). Individuals who hold these values are likely to accept the organizational value system as one way of expressing loyalty and duty. For example, certain classes of people, such as athletes and soldiers, are likely to value loyalty and duty. These values may impel them to accept other values that their respective organizations and their leaders espouse.

American Values and Sport

The growth of the field of sport management largely is based on the popularity of sport in several of the industrialized nations, particularly in the United States and Canada. Several reasons are advanced for the popularity of sports in American society. The more significant reasons are

- sport as a means of entertainment and diversion for the alienated masses in urban and bureaucratic society,
- the influence of mass media that extensively cover sporting events, and
- the increase in leisure time and a relatively high standard of living (Eitzen and Sage 1986).

In a Nutshell

Values affect significant processes in organizations including the setting of organizational goals, organizational communication, and expectations for others' behaviors. They also influence perceptions of leadership and manager-employee relationships.

According to these authors, the important underlying factor is that sport mirrors society and its values. Eitzen and Sage (1986) noted that the dominant **American values** are success, competition, hard work, continual striving, deferred gratification, materialism, and external conformity: "In learning the culture (through the socialization process), most Americans have internalized values that predispose them to be interested in the outcome of competitive situations—and competition is the sin qua non of sports" (p. 59). To attain success in competition, the athletes participate in prolonged and hard training. Consider the case of a 100-meter sprinter. For every 10 seconds of competition (the duration of the race), the athlete spends hours of practice each week, which may extend to months. During periods of training, athletes sacrifice gratification of ordinary pleasures (e.g., partying). Of course, most often these sacrifices are made in the hope of reaping intrinsic and extrinsic (i.e., material) rewards later. Excellence of the athletes and the enormity of monetary rewards that they garner characterize modern professional athletics. Strict acceptance of the authority of the coaches shows conformity. Athletes tend to adhere to the rules that coaches establish even when those rules affect their personal and family life. Finally, the hallmark of athletics is the constant striving to better one's performance, even by those at the top of the rankings. Society expects the athletes to better their own marks. Because all of these characteristics mirror the values of American society, it is not surprising that sport is at the center of American life.

In Their View

It is evident that values affect sport. Just as important is the insight that sport in society, through its organization and the demands and emphases of those in power, reinforces societal values. This mutual reinforcement places sport squarely in the middle of society's "way of life." It is precisely because sport is so intertwined with the fundamental values of society that any attack on sport is usually interpreted as unpatriotic. Hence criticism of sport is rarely taken seriously. (Eitzen and Sage 1986, 67)

Summary

Earlier chapters identified the values of knowing, doing, and helping as the underlying values of volunteerism and professionalism. Differences also may be present within these two groups on more specific values.

As Eitzen and Sage (1986) pointed out, racial and ethnic diversity in the United States allows for greater differences in the value systems that subgroups hold, and values are not always consistent with each other (e.g., individualism with conformity or competition with cooperation).

It is fashionable to speak of value-free organization science or management. However, by accepting the notion that one's values influence an individual's perceptions and behaviors, society has to concede that values that managers hold also govern managerial actions. The view that values and value systems are significant in the analyses of organizations and their management is gaining strength (Barney 1986, Keeley 1983). According to Barney (1986), "Organizational culture typically is defined as a complex set of values, beliefs, assumptions, and symbols that define the way in which a firm conducts its business" (p. 657).

The values of managers affect the decision that they make, and the values of the members affect the reactions to those decisions. The value systems of managers set the tone and direction of organizational goals and processes. The influence of values manifests itself in the plans, the organizational structure, the leadership patterns, and the evaluation of individual performance and organizational effectiveness. If the employees also share the values that underlie the organizational goals and processes, then they are likely to be more motivated and to execute the plans and decisions that have been made.

Thus, the significance of values in the organizational context cannot be minimized. The values that managers of an organization and its members hold need to be somewhat congruent at least in those values that guide organizational processes. For example, one can pursue excellence or pursue pleasure in youth sports. However, as noted earlier, the values underlying the pursuit of excellence are success, competition, hard work, delayed gratification, and conformity and obedience. These val-

ues are not consistent with pursuit of pleasure in which gratification is immediate and is limited to sport experience. If coaches and others who organize and conduct youth sports differ on the mentioned values, then conflict is bound to occur. Therefore, clarifying for all organizational participants the goals of the enterprise and the values that underlie those goals behooves the manager. Moreover, in recruiting clients and volunteer and professional workers, the manager should make some effort to ensure that they share those organizational values.

Key Terms

values, beliefs, attitude, norms, terminal values, instrumental values, hierarchy of values, value system, management values, American values

Your Perspectives

- Physical education teachers in high schools teach sports to several classes of students and coach competitive sports. Distinguish between those two situations (i.e., teaching and coaching) and identify the specific values that each situation may evoke.

- Compare and contrast professional sports and Division I intercollegiate sports in terms of the dominant values associated with each. Can we also make value-based distinctions between Division I and Division III intercollegiate sports?

- Identify the terminal and instrumental values that are dominant among your friends and family and explain how those values affect your behavior and decisions.

- Discuss the relationships between those values associated with sport and the dominant American values. To what extent are these sets of values consistent with each other? Do any of the sport-related values conflict with any of the societal values?

7 Motivation

Learning Objectives

After reading this chapter you will be able to

- understand the process by which individuals are motivated in an organizational context;
- recognize that motivation leads to desired performance only when requisite ability and clear role perception are present;
- distinguish between intrinsic and extrinsic rewards;
- explain the origins of perceived inequity and its effects on motivation; and
- understand motivation as personal investment and explain it in terms of its direction, persistence, continuing motivation, intensity, and performance.

The discussion of individual differences in ability, personality, and values in chapters 4 through 6 highlighted what individuals bring to the work organization. The implication is that people who have differing abilities carry out different tasks with varying levels of effectiveness. People who have different personalities and hold different values react differently to organizational processes. The focus in this chapter is on the extent to which and the processes through which individuals are inclined to work toward the attainment of organizational goals. The inclination to work is generally labeled motivation. Individuals differ not only on the strength of their motivation but also on the processes through which they are motivated. A clearer understanding of the motivational processes in the workplace is critical for effective management. In fact, several of the managerial practices, such as job enrichment and performance-based pay schemes, have been advanced based on one or more theories of motivation.

This chapter presents several perspectives on work motivation. Its central thrust is to present a comprehensive model of motivation, which Porter and Lawler (1968) proposed, integrating significant aspects of other theories of motivation in organizations. Brief descriptions of other relevant theories appear in sidebars to the chapter and include Adams' (1963) theory of inequity, Herzberg's (1968) motivation-hygiene theory, Maslow's (1943) need hierarchy theory, and Vroom's (1964) expectancy theory. The final section of the chapter describes Maehr and Braskamp's (1986) theory of personal investment.

Definition of Motivation

What is **motivation**? Hoy and Miskel (1982) defined it as "the complex forces, drives, needs, tension states, or other mechanisms that start and maintain voluntary activity toward the achievement of personal goals" (p. 137). They explained that

> Activating forces are assumed to exist within individuals. Examples of such internal forces include memory, affective responses, and pleasure-seeking tendencies. Motivation also directs or channels behavior; that is, it provides a goal orientation. Individual behavior is directed toward something. (p. 137)

While Hoy and Miskel's (1982) definition applies to behavior in all contexts, our interest is on behavior in organizations. In this context, Robbins (1997b) defined motivation as "the willingness to exert a persistent and high level of effort toward organizational goals, conditioned by the effort's ability to satisfy some individual need. . . . The key elements in our definition are intensity of effort, persistence, direction toward organizational goals, and needs" (p. 388).

The given definitions suggest that motivated behavior is behavior directed toward the fulfillment of a need, motive, or desire that has been deprived. Robbins' (1997b) definition also includes the attributes of motivated behavior (i.e., intensity, direction, and persistence). An individual's experience with and expectations for the consequences of such behavior also influence behavior.

Several theories of human motivation exist and include some that address human behavior in general and some that address behavior within organizations. Our interest is with individual motivation in the organizational context. Authors have classified the theories of motivation pertaining to organizational behavior as need-based or content theories (Herzberg, Mausner, and Snyderman 1959; Maslow 1943) or process theories (Adams 1977, Vroom 1964). The general paradigm for motivational theories based on needs is that when a need is deprived, the individual is aroused and driven to seek the sources for the satisfaction of that need and to take some action to achieve such satisfaction. The need-based theories also are called **content theories** because they indicate what (i.e., content) motivates individuals to engage in specific behaviors.

While the content theories are concerned with the factors that motivate the worker (i.e., personal factors, such as individual needs, or organizational factors, such as the task assignment and rewards), they do not explain how individuals choose one behavior from the several open to them. The **process theories** of motivation address the individual's evaluation and choice of certain courses of action and how other factors influence the outcomes of such courses of action.

An understanding of these theories provides the manager with a gestalt view of the intricacies and complexities of human motivation as well as insight into the appropriateness of the theories and their concepts to specific situations. For instance, when an employee of an athletic department is not excited about the routine nature of his or her job, the content of the job is in question. Therefore, the content theories of motivation (Maslow 1943, Herzberg 1968) may be more relevant in addressing the issue. In contrast, when the same employee complains that he or she received a smaller pay increase than other comparable employees received, the issue is a question of **equity**. Adam's (1963, 1977) theory of inequity may be more relevant in resolving this issue. For our purposes, I discuss Porter and Lawler's (1968) model of work motivation, which is comprehensive enough to include the significant concepts from other content and process theories. I also highlight aspects of four other relevant theories.

In a Nutshell

Two classes of theories of motivation exist. One class is called content theories (e.g., Herzberg's [1968] and Maslow's [1943] theories), which address the factors (or content) that motivate individuals. The other class is called process theories (e.g., Adam's [1977] and Vroom's [1964] theories), which address the process by which individuals choose one behavior over others. Both approaches have substance, and both are relevant to organizational contexts.

A Model of Motivation

The model of motivation that Porter and Lawler (1968) proposed is schematically represented in figure 7.1. In order to facilitate the discussion of the model, I placed numbers in the boxes in the figure and refer to them in the following sections.

Effort

Effort (see figure 7.1, box 3) refers to the motivation behind an individual's expended energy in the work context. That is, the degree of effort expended is a reflection of an individual's motivational state. The level of effort that an individual is willing to put forth (or the level of motivation behind it) is a function of the value that the individual attaches to the possible rewards (box 1) and of the individual's perceptions of the probability that effort will result in reward (box 2).

Value of Rewards

Every organization offers some type of rewards (e.g., pay, bonus, and promotion). In addition to these extrinsic rewards, there may be other intrinsic rewards, such as mastering a challenging task or helping others. It is expected that an individual will desire one or both types of rewards (intrinsic and extrinsic) to some extent. If a person does not value

the rewards available in the organization, then he or she may not join it in the first place. On the other hand, the organization can expect people who desire those rewards to join it and to work hard to gain those intrinsic and extrinsic rewards. The linkage between value of rewards (box 1) and effort (box 3) implies that essential thrust.

Note that all members may not value equally the rewards that the organization offers except, perhaps, in the case of monetary rewards. For example, all members should value a promotion to a higher position. However, some members may not value it (in fact, they may despise it) because of the possibility of transfer to a distant location.

Effort-Reward Probability

From a different perspective, a person may believe that his or her own efforts might not lead to the desired rewards. Two components compose the estimation of effort leading to the rewards. The first component relates to the person's belief that his or

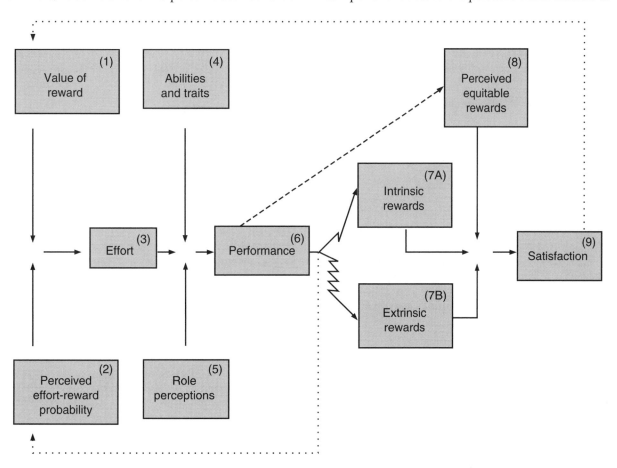

Figure 7.1 Porter and Lawler's model of motivation.

Adapted, by permission, from L.W. Porter and E.E. Lawler, 1968, *Managerial attitudes and performance* (Homewood, IL: Richard D. Irwin. Library of Congress Catalog Card No. 67-29148).

In Their View

In clearing up the myth, "young people today aren't motivated," Robbins (1997b) wrote that

> Young workers today, the so-called Generation X, have different work values than baby boomers. Generation X workers value flexibility, job satisfaction, and loyalty to relationships. They are much more individualistic than boomers. . . . And Xers are not loyal to a single employer. . . . They want to build a diverse set of skills that will maintain their marketability. . . . Young people today can be highly motivated workers. But managers have to accommodate their needs. (p. 387)

her effort will lead to performance as the organization expects. If, for example, an employee of an intercollegiate athletic department believes that his or her efforts will result in attaining the sponsorships target that the department set, that person is likely to put forth much effort in this regard. If, however, the person does not expect to achieve the target despite the best efforts, then the motivation decreases.

The second component relates to the relationship between performance (i.e., achieving the sponsorship target) and rewards that the person seeks (e.g., salary increase or promotion). If the person does not see a strong relationship between performance and rewards, then motivation decreases. For example, an employee of a city recreation department desires a promotion but does not put forth his or her best efforts to that end because of a perception that the promotion is based on seniority or that other colleagues are better performers. In contrast, another employee is convinced that his or her efforts will lead to the desired performance and subsequent promotion, so he or she works toward that promotion.

The linkage between perceived effort-reward probability (box 2) and effort (box 3) emphasizes these relationships. In sum, effort or motivation is maximized when an individual places high value on the rewards available through participation in the organization and its activities and when that person also believes that his or her efforts would lead to the desired rewards. The concepts of value of reward and perceived effort-reward probability are similar to the concepts contained in Vroom's (1964) expectancy model of motivation that is described on page 99.

In a Nutshell

According to Porter and Lawler (1968), two conditions must exist for a person to be motivated in the work context. First, that person must value rewards that are supposed to be available in that context. Second, the person must see a connection between his or her efforts and expected performance level and between his or her performance and the rewards.

Performance

Assuming that a person values the rewards that the organization offers and believes that his or her efforts will get the rewards, the organization can expect the individual to put forth much effort. The organization also can expect that the effort that the employee expends will result in a certain level of performance (box 6). **Performance**, in this context, refers to what the organization expects of the employee. That is, individuals may have their own standards of performance, but an organization measures performance in terms of things such as organizational standards, rules, and expectations.

Abilities and Traits

One of the significant contributions of Porter and Lawler's (1968) model is that it highlights the complexity of the effort-performance relationship. Effort does not always lead directly to good performance. For effective performance to occur, an individual must have the necessary abilities and traits (box 4), which were discussed in chapters 4 and 5, respectively. In general, every job requires certain kinds and levels of abilities and particular psychological dispositions. Individuals who do not possess those qualities will have difficulty performing well in that job. For example, a player who is five feet tall (which is a trait) cannot adequately perform in the position of a basketball center. A person who is seven feet tall but has no ability cannot be effective as a basketball center. Similarly, a successful fitness instructor needs to possess psychomotor abilities, such as agility, flexibility, and endurance. In addition, that person must have leadership traits to be able to motivate the clients. A person volunteering to market a sport program can be effective only if he or she has the communication and marketing skills. Recall that while traits are enduring and stable characteristics, abilities are transient and trainable qualities.

Vroom's Expectancy Model of Motivation

The main postulate of Vroom's (1964) expectancy theory is as follows:

> The force on a person (motive) to perform a given act is based on the weighted value (or utility) of all the possible outcomes of the act multiplied by the perceived usefulness of the act in the attainment of these outcomes. Whenever an individual chooses between alternatives that involve certain outcomes, it seems clear that his [or her] behavior is affected not only by his [or her] preferences among outcomes, but also by the degree to which he [or she] believes these outcomes to be probable. (p. 18)

Vroom's expectancy theory incorporates four major variables (or concepts): valence, outcome, expectancy, and instrumentality. The interplay of these variables is illustrated in figure A.

A

Expectancy   Instrumentality

| Force =
net valence x
expectancy x
instrumentality | → | First-level
outcomes

(organizational
expectations) | → | Second-level
outcomes with
valences

(individual's goals) |

An individual's preferences for particular outcomes is referred to as **valence**, which is the same as value of rewards in Porter and Lawler's (1968) model. Valence of outcomes may range from +1 where the outcome is strongly preferred (e.g., promotion) to −1 where the outcome is strongly detested. (e.g., transfer to a distant locality). Note that this example of concomitant outcomes of a promotion and a transfer may elicit both positive and negative valences as shown in figure B.

The two sets of outcomes are first-level outcome, which refers to the performance standards achieved by the employee, and second-level outcome, which refers to the rewards for that performance. Note that the organization mainly is concerned with the first-level outcome, and the member largely is interested in the second level-outcome.

B

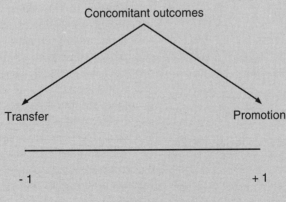

(continued)

Expectancy is the probability estimate that effort will lead to the first-level outcome. The individual's estimate of the relationship between the first-level outcome and the second-level outcome is called **instrumentality**. Expectancy connects individual effort to first-level outcome, and instrumentality links the first- and second-level outcomes. These values may range from +1 where the individual perceives strong relationship to 0 where the individual perceives no linkage.

In Vroom's expectancy theory, the force (equated here with motivation) with which an individual engages in an activity depends on the valence or attraction for the rewards or incentives that the organization has to offer, on the expectancy that effort results in a certain level of performance, and on the instrumentality of such performance in the attainment of the rewards sought.

Role Perception

Another factor that affects the effort-performance relationship is the accuracy of the individual's role perception (see figure 7.1, box 5). Each employee must have a complete understanding of what activities are necessary and of how he or she should do them. A university expects a faculty member in sport management do an adequate job in teaching, research, and community work. The individual could do an outstanding job of coaching various community volleyball clubs, but this would be of minimal value if his or her teacher ratings were low and he or she did little research and writing. The professor's time and effort should be spent in course design and the preparation of lectures and examinations in order to effectively carry out the teaching function. Similarly, the director of a city recreation department needs to engage in several managerial activities including public relations. However, if the director spends most of his or her time outside of the office participating in several civic activities in the name of public relations, performance in other areas would be less than what the city administrators expect. Hence, correct perceptions of the role assigned to a worker is important.

In a Nutshell

In Porter and Lawler's (1968) model, performance refers to performance that the organization defines or expects. More significantly, attainment of such expected performance depends on the member having the necessary abilities and traits and perceiving his or her role correctly.

Rewards

If the individual has the necessary abilities and traits and perceives his or her role correctly, it is reasonable to expect that the individual will accomplish an acceptable level of performance (i.e., acceptable in terms of organizational expectations). Such a performance results in certain rewards. These rewards can be categorized as intrinsic rewards (box 7A) and extrinsic rewards (box 7B).

Intrinsic Rewards

When a person completes a task, he or she may experience a sense of accomplishment and achievement. A challenging and meaningful task may heighten such feelings. For example, a new director who is hired to supervise an athletic department riddled with various kinds of NCAA rule violations and internal conflicts may find the task challenging and, at times, insurmountable. If and when the director brings the department back to order and builds a cohesive and successful unit, he or she may gain an extreme sense of accomplishment and the sense of having done something good for the athletes, the university, and the community. A volunteer coach may enjoy similar feelings when he or she helps young athletes master the skills of a sport. In the process, the individuals also may feel a sense of growth to the extent that they themselves have enhanced their capability to manage challenging tasks. In these cases, others may compliment the persons involved on having done a good job. However, the feelings that the individuals derive directly from the experience are truly intrinsic. These feelings are personal to the individuals, and others cannot necessarily enhance or diminish the effects of such feelings. In other words, the persons themselves administer the rewards. These **intrinsic rewards** relate to higher-order needs of Maslow's (1943) need hierarchy theory described on page 101.

Extrinsic Rewards

In contrast to the intrinsic rewards that are personally derived, external agents (e.g., supervisors) administer the **extrinsic rewards**. They usually are

Maslow's Need Hierarchy Theory

The essence of Maslow's (1943) need hierarchy theory lies in its specification of five classes of needs that are ordered in a hierarchy of prepotency (i.e., power or force). After stating that only unsatisfied needs are the basis of behavior and that satisfied needs lose their potency to instigate behavior, Maslow argued that people focus on meeting their basic needs then move up the scale of the hierarchy of needs when the lower-order (i.e., prepotent) needs are satisfied. In a commentary on the concept of a hierarchy of needs, Maslow (1943) stated that

> It is quite true that man [or woman] lives by bread alone—when there is no bread. But what happens to man's [or woman's] desires when there *is* plenty of bread and when his [or her] belly is chronically filled? *At once other (and "higher") needs emerge* and these, rather than physiological hungers, dominate the organism. And when these in turn are satisfied, again new (and still "higher") needs emerge and so on. This is what we mean by saying that the basic human needs are organized into a hierarchy of relative prepotency. (p. 375)

Maslow proposed five categories of needs in order of importance to the individual: physiological, safety and security, love, esteem, and self-actualization needs. Physiological needs relate to the more fundamental and biological requirements of a human being, such as food and shelter and the need to avoid pain. From an organizational perspective, the organization must provide the employee with sufficient financial rewards (e.g., salary or bonus) to ensure that the physiological needs are satisfied. Safety and security needs refer to an individual's preference for "a safe, orderly, predictable, organized world, which he [or she] can count on, and in which unexpected, unmanageable or other dangerous things do not happen" (Maslow 1943, 378). In an organizational context, job security, health coverage, and retirement schemes are related to security needs, and safe working conditions, precautions against accidents, and other such organizational efforts are aimed at satisfying the safety needs of employees. Love needs represent the desires of people for friendship and warm interpersonal interaction with others (i.e., to be associated with and accepted by others). The satisfaction of the social needs in an organization depends on the employee's co-workers, workgroups, supervisors, and the intensity of their social needs. Esteem needs are higher order needs that relate to a person's desire to have others recognize him or her and to have status among them. According to Maslow, the esteem needs include a desire for strength, achievement, adequacy, confidence (i.e., self-esteem), recognition, and respect (i.e., esteem) from others. The title and status accorded to individuals in an organization and the respect that peers give them are the kinds of factors that cater to esteem needs. Finally, the need for self-actualization is at the highest level

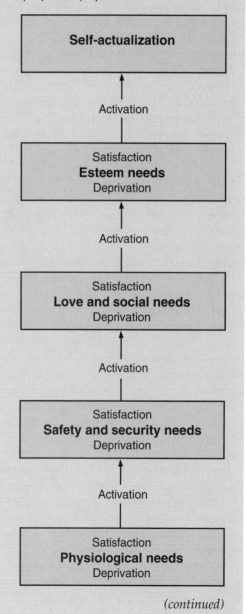

(continued)

in Maslow's hierarchy. Individuals operating at this level endeavor to be what they can be potentially: "To become everything one is capable of becoming" (Maslow 1943, 382).

One important component of Maslow's theory is often overlooked. Conventionally, the deprivation of a need is seen as the driving force, and scant attention is given to the effects of gratification of that need. In Maslow's theory, gratification of a need is as important as deprivation because gratification releases the organism from one set of needs and activates another set. The process of the deprivation of a need dominating the individual and of its gratification activating the next higher level need is illustrated in the figure.

reflected in factors such as salary increases, bonuses, or promotions. These are tangible rewards and are known to everybody. The problem with the extrinsic rewards is that the criteria on which they are distributed may not always be related to performance. As an example, the organization could base promotion on seniority and not on performance. Likewise, the organization could fix the same salary increases for every employee at a particular level; it may not consider relative performance. This latter practice would be the case in many government bureaucracies and those organizations where the unions have a very strong voice.

Note the differences in the lines connecting performance (see figure 7.1, box 6) to intrinsic (box 7A) and extrinsic (box 7B) rewards. Because intrinsic rewards are derived personally, they should be related more directly to personal performance. However, the job itself should provide the challenge and variety for one to feel good about the performance. A simple and routine job leaves little room for intrinsic rewards. To represent the contingent effect of job on intrinsic rewards in figure 7.1, a semi-jagged line is used to connect performance to intrinsic rewards. On the other hand, to represent how other considerations that are not related to performance (e.g., faulty performance evaluations by others, seniority-based reward systems, and favoritism in allocation of rewards) mediate extrinsic rewards, a relatively more jagged line has been used in figure 7.1 to link performance and extrinsic rewards.

The distinction between intrinsic rewards and extrinsic rewards is analogous to the distinction that Herzberg, Mausner, and Snyderman (1959) made between hygiene factors and motivators in their theory of motivation. Their theory states that the contents or the nature of a job and the opportunities it offers for the individual to gain intrinsic rewards are more critical in motivating an employee than salary and other extrinsic factors surrounding the job. Their theory is explained on page 103.

Satisfaction

The receipt of rewards generally should lead to **satisfaction** (box 9). A more detailed discussion of job satisfaction is provided in chapter 14. For the moment, note that the relationship between receipt of rewards and satisfaction depends on the individual's perception of whether the rewards are equitable (box 8). Adams (1963, 1977) first clarified the dynamics of perceptions of equity in his theory of inequity (see page 105).

In Their View

Many of the behaviors that I/O (industrial/organizational) psychologists study are more or less objective; they can be measured in fairly (although absolutely) unambiguous ways. Productivity, turnover, and absenteeism are some examples. Other variables are not so clear-cut. Motivation is a psychological state of the individual worker, and although it may influence people's observable behaviors, it is not the same as those behaviors. Because we cannot observe motivation directly, we must *infer* it from our observations of the behavior that we can see. Unless everyone with the same level of motivation behaves in the same way (and they do not), this presents a problem for studying and understanding motivation. (Saal and Knight 1995, 245-246)

Equity of Rewards

In general, the notion of equity refers to an individual's perception that the rewards were distributed fairly according to previously specified standards and on the basis of performance. For example, if person A in the public relations unit of the athletic department was more effective than

Herzberg's Motivation-Hygiene (Two-Factor) Theory

The theory of Herzberg and his associates (Herzberg, Mausner, and Snyderman 1959; Herzberg 1968) began with a study of engineers whom the researchers asked to recall the most satisfying event in their work experience and to identify the factors that led to such satisfaction. The researchers also asked them to identify the most dissatisfying event and to narrate the incident. The analyses of these responses revealed that

> The factors involved in producing job satisfaction (and motivation) are separate and distinct from the factors that lead to job dissatisfaction. Since separate factors need to be considered, depending on whether job satisfaction or job dissatisfaction is being examined, it follows that these two feelings are not opposites of each other. The opposite of job satisfaction is not job dissatisfaction, but *no* job satisfaction; and, similarly, the opposite of job dissatisfaction is not job satisfaction, but *no* job dissatisfaction. (Herzberg 1968, 56)

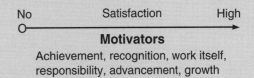

No   Satisfaction   High

Motivators

Achievement, recognition, work itself,
responsibility, advancement, growth

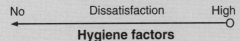

No   Dissatisfaction   High

Hygiene factors

Company policy and administration;
supervision; relationship with superiors,
peers, and subordinates; working conditions;
salary; personal life; status; security

**Relative contribution of motivators and hygiene factors to
job satisfaction and dissatisfaction**

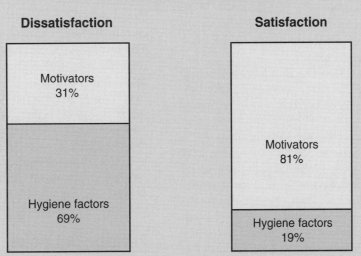

(continued)

The fundamental postulate of the theory is that only higher-order needs affect satisfaction and lower-order needs are associated with dissatisfaction. As a consequence, Herzberg and associates' theory is called a two-factor (or dual factor) theory (Herzberg, Mausner, and Snyderman 1959; Herzberg 1968). Their research showed that one set of factors (called the satisfiers or motivators) was associated more often with satisfaction than with dissatisfaction. Another set (called the dissatisfiers or hygienes) was referred to more often in incidents of dissatisfaction than in incidents of satisfaction. All of the satisfiers or motivators were related to higher-order needs, and the dissatisfiers were associated with lower-order needs. Herzberg and his associates replicated these results in several of their studies. The figure shows the relative percentage contributions of motivators and hygiene factors to both satisfaction and dissatisfaction. These figures, which are composites of the results of various studies, show that motivators accounted for 31% of the incidents of dissatisfaction and 81% of the incidents of satisfaction. On the other hand, the hygiene factors accounted for 69% of the incidents of dissatisfaction and 19% of the incidents of satisfaction. These results support Herzberg's idea that different sets of factors are associated with satisfaction and dissatisfaction.

The most important finding of Herzberg's work was that the motivators (or growth factors) all were related to the content of the work itself, and the hygiene factors all were related to the context in which the work was carried out. As shown in the figure, the content factors are achievement, recognition for achievement, the work itself, responsibility, and growth or advancement. The contextual factors are company policy and administration, supervision, interpersonal relationships, working conditions, salary, status, and security. The implication of the theory is that management must be concerned with eliminating dissatisfaction by improving the hygiene factors, i.e., providing adequate salary and wages, providing good working conditions, and having meaningful company policies and quality supervision. However, these hygiene factors alone do not result in motivated or satisfied workers. Therefore, management also must change jobs in order to provide for the psychological growth of employees. This issue of changing the content of jobs (or job enrichment as it is called) is discussed in chapter 8.

person B in managing the media and in projecting the image of the department, person A should be rewarded more than person B. However, if the director rewards them equally, then person A feels the inequity of rewards; therefore, the satisfaction from the rewards is decreased.

Individuals who believe that they have performed well tend to emphasize performance as a standard for equity of rewards rather than the cost-benefit comparisons that Adams' (1965, 1977) theory suggested. An NBA player is not as concerned about the effort he put in to get to the NBA (or the effort put in during the season) as he is about receiving a salary comparable to other players whose performance contributions are similar. Thus, the dotted line between performance (see figure 7.1, box 6) and perceived equitable rewards (box 8) illustrates the importance of performance in the determination of equity of rewards. In addition, the effect of perceived equity of rewards on the relationship between intrinsic rewards and satisfaction is minimal because this relationship is experienced internally.

In a Nutshell

When an individual achieves a level of performance, certain intrinsic and extrinsic rewards are available. The individual's perception of how equitable the rewards are relative to one's inputs influences the relationship between these rewards and satisfaction. Equity judgments are made based on some internal standards (e.g., what did I get on the previous occasion?) or external comparisons (e.g., what did my colleague get?). In an organizational context, the comparisons tend to be what one gets in return for one's inputs compared with what another person may get in return for his or her inputs.

Feedback Loops

Finally, figure 7.1 shows two feedback loops—one leading from satisfaction back to value of rewards and the other leading from the relationship between performance and rewards back to perceived effort-reward probability. The first feedback loop reflects

Adams' Theory of Inequity

In his theory of inequity, Adams (1963, 1977) stated that on receiving a reward, a person compares that reward with some internalized standard. If the comparison is favorable, then the person has satisfaction. If the comparison is unfavorable, however, he or she has dissatisfaction. For instance, it is not enough for a student to receive a B grade in a course. That grade must be comparable with what other students receive. Similarly, a merit raise of $1,000 does not provide happiness in a professor if every other professor received $1,001. The important point in both of these examples is that the absolute amount does not have a bearing on the estimation of equity; it is the relative amount that is critical.

The individual's internalized standard could be simply a comparison between personal effort (i.e., inputs) and the rewards of that effort (i.e., outcomes). For example, if a person makes great sacrifices to lose weight but only loses two pounds in six months, the individual would have a feeling of inequity. This feeling would result from a simple comparison of personal cost with personal benefit. However, in an organizational context, the cost-benefit comparison extends to referent others in the organization. That is, an individual compares the personal cost-benefit balance with the cost-benefit ratio of others in the workgroup. Adams' theory is anchored on this comparison to a referent others. He noted (see figure) that

> Inequity exists for *Person* whenever he [or she] perceives that the ratio of his [or her] outcomes to inputs and the ratio of *Other's* outcomes to Other's inputs are unequal. (Adams 1977, 113) (emphasis added)

The other in Adams' theory could be a subordinate, a supervisor, a co-worker, or an employee in another comparable organization or occupation.

The concept of inputs in his theory refers to the personal contributions in terms of intelligence, education and training, experience and seniority, personal appearance or attractiveness, health, and effort on the job. Outcomes in an organizational context include pay, seniority and other fringe benefits, working conditions including status and perquisites, and the psychological or intrinsic rewards of the job.

When a person perceives inequity and feels the tension and discomfort associated with such inequity, he or she may make an attempt to restore equity (or reduce the inequity) in a number of ways. Obviously, the person may attempt to alter the values of any of the four elements of the inequity formula: personal outcomes, personal inputs, other's outcomes, and other's inputs. The most frequently used strategy is to attempt to increase personal outcomes. Thus, an individual is most likely to approach an employer and ask for more pay, greater benefits, and so on. Of course,

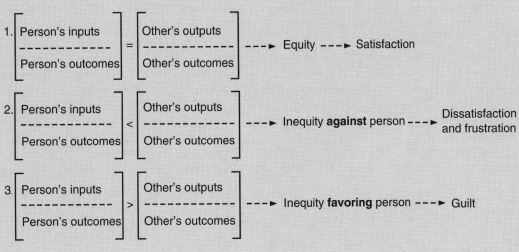

(continued)

the person also can reduce the feeling of inequity by reducing personal inputs through decreased productivity or increased absenteeism. He or she also could reduce inequity by reducing other's outcomes or inputs. However, the individual may be constrained from adopting this strategy. Superiors are most likely to determine other's outcomes (i.e., pay or promotion), and that other individual is most likely to strongly influence the other's inputs. More importantly, a strategy that focuses on other's inputs or outcomes may not be psychologically acceptable to the person. For instance, a facility supervisor in an athletic department or a recreation department is not likely to ask to reduce the rewards to another supervisor. In addition, a supervisor is not likely to sabotage the efforts of the other supervisor.

Apart from manipulating personal outcomes and inputs, there are other ways of reducing inequity. Adams suggested that individuals may alter their perceptions of personal and other's outcomes and inputs in such a manner that equity is perceptually restored. A person also may change the other of comparison—i.e., the other to whom he or she compares himself or herself. Another possibility is that the person could leave the organization and go elsewhere.

The significance of Adams' theory lies in the fact that organizational reward systems are considered to be meaningful and effective only in so far as they create a sense of equity among the members of the organization. Porter and Lawler (1968) further elaborated on this notion in their model of motivation.

the fact that the receipt of rewards affects the values attached to those rewards. In the case of an extrinsic reward, such as pay, the value that employees attach to these rewards is likely to be lowered as more and more of it is received. Thus, an athlete who receives a high salary is less likely to emphasize salary increases as much as an athlete on the low end of the pay scale. This view is also consistent with Herzberg's theory that suggested that gratification of lower-order needs do not contribute much to motivation (see page 103). However, Porter and Lawler (1968) acknowledged that the satisfaction derived from the intrinsic rewards is likely to lead the individual to value them more. Figure 7.2 shows the differential effects of receipt of intrinsic and extrinsic rewards on the values attached to them.

The second loop in figure 7.1 relates to the employee's perception of the probability that his or her efforts will result in the rewards sought. As noted before, there are two components to this effort-reward probability estimate made by the individual. First, there is the issue of whether one's effort will result in performance expected by the organization (box 6). If, for example, a volunteer worker did not reach the objectives despite the best efforts, then the perceived relationship between one's efforts and performance will be weakened.

The second component relates to the performance-reward relationship. Suppose our volunteer achieves the objectives; his or her sense of "can do" would be strengthened. While the volunteer would enjoy the rewards of achievement internally, the others may not recognize the performance and reward the volunteer in terms of recognition, praise, and gratitude. Instead, other volunteers with similar or less achievement may be praised. This lack of a relationship between performance and rewards from others may negatively influence the volunteer's enthusiasm for the work. Thus, the effort-reward probability combines a person's beliefs about his or her own capacity to perform and the organization's practice of rewarding good performances.

In Their View

The theories described throughout this chapter cannot explain all behavior within an organization. In the views of Pinder (1984) and Landy and Becker (1987), these are, in fact, middle-range theories capable of explaining only very specific processes or outcomes in an organization. For example, Landy and Becker (1987) suggested that the two-factor theory of Herzberg, Mausner, and Snyderman (1959) is more relevant to explaining affective reactions to certain job characteristics or job satisfaction. The equity theory (Adams 1965, 1977) also relates perceptions of inequity to negative feelings and dissatisfaction. On the other hand, the expectancy theory (Vroom 1964) can explain choices that individuals make from among several discrete ways of behaving without reference to satisfaction or dissatisfaction. Porter and Lawler's (1968) model of motivation is more comprehensive and tends to integrate the other theories explained in this chapter.

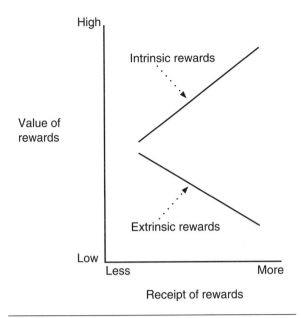

Figure 7.2 Values of intrinsic and extrinsic rewards as a function of their receipts.

A baseball organization that habitually promotes its managers on the basis of seniority weakens the employee's perception of the relationships between effort, performance, and promotion. That is, an individual desiring promotion might not be triggered to work hard because he or she perceives that the best way to get a promotion is to get old. Thus, as Porter and Lawler (1968) pointed out, the organizational practices have a great influence in determining the perceived connection between performance and rewards.

In a Nutshell

An individual's experience in performing and receiving rewards in an organizational context affects subsequent motivation in two different ways. First, the value of rewards can change (e.g., the more the extrinsic rewards, the less the value of those rewards, and the more the intrinsic rewards, the higher the value placed on them). Second, if organizational rewards are not tied to performance, motivation to perform may weaken.

Motivation as Personal Investment

Maehr and Braskamp (1986) provided an alternate and a more recent view of individual motivation.

They suggested that motivation is inferred from the observed behavior of individuals. For example, when we see a young person shooting basketball free throws by himself or herself, we conclude that he or she is motivated (i.e., he or she is making a **personal investment**). This approach would be useful for practicing managers because it explains motivated behavior and, more importantly, how they can identify it.

Behavioral Indicators of Personal Investment

Maehr and Braskamp (1986) argued that observed behaviors can be evaluated on five interrelated dimensions—direction, persistence, continuing motivation, intensity, and performance. In their model, Porter and Lawler (1968) equated effort with motivation. Recall Robbins' (1997b) definition of motivation that included similar concepts of intensity of effort, persistence, and direction. Maehr and Braskamp's work is more detailed and comprehensive.

• **Direction**—Direction refers to the choices that an individual makes among different behavioral alternatives. For example, a volunteer coach attends a coaching clinic during the weekend instead of going fishing. Others infer that he or she is motivated based on the choice of one behavior over another.

• **Persistence**—Persistence refers to the extent of time that an individual spends on a particular job or project. For example, basketball players spend much time practicing their shots. Others rate them as highly motivated based on their persistence with the job at hand.

• **Continuing motivation**—Continuing motivation refers to the tendency of individuals to return to a task after being away from it for a period of time. For instance, other demands often interrupt a fitness club manager who is developing a strategic plan for the firm. Yet, the manager keeps returning to work on the plan. Those who observe this tendency of the manager continuing to work even after several interruptions infer that the manager is motivated to complete the plan. Note the difference between persistence, which is continuous activity, and continuing motivation, which is resumption of the activity after interruptions.

• **Intensity**—Intensity refers to the energy expended and the activity level of individuals involved in a task. Two coaches of juvenile teams may differ in the level of activity and energy expended in getting ready for a coaching session although they may spend an equal amount of time on the task. Others are likely to believe that the more active person is more motivated. Maehr and Braskamp (1986) cautioned that this difference in activity may be a function of physiological factors; therefore, intensity is not as reliable a measure of motivation as direction. Additionally, one's traits and abilities also may influence the activity level. For instance, a more anxious person is likely to be more active in getting ready for a coaching session than a less anxious person. Similarly, one who has the required abilities and coaching experience is likely to be less active than the other individual.

• **Performance**—Whenever performances between two individuals or within one individual vary, others tend to ascribe such variations to motivation. This ascription is particularly true when one individual performs differently at different times. However, be cautious about the inferences made about motivation based on performance. Several coaches and media persons tend to fall into this fallacy. Whenever a particular athlete performs well, these persons most often attribute the performance to the dedication and motivation of the athlete. These inferences also imply that the other athletes were not as motivated as the good performer. This implication is far from the truth. Managers should not place much confidence in performance as a measure of motivation because performance "is a product of acquired skills, ability, and a combination of the behavioral patterns already reviewed" (Maehr and Braskamp 1986, 5). The performances of the other members on the team also may affect performance in a team setting. Therefore, performance is only a crude measure of motivation and should be used rarely.

In a Nutshell

A person's choice of a behavior, the persistence and intensity with which such a person engages in that behavior, the tendency to return to that behavior when interrupted, and the performance achieved indicate a person's level of motivation.

The major thrust of Maehr and Braskamp's argument is that when one considers all of the discussed behavioral patterns as a collective, the patterns indicate the extent to which individuals invest themselves in a given activity. Just as persons may differ in the ways in which they invest their money, people

also differ in the ways in which they invest their personal resources (e.g., time, talent, and energy) in various activities. This view has two implications. The first implication is that everybody is motivated to do something; that is, they do invest their personal resources in some activities. For example, one fitness instructor invests the available free time in a bar with friends, while another spends the time in the library to learn more about fitness and wellness. The former instructor is as motivated to be at the bar as the latter is to be at the library.

> The issue is really not *whether* a person is motivated but, rather, how, to what ends, and in what ways the person is motivated. The assumption is that all people are motivated to do something; the question is *what* they are motivated to do. (Maehr and Braskamp 1986, 6-7)

The second implication is that personal investment is a course of action: "A process whereby people take certain available resources—their time, talent, and energy—and distribute them as they choose" (Maehr and Braskamp 1986, 7). The concept brings together several behavioral patterns that reflect a degree of attraction toward something. However, as Maehr and Braskamp (1986) noted: "The emphasis is on something that is done that is observable, objective, and quantifiable" (p. 9).

The advantage of viewing motivation as personal investment is that "one can consider motivation not only as an enduring trait of individuals or groups but as a direct product of the situation in which the person or group is placed. And situations are easier to change than people" (Maehr and Braskamp 1986, 8). This is a critical issue for sport and recreation managers. When a manager sees persons not investing their personal resources in organizational activities, it is not profitable to label them unmotivated. Instead, the manager should find out what is in the situation that makes these members invest their resources elsewhere and how he or she can make the situation more attractive to the members. For instance, an employee of a university recreation department may not invest as much of his or her resources in assigned departmental tasks as in coaching a youth soccer team outside of the job responsibilities. An analysis may show that his or her job does not provide as much challenge or autonomy as coaching a youth team provides. Redesigning the employee's job to include relatively more autonomy and challenge may accomplish the redirection of the investment of the employee's resources. Based on this line of reasoning, Maehr and Braskamp (1986) proposed the motivational process shown in figure 7.3. According to the model, external factors, such as task design, social norms, and options available to the individual, interact with that individual's personal thoughts, emotions, and preferences to determine the investment of that person's resources in specific activities. The model also suggests that such investment leads to certain outcomes (or payoffs) for the individual. These outcomes are described in the following section.

Outcomes of Personal Investment

Maehr and Braskamp (1986) suggested that if managers think of motivation as investment, then they also should consider the payoffs or the outcomes of such investments. Because individuals invest their personal resources, the outcomes to be considered also should be from individuals' perspectives. However, individuals, organizations, and societies may place differential values on these outcomes. In their view, the outcomes of any personal investment can be categorized into three broad classes: achievement, personal growth, and life satisfaction.

Achievement

Achievement involves "a personal accomplishment—something that is attributed to one's ability and effort. But it is an accomplishment that is not only valued by the person; it also has social signifi-

cance" (Maehr and Braskamp 1986, 13). Note that anything good that happens to an individual is not considered achievement because the good thing cannot be attributed to the individual's ability or effort. These authors also note that achievement refers to an outcome that was in doubt. Thus, routine performances, such as a professional basketball player making 60% of his or her free throws, are not considered achievement. A more significant criterion is that other people or organizations must value the accomplishment. For example, the university where I work is not likely to value a professor's expertise and accomplishments in shooting marbles. For that matter, the professor's family may not have any appreciation for such accomplishments either. This does not deny the fact that the professor may value these accomplishments immensely. However, others need to value them if managers are to label them as achievement. The values that the individual holds falls under one of the other two categories described: personal growth and life satisfaction.

Personal Growth

Personal growth refers to the enhancement of one's ability, skill, or competence. To modify Maehr and Braskamp's (1986) example, consider three sport managers who spend their free time differently. The first manager joins a master of business administration program to further his or her expertise in management. The second gets involved in ceramics to gain the fulfillment from creating things with one's

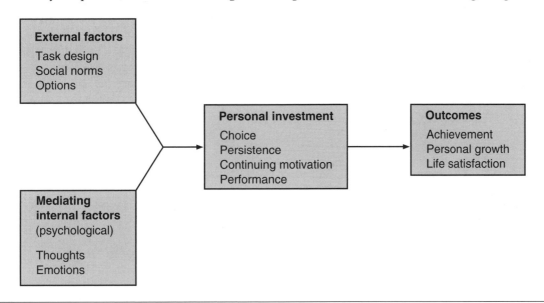

Figure 7.3   Model of motivation as personal investment.

Adapted, by permission, from M.L. Maehr and L.A. Braskamp, 1986, *The motivation factor: A theory of personal investment.* (Lexington, MA: Lexington Books).

hands. The third tries skydiving to face the danger, conquer the challenge, and experience the vertigo. "Enhancement of ability is involved in each case, but clearly the goal in the first case is achievement, whereas in the other two it is personal growth" (Maehr and Braskamp 1986, 14). Note that while the respective individuals equally may value the three different payoffs, the first—achievement—is more critical in an organizational context because it leads to organizational effectiveness.

Life Satisfaction

The final category of outcomes in Maehr and Braskamp's (1986) scheme is life satisfaction and general well-being. In their view, although personal growth and achievement are desired and valued outcomes, other personal investments may lead to neither of the outcomes. However, such investments still may lead to what they call life satisfaction. Consider, for example, a person who has been fishing regularly for the past several years. Any payoff from this investment cannot be considered achievement or personal growth. However, the satisfaction that the person receives from such investment is of great value to the individual and contributes greatly to his or her life satisfaction and well-being.

In a Nutshell

The outcomes of personal investment in an activity as Maehr and Braskamp (1986) described could be achievement of some significance as a result of one's ability and effort; personal growth reflected in the enhancement of one's ability, skill, or competence; and life satisfaction including the former two and a sense of well-being.

Summary

I described in detail two theories of motivation— Porter and Lawler's (1968) expectancy model of motivation and Maehr and Braskamp's (1986) theory of motivation as personal investment. Porter and Lawler's (1968) model included concepts from the theories of Adams (1963, 1977); Herzberg (1968); Herzberg, Mausner, and Snyderman (1959); Maslow (1943); and Vroom (1964), which I also partially described. These theories clearly show that sport organizations and their managers can manipulate several of the factors under their control in an effort to enhance members' motivation.

All of the theories discussed refer directly or indirectly to intrinsic rewards, and they also suggest that the worker directly derives these intrinsic rewards from the performance of a job. It is evident, therefore, that the job and the tasks associated with the job are sources of motivation. Because the managers control the design of the job, they can design the jobs to increase the motivating potential of these jobs. Chapter 8 focuses on this subject.

The motivational theories described in this chapter also provide a framework for managers to analyze and understand behaviors of their members and to identify ways of reinforcing desirable behaviors and modifying undesirable ones. In fact, some theories of leadership discussed in chapter 10 are based on the expectancy model of motivation.

Another significant contributor of motivation in organizations is the fairness in organizational procedures and in the distribution of organizational practices. The theories of Porter and Lawler (1968) and Adams (1963) pointed out that the rewards that the organization offers lose their motivating potential if they are perceived to be inequitable. To make them equitable, some organizations may distribute the rewards equally among all employees. Such a practice overlooks the different levels of performance that different people achieve; therefore, it cannot enhance motivation to perform. If rewards are to serve as motivators, then they should be tied to performance, which entails the accurate assessment of individual performance and the institution of fair reward systems. Chapters 11 and 12 address these issues.

Key Terms

motivation, content theories, process theories, equity, performance, valence, expectancy, instrumentality, intrinsic rewards, extrinsic rewards, satisfaction, personal investment

Your Perspectives

- Consider your school work in your present institution or various job functions in your current position. Do you spend more time and effort in some courses or tasks than in others? Explain what factors contribute to this differential emphasis you place on courses or tasks.

- Explain the feelings you have when you complete a course or task. What intrinsic and extrinsic factors are associated with those feelings?

- Think of a paid job with which you were quite satisfied. What factors contributed to that satisfaction?

- Think of a paid job in which you were very dissatisfied. Explain the reasons for such dissatisfaction.

- Think of a co-worker or a classmate whom you think was motivated highly. Explain why you think he or she was motivated highly. Identify the specific factors that influenced your opinion of that person.

Part III

Human Resource Practices

The preceding sections outlined the classes of human resources in sport and recreation organizations and the differences among them in abilities, personality, values, and motivation. Such individual differences have functional utility from the societal point of view. A high degree of division of labor and a multitude of vocational pursuits characterize every society. All of these vocations and occupations require a diversity of aptitudes, abilities, and temperaments. Fortunately, great variety in these individual difference variables also characterize people in a society.

However, an organization can harness the functional utility of individual differences only if it matches these differences with the requirements of the tasks. That is, the performance of the individuals in an organization and the effectiveness of the total organization largely depends on the fit between the individuals and their differences on the one hand and the tasks assigned to them on the other hand. In addition, the organizational processes of evaluating and rewarding task performance also play a significant part in the effective use of the human resources. Therefore, an organization must assign jobs to individuals that are consistent with their abilities and orientations, influence them to perform their jobs adequately, evaluate their performance on specified criteria, and reward them for effective performance.

As noted earlier, our interest in individual differences stems from the concept of person-task fit. That is, our major concern is in creating a fit between the task assigned to an individual and that person's profile on individual difference factors. The concept of person-task fit is critical from the perspectives of both the organization and the individual. The organization can expect greater productivity if the members possess attributes that the assigned tasks require. On the other hand, the individual member feels competent, confident, and satisfied if the assigned task matches his or her attributes.

The foregoing discussion highlights two significant analyses. First, the manager must assess the members' abilities that are relevant to the organization. Second, the manager must analyze the jobs and their attributes and must identify the characteristics of individuals that are needed to perform those jobs well. Such assessment of jobs, as well as the individuals, helps the manager select the individuals for specific jobs. In addition, such analyses also reveal to the manager which of the current members need to be trained and in what abilities they need to be trained. These two types of assessments are the content of the chapters 8 and 9.

In chapter 8, I discuss the nature of the jobs in terms of their attributes and motivational properties. The central focus of the chapter is on the Job Characteristics Model that offers some guidelines for increasing the motivating potential of the jobs themselves.

One of the critical managerial concerns is recruiting workers and assigning them to appropriate jobs. In this staffing procedure, the manager must take care in matching individual difference characteristics with characteristics of the task. Chapter 9 presents the approaches to assigning the appropriate jobs to members of the organization. The procedures regarding the recruitment, selection, and promotion of personnel are also discussed.

The focus of chapter 10 is on a discussion of leadership and decision making. After recruiting the workers and assigning them to specific jobs, management must be concerned with influencing and motivating employees to achieve the assigned tasks. The chapter explains this function of leadership in greater detail. Significant theories of leadership are explained and then synthesized into a more comprehensive model labeled "multidimensional model of leadership." The chapter also discusses the advantages and disadvantages of participative decision making. It includes a description of vari-

ous problem situations and specifies the appropriate level of member participation (ranging from purely autocratic to purely group decision making) for every problem situation.

In chapter 11, I discuss the evaluation of individual performances. The evaluations serve two functions: formative and evaluative. The member may see the evaluations as tools to foster the growth and performance of the individual member. Evaluations also serve the purposes of the organization in identifying good performances and rewarding them accordingly. The subject of chapter 12 is the various reward systems that have been advanced and their relevance to sport organizations.

Organizational justice is the subject of chapter 13. The fundamental notion pervading society is that individuals must be treated fairly and justly in all circumstances. Within an organization, this notion relates to the distribution of rewards to all of the organization's members in a just manner, and it relates to the procedures employed to assign members to organizational positions (including promotions) and to evaluate them on their performance in a fair and uniform manner. The former notion is termed "distributive justice"; the latter, "procedural justice." These issues are addressed in the context of sport organizations.

8 Job Design

Learning Objectives

After reading this chapter you will be able to

- distinguish among job simplification, job rotation, and job enlargement;
- understand the concept of job enrichment;
- explain the various attributes of jobs and their motivational properties;
- understand the concepts of interdependence among tasks and the variability of tasks;
- distinguish among standardization, planning, and mutual adjustment as methods of coordinating jobs; and
- select an appropriate method of coordinating tasks based on their interdependence and variability.

It is not uncommon to hear people say, "A job is a job is a job," "I love my job," "My job is not a great one, but it pays well," "My job is like any other, but the people I work with are absolutely wonderful," or "My job is OK, but my supervisor is intolerable." For some people, jobs may be quite interesting and satisfying, and these jobs may serve as a retreat from the worries and turmoil of the outside world. Others may perceive their jobs as the penalty they pay for the enjoyment of life outside the workplace.

These differential reactions can be found in all kinds of jobs. That is why "white collar woes" and "blue collar blues" exist. These reactions illustrate that all jobs are not necessarily alike. They may differ either in the content of the job (e.g., it is exciting) or in the context (e.g., the workgroup or the leader). The rewards of task performance may be intrinsic (e.g., it is challenging) or extrinsic (e.g., it pays well). In chapter 7, I introduced these concepts in the discussion of Herzberg's (1968) two-factor theory. I will elaborate on the nature of the task in this chapter.

First, I define a job and job design. Schermerhorn, Hunt, and Osborn (1985) defined a job as "one or more tasks that an individual performs in direct support of the organization's production purpose," and they defined **job design** as "simply the specification of task attributes and the creation of work settings which include work groups" (p. 203).

Job Designs

Given the significance of jobs, it is not surprising that theorists and practicing managers have attempted to modify the design of jobs to increase worker motivation and productivity. This chapter outlines four of the general procedures that have been in vogue: job simplification, job rotation, job enlargement, and job enrichment.

Job Simplification

Industrial engineers, whose intent was to make each job as simple and as specialized as possible so that greater efficiency could be achieved, initiated **job simplification** in the early part of the 20th century. They even studied the time taken for each motion in performing a task and attempted to simplify these motions. These time-motion studies permitted them to break down tasks into activities and to specify in detail how each activity should be carried out. This approach is still found in the assembly line operations that many manufacturing firms adopted. Even office work has a number of simplified and specialized jobs (e.g., jobs of a filing clerk, typist, or receptionist). In a system of specialized and simplified tasks, employees do not have much room to vary from the specified routines. The potential advantages of job simplification is the increased economy of operation. This increase is achieved because simplified jobs promote specialization that, in turn, increases productivity. The other advantages are that low-skilled employees requiring little training can staff simplified jobs and that the employees are transferable from one job to the other. Further, management can easily monitor the productivity in these simplified jobs. On the other hand, several potential reactive outcomes undermine the potential advantages of job simplification. Job simplification makes the job routine, monotonous, and boring. In time, workers begin to dislike the job; therefore, absenteeism and turnover increase. Even when they attend work, workers may not put forth their best efforts, and they may be prone to make mistakes.

Job Rotation

In order to counter the negative ramifications of job simplification, researchers have advanced two strategies (Saal and Knight 1995). The first strategy is **job rotation**, i.e., moving the workers periodically from one job to another. For example, two workers in a fitness club alternate each week or month between the jobs of facility and equipment maintenance and

of receiving clients. This job rotation has an immediate effect of exciting the individuals because of the novelty of the job, the location, and workgroup. However, once the novelty wears off, workers still may be alienated from their jobs if each of the jobs they move into are still simplified, routinized, and boring. Overall, however, rotating into different jobs is more motivational than performing one simplified job because of the variety involved. Further, job rotation has an added advantage in the form of training the workers: "It allows workers to become more familiar with different tasks and increases the flexibility with which they can be moved from one job to another" (Schermerhorn, Hunt, and Osborn 1997, 155). This flexibility in movement among jobs becomes particularly significant when one or more individuals are absent (e.g., due to sickness or injury).

In Their View

Noting that classical approaches to job design (e.g., job simplification) have disregarded the psychological implications, such as boredom and isolation, Rees (1996) remarked that

> too often the Procrustean approach is taken to job design. Procrustes was a legendary figure in Greek mythology who had a special bed. He was obsessive about guests fitting his bed exactly. If they were too long for the bed he cut off their feet; if they were too small he stretched them on a rack until they fit! The moral is that jobs can be designed with little or no thought to matching with the individual—the assumption being that people can always be found who can be made to fit the job, however badly they are designed. (p. 145)

While this assumption is not widely held in modern times, some people's abilities, personality, and values (discussed in chapters 4 through 6) are consistent with simplified jobs.

Job Enlargement

Another strategy to motivate the workers is to enlarge their jobs. That is, instead of being locked into one specialized and routinized job (e.g., filing), the worker is asked to do more things (e.g., typing and answering the phone in addition to filing). In the previous example of a fitness club, the two employees may both be involved in facility and equipment maintenance as well as the reception work. As in job rotation, **job enlargement** may have only minimal impact on workers' motivation and satisfaction as long as the added tasks are still simplified. However, as noted earlier, the opportunity to do a variety of jobs is better than doing just one simplified task. Management may undertake job enlargement because of the belief that it will satisfy workers' needs or because the increasing workload is better assigned to those who do similar work (Saal and Knight 1995). Therein lies a problem. Even when managers undertake job enlargement with the workers in mind, the workers may perceive it as management tactics to extract more work from the workers. One way that managers can counteract these negative perceptions is to explain clearly the reasons for job enlargement and to explain that the process results in a mix of tasks and not in more work. Further, if the workers themselves are involved in the process of job enlargement, they are likely to comprehend better the rationale for the process. The two employees from the fitness club will understand the ramifications of the process and accept the decision to enlarge their jobs if they are asked to participate in the decision.

Job Enrichment

Recall that Herzberg's (1968) motivation-hygiene theory proposed that the content, rather than the context, of the job best serves the higher-order needs of an individual. In addition, the intrinsic rewards of working are derived more from the job itself than from other factors. The practical implication of the theory is that the jobs need to be redesigned so that more of the motivators (i.e., sources of higher-order need satisfaction) are present in job performance.

According to Herzberg (1968), neither job rotation nor job enlargement addresses the issue of meaninglessness of the jobs. In these efforts, either

In a Nutshell

One method of achieving efficiency is to make jobs simple and specialized. This method ensures uniformity of operations and greater productivity in certain forms of operations. Because job simplification makes jobs routine and boring, employees may become less motivated and involved. To counter this trend, managers may try job rotation (i.e., moving a worker from job to job) or job enlargement (i.e., assigning a worker different kinds of work). However, managers must note that the advantages of job rotation and job enlargement may be limited if the different jobs themselves are routine and simplified.

a worker is moved into different meaningless jobs or more meaningless jobs are heaped on the worker. He considered job rotation equivalent to substituting one zero for another and considered job enlargement equivalent to adding one zero to another. His concept of job design involves vertical loading, or **job enrichment**. Table 8.1 lists his proposal of seven principles for enriching jobs and the motivators involved.

As shown in table 8.1, the purposes of vertical loading of a job are to make the worker

- feel responsible for the job,
- experience achievement and growth in a challenging job, and
- gain recognition (both internal and external) for a job well done.

These purposes can be achieved through allowing the workers more authority to decide how they will carry out the assigned work, making them more responsible for their work, and providing fast

The job design approaches of job simplification, job rotation, job enlargement, and job enrichment are equally applicable to both volunteer and paid workers. The focus in these discussions is on how to make the job itself motivating without reference to whether one is paid for the job. For instance, a volunteer association running a soccer league may simplify the task of sending out notices to interested parties by breaking it into simpler units of typing, writing out addresses on envelopes, and stuffing the envelopes. The association can assign these simplified units to individual volunteers (i.e., job simplification). Job rotation means that the volunteers take turns typing, writing, and stuffing. Job enlargement implies that every volunteer performs all three tasks. Finally, job enrichment requires the managers to assign more difficult and challenging jobs to the volunteers. For example, the volunteers who sent out the information also may be asked to form teams from individual clients or to categorize the teams based on specific criteria (e.g., age or skill) and may be asked to draw up the schedule of competitions.

Table 8.1   Principles of Vertical Loading

Principle	Motivators involved
Removing some controls while retaining accountability	Responsibility and personal achievement
Increasing the accountability of individuals for own work	Responsibility and recognition
Giving a person a complete natural unit of work (e.g., module, division, area)	Responsibility, achievement, and recognition
Granting additional authority to an employee in his activity and granting job freedom	Responsibility, achievement, and recognition
Making periodic reports directly available to the worker himself rather than to the supervisor	Internal recognition
Introducing new and more difficult tasks not previously managed	Growth and learning
Assigning individuals specific and specialized tasks and enabling them to become experts	Responsibility, growth, and advancement

and accurate feedback directly to the workers. Monitoring and directing by supervisors are minimized. Vertical loading of a job also involves assigning more new and more difficult jobs to the workers. In the previous example of a fitness club, the two workers may be allowed to decide among themselves how they will fulfill the responsibilities of facility and equipment maintenance and reception.

In a Nutshell

A superior method of designing jobs to ensure worker motivation and involvement is job enrichment. Jobs are designed in such a way that they allow employees greater autonomy in carrying out the tasks, responsibility for outcomes, increasing challenge in the job, progressive growth and sense of achievement, and periodic and accurate feedback.

Task Attributes

While the foregoing approaches are grounded in the notion that jobs do have an impact on employees, the proponents of these approaches did not articulate well the causal relationships among the job, the individual, and the outcome variables. That is, they did not indicate which elements of a task affect what aspects of the individual to result in positive reactions from the worker and increased productivity. This is the focus of the remainder of this chapter.

We know that the jobs in sport and recreation are not alike. The sport lawyer's job is different from that of the public relations officer of a professional sport franchise. By the same token, the job of the director of a city recreation department is different from that of facility manager in that department. Yet another example is the contrast between the job of the employee at the ticket counter and the job of the director of ticketing operations of a university athletic department.

The obvious distinctions among these jobs relate to the domain in which they operate (e.g., sport law compared with public relations) and to the scope of operation (e.g., management of a single facility compared with management of the entire department). It is also possible to distinguish among these jobs on the basis of how variable the tasks associated with each job are or how much variety exists in each of these jobs. For example, the employee at the ticket counter experiences less variability and less variety than employees in other jobs cited earlier. These concepts of variability and variety are just two of several task characteristics, or **task attributes**, that distinguish one job from another. In the discussion of consumer, professional, and human services in the introduction, I alluded to some of these concepts (see table 1).

The study of the impact of the task and its attributes has been extensive. Researchers report that the task attributes affect

- an employee's motivation (Hackman and Lawler 1971, Hackman and Oldham 1980, Herzberg 1968, Turner and Lawrence 1965),
- an employee's growth and adjustment and his or her sense of competence (Lorsch and Morse 1974, Morse 1976),
- the effectiveness of leadership style (Fiedler 1967),
- the structure of work units (Van de Ven and Delbecq 1974), and
- the control and integration of work units (Lawrence and Lorsch 1967, Thompson 1967).

This section describes the task attributes as various authors outlined them (Hackman and Lawler 1971, Hackman and Oldham 1980, Thompson 1967, Turner and Lawrence 1965) and the processes by which they affect one's motivation. It also discusses how these attributes warrant different forms of control and coordination.

In Their View

Referring to the myth that everyone wants a challenging job, Robbins (1997b) noted that scholars and consultants hold the view that employees want challenging and meaningful jobs: "Well, not *everyone* wants a job like that. There are still a lot of people who prefer jobs that make minimal psychological demands. Work to them is merely a means to some other end; it is not an end itself. They use their hours off the job to fulfill their needs for responsibility, achievement, growth, and recognition" (p. 387). Schermerhorn, Hunt, and Osborn (1997) noted that individuals who may prefer job enrichment are "those who need achievement, who hold middle-class working values, and/or who are seeking higher order growth-need satisfaction at work" (p. 159).

Task Variety

Skill variety refers to "the degree to which a job requires a variety of different activities in carrying out the work, involving the use of a number of different skills and talents of the person" (Hackman and Oldham 1980, 78). As the definition implies, variety may relate to the number of tools and controls a worker uses (i.e., object variety) or to the change in work pace, physical location, or physical operation (i.e., motor variety) (Turner and Lawrence 1965).

In this context, an employee in a club who leads an aerobics class, teaches tennis to juniors, and

manages the accounting books enjoys more variety in the job than another person performing just any one of those tasks. For an example of clients in sport, the task of a rower involves only one movement pattern, but the task of a basketball player involves several patterns of movement. Even within one sport, one could identify differences in variety, such as in the case of a quarterback and a place kicker in football.

Task Variability

A closely related, but different, attribute is **task variability**. This attribute refers to the number of exceptional cases encountered in the work that require different methods or procedures for doing the work (Van de Ven and Delbecq 1974). For example, the jobs of a fitness consultant and a coach are variable to the extent that the clients are all different and their needs and requirements are unique. Therefore, the methods and procedures that they use to help their clients are variable. In contrast, the job of a locker-room attendant is less variable than those jobs because his or her job involves assigning lockers and handing out towels to qualified people. Task variability is related closely to the extent to which the environment of the task provider is stable or turbulent. The environment of the fitness consultant is less stable than that of the locker-room attendant because the clients' needs and the appropriate services are constantly changing in the former job. In addition, to the extent that new information and technology of providing those services are available, the consultant's job is more variable.

The difference between teeball and softball also clearly demonstrates variability. In teeball, the batter, whose environment is stable and predictable, initiates his or her own movement and performs a closed skill. On the other hand, the softball batter also exhibits hitting ability; however, the stimulus conditions in his or her environment are unstable and unpredictable, and the location and velocity of the ball and other players externally pace his or her movements. In that sense, he or she is involved in an open skill. The terms "routine" (or nonvariable) and "nonroutine" (or variable) also describe the extent of variability in jobs.

Task Autonomy

Autonomy means "the degree to which the job provides substantial freedom, independence, and discretion to the individual in scheduling the work and in determining the procedures to be used in carrying it out" (Hackman and Oldham 1980, 79).

For example, the coach of a basketball team has considerable autonomy in the recruitment of players, methods of training, and competitive strategies (Chelladurai and Kuga 1996). Similarly, the marketing director of a university athletic department may enjoy autonomy in terms of contacts that he or she makes, the manner and substance of his or her communications, and the final transactions. In contrast, the clerks in the ticket office or the accounting office may not have such autonomy to the extent that the tasks they need to do, how they carry out those tasks, and when they do the tasks (i.e., hours of work) are specified for them. Even in blue collar jobs, autonomy may be reflected in the freedom that the worker has in the choice of material and tools used and in the sequence in which he or she carries out different activities (Turner and Lawrence 1965). For example, a caretaker in a fitness club may have considerable autonomy in carrying out the task and in deciding what materials to use.

Task Identity

Task identity refers to "the degree to which a job requires completion of a 'whole' and identifiable piece of work; that is, doing a job from beginning to end with a visible outcome" (Hackman and Oldham 1980, 78).

Hackman and Oldham (1980) suggested that a social worker who manages all of the needs of a client finds the job more meaningful than one who manages only one problem. According to this view, a person who evaluates the fitness level of a client, prescribes an exercise regimen for the client, and leads and supervises the exercise session perceives the job of rehabilitating the client as his or her own (i.e., task identity) and, therefore, finds it more meaningful than does a person who performs only one of the tasks. Chelladurai (1985) noted that

> high task identity would be available to high school coaches. They develop the athletic potential of the few students who report for the team. This development is easily identified and attributed to the coach, who is usually the sole individual responsible for that task. In contrast, classroom teachers cannot easily identify their end product or their personal contributions to that end product. (pp. 120-121)

Take the case of the clients in sport. Obviously, people engaged in individual sports (e.g., tennis or wrestling) experience task identity to a greater extent than those engaged in team sports. In team sports, the participant cannot do "a whole piece of work." However, within a given sport, some may be involved in the initiation of the task and some in the completion of the task. Others may be involved peripherally with the main objective of the group.

Job Feedback

Job feedback is "the degree to which carrying out the work activities provides the individual with direct and clear information about the effectiveness of his or her performance" (Hackman and Oldham 1980, 80). That is, the feedback must emanate from the performance of the job itself. Job feedback is different from the feedback that comes from other agents, such as a supervisor or a client. For example, a sport marketer may have the "gut feeling" that the presentation just finished was good (or bad). Facility managers may get positive feedback as they ready the facility for a competition. For an example from sport clients, the goalkeeper in hockey gets an immediate and objective feedback when he or she stops the puck or otherwise. In contrast, the diver or gymnast has to wait for judges' ratings that may or may not be objective. The contrast between feedback from the job and from others is illustrated when a basketball player gets an immediate and positive feedback as his or her shot goes in. That is the feedback inherent in the task. However, the coach may point out that the shooting movement was not proper or that the shot should not have been attempted in the first place.

Task Significance

The significance of the task reflects

> the degree to which a job has a substantial impact on the lives of other people, whether those people are in the immediate organization or in the world at large. . . . When we know that what we do in our work will affect someone else's happiness, health, or safety, we care about that work more than if the work is largely irrelevant to the lives and well-being of other people. (Hackman and Oldham 1980, 79)

An exercise leader's job with cardiac patients is likely to be perceived as more significant than a similar job with young adults. Similarly, the job of a coach in youth sports is accorded greater significance than the job of a custodian in charge of the facility because the coach has a direct impact on the clients and their welfare.

Interaction

Turner and Lawrence (1965) stipulated two levels of interaction in a job: required and optional. Required interaction is the degree of interaction that is prescribed to facilitate more efficient operation. This attribute also has been called dealing with others and interdependence. Consider the number and type of people with whom an event manager necessarily has to interact in staging a football game at a large university. The event manager has to interact with the city police, university security officials, the media, the athletic director and other superiors, and the personnel of the event department. For another example, coaches and assistant coaches or exercise physiologists and exercise leaders have to interact with each other in assisting their clients (i.e., athletes and cardiac patients, respectively). Optional interaction refers to interaction that takes place at the discretion of the worker but that is not required of the job. For example, an accounting clerk in the athletic department does not have to interact with others in performing his or her job. However, the clerk may still have the opportunity to interact with other employees and form friendships at his or her discretion. Similarly, the locker-room attendant has the opportunity to discuss the weather or gardening with the "jogging" professors.

Strategic Position

Strategic position refers to the importance of a specific job in terms of the accomplishment of the total group (Turner and Lawrence 1965). The total group's performance may rely heavily on the performance of specific positions. For example, the performance of the pitcher is more crucial to the baseball team's success than the performance of any other position on the team. The quarterback in football and the goalkeeper in hockey are other examples of strategic positions. In the organizational context, the strategic positions are frequently the administrative positions. However, some jobs are at the center of activities, so they gain some strategic importance. For example, the secretary of the general manager of a professional sport team occupies a strategic position to the extent that he or she is a conduit to much of the confidential information and a buffer between the manager and the coaches, athletes, and media.

Risk of Injury

Some jobs, such as those of electricians, welders, and construction workers, carry a risk of injury. In athletics, contact sports, such as football, hockey, and boxing, possess a greater risk of injury than other sports. Even in other physical activities, the danger of some form of injury is always present. For example, the aerobics instructors and their clients are susceptible to injuries due to the nature of their activities. Therefore, sport managers are burdened with additional concerns about the safety of their employees and clients. To minimize the risk of injuries in their operations, sport managers must keep pace with the vast advances being made in securing the safety and health of workers and clients. These concerns stem not only from the humanistic perspective (i.e., the concern is with the employees and clients) but also from the legal perspective (i.e., the concern is with the organization and manager).

In a Nutshell

Jobs can be differentiated on the basis of specific attributes associated with them. The more significant attributes are variety, variability, autonomy, task identity, job feedback, task significance, interaction, strategic position, and risk of injury. In analyzing jobs, managers first must consider these attributes in addition to other job factors.

Motivational Properties of Tasks

From the practical standpoint, the analyses of tasks and their attributes should lead to

- better description of the jobs,
- more effective recruitment of personnel with requisite ability to perform a given job,
- better coordination of the jobs, and
- better employee motivation on the job.

Chapter 9 covers the topics of job description and recruitment. At this point, I explore the process by which the task itself affects employee motivation (i.e., the **motivational properties** of the task) and how the differences among tasks warrant different forms of mechanisms of coordination.

Among the studies of the effects of jobs on employee attitudes, satisfaction, and productivity, the work of Hackman and his associates (Hackman and Lawler 1971, Hackman and Oldham 1976, Hackman and Oldham 1980) is the most comprehensive and useful for our purposes. Figure 8.1 illustrates their job characteristics model of motivation.

According to the model, certain job characteristics enhance the psychological states of the workers: experienced meaningfulness of the work, experienced responsibility, and knowledge of results. These **psychological states**, in fact, represent the intrinsic rewards of performing the job and, therefore, are instrumental to enhanced internal motivation, job satisfaction, work effectiveness, and personal growth satisfaction. As shown in figure 8.1, a major supposition in Hackman and Oldham's theory is that designing jobs to include the significant characteristics of skill variety, task identity, task significance, task autonomy, and job feedback, which were described earlier, can cultivate these psychological states. The authors considered these characteristics as the core characteristics of a job.

Experienced Meaningfulness and Task Attributes

Experienced meaningfulness of the work enhances motivation, performance, and satisfaction. That is, "the person must *experience the work as meaningful*, as something that 'counts' in one's system of values" (Hackman and Oldham 1980, 73).

According to the model, the attributes of skill variety, task identity, and task significance enhance the meaningfulness of the job as the worker experiences it. However, note some reservations in these general relationships. If skill variety is to be related

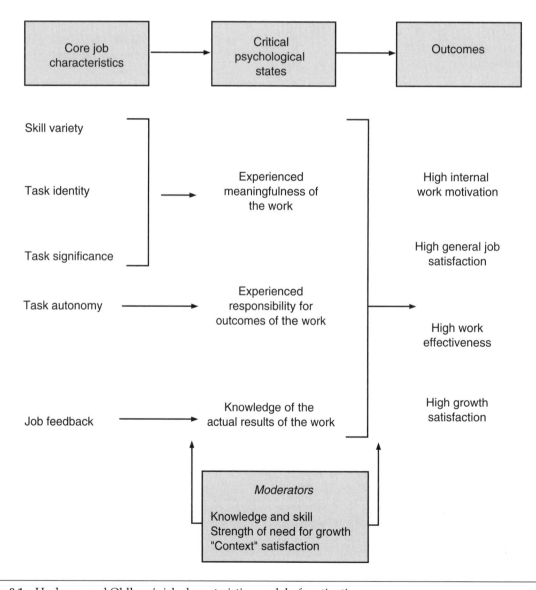

Figure 8.1 Hackman and Oldham's job characteristics model of motivation.

J.R. Hackman/G.R. Oldham, *Work redesign,* (figure 4.6—page 90). © 1980 by Addison-Wesley Publishing Co., Inc. Reprinted by permission of Addison Wesley Longman.

to meaningfulness of the job, such variety must use the member's skills and talents and develop them further.

Regarding task significance, Chelladurai (1985) noted the distinction between the significance that an employee personally experiences and the significance that other external agents attach to that job. For example, a fitness instructor may perceive his or her job to be significant insofar as it contributes to the fitness and health of the clients. However, the lay public, and perhaps even the owners and managers of the club, might believe that the instructor is simply "bouncing around." If external agents attach low significance to the domain, the fitness instructor may not be able to maintain for long the personal conviction that the job is significant. This same issue arises when the jobs of a physical education teacher and a coach are compared. While individuals may perceive significance in either or both of the jobs, the administrators, media, and community are likely to distort the relative significance of the two jobs. That is, the coaching job is likely to be treated as more significant than the teaching job (Chelladurai and Kuga 1996).

Finally, while each of the three characteristics (skill variety, task identity, and task significance) contributes to the experienced meaningfulness of the task, they need not all be present for a job to be meaningful.

> For instance, welders working on a large bridge could find their job very meaningful because it contributed to the safety of the bridge, and, consequently, to the safety of the public. Nonetheless, the job would rank very low in terms of skill variety and/or task identity. Similarly, an individual who welds a wrought iron fence might find the task meaningful because all of the work, when finished, would represent a personal accomplishment. (Chelladurai 1985, 121)

For another example from the field of sport management, consider the task of individuals who carry an injured athlete off the field. The task itself is devoid of any variety or variability. However, it is highly significant from the perspective of those carrying out the task because their primary concern is the safety and welfare of the athlete.

Experienced Responsibility and Job Autonomy

The perception of personal responsibility also enhances internal work motivation when the individual feels largely responsible for the successful completion of a task. To the extent that personal responsibility is reduced, the internal motivation is likely to be affected negatively.

Autonomy is the only task attribute directly related to experienced responsibility. For an individual to feel personally responsible and accountable in a job situation, the person must be allowed considerable freedom to decide on the processes of carrying out the assigned job. To the extent that rules and regulations govern the person's activities, the person would not feel that he or she is personally responsible for the job. As noted earlier, coaching a sports team carries considerable autonomy. Therefore, an individual may feel more responsible for the outcome of his or her coaching. In a similar fashion, a person who has been given complete charge of a sponsorship drive may feel more responsible for the outcomes of such a drive.

In Their View

In illustrating the significance of all three psychological states, Hackman and Oldham (1980) cited the example of golfing:

> Knowledge of results is direct and immediate; the player hits the ball and sees at once where it goes. . . . Experienced personal responsibility for the outcomes also is clear and high, despite the tendency of the golfers sometimes to claim that the slice was due to someone whispering behind the tee. . . . Experienced meaningfulness also is high, despite the fact that the task itself is mostly devoid of cosmic significance. . . . So, in golf, the three psychological states are present, and internal motivation among regular golfers is usually quite high. Indeed, golfers exhibit an intensity of behavior that is rarely seen in the workplace; getting up before dawn to be first on the tee, feeling jubilation or despair all day depending on how well the morning round was played, sometimes even destroying the tools and equipment—not out of boredom or frustration with the work (as is sometimes seen in the industrial setting) but rather from anger at oneself for not playing better. (pp. 74-75)

Knowledge of Results and Job Feedback

Knowledge of results is fundamental to the realization of how well the job has been accomplished and to subsequent feelings of satisfaction or dissatisfaction. Further, knowledge of results serves to modify one's efforts to match the requirements of the job. This knowledge also may help the individual shape his or her performance aspirations to match the job requirements. As noted earlier, job feedback must be distinguished from the feedback that other people, such as a supervisor, provide. Although both feedback from the job and from others are motivational, the Hackman and Oldham model emphasizes the feedback mechanisms inherent in the job itself.

In summary, the job characteristics of skill variety, task identity, and task significance enhance the meaningfulness of the job. The autonomy to decide the manner in which effort is expended enhances the perception of responsibility for the outcomes of the work. The feedback from the job provides knowledge of the results of the work activities. While these attributes individually affect motivation, the joint effects are more complex. According to Hackman and Oldham (1980), the joint effects are the motivating potential of a job. They even advanced the following formula to assess the motivating potential score for a job.

$$MPS = \frac{\frac{Skill}{Variety} + \frac{Task}{Identity} + \frac{Task}{Significance}}{3} \times Autonomy \times Feedback$$

As noted earlier, higher levels of the other two attributes can offset a task's deficiency in one of the attributes of skill variety, task identity, or task significance. Averaging the effects of those three attributes in the formula indicates that effect. In contrast, the effects of autonomy or feedback are multiplicative in nature, meaning that the lower the score on either or both of those attributes, the lower the total motivating potential score.

Outcomes

The outcomes outlined in Hackman and Oldham's model are

- internal work motivation,
- general job satisfaction,
- work effectiveness, and
- growth satisfaction.

Two of these outcomes are critical to the organization, and the other two are critical to the individual. Work effectiveness, which, in fact, is a function of high internal work motivation, is an outcome that is necessary for the survival and growth of the organization. However, the individual also needs to be satisfied with the work and the context in which it takes place. These feelings and attitudes toward the job generally are labeled as job satisfaction. Chapter 14 covers this concept in greater detail. In addition to being satisfied with the job, the worker

In a Nutshell

Hackman and Oldham (1980) believed that jobs may be motivational by themselves by elevating the psychological states of experienced meaningfulness, experienced responsibility, and knowledge of results. Job attributes of skill variety, task identity, and task significance enhance workers' perceptions of meaningfulness of their jobs, job autonomy enhances their sense of responsibility for their job, and job feedback enhances their knowledge of results. These psychological states in turn contribute to increased motivation, job satisfaction, personal growth, and productivity.

Bear in mind that Hackman and Oldham's model links task attributes to the motivational aspects of a job. However, such motivational impact depends on how the worker perceives the task. Therefore, a worker's perception of the job attributes is more critical than the actual properties of that task. Two individuals performing the same task may perceive different levels of attributes in the job, and, thus, the job may differentially motivate them. For instance, one aerobics instructor may perceive his or her job to be autonomous enough, to have considerable variety, and to be helping his or her clients get fit. Another aerobics instructor in the same organization may perceive his or her job to be physically tiring and to be repetitious because he or she performs the same routines class after class to similar groups of clients. As another example, Chelladurai, Kuga, and O'Bryant (in press) found that male students in physical education degree programs who had some experience as volunteer coaches perceived greater variety in the coaching job than female students perceived. Therefore, sport managers must be attuned not only to the objective characteristics of the jobs but also to workers' perceptions of those jobs. Managers also need to clarify the job characteristics to their employees to correct any misperceptions about them.

must also feel that the experiences in the workplace contribute to his or her personal growth.

Implementing Task Attributes

Hackman et al. (1975) advanced five implementing concepts for enriching jobs. Figure 8.2 shows the linkage between their implementing concepts and the five task attributes of Hackman and Oldham's model (see figure 8.1).

Combining Tasks

In implementing this concept, several pieces of fractionated work are put together to form new and larger modules of work. Instead of making several employees put together a product, such as on an assembly line, each one of the employees may assemble the whole unit. Combining tasks in this manner enhances both task identity and skill variety. For instance, a clerk in a city recreation department may be assigned the task of receiving applications for a youth sports program organized by the department. Another clerk may be assigned the task of scrutinizing these applications and placing them in appropriate categories (e.g., categories by age or locality). A third clerk may be asked to contact the applicants to let them know the status of their applications. With a view to combine these tasks, the supervisor may ask each individual clerk to

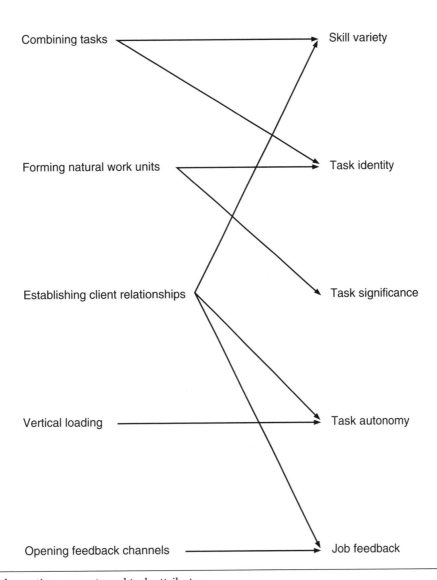

Figure 8.2 Implementing concepts and task attributes.

handle all three phases of the process with reference to a restricted number of applications.

Forming Natural Work Units

The concept of forming natural work units emphasizes that the work unit offers a sense of ownership of the job, or "a sense of continuing responsibility for an identifiable body of work" (Hackman et al. 1975, 63). Hackman et al. (1975) contrasted several typists typing bits and pieces of many papers with each typist typing a whole paper or all of the papers for a department. They reported that this notion of a natural work unit enhanced task identity and task significance.

Establishing Client Relationships

Hackman et al. (1975) argued that by allowing the workers direct contact with their clients, managers can simultaneously gain three advantages. First, the clients' reactions enhance the feedback inherent in the job. Second, skill variety increases because the employee has to use interpersonal skills including communication. Third, the worker enjoys greater autonomy because he or she has to manage the interactions with the client without any directions from external sources.

Vertical Loading

Like Herzberg (1968), Hackman et al. (1975) suggested that the employee must be allowed not only to do the job but also to control it. Control refers to the extent of a worker's discretion in performing the task (e.g., choice of methods, scheduling of activities, solving problems, and financial control). The suggestion that an individual must be given more control over his or her own job is a major component of job enrichment (see table 8.1). Such assignment of control over the job to the worker (i.e., vertical loading) contributes to the worker's feeling of increased autonomy.

Opening Feedback Channels

In the view of Hackman et al. (1975), management must remove the obstacles that block feedback to the worker. They argue that having another individual or unit at another place and time perform quality control denies the worker the immediate feedback. If management involves the worker in quality check, then the worker gets immediate feedback. The results of any performance evaluation should be immediately passed on to the individual instead of being filed or sent upward to higher-level management. Such efforts increase the task feedback and let the worker know immediately how well he or she has performed the work. If he or she has made any errors, then having them corrected immediately is better than continuing to have the same mistakes made.

In a Nutshell

Managers can increase the motivating potential of a job by combining various jobs to create natural work units, allowing employees direct contact with clients, increasing workers' control over their jobs, and opening feedback channels. Whether these actions will have the desired effects depends on workers' knowledge and skill level, their need to grow, and their satisfaction with other contextual factors, such as salary and safety.

Task Attributes and Individual Differences

Perhaps the most significant contribution of Hackman and Oldham (1976, 1980) lies in their specification that the relationship between the job characteristics on the one hand and internal motivation, satisfaction, and performance on the other depends on an individual's knowledge and skills, growth need strength (i.e., strong needs for personal accomplishments, learning, and growth), and satisfaction with other organizational factors. A job that has a high level of motivating potential may be frustrating to an individual if that person does not possess the required knowledge and skill (i.e., competency) to perform the task. Similarly, the task may lose its motivating potential if the person has a low level of growth need strength. The final individual difference factor to which Hackman and Oldham refered is an individual's satisfaction with other organizational factors, such as pay and job security. The great dissatisfaction with factors surrounding the job may overwhelm the potential of the job to motivate.

In overview, Hackman and Oldham's job characteristics model extends the content theories referred to in chapter 7 by highlighting the nature of the job and the motivating potential of various characteristics of the job. In addition, it modifies the content theories by emphasizing the differences among individuals that affect their reactions to the job and its characteristics.

In Their View

In an attempt to explain the tendency of school physical education teachers to be more inclined toward coaching than teaching, Chelladurai and Kuga (1996) analyzed the tasks of teaching physical education and coaching a sport. In addition to Hackman and Oldham's (1980) five task attributes, they included five other attributes that set apart coaching from teaching (i.e., size of the group, homogeneity in members' ability, group's acceptance of goals, duration of the contact, and member motivation to participate). They suggested that the differences in these task attributes may make coaching more amenable to the leader (i.e., coach) exercising influence and, therefore, more motivational than teaching.

While the job characteristics model is intuitively appealing and conceptually elegant, the research results have not yielded consistent support for the model (Saal and Knight 1995). In some studies the distinctions made between the five job attributes do not appear. In some others, the relationships among the job attributes, individual differences, and outcome measures are not in accordance with the specifications of the model. In the context of sport management, Cleave (1993) applied the model to the administrators of university athletics, recreational sports, and physical education programs in Canada and Illinois. She found that they supported most of Hackman and Oldham's (1980) propositions. The notable exception was that the job characteristic of autonomy had a direct effect on outcome variables independent of the psychological states.

Theoretical models developed in other fields can provide useful frameworks for understanding phenomena in sport management. However, researchers and others should not simply assume that such models can be transferred directly. To enhance the understanding of the field of sport management, not only must research be based on theoretical models, but these models must be tested within the field. (Cleave 1993, 241)

However, researchers generally agree that this issue is more related to the problems in measurement and analyses than to the model itself (Saal and Knight 1995). Despite some of the negative results, the model can serve as a basis for redesigning the jobs in sport organizations to match the needs and desires and the skills of the paid and volunteer workers.

Remember that a job is not limited to the five attributes included in Hackman and Oldham's (1980) model. For instance, the required and optional interactions, the risk of injury referred to earlier, and the psychomotor aspects of the job could affect the worker. For instance, Stone and Gueutal (1985) identified three dimensions of jobs that their subjects perceived. The first factor is complexity, which incorporates all five task attributes that Hackman and Oldham (1980) outlined. The second factor is named serves the public, and it refers to interacting with and serving people outside of the organization. The third factor is physical demand, which refers to the strength and physical activity required to perform the task and the hazards to health.

As noted in chapters 1 and 2, a high level of the sense of service to others characterizes the professional and volunteer workers in sport management;

Several of the jobs in sport and recreation do possess the attributes that are motivational. For example, coaches of youth and adult sports, fitness specialists, marketing directors of intercollegiate athletics and recreational sports, and such other people do have the attributes of skill variety, task identity, task significance, autonomy, and job feedback (i.e., Hackman and Oldham's attributes with motivational impact). Stone and Gueutal's (1985) dimension of serving the public is also a hallmark of several of the jobs in sport and recreation. Finally, Stone and Gueutal's (1985) dimension of physical demand is characteristic of many of the jobs in the context of sport management. Note that sport and recreation managers do have some discretion in changing the nature of some of the jobs under their jurisdiction. However, enriching the jobs without reference to the abilities, personality, and values of concerned employees or volunteers may result in dysfunction. That is, if an employee or a volunteer does not have the ability or the personality to manage an enriched job, then such a job will not be motivational to that individual. Hence, the manager must take great care in redesigning jobs. One useful approach in this regard is to involve the employees and volunteers themselves in redesigning their jobs.

therefore, they experience a great sense of meaningfulness in their jobs. Thus, Stone and Gueutal's (1985) dimension of serving the public is meaningful to the context of sport management. In addition, many of the workers in sport management, particularly in participant services, are engaged in physically demanding jobs, such as coaching and fitness instruction. As is evident, Stone and Gueutal's (1985) dimension of physical demand also is relevant to sport management. In the final analysis, both Hackman and Oldham's (1980) job characteristics model and Stone and Gueutal's (1985) three-dimensional scheme are applicable to the context of sport and recreation management.

Other Approaches to Job Design

Our discussion of job design has focused largely on the psychological impact of task attributes on employee motivation. However, the job design also can be approached from other perspectives, such as safety, stress, and health. As noted earlier, although they are not linked directly to worker motivation, attributes, such as risk of injury and physical demand, also are critical. Campion and Thayer (1985) summarized these differing perspectives on job design. Reviewing the perspectives of different disciplines, they isolated four approaches to designing

jobs: motivational, mechanistic, biological, and perceptual or motor. These four dimensions and the expected job outcomes of each approach are outlined in table 8.2.

The works of Herzberg (1968) and Hackman and Oldham (1980) exemplify the motivational approach. This approach largely is based on the discipline of organizational psychology and emphasizes job enlargement and job enrichment. The mechanistic approach is drawn from the classic scientific management and time-motion studies and from industrial engineering. This approach advocates work simplification, specialization, and routinization. The biological approach is based on work physiology, biomechanics, and anthropometry and focuses on the physical well-being of the worker in executing the assigned tasks. Finally, the perceptual, or motor, approach aims at creating "person-machine fit by attending to people's perceptual/motor capabilities and limitations, thus preventing errors and accidents and reducing boredom and task aversion" (Campion and Thayer 1985, 33). The principles of this approach are drawn from experimental psychology.

In addition to outlining the four task-design approaches, Campion and Thayer (1985) also isolated four sets of outcomes from among many that organizations seek. They labeled these four outcome groups satisfaction, efficiency, comfort, and reliability (see table 8.2). Satisfaction refers to workers'

Table 8.2 Campion and Thayer's Task-Design Approaches and Outcome Clusters

Job design approaches	Job outcomes
Motivational	**Satisfaction**
Job enlargement	Intrinsic work motivation
Job enrichment	Job involvement
Vertical loading	Job satisfaction
Mechanistic	**Efficiency**
Work simplification	Resource use
Work routinization	Less idle time
Work specialization	Less training time
Biological	**Comfort**
Physical well-being	Comfort
Seating and tool design	Physical fatigue
Noise, climate, and stress	Health problems
Perceptual	**Reliability**
Information processing	Safety
Memory requirements	System reliability
Visual-auditory links	Accident rates

internal work motivation, involvement in their jobs, and satisfaction with their job. Maximal use of people and machines (i.e., less idle time) and less training time for the job indicate efficiency. Comfort is concerned with physical well-being and includes lack of physical fatigue, back problems, and muscle strain. Reliability refers to the safety of the worker in terms of the reliability of the worker-machine system, which is measured by things such as accident rates and injuries. One of the serious concerns within sport management is ensuring the safety of the workers and clients. This concern is particularly true when engaging in risky activities and employing machines and tools to deliver the services. For example, all of the weight-training equipment used in a fitness firm are sources of serious injuries. Therefore, the manager should attempt to keep the equipment in good repair and to ensure the proper use of them.

Campion and Thayer noted the logical correspondence between these four sets of outcomes and the four task-design approaches outlined earlier. Their research confirmed that each approach was more highly related to one of the four sets of outcomes than to the other three outcomes. These relationships are shown in table 8.2.

Task Dependence, Coordination, and Variability

As noted earlier, the nature of the job has an effect not only on worker motivation but also on other managerial aspects. This section addresses the concept of **task dependence** and the methods of coordination.

In a Nutshell

Managers can orient job design efforts toward worker motivation and satisfaction (e.g., job enlargement and job enrichment), efficiency (e.g., job simplification and specialization), worker comfort (e.g., seating, tool design, and noise and climate control), and reliability of the worker-machine system (e.g., assessing information processing and memory requirements).

If an organization is a collection of members who contribute their efforts toward a common goal, then a fundamental task of that organization (or any group) is to coordinate the activities of its members. The multiple and different contributions of the members may all be wasted if no mechanism is available to ensure that these contributions are all geared toward the attainment of organizational objectives.

The relative ease or difficulty with which such coordination can be secured depends on the nature of the tasks, particularly on the extent to which they depend on each other (i.e., the extent to which there is required interaction among the tasks) and on the extent to which the tasks are variable (i.e., the extent to which the environment keeps changing and, therefore, the task goals and procedures need adjusting).

In discussing the relationship between cohesion and performance in sport, Carron and Chelladurai (1981) proposed a classification of sport tasks based on the concept of required interaction. They based their scheme on the frameworks that other

Campion and Thayer's (1985) description of four approaches to job design should not be viewed as some theoretical exercise. Each one of the approaches is relevant to sport and recreation management. The motivational approach leads to the suggestion of enriching the jobs in sport and recreation (e.g., those of clerks and receptionists). It was noted earlier that such job enrichment should be considered in conjunction with member potential and preferences. The mechanistic approach to job simplification and routinization may indeed prove to be beneficial to the extent the resources are better used and the work processes are made more efficient (e.g., ticketing operations in an athletic department). In fact, some sport volunteers may prefer such simplified assignments because of their involvement with highly enriched jobs elsewhere. The importance of attending to the biological and perceptual/motor approaches to job design is illustrated by the fact that some of the recommendations emanating from those approaches are mandated by law. For instance, the temperatures in the workplace cannot vary beyond specified limits. The seating and lighting arrangements may also be regulated. Similarly, the concerns with appropriate shoes, helmets, and other protective equipment are borne partly out of the need for performance improvements and partly out of the need for the safety of athletes. In either case, they fall under the biological and perceptual/motor approaches.

researchers proposed for organizational tasks (Thompson 1967, Turner and Lawrence 1965) and that classify sport tasks (Ball 1973, Poulton 1957). The basic proposition of their model is that tasks vary in the degree of interdependence required of them and that the type of coordination also varies with the degree of interdependence. Although Carron and Chelladurai (1981) proposed their model in the context of sport teams, they largely drew from the fields of management and organizational behavior. Therefore, the scheme is readily applicable to organizational tasks. The following section explains it in greater detail.

Types of Interdependence

Carron and Chelladurai (1981) classified tasks as independent, coactively dependent, proactively-reactively dependent, and interactively dependent.

Independent Tasks

An independent task is a task that one person can carry out successfully without interacting with people performing other tasks. Carron and Chelladurai (1981) cited the tasks of archery, bowling, individual events in track and field, and swimming as examples. In these examples, individual performance can be assessed and rewarded. If two people volunteer to collect donations for the junior soccer league in their respective neighborhoods, their tasks are independent of each other. They need not interact with each other in any way. They go door-to-door in their own neighborhoods, and the league manager can easily assess their performance (e.g., how much did each collect?) and reward them (e.g., a merit badge). The coaches of various youth teams in city leagues are involved in largely independent tasks.

Coactively Dependent Tasks

Coactively dependent tasks are tasks that depend on a common, but external, source for initiation or control of their activities. Usually in these tasks, the members perform more or less similar tasks, and their collective contributions determine the group's success, such as in the case of a rowing-eights team or a tug-of-war team. In the organizational context, the tennis, swimming, and fitness units of a city recreation department depend on each other only to the extent that they receive their directions and funding from a common source. Their reliance on a common, but limited, budget best illustrates the

nature of their interdependence. That is, if one unit gets more, another unit gets less. The coaches of a university athletic department are involved in coactively dependent jobs because their jobs are sufficiently independent of other coaching jobs but all jobs depend on a common source for the scheduling of facilities and the distribution of needed resources.

In Their View

Before 1800, very few people had a job. People worked hard raising food or making things at home. They had no regular hours, no job descriptions, no bosses, and no employee benefits. Instead, they put in long hours on shifting clusters of tasks, in a variety of locations, on a schedule set by the sun and the weather and the needs of the day. It was the Industrial Revolution and the creation of large manufacturing companies that brought about the concept of what we have come to think as *jobs*. But the conditions that created "the job" are disappearing. Customized production is pushing out mass production; most workers now handle information, not physical products; and competitive conditions are demanding rapid responses to changing markets. In twenty-five years or so it's possible that very few people will have jobs as we have come to know them. (Robbins 1997b, 216)

While this perspective may hold in several industries, jobs in service industries (particularly those involving human services) are likely to mirror the existing ones for a long time to come.

Reactively-Proactively Dependent Tasks

Reactively-proactively dependent tasks are tasks that one member initiates and another member completes. The first person depends on the second person to complete the task, and the second person depends on the first to begin the task. All assembly line tasks fall under this category. In a four-person track relay team, the first person is proactively dependent on the other three to complete the task, and the last person is reactively dependent on the previous three for initiating the task. Both the second and third runners are reactively dependent on the previous runner and proactively dependent on the next runner.

Reactive-proactive dependence exists wherever a series of tasks are arranged sequentially. For example, the accounting clerk in a recreation department is reactively dependent on employees in other units to submit statements of receipts and expenses before he or she can prepare a master document. By the same token, the director of the department is proactively dependent on the subordinates to carry out his or her policies and directions.

Interactively Dependent Tasks

Interactively dependent tasks require the greatest amount of interaction. In these tasks, members performing various assignments need to interact with each other effectively in order to complete the group task. These tasks tend to be variable; that is, they are open to environmental influences. Good examples from sport include basketball and hockey in which the players are interactively dependent on each other in order to achieve personal and group goals. Individuals involved in organizing a major sport event (e.g., event managers, facility managers, security officials, media, and public relations personnel) are all interactively dependent on each other to carry out their respective assignments and, in turn, the total work.

Methods of Coordination

Managers can achieve **coordination** among tasks in a number of ways. However, some of the ways are more efficient and less costly given a certain type of interdependence among tasks. Carron and Chelladurai (1981) applied Thompson's (1967) three methods of coordination (i.e., standardization, planning, and mutual adjustment) to the four types of interdependent tasks outlined earlier.

- **Standardization** is the process of specifying a set of rules, regulations, and procedures for each task. In essence, such standardization tends to constrain and direct individual actions. As long as the different sets of rules, regulations, and procedures relating to various tasks are consistent with each other, the manager can expect the tasks to be coordinated properly. However, as Thompson (1967) noted, standardization is appropriate only with tasks performed in a stable environment.

- **Planning** is the process of establishing goals for individuals and scheduling their activities. Thus, the manager gives each member of the group a goal and expects him or her to achieve it within a specified time.

- In some tasks, coordination can be achieved only by the **mutual adjustments** among members involved in the tasks. Where the tasks tend to be highly variable and complex, previously established rules, procedures, and plans may be irrelevant. Under those circumstances, members need to interact with each other and make necessary adjustments in their goals and activities in order to attain the group's goals.

The final segment of Carron and Chelladurai's (1981) model is matching the method of coordination with the type of interdependence inherent in the tasks. Figure 8.3 illustrates the appropriateness of each form of coordination to different types of interdependencies. The solid lines in figure 8.3 indicate the primary mode of coordinating jobs of a particular dependence type. The dotted lines suggest that the mode of coordination in question also is applicable as a supplemental mode of coordination.

Although all forms of coordination may be pertinent to interactively dependent tasks, the predomi-

While some jobs are inherently interdependent on each other, management itself can make some others more or less interdependent. Consider, for example, several aerobics instructors that a university department of recreational sports employs. The department may permit the instructors to make decisions jointly about their own schedules, the specific groups of clients that they manage, and the locations of their classes. In this scenario, the department has created interdependence among the aerobics instructors. Mutual adjustment among the instructors is relevant as a coordinative mechanism.

On the other hand, the supervisor may schedule the aerobics classes in terms of time, location, and client groups. Further, the supervisor also assigns the specific instructors to specific classes. In this case, the interdependence among the aerobics instructors is minimized, and the need for mutual adjustment as a means of coordination is reduced. The choice of one approach over another is a function of both the managerial style and the members' preferences.

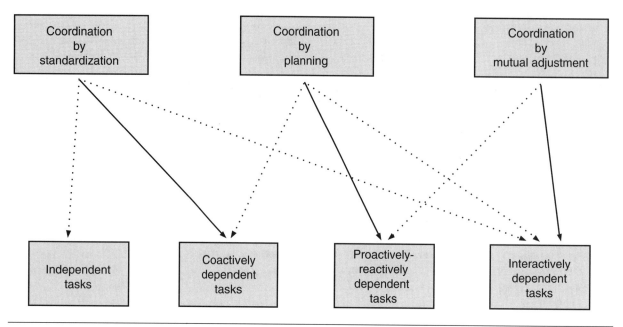

Figure 8.3 Types of task dependence and coordination.

Reprinted by permission of Sage Publications Ltd. from A.V. Carron and P. Chelladurai, 1981, "Cohesiveness as a factor in sport performance," *International Review of Sport Sociology* 2 (16): 21-41. Copyright 1981 by Sage Publications Ltd.

nant form of coordination is by mutual adjustment. As noted earlier, to the extent that the environmental demands and constraints keep changing, previous standardization and planning will become obsolete, and it is mutual adjustment by members that will prove to be the most dominant and appropriate mode of coordination.

Similarly, coordination by planning is the most dominant and appropriate coordinative mechanism for proactively-reactively dependent tasks; coordination by standardization, for coactively dependent tasks. In the case of independent tasks, the need for coordination is minimal, and the necessary coordination is achieved by standardization.

As noted, the cost of coordination (in terms of effort, time, money, and efficiency) increases as the form of coordination moves from standardization through planning to mutual adjustment. In addition, the actual control by top management diminishes with the movement away from standardization and to mutual adjustment. Therefore, it is not surprising that theorists and practicing managers have advocated simplification, fragmentation, and routinization of jobs so that they can be coordinated and controlled through standardization or planning.

Task Variability

Just as the extent of interdependence affects the type of coordinative mechanism employed, task vari-

In a Nutshell

Coordinating the efforts of various workers becomes progressively difficult with increasing interdependence among them. The major mechanisms of coordination in order of increasing cost and difficulty are standardization in which management sets extensive rules and regulations to govern the work activities; planning in which management sets the goals, work schedules, and timelines; and mutual adjustment in which management expects the workers to adjust with each other to manage the varying circumstances affecting their jobs.

ability also affects the extent of standardization and supervision. Recall that task variability refers to the number of exceptional cases encountered in the work that require different methods or procedures for doing the work (Van de Ven and Delbecq 1974). If task requirements are changing constantly, managers will find it more difficult to specify rules and regulations for every contingency that the employee faces. Therefore, managers will find it necessary to allow the members the discretion to communicate with other members both horizontally and vertically as and when necessary and to make appropriate decisions. On the other hand, if the task requirements are stable, standardizing the tasks is

Examples of jobs that managers can coordinate through standardization, planning, and mutual adjustment can be drawn from an athletic department of a university. The locker-room attendants in different locations are involved in independent tasks, but the attendants in one location may be coactively dependent on each other to the extent that their schedules are arranged sequentially. The major form of coordination is standardization whereby management standardizes the tasks for each attendant through specification of the assigned tasks.

As noted in the text, coaches of the athletic department are coactively dependent on the athletic director and his or her assistants for coordinating their activities and for planning in the form of setting goals for each team, budgeting the resources for the teams, and scheduling their practice sessions and games. In addition, the administrators may set specific guidelines individually for each team or collectively for all teams regarding recruiting practices, treatment of athletes, and such other critical operations. The relationships among facility managers, event managers, those who schedule the events, and the coaches themselves best illustrate the proactive-reactive dependence. Facility managers and event managers need to know in advance the schedule of events so that they can prepare for the events. That is, the individuals who schedule the events should plan in advance and notify the others. If a coach wants specific arrangements for a competition, he or she plans those arrangements in advance and informs the facility and event managers. Thus, planning becomes the major mode of coordination in proactively-reactively dependent tasks.

In the case of a marketing department, the tasks of the senior marketing executives can best be coordinated through mutual adjustment among those executives. For instance, the athletic director may set the overall target for sponsorship, and the marketing executives seek sponsors. They need to adjust to each other in seeking different sponsors and accommodating each individual's style of operation. In so far as they are addressing idiosyncratic ways of the would-be sponsors and in so far as there is competition for sponsorship money, the environment is turbulent (i.e., their jobs are variable), and mutual adjustment is the dominant mode of coordination.

more efficient (i.e., specify extensive rules and procedures). Under those circumstances, managers can ensure proper control and coordination of the activities through proper supervision.

Summary

In summary, I presented various approaches to designing jobs, ranging from job simplification to job enrichment. I also presented Hackman and Oldham's (1980) model outlining the motivational properties of jobs. Note that although sport managers must attempt to enhance the motivational aspects of a job under their supervision, they must also be aware of the constraints. First, higher-level management may not permit the sport manager to change the jobs under his or her jurisdiction. Second, the members may not have the ability and skill to carry out enriched jobs. Third, members may be content and satisfied with the current level of enrichment in their jobs and may not desire any more of it. Fourth, effort and time involved in enriching and coordinating jobs constitute a cost . Sport managers must also be concerned with the internal and external elements of jobs that may be detrimental to the comfort, health, and safety of the workers and those surrounding them.

Note also that tasks may vary in the degree of interdependence among them and that they can be categorized as independent, coactively dependent, proactively-reactively dependent, and interactively dependent. Coordination among the jobs is more difficult with increasing interdependence, and the manager must employ different types of coordination, which include, standardization, planning, and mutual adjustment.

Key Terms

job design, job simplification, job rotation, job enlargement, job enrichment, task attributes, task variability, motivational properties, psychological states, task dependence, coordination, standardization, planning, mutual adjustments

Your Perspectives

- In chapter 7, you responded to questions related to your motivation. Now consider the job that you enjoyed very much and focus only on the characteristics of the tasks associated with that job. Describe the attributes of the job that were attractive to you and those attributes that you detested.

- Consider three jobs that offered one of the following: sense of meaningfulness, autonomy in performing the job, and feedback from the job itself. If you had a choice among these three jobs, which one would you choose and why?

- Bearing in mind Hackman and Oldham's (1980) job characteristics model, describe a job in sport management with a high motivating potential and a job with low motivating potential. How does your assessment relate to your own abilities, predispositions, and values?

- Consider the athletic department of a large university. Which of the units within that enterprise can be coordinated through standardization (i.e., extensive rules and regulations), planning (i.e., setting goals, schedules, and time lines), and mutual adjustment (i.e., workers themselves adjust to each other in achieving the goals)?

9 Staffing and Career Considerations

Learning Objectives

After reading this chapter you will be able to

- understand the purpose and focus of job analysis, job description, and job specification;

- explain the process of matching people with jobs through recruiting, hiring, and training;

- discuss the concept of psychological contract in terms of individual contributions and organizational inducements;

- explain what a career means from the perspectives of the individual and the organization;

- gain an insight into career orientation and career anchors; and

- understand the functions, processes, and outcomes of mentoring.

As noted at the beginning of this text, the employees of the organization make the organizational systems work. All the plans and procedures of the organization will be effective only if you have the right people to execute those plans and procedures. This is particularly true in the case of service organizations, which most sport and recreation organizations are. Therefore, sport managers must be concerned with staffing their organizations. As Sullivan (1997) noted, this is not an easy process, and it is different from addressing clients, customers, and other external agents. Sullivan also pointed out that typical managers, particularly in small enterprises, spend more waking hours with their employees than with their own families.

> Building good staff is like making homemade soup. The people you hire are the ingredients you mix in. High quality ingredients guarantee a first rate meal. . . . It is not magical. It takes patience and effort to make it work. The sweat equity invested will reap high dividends. (Sullivan 1997, 2)

Chapter 9 outlines the following significant steps in the staffing process: staffing needs assessment, job analysis, job description, job specification, recruiting, hiring, and training. In addition, the concepts of psychological contract and careers are also discussed.

In Their View

The staffing problem can be brought into focus for the reader if he or she thinks of a football team or a symphony orchestra, since these are relatively small organizations with clearly indentifiable roles. . . . First, there is the problem of attracting the best players. Not all of them want to work for the same organization and, as a result, the pool of individuals applying for work in the organization is likely to be less than ideal. Secondly, there is the problem of selecting the individuals who will develop into the best players. Sometimes, the wrong decisions are made despite a careful analysis of the applicants. In football, for example, players who are not drafted or who are released by teams occasionally end up as stars (such as Johnny Unitas of the Baltimore Colts). Finally, there is the problem of developing the individual players so that when a job opening appears (either because of personnel changes or a new job has been created), someone will be available to fill it. (Nadler, Hackman, and Lawler 1979, 41-42)

Purposes of Staffing

The goals of **staffing** can be viewed from two perspectives—technical and citizenship (Jackson and Schuler 1992). The concern in the technical perspective is to ensure that a person in a job has the right skills to effectively perform that job. Accordingly, the emphasis is placed on hiring the people with the right technical skills and training them further in those skills. In the other perspective, labeled citizenship perspective (Jackson and Schuler [1992] call it the control perspective), the focus is on the predictability and reliability of social interactions to ensure behavior according to organizationally approved norms and values. That is, as Jackson and Schuler (1992) noted, the process of staffing should be geared to ensuring social performance (i.e., citizenship) in addition to job performance (i.e., technical performance).

This view leads to the suggestion that the staffing practices need to encompass the requirements of the job as well as those of the organization (Schneider and Bowen 1992). That is, these practices should be aimed at person-organization fit instead of the traditional person-job fit. Organizations must attempt to attract people with requisite personality and ability to participate and promote the organizational climate for service and, at the same time, to perform effectively the tasks of a particular job. The person-organization fit consists of the fit between one's knowledge, skills, and abilities and the task demands and the fit between overall personality (e.g., needs, interests, and values) and the climate of the organization. In other words, the person must fit both the content and the context of the job. That is, "applicants are hired based upon who they *are*, not just what they can *do*" (Schneider and Bowen 1992, 11).

In a Nutshell

The purposes of staffing procedures are twofold. The first concern is with creating a fit between the individual's skills and the job requirements. This technical aspect of staffing is to ensure that individuals are capable of performing the assigned tasks. The second concern is with matching the individual orientations with organizational goals, values, and culture. This citizenship aspect is to ensure that individuals fit into the culture and climate of the organization.

Focuses of Staffing

The foregoing discussion clearly indicates that the focus of staffing is twofold. First, the job itself is brought under scrutiny to determine the number and types of jobs to be filled. In other words, the focus is on the content of the job. The second focus is on the people to ensure that appropriate members are hired. The concepts of task and its characteristics (discussed in chapter 8) and individual differences in abilities, personality, and values (discussed in chapters 4 through 6) become relevant in creating a match between the task and the individual.

Focus on Jobs

Every job exists only to contribute to the attainment of organizational goals. That is, every job is a piece of the puzzle that makes up the total effort to achieve the expected outcomes. Thus, the manager must ensure the nature of each job and its requirements so that it fits nicely into the total picture. The focus on jobs in staffing consists of

- assessing staffing needs,
- analyzing the job,
- describing the job,
- specifying what is required of the individual for successful performance of the job,
- recruiting prospective applicants, and
- screening and selecting suitable candidates.

Staffing Needs Assessment

The first step, of course, is to determine how many jobs are vacant and need to be filled. This analysis takes into account the immediate necessity to fill a job and the short- and long-range requirements. Factors such as an organizational plan to expand (or contract) or projected retirements in the near future have an influence on the staffing requirements. For instance, the manager of a large fitness club needs to determine how many fitness instructors, facility and equipment personnel, secretaries, and accounting clerks he or she needs. Such an estimation is based on the number and type of current employees, the prospects of some of them leaving (e.g., retiring or moving on to other locations or jobs), and the plans to expand or reduce organizational activities. After deciding on the staffing requirements, the manager next analyzes the job, which leads to job description and job specification.

Job Analysis

As the name implies, **job analysis** is simply studying the job and the various tasks associated with it and collecting information on the operations and responsibilities of the job. Job analysis can be carried out in several ways. First, if the proposed job is a new creation, the manager may have to list all of the operations that he or she perceives to be essential for job performance. This conceptually developed list may have to be modified through subsequent experiences. In addition, the manager possibly may observe and analyze a similar job in other organizations and may generate a list of activities associated with that job.

If such a job is already in place, observing the job being carried out facilitates job analysis. The manager also can collect the necessary information by interviewing the employee carrying out the job or the supervisor of that employee. Another approach is to ask the employee to respond to a job analysis questionnaire. Finally, the manager can ask current employees performing those jobs to keep a daily log

of all of the activities in which they engage and of the time needed for each activity. The purpose of job analysis is to gather the information on the job, the operations, the duties and responsibilities involved in that job, the working conditions, and such other critical elements of a job. Table 9.1 provides a list and description of the major items included in job analysis.

The information gathered from a job analysis is used to generate a job description. In addition, job analysis also provides information on what kinds of abilities and talents, education, and experience is required to perform the job adequately. This latter information results in the job specification.

In Their View

Saal and Knight (1995) classified the approaches to job analysis into job-oriented, worker-oriented, and trait-oriented. Job-oriented approach focuses on the job outcomes or results and the factors that facilitate those outcomes. In essence, this approach establishes the reasons why a job exists. For example, the tasks a locker-room attendant (or a receptionist, or a tennis instructor) is expected to accomplish (i.e., the outcome), and how these accomplishments contribute to the overall objective would be the concern in this approach. The worker-oriented approach centers on the behaviors and activities of the workers in performing their jobs. For example, what behaviors and activities of the locker-room attendant would lead to the outcomes expected of that job is the issue. It would be expected that the attendant would be organized and methodical in issuing, retrieving, and storing the equipment (balls, rackets, towels, etc.). The attendant also needs to be courteous and pleasant toward the clients. Finally, the trait-oriented approach emphasizes the traits that contribute to job performance. For instance, the need for the attendant to be pleasant and courteous may be tied to the personality trait of service orientation (discussed in Chapter 5). Saal and Knight (1995) note that the trait-oriented approach, which is the least known approach, calls for more complex procedures because a single trait may contribute to performance in more than one activity. By the same token, more than one trait can facilitate performance in an activity. More importantly, those authors alert us to the "unpleasant possibility that an emphasis on human characteristics can degenerate into destructive and illegal group stereotypes based on race, sex, age, and other demographic variables" (p. 62).

Table 9.1 Critical Elements in a Job Analysis

Element	Description
Job identification	Including job title, its department or division, and titles of supervisors
Job summary	Brief description of the job including its purpose and activities
Duties	Primary duties classified as technical, clerical, or professional; major duties and the proportions of time involved; and other duties and their time involvement
Responsibility	Extent of responsibility over use and care of equipment and tools, personal safety and safety of others, and the performance of others
Human characteristics	Extent to which certain human characteristics are required including physical attributes such as vision, eye-hand coordination, strength, height, initiative, ingenuity, judgement, writing, education, experience, and training
Working conditions	Description of the physical conditions (usual or unusual) under which the job is to be carried out and any unusual psychological demands
Health and safety features	Description of health or safety hazards including special training or equipment needed
Performance standards	Description of how performance on the job is measured and the identifiable factors that contribute to successful performance

Job Description

A **job description** is a "written statement that explains the duties, the working conditions, and other aspects of a specified job" (Werther et al. 1985, 117). More specifically, a job description outlines the specific duties, activities, and responsibilities involved in that job. Typically, a job description includes information on the job title, the immediate supervisor of the job, the number and type of jobs that the incumbent supervises, and specific activities of the job. Figure 9.1 provides an example of a job description for an assistant coordinator in the Department of Campus Recreation at The University of Western Ontario.

When developing a job description, the manager must ensure that it is concise and clear. The job description must define broadly the scope of the job in terms of the nature of the work and its relationships with other jobs. At the same time, it also should be specific to indicate the complexity of the job, the skill required to manage it, and the worker's responsibility for each phase of the work.

Focus on People

After assessing the need for specific jobs and analyzing and describing each of those jobs, the focus shifts to the type of person who would best fit the job. This focus is reflected in what is termed **job specification**.

While a job description outlines what needs to be done within a job, job specification outlines the human qualities needed to carry out the job. Werther et al. (1985) noted the distinction between job description and job specification as follows:

A *job description* defines what the job does; it is a profile of the job. A *job specification* describes what the job demands of employees who do it and the human factors that are required. It is a profile of human characteristics needed by the job. These requirements include experience, training, education, physical demands, and mental demands. (p. 121)

For instance, a job specification for an aerobics instructor should include the psychological characteristics, such as a pleasant disposition and the ability to motivate the participants, as well as the physical characteristics, such as agility and stamina. A job specification for a marketing director may not mention anything about physical characteristics but may emphasize the conceptual and human skills including the ability to persuade prospective donors and customers.

The University of Western Ontario
Faculty of Kinesiology
Department of Campus Recreation

Position	Assistant Coordinator
Supervisor	Marketing and Membership Coordinator
Purpose	Contributes to the mission of the program by administering and supervising the personnel and programming portions of the Membership Services Unit. Personnel includes recruitment, selection, orientation, training, performance evaluation, and record keeping. Programming includes scheduling, facility management, inventory management, record keeping, and program evaluation.
Supervises	Membership Services Staff—25 Number of participants—approximately 2,600
Specific responsibilities	Personnel Recruitment (planning and administering an advertising campaign), selection (screening applications and qualifications, interviewing, and hiring), orientation (planning and conducting appropriate orientation and social activities), training of personnel (planning and conducting appropriate training activities), and evaluating their performance (providing employees with feedback on performance, support, and supervision). Programming Scheduling and facility management (use of locker rooms, racquet courts, gymnasium, and campus recreation areas), inventory management (determining equipment and supply needs, securing high-quality equipment and supplies, and maintaining them in good repair), record keeping (ensuring all information is updated weekly, and producing reports as needed), program evaluation (collecting information from customers and staff both formally and informally, and submitting annual reports to the chairperson), and special assignments (completing special tasks that the Marketing and Membership Services Coordinator assigns).
Work schedule	Because the activities are scheduled throughout the week, the incumbent has a flexible work schedule.
Qualifications necessary	The incumbent should possess excellent organizational skills accompanied by strong oral and written communication skills. Proven leadership abilities, outstanding interpersonal skills, and strong computer skills are essential. In addition, he or she must have a solid background of experience in recreational sports administration.
Discretion allowed	An action plan for each job function is to be discussed with the Marketing and Membership Services Coordinator.
Critical working relations	Marketing and Membership Services Coordinator, Membership Services staff, unit coordinators, and other part-time campus recreation staff.

Figure 9.1 Example of a job description.

Adapted, by permission, from the University of Western Ontario Campus Recreation, 1998.

Matching People and Jobs

So far, the emphasis has been on the analysis of the type and number of jobs to be filled, the activities and responsibilities of a specific job, and the human characteristics that a job requires. The next set of steps addresses finding the right people to join the organization and training them to perform the appropriate jobs. These managerial tasks are termed recruiting, hiring, and training, which the next sections discuss.

In a Nutshell

Job analysis identifies the activities/tasks, and the skills and predispositions associated with a specific job or a group of jobs. Job description outlines the duties and responsibilities of a job, its relationships with others in the organization, and the working conditions. Job specification specifies the human requirements of the job including education, experience, abilities, and personality.

Recruiting

Recruiting is the process of gathering a pool of prospective and capable applicants and encouraging them to apply for a position. This step is similar to how one goes about buying a car, a suit, or a computer. Take the case of buying a car. After deciding on the type of car he or she wants, an individual visits more than one car dealer to ensure that he or she has a selection of that particular type of car from which to choose. In a similar manner, an organization in search of employees also must reach out to many different types of sources of future employees.

The most obvious way of recruiting applicants is to advertise the position in several newspapers, journals, and trade publications. One recent, and seemingly effective, way of advertising a position is through the electronic mode of the world wide web. The advantage of advertising is that the notice has wide distribution and, thus, generates a larger pool of potential candidates. This idea of a larger pool of candidates could be a drawback itself in the sense that the manager has to sift through all of those applicants, some of whom may be totally unqualified.

Campus recruiting is another option. Because universities and colleges are the best source of young professionals, campus recruiting may prove to be the best source if an organization is seeking professionals at the entry level. The advantage of campus recruiting is that the recruiter gets to meet with several potential candidates and make a preliminary assessment of the candidates. The manager can contact the more impressive candidates later and encourage them to submit their applications. The drawback is that the recruiter may have to interact with several students who may not be interested in the job or the organization.

In addition, managers can encourage current employees to approach qualified friends and relatives to apply for positions. This process is known as employee referral. Because an employee knows the organization, its goals, and its processes well, he or she may have a good grasp of who will fit in well in the organization and carry out the job effectively. Thus, this process is likely to produce strong candidates. Further, because the image of the employee

Addressing the issue of recruiting older volunteers, Kouri (1990) noted that "there are two transition points in older adulthood when individuals are apt to seek rewarding, meaningful ways to structure time and channel their skills and energies. These are times when individuals are likely to be receptive to invitations for volunteer commitments. The first transition point is retirement; the second occurs around age 75" (pp. 65-66).

She also suggests that the recruiter may profit by participating in retirement-planning programs and company-sponsored gatherings of retired employees to explain volunteer opportunities. In the case of sport and recreation, managers can adopt this strategy and approach preretirees and retirees with brochures on the organization, its goals and volunteer opportunities, and the job descriptions. Similarly, they also can visit residences for senior citizens and advertise the opportunities for volunteers in their programs. She also points out several wrong assumptions people make about older persons. Among these assumptions are that older persons want to do the same work as they did before retirement, that all have difficulties with hearing or vision, that they will not change, that they want minimal responsibility, and that they will all come forward to help on their own.

who sponsors a candidate is at stake, the employee probably will recommend only strong candidates. The drawback of this process is that employees are likely to recommend only those who are similar to themselves. Thus, employee referral may result in homologous reproduction (i.e., a state in which only similar people are employed). In other words, the process may restrict diversity in terms of sex, race, ethnicity, and other demographic characteristics.

In Their View

Despite the hassle of filling out forms, the application form does play an important part for the following reasons:

- It is the first document an applicant completes on your terms and in your format.
- It captures essential data needed to make more complete candidate evaluations.
- It communicates important legal information designed to protect your organization.
- It is a key information source when putting new hires on the payroll.
- It is a form of test to see who can write clearly and follow instructions (Sullivan 1997, 21).

While the foregoing approaches are aimed at qualified candidates from outside the organization, the possibility also exists that several current employees may qualify for the advertised positions. This internal search is cost effective because the manager or recruiter knows the potential candidates and their performances well. He or she has no need for further assessment of the individuals. Further, such a focus on internal candidates is motivational in the sense that every employee can aspire to higher positions. If the jobs are at higher levels, the current employees may prove to be quite suitable and valuable. Ignoring them is disadvantageous to the organization and unfair to its employees. However, if the jobs are at the entry level, current employees may be overqualified, and the number of potential candidates would be limited. Internal search also might restrict diversity in the workplace.

Managers also can approach their counterparts in other organizations to ask qualified candidates to apply for the position. The essential point is that the organization must make every effort to reach out to qualified prospects for a job.

In a Nutshell

Recruiting is the process of attracting a number of prospective employees from whom the manager can select and hire the best. Advertising in the media, campus recruiting, and employee referrals are some useful ways of attracting qualified candidates. In addition, search within the organization may yield a list of employees qualified for the position.

Hiring

Hiring is the process of selecting a person from the pool of qualified applicants gathered during the recruiting process. Because the manager has analyzed and described the job and has specified the appropriate human factors, selecting suitable candidates should be easy. The ease of the selection process appears to be true particularly if the application form is well designed to elicit the most relevant and critical information. However, the process is much more complicated than what appears on paper. The major reason why the process is complicated is, as noted earlier, the need to forge a fit between the individual and the job as well as a fit between the individual and the organization. The job analysis, job description, job specification, and advertisements are aimed at the individual-job fit. However, they do not capture the essence of individual-organization fit, which encompasses personal needs, attitudes, values of the individual, and values and culture of the organization. Therefore, organizations and their managers commonly resort to other procedures to select an individual who fits the organizational context. These procedures include checking biographical background, considering reference letters, conducting interviews, and using personal judgment.

The problem here is that these latter processes may elicit personal biases in hiring people. The manager must make these processes free of any discriminatory practices. Federal and state governments make many provisions that govern the employment practices of organizations. Table 9.2 provides some of those regulations that govern the employment practices. Although these are legal requirements that organizations must follow implicitly, they also highlight the need for managers to be on guard and prevent any personal biases from surfacing in the hiring process. Managers must be wary of asking unwarranted and irrelevant questions of prospective candidates for jobs.

Some questions may appear to be innocuous, but they may be damaging to both the individual and the organization. Some of the proscribed questions are listed in table 9.3. The point is that selection of a candidate must be based on criteria that are relevant to the job and organizational requirements and that other attributes of the candidate must be made absolutely irrelevant to the selection process.

Another danger is that during the recruiting and hiring processes, either the individual, the organization, or both may not be truthful in what each one has to offer to the other. For instance, prospective candidates may project themselves as more capable than they really are and suggest that they can perform several different tasks (e.g., computer analysis, which they may know nothing about) required in the organization. On the other hand, the manager may portray the organization as something different from what it really is. For instance, the manager of a professional sport club may proclaim that the organization recognizes performance and that all salary and merit increments are based only on performance. Yet, in actuality, the club may emphasize seniority or may promote the owner's nephew or niece. The effects of false claims on the part of the individual or the organization have negative consequences (see figure 9.2 on page 145).

Table 9.2   Significant Government Regulations Governing Staffing Procedures

Laws and executive orders	Purpose or intent
Equal Pay Act (1963)	Forbids sex-based discrimination in rates of pay for men and women working in the same or similar jobs.
Age Discrimination in Employment Act (1967)	Forbids discrimination against individuals between 40 and 70 years of age.
Title VII, Civil Rights Act (1972)	Forbids discrimination based on race, sex, color, religion, or national origin.
Rehabilitation Act, as amended (1973)	Forbids discrimination against persons with disabilities and requires affirmative action to provide employment opportunity for persons with disabilities.
Vietnam-Era Veterans Readjustment Assistance Act (1974)	Forbids discrimination in hiring disabled veterans with a 30% or more disability rating, veterans discharged or released for a service-connected disability, and veterans on active duty between August 5, 1964, and May 7, 1975.
Equal Employment Opportunity Commission Guidelines (1978)	Created by the 1964 Civil Rights Act, this commission investigates and eliminates employment discrimination against certain groups of individuals (e.g., women and African, Asian, Hispanic, and Native Americans).
Pregnancy Discrimination Act (1978)	Requires pregnancy to be treated as any other medical condition with regard to fringe benefits and leave policies.
Immigration Reform and Control Act (1986)	Prohibits hiring of illegal aliens.
Americans With Disabilities Act (1990)	Provides for increased access to services and jobs for persons with disabilities.
Older Workers Benefit Protection Act (1990)	Provides protection for employees who are more than 40 years of age regarding fringe benefits and gives employees time to consider an early retirement offer.
Civil Rights Act (1978)	Allows women, persons with disabilities, and persons of religious minorities to have a jury trial and to sue for punitive damages if they can prove intentional hiring and workplace discrimination.

Table 9.3 Sample of Irrelevant Questions Asked of Candidates

Inquiries before hiring	Lawful	Unlawful*
Name	Name	Inquiry about any title that indicates race, color, religion, sex, national origin, disability, age, or ancestry
Address	Inquiry about place and length at current address	Inquiry about any foreign addresses that would indicate national origin
Age	Inquiry limited to establishing that the applicant meets a minimum age requirement that may be established by law	Requiring a birth certificate or baptismal record before hiring Any inquiry that would reveal the the date of high school garduation Any inquiry that would reveal whether the applicant is at least 40 years of age
Birthplace, national origin, or ancestry	—	Any inquiry about place of birth Any inquiry about place of birth of parents, grandparents, or spouse Any other inquiry about national origin or ancestry
Race or color	—	Any inquiry that would reveal race or color
Sex	—	Any inquiry that would reveal sex Any inquiry made of members of one sex but not of the other
Height and weight	Inquiry about the ability to perform the actual job requirements	Considering height or weight to be a job requirement without showing that no employee with the ineligible height or weight can do the work
Religion or creed	—	Any inquiry that would indicate or identify religious denomination or custom Telling the applicant the employer's religious indentity or preference Requesting the pastor's recommendation or reference
Disability	Any inquiry necessary to determine the applicant's ability to substantially perform a specific job without significant hazard	Any inquiry about past or current medical conditions not related to the position for which the applicant applied Any inquiry about Workers' Compensation or similar claims

(continued)

Table 9.3 *(continued)*

Inquiries before hiring	Lawful	Unlawful*
Citizenship	Inquiry about whether the applicant is a U.S. citizen Inquiry about whether a noncitizen applicant intends to become a U.S. citizen Inquiry about whether U.S. residence is legal Inquiry about whether the applicant's spouse is a U.S. citizen Requiring proof of citizenship after hiring Any other requirements that the Immigration Reform and Control Act of 1986, as amended, mandates	Inquiry about whether the applicant is a native-born or naturalized U.S. citizen Requiring proof of citizenship before hiring Inquiry about whether the applicant's parents or spouse are native-born or naturalized U.S. citizens
Photographs	Requiring photograph after hiring for identification	Requiring photograph before hiring
Arrests and convictions	Inquiry about conviction of specific crimes related to qualifications for the job for which the applicant applied	—
Education	Inquiry about the nature and extent of academic, professional, or vocational training Inquiry about language skills, such as reading and writing of foreign languages, if job-related	Any inquiry that would reveal the nationality or religious affiliation of a school Inquiry about what the applicant's mother tongue is or how foreign language ability was acquired
Relatives	Inquiry about name, relationship, and address of person to be notified in case of emergency	Any inquiry about a relative that would be unlawful if made about the applicant
Organizations	Inquiry about membership in professional organizations and offices held, excluding any organization that has a name or character indicating the race, color, religion, sex, national origin, disability, age, or ancestry of its members	Inquiry about every club and organization where membership is held
Military service	Inquiry about service in U.S. armed forces when such service is a qualification for the job Requiring military discharge certificate after being hired	Inquiry about military service in armed service of any country but the United States Requesting military service records Inquiry about type of discharge

Inquiries before hiring	Lawful	Unlawful*
Work schedule	Inquiry about willingness or ability to work required work schedule	Inquiry about willingness or ability to work any particular religious holidays
Miscellaneous	Any inquiry required to reveal qualifications for the job for which the applicant applied	Any inquiry that is not job-related and that may elicit or attempt to elicit any information concerning race, color, religion, sex, marital status, national origin, disability, age, or ancestry of an applicant for employment or membership
References	General personal and work references that do not reveal the race, color, religion, sex, national origin, disability, age, or ancestry of the applicant	Requesting references specifically from clergymen or any other persons who might reflect race, color, religion, sex, national origin, disability, age, or ancestry of applicant

I. Employers acting under bona fide affirmative action programs or acting under orders of equal employment law enforcement agencies of federal, state, or local governments may make some of the prohibited inquiries listed to the extent that these inquiries are required by such programs or orders.

II. Employers having federal defense contracts are exempt to the extent that otherwise prohibited inquiries are required by federal law for security purposes.

III. Although not specifically listed above, any inquiry is prohibited that elicits information as to, or which is not job-related and may be used to discriminate on the basis of, race, color, religion, sex, national origin, disability, age, or ancestry in violation of law.

*Unless bona fide occupational qualification is certified in advance by the Ohio Civil Rights Commission.

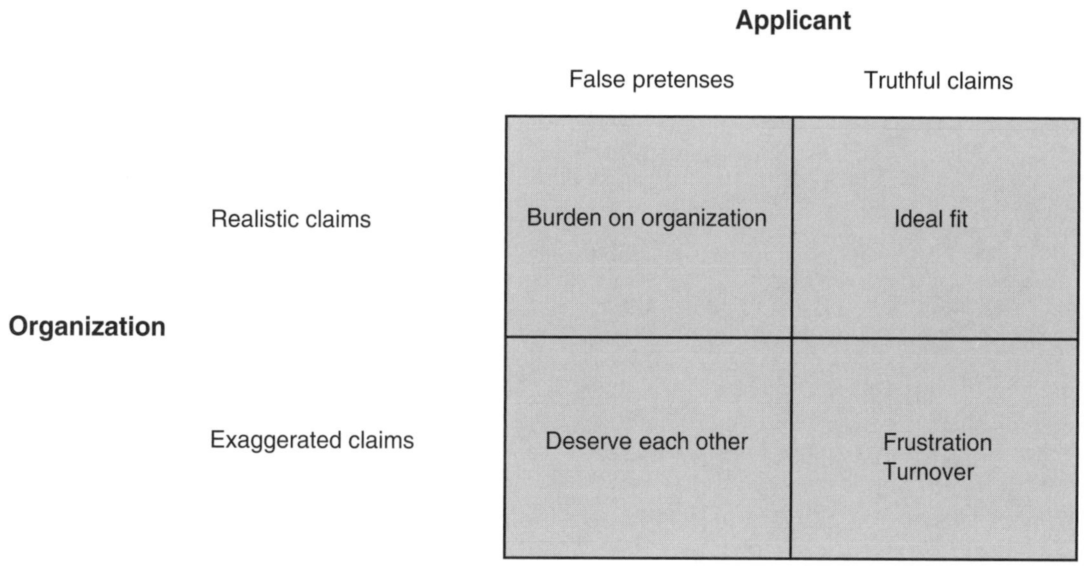

Applicant

	False pretenses	Truthful claims
Realistic claims	Burden on organization	Ideal fit
Exaggerated claims	Deserve each other	Frustration Turnover

Organization

Figure 9.2 Effects of false claims by the organization and the applicant.

In a Nutshell

Hiring is the process of selecting a person to fit the job as well as the organization. Managers must employ only those criteria that relate to job performance and must disregard irrelevant factors. The manager must also conform to government regulations that govern the employment process.

Training

With regard to **training**, Grönroos (1990) stated that human resource management should focus on "developing a *holistic view* of the service organization; developing *skills* concerning how various tasks are to be performed; and developing *communication and service skills*" (p. 253). Similarly, Schneider and Bowen (1992) suggested that the training program should develop both technical job skills and interpersonal or customer relationships skills. In addition, the training program should facilitate the assimilation of cultural values and norms of the organization. In essence, the training programs are designed to further the fit between the individual and the organization.

Another useful scheme in the development of training programs is that of Humphrey and Ashforth (1994) who pointed out that two types of knowledge structures are necessary for effective service encounters: script and categorical. A script knowledge structure refers to a service worker's expectation for a series of coherently organized events in a successful service encounter and for the alternative courses of action available for every event. Categorical knowledge structure refers to an understanding of the different types of clients with specific needs and wants and of personal characteristics. Such knowledge results in the development of prototypes of clients. As Humphrey and Ashforth (1994) pointed out,

> agents must have both categorical and script knowledge. Categorical knowledge helps them understand customers, whereas scripts help them understand the service options available to meet customers' varying needs. (p. 176)

In the context of sport and recreation management, the training on categorical knowledge emphasizes the distinction among various classes of customers (e.g., youth, women, and the elderly) and their motives for participation (e.g., pleasure, excellence, or health). The script knowledge entails training in the technical skills needed to provide the service (e.g., techniques and strategies of coaching)

Martin (1990) presented one way of training service employees. In studying the employee-customer interface in bowling centers, he identified several employee behaviors that influence customer relations. The positive behaviors included greeting the customers sincerely, thanking the customers when they pay, encouraging the customers to visit again, thanking the customers for reporting problems, and making a positive comment on the customers' performance. The negative behaviors included preoccupation with noncustomer tasks when the customer approaches the employee to obtain a lane, to pay for bowling, or to order a soft drink. The author also identified smoking or chewing during the interface with the customer as a negative behavior.

Martin (1990) found that bowling center employees generally failed to practice good customer relations behaviors. Based on his findings, he proposed the following steps to train the employees in customer relations behavior. These steps are relevant to all sport organizations.

- Provide a customer relations manual for each employee. The manual should cover a wide range of examples of encounters with customers. These encounters vary from one type of sport service to another.

- Ask the employees to conduct mystery-shopper audits in which the employee takes the role of a customer in other service firms. That experience should yield insights for the employee into good and bad customer relations behaviors.

- Meet with employees periodically to clarify and expand the contents of the manual. Employees themselves may provide additional cues on customer relations. Such discussions will also cover the complaints, as well as the compliments, received.

- Let the new employees serve alongside senior employees for a set training period before they are left on their own.

Staffing and Career Considerations **147**

In a Nutshell

Training is the process of cultivating job-related skills, interpersonal skills, and organizational values among newly hired employees. Such training would help the employee perform the technical aspects of the job adequately, interact with different classes of customers effectively, and learn the culture of the organization.

and the various stages of providing that service (e.g., progressive training regimen during practice sessions).

Psychological Contract

When an individual joins an organization, the organization and the individual always make a written formal agreement. Such documents as a job description, employment contract, policies on salary scales,

The discussion in this chapter focuses on recruiting suitable candidates for existing jobs. The other side of the coin is what managers can do when they find out that their organization is overstaffed. Due to technological advances, foreign competition, and dwindling markets for a given product, organizations may be forced to reduce their workforce. Currently, many organizations are downsizing, or "right sizing," their staffs. Decruitment is the name that Robbins (1997b) gave to this process of reductions in staff of an organization: "Decruitment is not a pleasant task for any manager to perform. But as many organizations are forced to shrink their size of their workforce or restructure their skill composition, decruitment is becoming an increasingly important part of human resource management" (p. 283).

Sport and recreation managers also may face this predicament. For instance, faced with reductions in the budgets allotted to them, city recreation departments, university athletic departments, and such other organizations may have to decruit their employees. Similarly, private profit-oriented firms, such as fitness clubs, may have to decruit if their client or customer base shrinks for any number of reasons. How can managers go about the process of decruiting? Robbins (1997b) identified the following options:

- Firing (i.e., permanent termination)
- Layoffs (i.e., temporary termination)
- Attrition (i.e., not filling positions falling vacant due to voluntary resignations or normal retirement)
- Transfers (i.e., moving employees laterally or downward)
- External loans (i.e., loaning employees' services to other organizations)
- Reduced work weeks (i.e., reducing the work hours each week or letting employees share their work)
- Early retirement (i.e., encouraging employees through incentives to retire early)

Of these options, firing (i.e., termination) is actually a severe form of punishing an employee for some violations (e.g., drinking on the job or being usually late to work). Because of the dramatic effects a firing has on the employee, his or her family, and even the manager who orders the firing, such an action should be taken only after careful deliberations. While some violations like drinking on the job or vandalizing can be cause for immediate dismissal, some others like tardiness and absenteeism may require three warnings (Mondy and Noe 1993). Continued poor performance may itself be a cause for firing. But a sport manager needs to document this poor performance based on the job description and actual data on employee performance. While a clear job description is fundamental to make informed decisions on firing and defense against subsequent legal troubles, it is also important to announce to all employees a list of violations justifying termination. It will also be helpful if immediate supervisors and co-workers are encouraged to monitor and warn against such violations.

and procedures for merit assessment and promotion constitute the formal contract. However, another aspect that is as critical to employment as the formal contract is the **psychological contract**. This contract simply refers to the implicit expectations between the organization and its members. The elements of the psychological contract include those of the formal contract as well as additional informal and implied elements, such as the privileges and obligations between the person and the organization.

Public and Real Psychological Contract

Tosi, Rizzo, and Carroll (1986) conceived of two boundaries of the psychological contract: public and real. The public boundary "includes those activities which the person wants others, especially his or her superior, to believe are the elements of the psychological contract" (p. 512). These tend to be the minimal set of activities that the formal contract defines. For example, fitness assessment and exercise prescription for the clients defines the public boundary of the psychological contract of a fitness consultant. The consultant also expects that he or she will undertake such activities between 8 A.M. and 5 P.M. on weekdays. As shown, these elements constitute the elements of the job description.

However, the real boundary of the psychological contract (i.e., the true limits) include the organizational expectation that the consultant will work overtime and during weekends and will also conduct a few exercise classes. Further, the organization (i.e., the managers who run it) also expect that the consultant will put forth his or her best efforts and not just put in the time. The consultant, while complying with these expectations, also has his or her own expectation of how the organization will reciprocate in terms of extra remuneration, benefits, and privileges.

For another example, consider the situation in which a branch of the ticketing operation of a professional sport club is closed and the employees in that branch are laid off. Despite the fact that the professional club followed all existing rules and procedures for such retrenchment of employees, an individual might still have the expectation that the organization will not undertake such procedures and will do its best to retain all of its employees. Thus, the released workers are not likely to question the basic causes of such closures but lament the breaking of the psychological contract.

Most often, such psychological expectations relate to one's needs, values, and attitudes. For instance, an individual joining an intercollegiate athletic department expects that the department will do everything to safeguard the health and welfare of the athletes (i.e., reflecting a personal value) and those of the employees (i.e., reflecting a personal need for security).

Individual Contributions and Organizational Inducements

From a different perspective, the psychological contract appears as a system of individual contributions and organizational inducements (Schermerhorn, Hunt, and Osborn 1985). That is, a psychological contract can exist and be meaningful only if the contributions by the member have some worth for the organization and if the member values the inducements by the organization. That is, the exchange of values between the organization and the member must be balanced and equitable.

The notion of a psychological contract is more critical to organizations that have volunteer workers. Because the material inducements of the formal contract (e.g., wages or salaries) are not relevant to them, the other elements within the psychological contract can attract and hold volunteers. The psychological contract includes elements such as the opportunity to express one's altruistic and helping tendencies through specified activities of the organization. Another critical element is the opportunity to engage in those activities in which the volunteer's valued abilities can be used. Chapter 1 presented the utilitarian, affective, and normative incentives that motivate volunteers. An organization that addresses those incentives in their personnel policies affecting volunteers is likely to be successful in recruiting and retaining volunteers. To the extent that the volunteer's contributions and the organization's inducements are not balanced, the psychological contract between the organization and the volunteers is tenuous, and, thus, the volunteers' commitment to the organization and their maximal efforts cannot be assured.

In a Nutshell

The psychological contract between the member and organization is the unwritten understanding that the member will contribute to the organization over and beyond the formal contract, and in return, the organization will extend its varied inducements (e.g., rewards).

A significant difference between paid employees and volunteer workers is that, by definition, the pay they receive to a large extent motivates paid employees. Pay cannot be used as a motivational tool in the case of volunteers. As noted in chapter 1, the goals of an organization, the context (i.e., people and processes) in which they work, and the tasks that they perform are likely to motivate volunteers. The underlying theme of this chapter, which is creating the person-job fit, should be extended to volunteers. With this in mind, managers can undertake several steps to create the volunteer-job fit (Kouri 1990). The concerns that are more critical to the context of sport and recreation management include the following:

- The skills the volunteer wants to use and not what the organization wants to be used
- The level of responsibility that the volunteer wants
- The type of people with whom the volunteer wants to work
- The volunteer's expectations for the job

These concerns reflect the incentives for volunteer motivation. The manager can best achieve the volunteer-job fit if the volunteers themselves are involved in designing the job and if the organization is flexible in creating jobs that the volunteers want.

Career Considerations

The staffing procedures including the analyses of jobs and their descriptions have long-term implications for individuals as well. Most Americans spend nearly one-third of their adult life (i.e., between 25 and 65 years of age) in various jobs in different organizational contexts. Stated otherwise, jobs form one of the central elements of one's life. If you ask your parents to describe their life, their description most probably would revolve around the jobs that they have held in different places at different times. By the same token, if you are asked about your future life, you are most likely to describe it in terms of the jobs you want to hold in the future. This notion of a succession of jobs is called a career. Because most of the readers of this text are likely to embark on a career, the topic needs some detailed discussion. Discussing the concept of career from both the individual's perspective and the organization's perspective would be useful.

Individual Careers

Johns (1988) defined career as "a sequence of work activities and positions, and associated attitudes and reactions, experienced over a person's life" (p. 617). Thus, a career refers to the preparation for a job or jobs, the jobs held during one's lifetime, and the movement from job to job. The concept also includes one's work-related attitudes, values, and beliefs, and the extent to which one's self-identity is related to work (Tosi, Rizzo, and Carroll 1986). Apart from the fact that career connotes the objec-tive movement of a person along a path of jobs (which may be orderly and sequential or discontinuous), the concept of career also implies a fit between what the individual does in a job and the organizational context or environment in which the person performs that job, and the person's needs and preferences and his or her abilities, skills, and talents.

The concept of person-task fit naturally leads to the notion of person-occupation fit. For instance, a person may identify more closely with marketing as an occupation than with teaching or coaching based on personal needs and aptitudes. While person-task fit refers to the congruence of personal needs and values with a specific job (e.g., marketing director of recreational sports or competitive sports), person-occupation fit refers to the fit between the person and the occupation (e.g., marketing or coaching) irrespective of the specific job. Note that such occupational identity is critical for one's personal overall identity. In some cases, occupational identity indeed may be the essence of overall identity (e.g., the so-called workaholics identify with the work so much that there is no room for any other identity).

Career Orientation

As early as 1909, Frank Parsons noted that

In the wise choice of a vocation there are three broad factors: (1) a clear understanding of yourself, your aptitudes, abilities, interests, ambitions, resources, limitations and their causes; (2) a knowledge of the requirements and conditions of success, advantages and disadvantages, compensation, opportunities, and prospects in different lines of work; (3) true reasoning on the relations of these two groups of facts. (p. 5)

To expand on his statement, an individual's needs, values, goals, and preferences; his or her expectations from a career; and his or her estimation of personal talents, skills, expertise, and experiences related to particular jobs and occupations jointly describe and define that individual's **career orientation**. Career orientation means a person's preferences for specific kinds of jobs in specific occupational categories.

In Their View

London (1991) suggested that career motivation (or orientation) consists of career resilience (i.e., capacity to manage career barriers), career insight (i.e., understanding personal career goals and capacities and work environments), and career identity (i.e., how employees define themselves by their work). London suggested that organizations can support career resilience by providing feedback and positive reinforcement, creating opportunities for achievement, and encouraging group and collaborative work. They can enhance career insight by encouraging employees to set their career goals, providing information relevant to career goals, and giving performance feedback. They can build career identity by encouraging professional growth and work involvement through challenging jobs, providing leadership positions, and rewarding good performance in terms of recognition or bonuses.

Career Anchors

Along similar lines, Schein (1978) viewed people as developing a sense of their own competencies, talents, needs, and values based on their early work experiences. Each individual learns over a period of work experiences that he or she prefers certain work roles over others. These preferred work roles are anchored in one's talents, needs, motives, attitudes, and values. The specific patterns of skills, needs, and values are called **career anchors**, and they keep the person moored within a specific domain of occupation. That is, people tend to gravitate toward those jobs and occupations that satisfy their needs, use their skills and competencies, and hold their values dear.

Schein's (1978) extensive research showed that five distinct types of career anchors exist (see table

9.4). Note that career anchors evolve over a period of time. That is, work experiences in the next few years can modify what seems to be a career anchor at the moment. An individual may learn that he or she has talents that he or she has not used so far, or an individual may learn that his or her basic needs and values are likely to be more satisfied in another line of work. Even within one line of work, certain aspects of the job may be more fulfilling than other aspects. For instance, some athletic administrators may seek greater fulfillment in contributing to the growth and welfare of the athletes, and others may be more attuned to accomplishments of the teams (e.g., win-loss records). These two kinds of athletic directors have differing career anchors or career orientations. Some physical education teachers in high schools also serve as coaches. Some of these teacher-coaches have spent more time and energy in coaching at the expense of teaching. While acknowledging the several external factors that make these people focus more on coaching, Chelladurai and Kuga (1996) argued that the nature of coaching as a job and the innate talents and tendencies of individuals also can influence them to focus more on coaching than on teaching. This view parallels Schein's (1978) notion of career anchors.

In a Nutshell

An individual's movement from one job to another over his or her lifetime is known as his or her career. Further, the concept includes not only the listing of the jobs held but also an individual's lifetime experiences in the workplace.

Career Stages

Hall (1976) proposed that individuals go through four career stages covering the period from adolescence to retirement. In the exploration stage (i.e., from 16 to 28 years of age), a person explores different occupations or roles, develops needed skills and competencies, and establishes a social network of peers and superiors. The summer jobs, volunteer work, and internships that university students undertake may serve as the forum for exploring different occupations. In the establishment stage (i.e., from 22 to 42 years of age), the person specializes and gains expertise in a particular area of activity and contribution to the organization and develops a clear and focused career plan. In the advancement and maintenance stage (i.e., from 32 to 55 years of age), the focus is on making progress within the

Table 9.4 Career Anchors

Anchor	Description
Technical functional	A preference for technical or functional content of the job, such as accounting and ticketing operations
Managerial competence	A preference for managerial positions and the belief that one has the ability simultaneously to analyze problems, manage people, and manage one's own emotions
Creativity	A preference for occupations that satisfy the need to create something (e.g., a sport product, marketing process, sport agency) and to place one's name on it
Autonomy and independence	A preference for those lines of work that permit people to be on their own and to be independent of others (e.g., an agent for athletes, a fitness consultant)
Security	A preference for long-term job security and a stable future with good income including retirement benefits

organization and achieving career goals. The person possibly takes on the role of a mentor to the junior members of the organization. Finally, in late career stage (i.e., from 55 years of age to retirement), the individual's value to the organization is his or her breadth of knowledge and experience; therefore, mentoring may continue to be a significant contribution. The individual may also develop interest in nonwork endeavors. The overlap in years among the various career stages is a function of individual differences; that is, some individuals may move from one stage to another at a faster rate than others. Despite these differences in the rate of progression, individuals are expected to follow sequentially the given pattern of moving from one stage to another.

Organizational Career Systems

The foregoing discussion focused on the career orientation and development of the individual. Organizations also have (or should have) some strategies on the careers within their domain. Sonnenfeld and Peiperl (1988) used the name career systems to describe the "collections of policies, priorities, and actions that organizations use to manage the flow of their members into, through, and out of the organizations over time." They argued that because organizations are characterized by different goals and technologies and because they face different environmental contingencies, they also are likely to have different strategic priorities. The career systems that they institute reflect these strategic priorities. Sonnenfeld and Peiperl (1988) proposed that the various career systems can be grouped

In Their View

Thoughts about careers take on a special relevance in the new workplace. We live and work in a time when the implications of constant change pressure us continually to review and reassess our career progress. In particular, businesses are becoming smaller in size and employing fewer people, and new, more flexible and adaptable forms are replacing the traditional organizational "pyramid." Accordingly, multifunctional understanding is increasingly important as organizations emphasize lateral coordination. . . . In general, the nature of "work" is changing; future work will require continuous learning and will be less bound by the "9 to 5" traditions. (Schermerhorn et al. 1991, 113)

These authors suggest that an individual must take on the responsibility for his or her own career instead of the traditional reliance on the organization. Thus, an individual should build a portfolio of skills and continuously develop the portfolio to keep pace with the changing workplace.

into four categories based on two dimensions. The two dimensions are "first, the movement into and out of the firm, the *supply flow*, and, second, the movement across job assignments and through promotions within the firm, the *assignment flow*" (pp. 589-590).

Supply flow refers to the "openness of the career system to the external labor market at other than entry levels" (p. 590). Some organizations recruit employees at the entry level but rely on their own members to fill the higher level positions (e.g., parks and recreation departments). In some other cases, the organization recruits outsiders to fill even higher-level positions. For instance, a university may hire the athletic director from outside the ranks of its athletic department. The latter type of organization is likely to experience a greater proportion of employee turnover because the local employees may exit to other organizations to obtain better positions.

Assignment flow refers to the criteria by which managers assign or promote individuals within an organization. Sonnenfeld and Peiperl (1988) suggested that the organization may use the criterion of individual performance, which favors the star performer, or the criterion of contribution to the group, which favors the solid contributor.

Based on these two dimensions, Sonnenfeld and Peiperl (1988) proposed four kinds of career systems each with its own unique way of maintaining membership. Figure 9.3 depicts these four systems, which are labeled baseball team, academy, club, and fortress.

In a Nutshell

Organizations may differ in the ways in which they manage the careers of their employees (i.e., the organizational career systems). The two dimensions on which they may differ are whether they rely on an internal or external source for higher-level positions and whether they use individual performance or the contribution to the group as the criterion for promotions.

In brief, organizations that resemble baseball teams favor individual performers; individuals are recruited, assigned, or promoted to various positions within the organization and are recognized and rewarded on the basis of their performance. Faculties and departments in a university resemble baseball teams to the extent that the university recruits and rewards professors on the basis of their performance including granting of tenure and pay raises. Similarly, the hiring of coaches in a large athletic department is based on individual performance. While the emphasis on individual perfor-

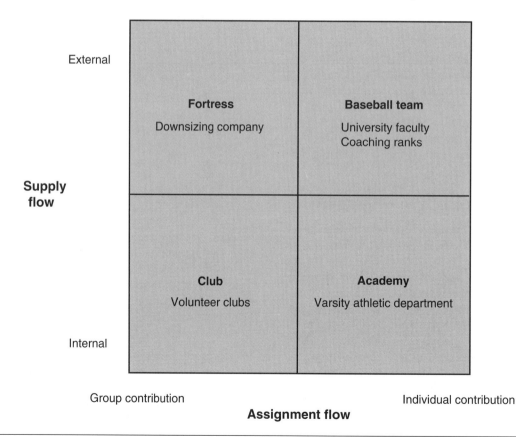

Figure 9.3   Sonnenfeld and Peiperl's four career systems.

Adapted, by permission, from J.A. Sonnenfeld and M.A. Peiperl, 1988, "Staffing policy as a strategic response: A typology of career systems," *Academy of Management Review* 13: 588-600.

mance reflects the assignment flow, the tendency of such organizations to go outside of their own ranks to hire qualified candidates indicates the external supply flow.

The academy-type organizations, like baseball teams, also use individual performance as the basis for promotion and rewards (i.e., the assignment flow); however, academies are closed to outside markets (i.e., external supply flow). They would rather rely on developing their own members' knowledge and skills and their commitment. Universities and athletic departments, in some circumstances, may rely on internal candidates for filling the positions. In such a case, they will resemble the academy as Sonnenfeld and Peiperl (1988) portrayed.

The organizations labeled clubs, like the academies, also are closed to external labor markets. However, unlike the academies, clubs use group contributions as the criterion for assignments and promotions. This criterion often is reflected in seniority being used as the basis for promotions.

Finally, these authors call the fortress "an institution under siege." In these cases, organizational survival is more critical than the members and their welfare. While it is open to external labor markets, the fortress does not exhibit any commitment to individual employees or their performances. The more critical concern is whether the group or unit is performing well. Recently, many firms in the business and industrial sector have attempted to survive by laying off a large number of their members or by replacing their senior staff (i.e., the highly paid staff) with new recruits. In a similar manner, when faced with declining membership, a fitness club may fire or lay off several of its employees.

The essential thrust of Sonnenfeld and Peiperl's (1988) argument is that a particular career system may be functional in certain types of organizations or its units. To add to this argument, one particular organization may adopt different systems at different times based on their particular circumstances. The particular circumstances at a point in time and, of course, the preferences of top-level decision makers dictate the choice of one system over another. For instance, a university athletic department may adopt the baseball team model in the case of hiring their coaches. That is, the department offers good salaries and benefits to outstanding coaches in order to recruit them. The department recognizes and rewards them as long as they perform well. However, if the coaches fail to perform (or their teams fail to perform), the department is likely to replace them with newly recruited, star performers. At another time, the department may be satisfied with promoting the assistant coach to the position of chief coach. From a different perspective, the directorate of the athletic program (i.e., the director and assistant directors) may resemble an academy that recruits the members when they are young, trains them in various positions, and promotes the better performers to higher positions.

Mentoring

In addition to training, managers can use the process of mentoring to groom members of an organization for advancement in their career. The young members who enter an organization must be aware of and capitalize on the opportunities for a mentoring relationship with significant others in the organization because such a relationship is quite critical for career advancement.

Based on the literature on mentoring, Weaver and Chelladurai (1995) defined mentoring as "a process in which a more experienced person serves as a role model, and provides guidance and support to a developing novice, and sponsors that novice in his/her career progress" (p. 1). Weaver and Chelladurai (1995) presented a schematic representation of

Despite the notion that individuals are responsible for their own careers and irrespective of their own career systems, organizations and their managers must endeavor to support their employees' career development. Robbins (1997b) identified the following as the critical aspects of such support:

- Communicate the organization's goals and future strategies so that interested employees can plan and prepare to participate in the company's future.

- Provide employees with opportunities for more interesting and challenging work experiences.

- Offer financial assistance (e.g., tuition fees) to help employees keep current in their fields.

- Offer employees paid time off from work for additional training elsewhere.

mentoring in organizations (see figure 9.4). The following sections present a brief description of the model.

Functions of Mentoring

The discussion begins with a description of what a **mentor** actually does. From a study of 15 executives, Kram (1983) identified two distinct sets of functions of mentoring: career and psychosocial, which are described in table 9.5. Career functions enhance career advancement by increasing the skills and abilities of the **protégé**, exposing the protégé to challenging tasks and to influential superiors, and sponsoring the protégé for advancement in the organization (Kram 1985).

In the psychosocial functions, the mentor facilitates the growth and development of the protégé by acting as a role model, accepting and confirming his or her abilities and talents, and providing counsel and friendship. These psychosocial functions enhance the protégé's sense of competence, identity, and managerial effectiveness.

Outcomes of Mentoring

Successful mentoring should result in significant outcomes for all three parties to the arrangement: the protégé, the mentor, and the organization.

Outcomes for the Protégé

Two kinds of outcomes result from a successful mentoring: advancement and growth (Hunt and Michael 1983, Zey 1985). These two outcomes parallel the two kinds of mentoring functions. As noted earlier, the mentor sponsors, coaches, and exposes

the protégé to top-level decision makers and to high-profile assignments. Therefore, the protégé is more likely to be noticed, recognized, and rewarded than a non-protégé is. Thus, the protégé may enjoy greater career success in terms of salary, bonuses, promotion, status, and power and may have greater job satisfaction (Dreher and Ash 1990, Fagenson 1989, Riley and Wrench 1985). The psychosocial functions of mentoring (i.e., role modeling, acceptance and confirmation, counseling, and friendship) facilitate the growth of the protégé in terms of competence, identity, and effectiveness (Kram 1985).

Outcomes for the Mentor

Mentors themselves gain in several ways. First, the rejuvenating challenge of guiding a young protégé and the intrinsic satisfaction derived from the mentoring process may not be available in the tasks associated with the regular work of the mentor (Hunt and Michael 1983, Kram 1985, Levinson 1978). Further, the process furthers the mentor's sense of competence and confidence in his or her own abilities (Noe 1988, Zey 1984). From a different perspective, mentoring brings several extrinsic rewards. The mentor gains in the status and esteem from peers and superiors (Jennings 1967, Kram 1980). Continued promotion of the mentor is made possible because the mentor trained the protégé to take over his or her responsibilities (Jennings 1967). The network of the protégé serves as a base of technical support, respect, power, and influence throughout the organization (Jennings 1967, Kram 1980). Finally, the protégé may help the mentor engage in new projects that, in turn, enhances mentor's reputation as an achiever and star maker (Newby and Heide 1992).

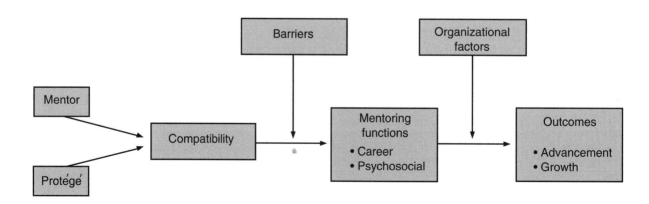

Figure 9.4 A model of mentoring in organizations.

Table 9.5   Functions of Mentoring

Career functions Sponsorship	The mentor highlights the protégé's potential and nominates him or her for advantageous transfers and promotions.
Exposure and visibility	The mentor provides the protégé with the opportunities to work with key people and decision makers who have an influence in the protégé's progress.
Coaching and feedback	The mentor teaches the corporate game and strategies and identifies strengths and weaknesses in the protégé's performance.
Developmental assignments	The mentor assigns challenging work to facilitate the development of key skills and knowledge crucial to further advancement.
Protection	The mentor shields the protégé from making mistakes and from those who may have an antagonistic view of the protégé.
Psychosocial functions Role modeling	The mentor models a set of attitudes, values, and behaviors for the protégé to imitate.
Acceptance and confirmation	The mentor confirms and expresses confidence in the protégé's abilities and talent and encourages him or her.
Counseling	The mentor counsels the protégé on personal concerns and anxieties.
Friendship	The mentor engages in friendly and social interactions that, in turn, relieve the pressures of work.

Source: Kram (1985).

Outcomes for the Organization

The major advantage accruing to the organization is the identification and grooming of good candidates with managerial potential for promotion to higher and more responsible positions. A protégé is likely to be more satisfied and committed to the organization and is likely to stay with that organization (Hunt and Michael 1983, Kram 1980). In sum, mentoring reduces the need to hire individuals from the outside. Because of these advantages, many organizations have instituted formal mentoring relationships (Zey 1985).

The above description of mentoring emphasizes the higher position of the mentor and the power and status associated with that position. While the idea of mentors with position and power is commonplace in organizations, it does not preclude the possibility that senior co-workers can fulfill many of the mentoring functions. Thus, a five-year assistant to the marketing director in an athletic department can and usually will help the newly hired assistant by teaching the technical and interpersonal aspects of the job, the interrelationships among the jobs and the units within the department, and the overall value system of the organization. It is also not uncommon for such a veteran to be a spokesperson for the newcomer. These are career functions indeed. By the same token, the veteran can also provide support by being a role model, accepting the newcomer for what he or she is, counseling, and offering friendship. These are the psychosocial functions. Thus, being a mentor is not restricted to senior executives. Even lower-level workers who have gained expertise through experience, and who have the inclination to help the novices can be effective mentors. Being aware of this opportunity, sport managers should encourage such mentoring relationships among workers.

In a Nutshell

Mentoring refers to a relationship between a mentor (i.e., a senior expert) and a protégé (i.e., a novice) in which the mentor offers his or her guidance for the personal growth of the protégé and sponsors the novice for promotion and career advancement. Effective mentoring leads to benefits for the protégé, the mentor, and the organization.

Mentor-Protégé Compatibility

While the process of mentoring is useful in many respects, it is highly dependent on the compatibility between the characteristics of the mentor and protégé (**mentor-protégé compatibility**). Typically, mentors are older and more experienced than the novice and have the knowledge and expertise to guide him or her (Burke 1984, Levinson 1978). Further, because of his or her seniority, the mentor is high on the organizational hierarchy and has cultivated an effective network inside and outside the organization (Hill, Bahniuk, and Dobos 1989; Hunt and Michael 1983). In addition, mentors should have a high need for influencing others including the protégés (Weaver and Chelladurai 1995). Other characteristics of the mentor that attract protégés are knowledge of operations and a positive attitude and open mind (Gaskill 1991).

Like the mentors, a high need for power characterizes protégés. Association with high-level executives who possess the real power satisfies such a need. Kanter (1977) called the association "reflected power." Other personal characteristics that mark a successful protégé are assertiveness, open-mindedness, and flexibility (Kram 1985, Noe 1988, Ragins and Cotton 1991, Scandura and Ragins 1993). The potential protégés need to have a strong faith in and appreciation for a mentoring relationship. In contrast, others may believe that their abilities and talents will carry them forward in their careers (Noe 1988). Protégés also have the potential for advancement, which is an assumption that is basic to the mentoring process. That is, when considering individuals for participation in the mentoring process, organizations usually select only those whom they believe are potential managers (Ragins 1989).

The sex of the protégé may have some bearing on the mentoring process. First, more men are found in the upper echelons of management, and, therefore, they form the larger pool of potential mentors (Gilbert and Rossman 1992). Researchers report that "women hold fewer than five percent of senior executive jobs in corporate America" (Schermerhorn, Hunt, and Osborn 1997, 3). Researchers have found similar statistics regarding low representation of women among administrative and coaching ranks in sport (Inglis, Danylchuk, and Pastore 1996). To that extent, women may have difficulty finding a female mentor.

Second, research also shows that women tend to be relatively more passive in seeking a mentoring relationship (Fitt and Newton 1981). This tendency may be due to a lack of faith in mentoring. Compared with men, women might tend to minimize the effects of the mentoring process, particularly with regard to their advancement in the organization, and might rely more on hard work for advancement (Hilliard 1990, Nieva and Gutek 1981, Noe 1988). In addition, compared with men, women tend to prefer more of the psychosocial functions from their mentors and less of the career functions (Burke 1984). In sum, the notion of mentor-protégé compatibility includes mutual adjustments in interpersonal relationships between the two parties and a sharing of interests and goals of mentoring and the directions thereof.

In a Nutshell

Several characteristics of the mentor and the protégé have to be compatible for an effective mentoring relationship to emerge and function. These characteristics include age differential between the two parties, willingness and relative ability or expertise of the mentor, and the flexibility of the protégé.

Intervening Variables

Readers also must be aware of those variables that may intervene in the mentoring process. Even when compatibility exists between the mentor and protégé, some barriers that hinder the emergence of a mentoring relationship may be present. These barriers include fear of sexual connotations, fear of tokenism, and lack of network opportunities (Gilbert and Rossman 1992, Hilliard 1990, Kram 1985, Shapiro and Farrow 1988). The close association between a mentor and protégé may be uncomfortable in the case of cross-sex mentoring. Either party in the relationship may not want to be seen as sexually motivated in the relationship. Even more significant is the fear that others may perceive the mentoring relationship as sexually oriented. Such fears and inhibitions may act as a barrier to successful mentoring.

In a similar manner, a woman or a person from a minority group may perceive the advances and concerns of a would-be mentor as gestures of tokenism (i.e., the tendency to hold the concern for one individual as the concern for the total group to which the individual belongs). Others outside of the mentoring relationship also may perceive it to be an indicant of tokenism.

Another barrier to forming effective mentoring relationships is a lack of opportunity to network with probable mentors. This barrier would be particularly true in the case of women and minorities.

To the extent that fewer women and minorities are present in higher ranks, the opportunity for networking is minimized. Further cultural and sexual differences may not permit interactions among mentors and protégés outside of work.

In Their View

In her study of perceptions of mentoring and networking among athletic administrators, Young (1990) found that the

> majority (94%) of administrators advocate that all young professionals establish mentoring relationships. The cross gender relationships should be considered a viable association. This is extremely important for a young woman because a high percentage of decision-making positions in athletics are held by men. . . . There is a larger pool of male administrators than females as potential candidates for mentors. Gaining the confidence and respect of a male administrator will help change the attitudes of some of the "old boys" concerning women and their ability to assume administrative positions. (p. 77)

Organizational factors may also inhibit the advancement or career outcomes expected of a mentoring relationship. The organization, its policies, and the politics therein largely determine the career outcomes, such as promotion, advancement, and increased salary. In some organizations such policies may emphasize seniority in the place of performance. In addition, more powerful officials of the organization may favor candidates other than the focal protégé. However, note that organizational factors do not affect the growth outcomes as much because these outcomes are administered within the dyad in the mentoring relationship and by the mentoring process itself. The extent to which the protégé grows in terms of knowledge, abilities, and performance accomplishments and gains a sense of achievement and fulfillment is in the domain of the mentor and the protégé.

Summary

In summary, this chapter presented the purposes of staffing and the steps involved in staffing. The preliminary steps include assessing the type and number of jobs that need to be filled, analyzing the tasks associated with a specific job, describing the job in terms of requirements and responsibilities, and specifying the human characteristics required to perform effectively in the job. Subsequent to these initial steps, the manager must recruit a large number of candidates for a position, identify and hire the best candidate for a job, and train the selected individual in the tasks associated with the job, in interpersonal skills, and in organizational values and norms.

I also outlined the concept and the significance of the psychological contract in contrast to the formal contract. I addressed the association between staffing procedures and career considerations from the perspective of the individual as well as the organization. Finally, I discussed the benefits of mentoring accruing to the protégé, the mentor, and the organizations and related them to career progress.

Key Terms

staffing, job analysis, job description, job specification, recruiting, hiring, training, psychological contract, career orientation, career anchors, mentor, protégé, mentor-protégé compatibility

Your Perspectives

- Following is a list of a set of jobs in sport management. Assume that you are offered all of these jobs and that the remuneration for these jobs is more or less equal. Rank these jobs in order of your preference. Explain your preferences in terms of the attraction of the jobs or organizations, your own estimates of how well you will do in each job, and the match between you and the jobs.
    - Director of a large YMCA sport and recreation program
    - Director of a metropolitan city recreation department
    - Executive director of a national sport governing body

- Manager in a sporting goods store
- Manager of a stadium or arena
- Marketing manager for a professional team
- General manager for a professional team

- One way of recognizing one's career anchor is to recall one's work experiences and the reactions to those experiences. Consider the following experiences and your reactions (i.e., positive, negative, or both) to them (Schein 1978). Relate these work experiences and reactions to your own perceived talents, needs, and values. A composite of all of these experiences and feelings would suggest which of the five career anchors is relatively more important to you?

  1. Why did you choose your major area of concentration in high school and your major in college? How did you feel about them?

  2. What were your expectations and experiences with your first job?

  3. How often have you changed jobs and why?

  4. Why have you chosen your current program of study? What do you expect to do after graduation? What are your expectations for the next 10 years?

Leadership

Learning Objectives

After reading this chapter you will be able to

- define leadership and describe forms of leader behavior;
- explain the multidimensional model of leadership, its components, and the relationships among these components;
- distinguish between transactional and transformational leadership and their effects;
- define charismatic leadership;
- explain the advantages and disadvantages of member participation in decision making;
- understand the varying degrees of participation by members; and
- know the critical attributes of a problem situation that determine the appropriate level of participation by members.

One of the significant processes in management of human resources is leadership. The leadership that the immediate supervisor and top-level administrators provide helps employees understand their roles and performance expectations and their relationships to organizational goals and reward systems. In addition, good leadership enhances employees' personal growth and development, motivation, performance, and job satisfaction. Therefore, managers need to have a clear understanding of the dynamics of leadership within organizations.

This chapter begins with a definition of leadership in the organizational context and presents the multidimensional model of leadership that synthesizes various approaches to leadership. I describe the more popular theories of leadership that the multidimensional model subsumes. I also explain the recent emphasis on transformational leadership and describe the critical differences between transformational and transactional leadership. The chapter concludes with a section on decision making. More specifically, the last section outlines the advantages and disadvantages of engaging members in decision making and the various methods of involving members in decision making.

The circumstances under which management should involve members in decision making also are discussed. An understanding of these various approaches to leadership and decision making will help the manager analyze the specific circumstances facing him or her and choose the leader behaviors or decision styles appropriate to a particular set of circumstances.

Definitions of Leadership

All of the definitions of **leadership** imply three significant elements of leadership:

- Leadership is a behavioral process.
- Leadership is interpersonal in nature.
- Leadership is aimed at **influencing** and motivating members toward group or organizational goals.

In Their View

The following are some excerpts from Drucker's (1992) book titled *Managing for the Future*. Drucker, who is one of the most renowned management scholars, emphasizes the great amount of work that leadership warrants. Although he is focusing on top-level managers, his pronouncements are equally valid at lower levels.

> Leadership does matter, of course. But, alas, it is something different from what is now touted under this label. It has little to do with "leadership qualities" and even less to do with "charisma." It is mundane, unromantic and boring. Its essence is performance. (p. 119)
>
> What then is leadership if it is not charisma and it is not a set of personality traits? The first thing to say about it is that it is work—something stressed again and again by the most charismatic leaders. . . . (p. 120)
>
> The foundation of effective leadership is thinking through the organization's mission, defining it and establishing it, clearly and visibly. The leader sets the goals, sets the priorities, and sets and maintains the standards. (p. 121)

For instance, Tosi, Rizzo, and Carroll (1986) suggested that "leadership is interpersonal influence which occurs when one person is able to gain compliance from another in the direction of organiza-

tionally desired goals" (p. 550). Although the term "compliance" in their definition may be offensive to some, the definition suggests that the organizational goals impose certain requirements on every member of an organization and that the function of leadership is to ensure that the members fulfill those requirements in the pursuit of organizational goals. Johns (1988) implied the same thing: "Effective leadership involves exerting influence in a way that achieves the organization's goals by enhancing the productivity and satisfaction of the work force" (p. 309). One underlying theme is that in the process of achieving organizational goals, increasing members' capacity for production and satisfaction thereof become central to the concept of leadership. Yukl and Van Fleet (1992) provided a more elaborate definition:

> Leadership is a process that includes influencing the task objectives and strategies of a group or organization, influencing people in the organization to implement the strategies and achieve the objectives, influencing group maintenance and identification, and influencing the culture of organizations. (p. 149)

In this definition, leadership includes shaping organizational objectives (i.e., setting new objectives or altering old ones) and maintaining the group and organizational culture. Thus, leadership pervades not only at the individual level but also at the group and organizational level.

If leadership is a behavioral process as noted, the focus is on what the leader does rather than on what the leader is. Therefore, managers must understand the various descriptions of leader behavior and their utility.

In a Nutshell

All definitions of leadership emphasize that it is a behavioral process aimed at influencing members to work toward achieving the group's goals. Thus the focus is on what the leader does rather than what the leader is. A critical purpose of leadership is to enhance members' productivity and satisfaction.

Leader Behavior Descriptions

Scholars from The Ohio State University and the University of Michigan were the first to describe and categorize the various forms of leader behaviors in industry and business. After considerable research over a period of time, the scholars from these two universities proposed two broad categories of leader behaviors—Ohio State proposed consideration and initiating structure (Halpin and Winer 1957), and Michigan proposed employee-oriented leadership and production-oriented leadership (Katz, Maccoby, and Morse 1950; Katz et al. 1951).

In the Ohio State scheme, consideration behavior reflects a leader's concern for members' well-being and for warm and friendly relations within the group. Initiating structure is behavior that clarifies the roles for both the leader and the members for effective performance on the group's tasks. Similarly, Michigan scholars defined employee orientation as the leader's concern with the human relations aspect of the job. On the other hand, production orientation reflects the leader's concern with the job and productivity.

A later attempt at synthesizing the foregoing efforts resulted in a four-dimensional description of leader behavior—support, interaction facilitation, goal emphasis, and work facilitation. Support behaviors aim at enhancing members' feelings of personal worth and importance. Interaction facilitation behaviors foster close and mutually satisfying relationships within the group. Goal emphasis behaviors emphasize the group's goals and their attainment. Work facilitation behaviors facilitate goal attainment by coordinating group activities and providing technical guidance (Taylor and Bowers 1972).

One of the criticisms of earlier attempts at describing leader behaviors was that just two or four dimensions cannot adequately describe leader behaviors. The second concern was that these earlier schemes confounded the extent to which the leader was participative with other forms of leader behavior. For instance, Ohio State's initiating structure included autocratic means of making decisions, and consideration included participative behaviors of the leader. Researchers have suggested that the style of decision making (i.e., participative or autocratic decision style) should be separated from the substance of those decisions (e.g., Chelladurai and Doherty 1998). For instance, the director of a recreation department may make a decision by himself or herself to install air conditioning in the workplace (i.e., reflecting an autocratic decision style), yet that decision is meant to enhance the comfort and welfare of the employees (i.e., consideration behavior). In contrast, another director may engage his or her employees in identifying and implementing ways to improve the performance of the group (i.e., a participative decision style reflecting initiat-

ing structure). In other words, a leader's concerns with task achievement or employee welfare should be treated independent of the extent to which the leader involves the members in making decisions. The issue of the appropriateness of autocratic and democratic decision making is discussed later in this chapter.

Given these concerns, later attempts at describing leader behavior have included several categories of leadership (House and Mitchell 1974, Stogdill 1963, Yukl 1989, Yukl and Van Fleet 1992). For instance, Yukl's (1989) managerial practices survey contains 11 behavior categories (see table 10.1).

In the context of sport and coaching, Chelladurai and Saleh (1980) identified five dimensions of leader behavior in sport situations—training and instruction, social support, positive feedback, democratic behavior, and autocratic behavior. These five dimensions are described in table 10.2. Training and instruction and positive feedback are related to the process of task accomplishment and the degree of task accomplishment, respectively. Social support is concerned with the social needs of members, individually and collectively. Democratic behavior and autocratic behavior are concerned with the degree to which the leader allows members to participate in decision making.

While the description of leader behaviors is necessary, it is not sufficient to understand the dynamics of leadership and its effects in their totality. The critical concern is whether the various forms of leader behavior described would be appropriate under all circumstances or whether their effectiveness depends on characteristics of the individuals or the situation. Because leadership involves the situations or organizational contexts in which both the leader and members are embedded, researchers have advanced several theories to suggest that certain forms of behaviors are appropriate in different situations. The following section outlines a synthesis of the various situational approaches to leadership.

Multidimensional Model of Leadership

The multidimensional model of leadership (Chelladurai 1978, Chelladurai 1993a) is an attempt to synthesize and to reconcile existing theories of leadership. A schematic illustration of the model is presented in figure 10.1.

Essentially, the model focuses on three states of leader behavior—required, preferred, and actual. It

Table 10.1 Dimensions of Yukl's (1981) Managerial Practices Survey

Dimension	Description
Networking	Socializing informally; developing contacts with people who are a source of information and support; and maintaining relationships through periodic interaction including visits, telephone calls, and correspondence and through attendance of meetings and social events
Supporting	Acting friendly and considerate, showing sympathy and support when someone is upset, listening to complaints and problems, looking out for others' interests, providing helpful career advice, doing things to aid others' career advancement
Managing conflict and team building	Encouraging and facilitating constructive resolution of conflict, fostering teamwork and cooperation, and building identification with the organizational unit or team
Motivating	Setting an example of proper behavior by one's own actions and using influence techniques that appeal to emotions, values, or logic to generate enthusiasm for the work and commitment to task objectives or to induce someone to carry out a request for support, cooperation, assistance, resources, or authorization
Recognizing and rewarding	Providing praise, recognition, and tangible rewards for effective performance, significant achievements, and special contributions and expressing respect and appreciation for others' accomplishments
Planning and organizing	Determining long-range objectives and strategies for adapting to environmental change; identifying necessary action steps to carry out a project or activity; allocating resources among activities according to priorities; and determining how to improve efficiency, productivity, and coordination with other parts of the organization
Problem solving	Identifying work-related problems; analyzing problems in a systematic, but timely, manner to determine causes and to find solutions; and acting decisively to implement solutions and to manage crises
Consulting and delegating	Checking with others before making changes that affect them, encouraging suggestions for improvement, inviting participation in decision making, incorporating the ideas and suggestions of others in decisions, and allowing others to have substantial discretion in carrying out work activities and managing problems
Monitoring operations and environment	Gathering information about the progress and quality of work activities, the success or failure of activities or projects, and the performance of individual contributors; determining the needs of clients or users; and scanning the environment to detect threats and opportunities
Informing	Disseminating relevant information about decisions, plans, and activities to others who need it to do their work; providing written materials and documents; answering requests for technical information; and telling others about the organizational unit to promote its reputation
Clarifying roles and objectives	Assigning tasks; providing direction in how to do the work; and communicating a clear understanding of job responsibilities, task objectives, deadlines, and performance expectations

Leadership in Organization 2/E by Yukl, Gary, © 1989. Reprinted by permission of Prentice-Hall, Inc., Upper Saddle River, NJ.

Table 10.2 Dimensions of Leader Behavior in Sports

Dimension	Description
Training and instruction	Coaching behavior aimed at improving the athletes' performance by emphasizing and facilitating hard and strenuous training; instructing them in the skills, techniques, and tactics of the sport; clarifying the relationship among the members; and structuring and coordinating the members' activities
Social support	Coaching behavior characterized by a concern for the welfare of individual athletes, positive group atmosphere, and warm interpersonal relations with members
Positive feedback	Coaching behavior that reinforces an athlete by recognizing and rewarding good performance
Democratic behavior	Coaching behavior that allows greater participation by athletes in decisions pertaining to group goals, practice methods, and game tactics and strategies
Autocratic behavior	Coaching behavior that involves independent decision making and that stresses personal authority

Source: Chelladurai and Saleh (1980).

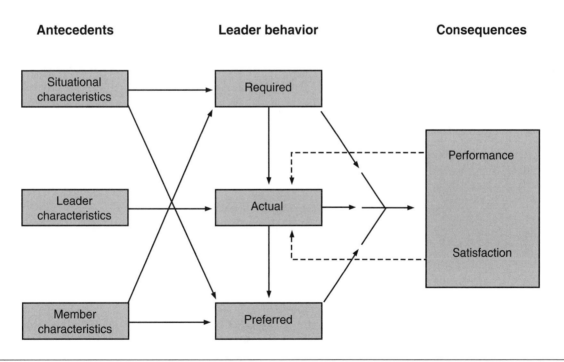

Figure 10.1 The multidimensional model of leadership.

From Chelladurai, P., "Leadership," in R.N. Singer, M. Murphey, and L.K. Tennant, Eds.: HANDBOOK OF RESEARCH ON SPORT PSYCHOLOGY, pp. 647-671. Copyright © 1993 by The International Society of Sport Psychology. Used by permission of Macmillan Reference USA, a Simon & Schuster Macmillan Company.

To facilitate a greater understanding of the role of leadership in sports, Chelladurai (1981) presented a modified version of the Porter and Lawler (1968) model of motivation (see chapter 7, figure 7.1) and discussed the relevance of the various dimensions of coaching behavior to the motivational process as shown in the figure below. The member's ability (box 6) and the accuracy of the perception of his or her role (box 7) moderate the effort-performance relationship (from box 2 to box 3). Finally, the member's perception of the equity of the rewards (box 8) influences the reward-satisfaction relationship (from box 4 to box 5).

Given this motivation-performance-satisfaction sequence, identifying the points at which the coach can profitably intervene to enhance the motivational state of the individual is easier. The coach's social support behavior (box A) makes the effort phase enjoyable and frees it from any interpersonal friction. Training and instruction behavior (box B) develops the member's ability and clarifies role expectations. Thus, training and instruction behavior strengthens the relationship between effort and performance. Democratic behavior increases the clarity of roles for the members and the feelings of involvement in decisions. Finally, positive feedback behavior (box C) ensures the equitable distribution of a coach's personal rewards (i.e., equal rewards for equal performance) and leads to a sense of equity and justice among the members.

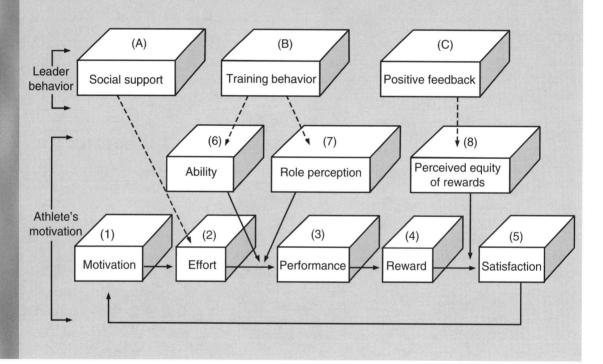

classifies the antecedent variables that determine these leader behaviors into situational characteristics, member characteristics, and leader characteristics. The consequences (i.e., outcome variables) in the model are group performance and satisfaction.

Required Leader Behavior

Stewart (1982) suggested that in any organizational context, the manager or leader faces certain de- mands and constraints that the organization imposes on the position. Demands are those activities expected of a leader in a given situation that he or she must fulfill in order for the group or organization to accept him or her. Constraints set the limits within which the leader can act. In other words, the leader is prohibited from acting in the domain beyond the boundaries that the constraints set. According to Stewart (1982), the area between demands and constraints of the situation represents the choices a leader has.

Situituation Characteristics and Required Behavior

What are those situational elements (i.e., demands and constraints) that have such strong influence on leader behavior? Osborn and Hunt (1975) labeled these **situational characteristics** as macro variables. They identified the size of the group, its technology, and its formal structure as some of the macro variables. In addition to these variables, the multidimensional model also includes the task of the group, the organizational goals, the norms of a particular social setting, and the nature of the group as other situational characteristics that influence and control leader behavior.

Because the construct of leadership refers to a group, it is necessary to study leader behavior in terms of the group's tasks, processes, and performance. For example, in a university department of sport or recreation management, different units (or groups) may be involved in the performance of different tasks (e.g., undergraduate or graduate programs in marketing or organizational behavior). Similarly, for each athletic team in a university, the group task becomes a part of the situation.

Organizational goals also affect the total group including the leader. For instance, the relative emphases placed on quality compared with quantity in a production firm affect both the manager's and the employees' behavior. In athletics, the differing goal orientations of professional and educational athletics lead to different behavioral expectations for the coaches and athletes in the two domains of athletics.

The norms and codes of conduct that are prevalent (or emerging) in a given social setting form a significant set of situational factors that impinge on leadership. Contrast, for instance, the social norms surrounding a coach with those surrounding a manager of a city recreation department. The social norms of the athletic setting permit a coach to yell and scream at the players, but such behaviors are proscribed in the case of the manager.

Member Characteristics and Required Behavior

Chelladurai (1993a) argued that the nature of the group as a whole would also influence that segment of leader behavior required in a situation. For instance, the differences in orientations between volunteers and professionals would impose differential demands on the leader (see chapters 1 and 2). One obvious difference between volunteer and paid professional employees is that one group is paid for their work and one is not. To the extent the supervisor has some control over such remuneration to the worker,

the supervisor also has the influence to motivate the members. In the case of volunteers, the leader has to resort to other means of influencing the members. From a different perspective, a leader's behaviors vary among youth volunteers, adult volunteers, and senior volunteers. Note here that the concern is with the nature of the group as a whole and not with individual differences within the group. For instance, House (1971) referred to perceived ability as an **individual difference variable**. Groups have differences in actual or perceived ability just as individuals do. Athletes at the Division I level of the NCAA are presumed to have higher ability than those from Division III. Similarly, recreation leaders of youth groups would behave somewhat differently from the leaders of senior citizens. When ability or maturity is viewed from the group's perspective, it has an impact on how the leader should behave in a given context (i.e., **required leader behavior**).

In a Nutshell

The situational variables (i.e., unit size, technology, formal structure, group task, organizational goals, the norms and behavioral expectations in a particular social context, and the nature of the group) influence and control a portion of a leader's behavior. The portion of leader behavior that situational factors control is referred to as the required leader behavior. These required behaviors tend to be task-oriented or instrumental in the realization of the group's objectives.

Preferred Leader Behavior

The preferences of members for specific leader behaviors (i.e., **preferred leader behavior**) stem from both the situational characteristics and the characteristics of the members themselves.

Situational Characteristics and Preferred Behavior

House's path-goal theory of leadership (House 1971, House and Dessler 1974), which is discussed on page 166, suggests that the impact of the task (particularly, its characteristics of interdependence and variability) is an immediate determinant of member preferences. For example, a maintenance worker in an athletic department who is engaged in independent and routine tasks is not likely to prefer higher levels of guidance from the supervisor. In contrast, marketing assistants involved collaboratively in the design and promotions of a new sports program may prefer more scrutiny and feedback from their marketing director. As noted earlier, the situational characteristics of unit size, technology, organizational goals, and norms place some constraints and demands on the leader.

The same situational characteristics also influence member preferences for specific forms of leader behavior. Therefore, their preferences for certain forms of leader behavior reflect the influences of the situation (Bass 1985, House 1971, Yukl 1989, Yukl and Van Fleet 1992). For instance, the preferences of an employee for interpersonal interactions with the athletic director (i.e., social support) would be lower in a large Division I institution than in a small Division III institution because the opportunities for such interactions are dependent on the size of the organization. By the same token, coaches in Division I may prefer greater scrutiny and guidance from the superiors regarding athletes' academic eligibility than coaches in Division III because of the strict rules enforced by the NCAA and the severe penalties imposed for violations of those rules.

Member Characteristics and Preferred Behavior

Individual difference factors were discussed at length in part II. These individual differences influence members' preferences for particular leader behaviors. For example, the path-goal theory highlights the effect of task relevant ability (House 1971, House and Dessler 1974). Consider, for example, two new employees A and B in the ticketing department of a university athletic department. Employee A perceives that he or she has sufficient ability to carry out the assigned tasks and, therefore, may not prefer much guidance and training. On the other hand, employee B believes that he or she does not have the understanding or the ability to perform the tasks and prefers that the supervisor spend more time clarifying, guiding, and coaching him or her.

Similarly, a number of personality traits, such as need for affiliation and need for achievement, influence members' preferences for different leader behaviors. Employees A and B in our example may differ in their need for affiliation. The person who has a greater need for affiliation may prefer the supervisor to interact more often at the social level in order to satisfy to some extent the need for affiliation. By the same token, employees A and B may differ in their need to achieve at moderately challenging tasks and to seek feedback (McClelland 1961). That is, the employee with a higher need to achieve may prefer that the director provide challenge, responsibility, and feedback (House and Dessler 1974).

House's Path-Goal Theory

The essence of House's (1971) path-goal theory of leadership is that the motivational function of the leader consists of increasing personal payoffs to subordinates for work—goal attainment and making the path to these payoffs easier to travel by clarifying it, reducing road blocks and pitfalls, and increasing the opportunities for personal satisfaction en route (p. 323).

The theory focuses on members' personal goals, their perceptions of the organizational goals, and the most effective paths to these goals. That is, the theory attempts to specify how leadership should clarify the path of members to desired goals or rewards.

The path-goal theory views the leader's function as a supplemental one. That is, leadership serves as an immediate source of rewards and satisfaction or as an instrument to future rewards and satisfaction, and it supplements the motivation that organizational factors provide (e.g., clarity of goals, preciseness of procedures, and guidance and support that the group provides).

The second proposition of the path-goal theory is that the motivational effect of leadership is a function of the situation that, in turn, comprises the members and the environmental pressures and demands. Members' personality and their perceptions of their ability affect their preferences for or reactions to specific forms of leader behavior. Similarly, leader behavior should be varied according to the nature of the tasks, that is the extent to which they are routine or variable, interdependent, and inherently satisfying. In the athletic context, athletes in interdependent sports (e.g., team sports) and athletes in variable sports (e.g., basketball) prefer more training and instruction than athletes in independent sports and nonvariable sports (e.g., track and field) (Chelladurai and Carron 1982).

In overview, the path-goal theory places greater emphasis on members, their ability, and their personal dispositions. Leadership is a process by which members' personal goals are aligned with organizational goals. Thus, achieving organizational goals leads to satisfaction of personal goals.

Lorsch and Morse (1974) and Morse (1976) suggested that an individual's attitude toward authority affects his or her reactions toward different types of supervision. Those whose respect for authority is high are more compliant to a leader's authority than those whose respect for authority is low. Thus, a director of marketing in an athletic department needs to vary the extent and manner of exercising his or her authority across members based on their attitude toward authority. Cognitive complexity refers to the way individuals process information and their capacity to manage different pieces of information. Researchers also expect it to determine, in part, the preference for structuring behavior from the leader (Wynne and Hunsaker 1975). For instance, the marketing director may have to spend extra time with those subordinates who have a low level of cognitive complexity to explain each of several aspects of a marketing project and the interrelationships among them.

In a Nutshell

Although all members are under the influence of the same situational characteristics, their preferences for specific forms of leader behavior may vary. These variations are a function of member characteristics including ability and personality.

Actual Leader Behavior

The third, and obviously the most central, state of leader behavior is actual behavior. As noted, two of the determinants of actual leader behavior are the requirements of the situation and the preferences of members. Osborn and Hunt (1975) divided the actual leader behavior into adaptive behaviors (i.e., adaptations to situational requirements) and reactive behaviors (i.e., reactions to member preferences). These two forms of leader behavior also are a function of a leader's personal characteristics, particularly personality and ability.

Personality and Actual Behavior

The leader's **personality** is the central focus of Fiedler's (1967) contingency model of leadership, which is summarized on page 168. According to Fiedler, leaders can be characterized as either task-oriented or relations-oriented leaders. The primary motive of task-oriented leaders is task accomplishment. Therefore, they tend to behave in a relatively more directing and autocratic manner in order to accomplish the task at hand. On the other hand, concern for positive group atmosphere motivates relations-oriented leaders, so they are likely to be more participative and less directive.

McClelland and his associates (McClelland 1961, 1975; McClelland and Burnham 1976; McClelland and Winter 1969) have isolated the needs for power, achievement, and affiliations as the most significant in the organizational context, particularly with reference to leaders or managers. Their theory of managerial motivation is summarized on page 170. Essentially, they noted how managers with differing levels of these needs behaved differently toward their subordinates. They found that those managers who had a high level of need for power moderated by their concern for the group and its productivity, a moderate level of need for achievement, and even lower levels of need for affiliation were more effective than those who had a low level of the need for power and a relatively higher level of the other two needs.

Ability and Actual Behavior

Ability of the leader is made up of two components. One of these components is the leader's specific knowledge and expertise concerning various aspects of the group task and the processes necessary for the attainment of the group's goals. Katz (1972) called it the technical skill. This specific ability varies with different leadership positions. In a city recreation department, knowledge of all the complex rules and regulations of the local government surrounding the activities of the department represents this type of technical ability.

The second component of ability includes the leader's capacity to conceptualize the organization as a whole and analyze the complexities of a problem and to persuade subordinates about the efficiency of a particular approach. According to Katz (1972), this is conceptual ability, which is a general ability that is transferable across situations. When a leader has the technical ability related to specific tasks and processes, he or she should be more confident in giving specific directions to members on how the tasks should be carried out. In the absence of such skills, the leader may rely on senior members to provide the guidance and coaching to other members. Similarly, when a leader has the conceptual ability, he or she can explain more easily the relationships of specific actions to a gestalt, or to the global picture of what is being sought. When the leader does not have conceptual ability, the leader may refrain from attempting to explain the actions in the context of the total picture or may be ineffective in his or her explanations.

Fiedler's Contingency Model of Leadership

In Fiedler's (1954, 1967, 1973) view, leadership effectiveness is contingent upon the fit between the leader's style and the situational favorableness. The leader's style (i.e., task orientation compared with employee or relations orientation) is a relatively stable personality characteristic. Fiedler measured this personality trait using the least preferred co-worker scale wherein the researcher asks subjects to recall an individual with whom they could work least well and to rate him or her on 16 to 20 bipolar items as follows:

Unpleasant   1   2   3   4   5   6   7   8   Pleasant

Those who score high on the scale (i.e., those who evaluate the least preferred co-worker more favorably) are relations-oriented leaders, and the low scorers are task-oriented leaders.

According to Fiedler, the situation may be more or less favorable to the leader for the exercise of influence over the subordinates. The favorableness of the situation is determined by

- leader-member relations (i.e., the extent of friendship and respect from the members),
- task structure (i.e., the clarity of goals and processes thereof), and
- power position of the leader (i.e., the authority and control over rewards and punishments).

Fiedler's research showed that task-oriented leaders (i.e., low scorers on the least preferred co-worker scale) were more effective in situations very high or very low in favorableness. On the other

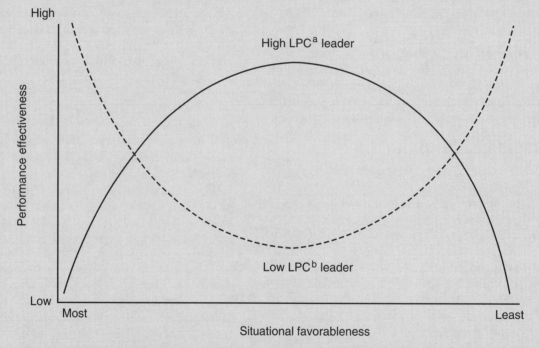

Leader-member relations	Good	Good	Good	Good	Poor	Poor	Poor	Poor
Task structure	Structured		Unstructured		Structured		Unstructured	
Leader position power	Strong	Weak	Strong	Weak	Strong	Weak	Strong	Weak

[a] High LPC=Scoring high on the least preferred co-worker scale.

[b] Low LPC=Scoring low on the least preferred co-worker scale.

Adapted from Fiedler 1967. (Top figure)

hand, relations-oriented leaders (i.e., high scorers on the least preferred co-worker scale) were more effective in moderately favorable situations. These contingent relationships between leader's style and situational favorableness are illustrated in the figure.

The lower part of the figure shows the continuum of situational favorableness beginning with the most favorable situation in which the leader-member relations are good, the task is structured, and the leader's power position is strong. At the other end of the continuum is the least favorable situation in which leader-member relations are poor, the task is unstructured, and the leader's power position is weak. Between the ends of the continuum are situations of varying favorableness to the exercise of influence depending on the configuration of the levels of leader-member relations, task structure, and leader position power.

The most important implication of Fiedler's theory is that any leadership style can be effective provided it is matched with the situation and its favorableness. In addition, because the leadership style is a stable personality characteristic, changing the situation is easier than changing leadership style. That is, the organization can change the situation by altering

- the composition of the group to create better leader-member relations (e.g., reassigning the manager or some employees of a sport facility to another facility);
- the task structure by varying the extent of rules and procedures in the task situation (e.g., letting the manager decide on how to manage the facility instead of following strict rules and procedures); or
- the power (or authority) of the leader (e.g., giving the facility manager the responsibility to evaluate the employees and recommend merit raises).

The sport situation might be most favorable to the leader (Chelladurai 1985). Because athletes participate voluntarily and choose the activity and the team, both the coach and the athletes share the organizational goal of pursuit of excellence. In addition, because all members of the organization clearly understand and accept the processes to achieve that goal, a great degree of **congruence** exists among the leader, the member, and the situation. Because the situation is favorable for the coach to exercise influence, an autocratic coach could be very effective. This view is consistent with the finding that coaches do tend to be generally autocratic and task-oriented in their leadership style (Hendry 1968, 1969; Ogilvie and Tutko 1966).

In a Nutshell

The demands and constraints that the situation imposes, the preferences of the members under his or her charge, and his or her own personal characteristics influence the actual behavior of a leader. Significant leader characteristics include ability, knowledge, experience, and personality. Some theorists, such as Fiedler, hold that leader personality is the most influential of these factors.

Performance and Satisfaction

The consequences included in the multidimensional model are **performance** and **satisfaction** (see figure 10.1). The degree to which the three states of leader behavior are congruent (i.e., the actual behavior is consistent with both the preferred and required behaviors) influences performance and satisfaction.

Thus, any of the states of leader behavior could be a limiting factor.

For example, in some bureaucratic organizations, outdated and dysfunctional rules and regulations might be a requirement within the system, and managers might enforce them. However, employees might intensely dislike these rules; therefore, performance and satisfaction would be reduced. For instance, employees in a city or a university recreation department spend considerable time and effort in interacting with the clients. Even so, the department requires the employees to punch a clock or keep a log of their activities on a daily basis. In addition, the organization expects the manager to enforce that rule. Such a bureaucratic requirement does not relate to the quality of the work done. Therefore, the employees are likely to be dissatisfied and may begin to work to satisfy the rule (i.e., just fulfill the minimal requirement). Similarly, if actual leader behavior deviated from

McClelland and Burnham's Theory of Managerial Motivation

McClelland and Burnham (1976) suggested that "the manager's job seems to call more for someone who can influence people than for someone who does things better on his own. In motivational terms, then, we might expect the successful manager to have a greater 'need for power' than 'need to achieve'" (p. 101). The need for power reflects "a desire to have impact, to be strong and influential" (p. 103). In addition, "the good manager's power is not oriented toward personal aggrandizement but toward the institution which he or she serves. . . . This is the 'socialized' face of power as distinguished from the concern for personal power" (p. 103).

According to McClelland and Burnham, the need for affiliation, which refers to the desire for the group to like and accept an individual, is least important to successful management. In fact, it could even be detrimental to successful management to the extent that it would lead to compromise on various rules in order to satisfy individual needs. In sum, "oddly enough, the good manager in a large company does not have a high need for achievement . . . although there must be plenty of that motive somewhere in his organization. . . . The top managers have a high need for power and an interest in influencing others, both greater than their interest in being liked by people" (p. 109).

the requirements of the organization or member preferences, it would detrimentally affect performance and satisfaction.

Feedback

In the multidimensional model, the leader is assumed to be flexible and capable of altering his or her behavior according to changing conditions. This perspective is consistent with the position that several scholars and researchers have taken (e.g., Bass 1985, House 1971, Yukl 1989). If a leader finds that his or her behavior has not resulted in increased performance of the group, the leader is likely to alter the actual behavior to enhance productivity (e.g., the manager of a fitness club may spend more time and effort in motivating the employees of the club). By the same token, if the leader finds that his or her group is not cohesive and integrated, the leader might begin emphasizing those aspects of his or her behavior that foster warm interpersonal relations within the group. In a similar manner, when the leader perceives low satisfaction among members, he or she might alter the behavior to enhance member satisfaction. The effects of the leader's perceptions of performance and satisfaction on actual leader behavior are indicated as feedback loops (or dotted lines) in figure 10.1.

Transformational and Transactional Leadership

In recent years, the transformation of organizations has raised great concern. Leaders are making frantic

In a Nutshell

The multidimensional model takes into account the characteristics of the situation, the leader, and the members, and it projects three states of leader behavior—required, preferred, and actual leader behaviors. The degree of congruence among these three states of leader behavior is assumed to be related to group performance and member satisfaction. While situational characteristics dictate a portion of the leader's behavior characteristics, that portion of behavior at the discretion of the leader is expected to have greater impact on member motivation and satisfaction. Thus, leadership plays a significant role in effective management of human resources.

efforts to change the structure and processes of all forms of organizations. Such efforts are called downsizing, right-sizing, re-engineering, restructuring, or refocusing. Any restructuring and repositioning of organizations requires strong leadership in the top positions. Those who guide their organizations to transform into innovative and profitable enterprises are called transformational leaders. The study of these leaders and transformational leadership also has intensified in the last two decades.

Several authors have suggested that most existing theories of leadership view the leader as transacting with his or her members (Bass 1990, Conger and Kanungo 1988, House and Podsakoff 1994). Such transactions involve the leader providing some resources including the leader's approval and support in return for the member's efforts toward the attainment of organizational goals. Transactional leadership is based on the assumption that the environment of the workgroup is somewhat stable and that both the leader and members are satisfied with the workgroup's purposes and processes. The members of the group have a stable set of needs and desires, and they are aware of the elements of transaction between themselves and the leader that would satisfy their needs and desires.

In Their View

Kerr and Jermier (1978) listed a number of factors that might serve as substitutes for leadership. These factors include members' characteristics (i.e., their professional orientation and affiliation), the nature of their task and the workgroup, and the organizational structure (including the policies and procedures). Those members who are highly trained may not need much guidance from the leader. The members also may receive such guidance from professional associations and from their peer groups. The workgroup also may provide the social support necessary when both personal and organizational problems arise. As noted before, organizational policies and procedures clearly may specify what the employee should do, how, and under what circumstances (as is the case in bureaucracies), making the leader's instrumental behavior redundant. Kerr and Jermier (1978) stressed that when numerous substitutes for leadership exist, a manager's attempts to influence members must be minimal; otherwise, the leadership might be viewed as interference.

In the multidimensional model described earlier, the leader operates within the confines of situational requirements. Further, the leader is expected to exercise his or her discretionary influence to motivate the members. Such discretionary influence may be in the form of rewards and punishments. The leader distributes rewards and punishments in exchange for member compliance or resistance to the leader's directions or requests. In this scenario, leadership is strictly a transactional process. That is, the leader offers something to the members in exchange for their efforts toward organizational goals. For instance, the owner of a sport-marketing company may be content with the business as it stands and with its management. The manager, in turn, operates as a leader in the transactional mode. That is, the manager may reward his or

her employees in the form of a bonus in proportion to the amount of business each employee brings in. This type of leadership with the creed, "You do this, you get that," is transactional in nature.

Transactional leadership is just a type of leadership, and it carries no moral tones. For instance, the exercise of a leader's discretionary influence entails the leader to set challenging goals for the members, helps them achieve those goals by enhancing their abilities, and supports them in their efforts (House 1971). In the example of the manager of a sport-marketing company, the manager may guide and coach the employees on how to get the business, set for them progressively challenging goals, and provide the necessary support for their efforts. However, the process is still transactional to the extent that the leader acknowledges and accepts situational demands.

In contrast, transformational leadership is defined as "the process of influencing major changes in the attitudes and assumptions of organization members (organizational culture) and building commitment for major changes in the organization's objectives and strategies" (Yukl and Van Fleet 1992, 174). According to this definition, the transformation occurs at three levels:

- Changes in organizational objectives and strategies
- Member commitment to the new set of goals and strategies
- Changes in the assumptions and attitudes of members

The basis for transformational leadership is a general discontent with the status quo, and transformational leaders are concerned with creating a new vision and order for the organization. In the process of changing the total organization, a transformational leader articulates the vision, convinces the members of the viability of the vision, and expresses confidence in their capacity to achieve that vision. Transformational leadership involves the arousal of members' higher-order needs that, in turn, elevates the level of effort beyond expectations (Bass 1985, Conger and Kanungo 1987). It also involves empowering the members to engage in innovative and creative ways to achieve the articulated vision. Note that transformational leadership involves a new vision, which is an alternative to the status quo. In fact, the terms transformational and visionary are used interchangeably to describe this form of leadership. The contrasts between transformational and transactional leadership are shown in table 10.3. The table shows that transactional

Table 10.3 Differences Between Transactional and Transformational Leadership

Leadership	Factors affected	Outcomes
Transactional	Cognition Abilities Exchanges	Lower turnover and absence Satisfaction Expected performance
Transformational	Emotions Values, goals, and needs Self-esteem	Higher aspirations Greater efforts Performance beyond expectations or call of duty Lower turnover and absence Satisfaction

Source: Bass (1985).

leadership influences the cognition and abilities of the member and influences the exchanges between the leader and member. Such exchanges lead to lower turnover and absence, member satisfaction, and expected performance. Transformational leadership, on the other hand, affects the emotions of members and their values, goals, needs, and self-esteem. These influences raise the aspirations of members who put forth greater efforts in order to achieve levels of performance beyond expectations. Note that these outcomes also are associated with higher job satisfaction and lower turnover or absence.

In the example of the manager of a sport-marketing company, the manager may believe that the business can be much better given the capacities of the members and the available opportunities in the market. Instead of operating within the existing constraints (i.e., the situational factors) and being confined to small scale operations limited to a few sports, the manager may see greater opportunities to expand not only in the magnitude of each individual project but also in the breadth of sport operations covered. This vision, of course, needs to be crystallized through a comprehensive analysis of present operations, market conditions, and the human and material resources available. The next step is to articulate this vision to the members and their place in the vision. The purpose here is to arouse members' need for achievement and self-esteem. In addition, the manager also may engage in creating a "can do" attitude and conviction in members. Equally important is the notion of encouraging and permitting the members to be creative in their approach to marketing in general and to their own projects and not to be confined to traditional methods. Finally, the manager also may express his or her

confidence in members' ability and determination to achieve that vision. Such a leadership orientation is likely to raise the aspirations of the members and nudge them to put in greater efforts in identifying and defining projects to secure new clients and fulfilling their needs. As a result, the members are likely to perform at a higher level than the level expected from a transactional perspective. In sum, such transformational leadership leads to members developing a psychological stake in their work.

In a Nutshell

Transactional leadership implies that the leader and members are satisfied with the status quo, and the leader's function is to motivate the members to attain the established goals. In contrast, transformational leadership refers to the extent to which the leader attempts to change the situation in terms of goals and processes, incites the higher-order needs of his or her followers, and exhibits confidence in their capacity to attain the elevated aspirations.

Transformational Leadership and the Multidimensional Model

In terms of Chelladurai's multidimensional model outlined earlier, a transformational leader attempts to alter the situational characteristics (i.e., goals and strategies) and the beliefs and attitudes of members including lower-level leaders or managers. In other words, instead of accepting the situational and member characteristics as a given, transformational leaders believe that those givens are alterable and they act accordingly. Thus, the behaviors and the effects of transformational leadership can be superimposed on the multidimensional model as shown in figure 10.2.

Many of the descriptions of transformational leadership imply that such leadership begins with the chief executive officer of an organization and that it begins to filter down to lower levels through the empowerment of successive levels of subordinates. For example, Lee Iacocca, former chief executive officer of the Chrysler Corporation, is renowned for transforming the corporation from the brink of bankruptcy to the innovative and profitable organization that it is today. He could not have done it without the wholehearted participation of lower-level managers and the workers. Other renowned transformational leaders, such as Mahatma Gandhi of India and Nelson Mandela of South Africa, could not have achieved what they did without active cooperation of their immediate followers.

In the context of sport and recreation, the current elevated image and status and, of course, the profitability of the NBA is largely attributed to the transformational leadership that Commissioner David Stern has provided. While he is eminently successful as a transformational leader, others, such as the owners, who bought into his vision and worked to achieve that vision, also deserve credit for the achievement. Similarly, Donna Lopiano of

the Women's Sport Foundation has transformed the women's movement in sport into an effective organization. On a global level, Juan Antonio Samaranch, president of the International Olympic Committee since 1980, has transformed the outlook and orientation of the International Olympic Committee members toward making the committee and the quadrennial Olympic Games a reservoir of revenue potential. In the process, he has enlisted the business and media communities to generate enough revenue to sustain the Olympic movement in general and to support athletic endeavor in developing countries.

However, the notion of transformational leadership need not be confined to large organizations with several levels of hierarchical structure. Smaller organizations with fewer levels of management and fewer members also can be the focus of transformational leadership. A typical example is that of a coach of an athletic team who transforms his or her team from a "perennial doormat" into a winning team. Such a coach begins with articulating a discontent with the current image of the team, articulating a vision wherein the team is performing in a winning fashion, and convincing the members that the vision is attainable and that they have the abilities to be a winning team. The only difference between the transformational leadership of a chief executive officer of a large corporation and that of

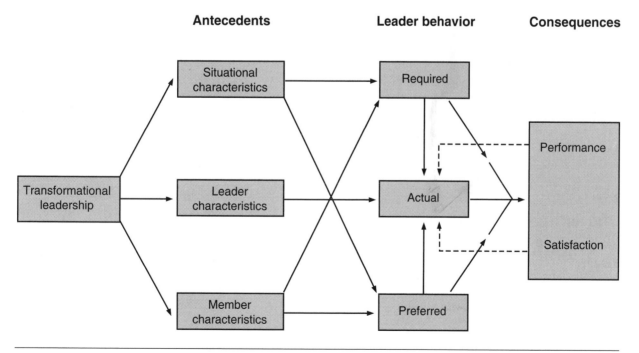

Figure 10.2   Modified multidimensional model of leadership.

From Chelladurai, P., "Leadership," in R.N. Singer, M. Murphey, and L.K. Tennant, Eds.: HANDBOOK OF RESEARCH ON SPORT PSYCHOLOGY, pp. 647-671. Copyright © 1993 by The International Society of Sport Psychology. Used by permission of Macmillan Reference USA, a Simon & Schuster Macmillan Company.

the coach is that the coach does not have to address several layers of managers. Instead, he or she interacts with the members directly.

In the context of sport organizations, Weese (1995, 1996) found that the directors of campus recreation in the universities belonging to the Big Ten and Mid-American Conferences varied in the extent to which they exhibited transformational leadership. Although he did not find a significant relationship between transformational leadership and organizational effectiveness as perceived by student participants in campus recreation, a telling finding was that the transformational leaders were able to cultivate the organizational culture (i.e., the system of values and beliefs) that, in turn, was positively associated with organizational effectiveness. The point is that the major contribution of transformational leadership is to change the values, beliefs, and aspirations of members (Weese 1995, 1996).

In a similar manner, Doherty and Danylchuk (1996) found that the coaches of university athletic teams in Canada perceived that their athletic administrators exhibited a considerable amount of transformational leadership. Further, such transformational leadership from the administrators was associated positively with coaches' perceptions of leadership effectiveness, their satisfaction with the leadership they received, and their extra effort to achieve organizational goals. In a later study of the same data, Doherty (1997) found that female and younger athletic administrators of Canadian university athletics exhibited more transformational leadership than their male and older counterparts. This interesting finding shows that women can be as effective as men in leadership positions and that both male and female subordinates are appreciative of such leadership. Further, Doherty (1997) speculated that the changing values and beliefs of younger administrators could be the source of their transformational leadership.

Transformational and Charismatic Leadership

Charismatic leadership is a term that is used often in conjunction with transformational leadership. While the two terms have been used synonymously in some contexts, considering them as distinct concepts is useful. Yukl and Van Fleet (1992) noted that charismatic leadership

> refers to the follower perception that a leader possesses a divinely inspired gift and is somehow unique and larger than life. . . . they [followers] also idolize or worship the leader

as a superhuman hero or spiritual figure. . . . Thus, with charismatic leadership the focus is on an individual leader rather than on a leadership process that may be shared among multiple leaders. (p. 174)

In this view, charisma is something that the leader is purported to have that enables him or her to transform the group or organization. Thus, charisma is a set of laudable attributes of the leader and a set of beliefs the members have about the leader. From this perspective, charisma is a personal resource that leaders exploit successfully in transforming their organizations and their members. Note that charisma is an attributional phenomenon, i.e., the attributions that the followers make regarding the extraordinary abilities of the leader. Such strong and positive attributions are the source of power that facilitates greater acceptance of the leader's pronouncements and the willingness to abide by his or her dictates and directions. Renowned coaches, such as Joe Paterno and Rick Pitino, have charisma. Donna Lopiano, to whom I referred earlier, has considerable influence because of the charisma she possesses and the judicious manner in which she uses that charisma.

In a Nutshell

Charismatic leadership refers to perceptions of members that the leader possesses some extraordinary gifts and talents. Effective leaders use these perceptions to engage the members in the transformation of the situation and themselves.

Leadership and Decision Making

All leaders are engaged in making decisions about critical issues, such as the group's goals and objectives, the appropriate means of achieving those goals, and the distribution of duties and responsibilities to members of the group. These decisions can be viewed as a cognitive process and as a social process.

Decision Making as a Cognitive Process

The emphasis in decision making as a cognitive process is on the rationality of the decision. That is, the concern is with evaluating the available alternatives and selecting the best one to achieve a desired end. Leaders can arrive at rational decisions only after defining the problem clearly, identifying relevant constraints, generating possible and plausible alternatives, evaluating and ranking the alternatives according to some selected criteria, and selecting the best alternative in terms of those criteria. In this view, generating alternatives and evaluating them become crucial to decision making. Thus, the focus here is on the objective and optimal use of available information. Because more information is available in a group than in an individual, the leader is well advised to include the members in the cognitive process of decision making. Such group involvement is beneficial in defining the problem and identifying alternate solutions to the problem. The extent to which the group can be involved in decision making and under what conditions are discussed later in the chapter.

Decision Making as a Social Process

The social process of decision making refers to the degree to which members of a group are allowed to participate in decision making and the varying degrees of influence the members have on the decisions. Thus, the social process of decision making may vary from strictly autocratic decision making by the manager to varying degrees of participation by members (e.g., consultation with one or a few members, consultation with all members, group decision making, and delegation). Chelladurai and Haggerty (1978) called these variations the decision styles of the leader.

Member involvement in decision making is a major concern in human resource management; therefore, this section focuses on the social processes of decision making in greater detail. Some leaders are described as autocratic and others as participative. For instance, Vince Lombardi, the famous football coach, was perceived to be autocratic in making decisions. As another example, the late Hal Ballard, former owner of the Toronto Maple Leafs hockey team, supposedly made decisions on his own. Successful managers have used the autocratic decision style in several other instances.

One obvious explanation is that their personality predisposes such individuals to be autocratic. A different perspective holds that instead of viewing individuals as autocratic or participative, society must view the situation as calling for autocratic or participative style of decision making (Vroom and Yetton 1973). In this view, being autocratic is neither evil nor immoral by itself. For instance, when a parent decides autocratically that the preschooler should go to bed, the parent is genuinely concerned about the welfare of the child and is deemed to make an optimal decision, albeit autocratically. On the other hand, the parent probably would permit a teenager to engage in discussions and participate in the decision regarding the choice of a university for higher education. The difference between the preschooler and the teenager in the capacity to participate meaningfully in decisions calls for different social processes of decision making. From the human resource management perspective, a manager must be aware of the benefits and drawbacks of participative decision making and of the appropriate degree of participation under varying circumstances.

Advantages of Participative Decision Making

The benefits of allowing members to participate in decision making can be summarized as

- higher rationality of the decisions,
- better understanding of the decisions,
- ownership of the decisions, and
- better execution of the decisions.

As noted earlier, the rationality of a decision is improved if more members participate in the decision because a group has more information and insight than an individual. This wider and deeper base of information and expertise assists the manager in clarifying the problem and in identifying and evaluating alternative solutions to the problem. Even more importantly, participative decisions enable the members to comprehend more clearly the problem and its solution. In addition, when members participate in decision making, they believe it is their decision and develop a sense of ownership over the decision. Finally, when members understand the decision and feel ownership of the decision, they are more likely to execute the decision more efficiently and effectively.

From an individual's perspective, participation in decision making makes the member more knowledgeable and more capable of analyzing problems and their attributes and of evaluating several options available. These experiences are critical to one's personal growth and development, which is one significant aim of human resource management. Further, such feelings of growth and development and the sense of ownership in decisions are likely to enhance the total job experience and job satisfaction.

Disadvantages of Participative Decision Making

Managers also must be aware of some of the drawbacks of participative decisions. The obvious problem is that participative decisions take time. For example, basketball coaches do not engage in participative decisions during timeouts because timeouts do not provide enough time for discussion and participation. In addition, the leader may have more information than the group as a whole. In such a case, participative decisions would be simply "pooling of ignorance" (Chelladurai 1985) and may not lead to higher-quality decisions. Another significant factor that affects the effectiveness of participative decisions is the extent to which the group is integrated. If a group is not so well integrated and is marked by conflicts among cliques within the group, the leader should be very careful in engaging that group in participative decisions.

Advantages of Autocratic Decision Making

The foregoing advantages and disadvantages of participative decision making point to some advantages of autocratic decision making. More specifically, the autocratic style is appropriate when the leader and the group do not have the time to engage in participative decision making. In addition, the autocratic decision making may be advantageous when the group is split into fractious cliques. Note that the autocratic style is functional only to the extent that the members understand and accept the decisions that the leader makes. In the absence of such understanding and acceptance, they are not likely to execute the decisions effectively.

In a Nutshell

Participative decision making capitalizes on the abilities and knowledge of the members, resulting in better decisions. In addition, such a participative process creates a better understanding of the problem and the solution and ensures the acceptance of a decision. The disadvantages of group decision making include the cost of time it takes to make decisions and the possibility of the group conflicts arising out of differences in preferred solutions to a problem.

Decision Styles

Note that participation in decision making may take several forms. For instance, Vroom and his colleagues identified five procedures of involving members in decision making (Vroom and Jago 1978, 1988; Vroom and Yetton 1973). These are described in table 10.4. Chelladurai and his associates (Chelladurai 1993b; Chelladurai and Arnott 1985;

Table 10.4   Decision Styles and Their Description

Decision style	Description
Autocratic I (AI)	The leader personally makes the decision based on the information available.
Autocratic II (AII)	The leader secures the necessary information from the members, and then makes the decision personally. The leader may or may not explain the problem, and members do not have any role in the decision.
Consultive I (CI)	The leader shares the problem with relevant members on an individual basis, takes their ideas into account, and then makes the decision alone.
Consultive II (CII)	The leader shares the problem with all the members as a group, takes their views into account, and then makes the decision alone.
Group II (GII)	The leader shares the problem with the group, lets the group generate and evaluate alternative solutions, and then arrives at a consensus solution. The role of the leader in this decision procedure is that of a chairperson.

Reprinted from *Leadership and decision-making*, by Victor H. Vroom and Philip W. Yetton, by permission of the University of Pittsburgh Press. © 1973 by University of Pittsburgh Press.

Chelladurai and Haggerty 1978; Chelladurai, Haggerty, and Baxter 1989; Chelladurai and Quek 1995) have labeled these varying degrees of participation as decision styles.

Note that only the last procedure (GII) shown in table 10.4 is truly participative, i.e., the members actually make the decision. In all the other situations, the leader makes the decision by himself or herself. However, the degree to which the leader allows members to influence his or her decision increases from a purely autocratic procedure (AI) to consultation with the total group (CII).

Problem Attributes

The question now is, Which of the decision styles is appropriate under what conditions? According to Vroom and Jago (1988), every decision situation can be described in terms of 12 attributes. Basically, these attributes relate to the leader, the members, and the problem itself. A leader may or may not have all of the necessary information to make the decision (i.e., leader information). Because information is critical to making a rational decision, the leader may vary the decision style based on the information available to him or her. Another attribute of the leader is that he or she has sufficient influence over the subordinates that the members will be committed to the decision should the leader make the decision autocratically (i.e., commitment probability). If the leader believes that the members would accept and commit to the leader's decision in a given situation, then the leader may be relatively more autocratic. Further, the leader may be motivated toward minimizing the time taken (i.e., motivation-time) or toward maximizing member development (i.e., motivation-development). When a leader prefers to minimize the time for making decisions, he or she tends toward more autocratic decision styles including consultative styles. On the other hand, if a leader is more concerned with developmental aspects of decision making, he or she should employ more participative styles.

The member-related attributes are goal congruence (i.e., whether members share the organizational goals), subordinate conflict (i.e., whether members are likely to be in conflict over the solutions), and subordinate information (i.e., whether members have the information to make a quality decision). When members do not share the organizational goals, they may not contribute to effective decision making. If the members are in conflict with each other, they may not participate in decision making with an open mind. Finally, if the members do not have the necessary information, they cannot make the decision any more rationally than the leader can.

The three attributes of the problem situation are quality requirement (i.e., Does the problem in question require a high-quality decision?), commitment requirement (i.e., Is member commitment required to execute the decision?), problem structure (i.e., Is the problem simple and structured or complex?), and time constraint (i.e., Should the decision be made quickly?). The final attribute is geographical dispersion of the members that makes assembling them for participative decision making expensive. If a high-quality decision must be made, involving the members in decision making is advantageous. Similarly, if member commitment is critical for the execution of the decision, the leader should get the members to participate so that they will understand and accept the decision as their own. In some instances, the problem may be as simple as deciding whether to buy a water cooler for the office. In this case, resorting to a group decision is meaningless and time consuming. The influence of the problem

In Their View

Chelladurai (1993b) cautioned against confounding the decision style that a person adopts in a given situation with the mannerisms and affectations of that person. For instance, consider a football coach who presents his playbook for the season to the quarterback with the apparently menacing comment, "This is your bible. You better master it." In contrast, another coach may present his playbook with a smile and the comment, "Here is the playbook I drew up during the summer. You may get a kick out of reading it." The obvious difference in their mannerisms should not be allowed to mask the fact that both coaches autocratically decided on the plays.

Chelladurai also suggested that we should not be misguided by what he called window dressing. That is, a person may project himself or herself as very democratic by letting members make decisions in trivial matters. For instance, the director of a recreation department may let the group decide on the type of water cooler to be bought and its location in the office. However, the director may autocratically make decisions on more critical matters such as sports programming and scheduling. Thus, the director creates a façade of democratic leadership.

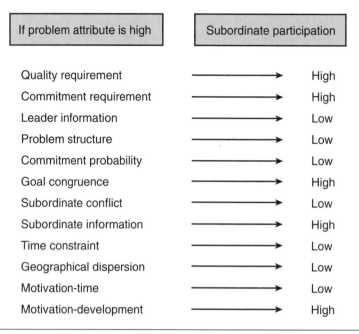

If problem attribute is high		Subordinate participation
Quality requirement	⟶	High
Commitment requirement	⟶	High
Leader information	⟶	Low
Problem structure	⟶	Low
Commitment probability	⟶	Low
Goal congruence	⟶	High
Subordinate conflict	⟶	Low
Subordinate information	⟶	High
Time constraint	⟶	Low
Geographical dispersion	⟶	Low
Motivation-time	⟶	Low
Motivation-development	⟶	High

Figure 10.3 Problem attributes and their effects on member participation.
Source: Vroom and Jago (1988).

attributes on the extent of member participation is shown in figure 10.3.

A mix of varying levels of the stated attributes characterizes every problem situation (i.e., decision situation). A leader or manager needs to make an objective assessment of these attributes and choose the decision style appropriate to that situation. While participative decision making is preferable in many situations, the manager needs to ensure that a participative style is functional in a given situation. As Vroom and Yetton (1973) pointed out: "The quality of the decision is dependent not only on the information and expertise of those participating in it, but also on their disposition to use their information in the service of the goal stated in the problem" (p. 29).

A consistent finding from the research on the model that Vroom and his associates proposed is that the influence of situational attributes was approximately four times the influence of individual difference (i.e., personal) factors on managers' choices of decision styles. Chelladurai and Arnott (1985) found a similar trend in the athletic context. Compared with individual differences among players, problem attributes influenced to a much greater extent basketball players' preferences for a particular decision style that their coaches use in a given situation.

In overview, sport and recreation managers need to analyze a problem situation in terms of the given

attributes and to select an appropriate decision style for that situation. Such a logical and rational approach maximizes the effectiveness of participative decision making and minimizes the importance of a manager's personal characteristics including personality as determinants of decision style choices.

In a Nutshell

While a leader would be better off to allow his or her members to participate in decision making, the extent to which such participation should occur is a function of the attributes of the problem including the characteristics of individual members and the group. A leader should evaluate these attributes and choose the most appropriate decision style in a given problem situation.

Summary

The focus of this chapter was on describing Chelladurai's multidimensional model of leadership. According to the model, situational characteristics, member characteristics, and leader characteristics lead to three states of leader behavior—required, preferred, and actual. Both the leader and the members have significant individual differences, and the influence of the characteristics of the situation affect the leadership process. One portion of actual leader behavior reflects the adaptation of the leader to the demands and constraints that situational characteristics place. The other portion of actual leader behavior is a function of the leader's reactions to members' preferences. A final proposition of the model was that the degree of congruence among the three states of leader behavior determines the extent to which members are satisfied and perform as individuals and as a group. The multidimensional model is a synthesis of existing leadership theories, such as House's path-goal theory and Fiedler's contingency model. In addition, the chapter contrasted transactional leadership and its effects with transactional leadership and its effects.

Finally, engaging members in making decisions has advantages and disadvantages. The degree to which a leader should allow his or her members to participate in making decisions is a function of the attributes of the situation. These attributes include characteristics of the members and the group as well as of the problem itself. An analysis of the varying configurations of the presence or absence of these attributes leads to concomitant decision styles.

Key Terms

leadership, influence, situational characteristics, individual difference variables, required leader behavior, preferred leader behavior, personality, ability, congruence, performance, satisfaction

Your Perspectives

- Define leadership and explain its significance in managing human resources.

- Think of a good leader with whom you are familiar. Describe him or her in terms of specific leader behaviors that impressed you most.
  - Which of those behaviors did situational requirements influence and which did member characteristics influence?
  - Would you prefer him or her to alter his or her behaviors? Why?
  - Would you consider that leader to be transformational? If yes, why? If no, why not?
  - Can that leader be described as charismatic? Explain.

- Describe the advantages and disadvantages of participative decision making.

- Explain the circumstances in which a participative style of decision making may not be tenable.

- Referring back to the leader you chose, would you label the person as participative or autocratic in decision making? Explain.

- If that leader varied the decision style, was he or she good in choosing the appropriate decision styles to different situations? Give examples.

Performance Appraisal

Learning Objectives

After reading this chapter you will be able to

- define the process of performance appraisal and explain its purposes,
- describe the steps involved in performance appraisal,
- understand the concept of performance domain and what constitutes that domain, and
- be familiar with various types of errors that may creep into the appraisal process.

The focus of this chapter is on an important managerial process that has a direct effect on member motivation and performance—performance appraisal. Performance appraisal is the basis for critical managerial decisions, such as training, retaining, promoting, and rewarding employees. Therefore, managers must carry it out periodically. Because performance appraisal has a direct impact on members' psychological and motivational state, it must be fair and based on valid criteria.

It is important that sport managers have a clear understanding of the ways in which performance appraisal can help the organization. This chapter elaborates on the two major purposes of performance appraisal—administrative and developmental. The administrative purpose focuses on evaluating the members on a comparative basis for administrative decisions such as salary increases and promotions. The developmental purpose is geared toward helping the members develop their skills and capabilities.

Every job is characterized by core and peripheral elements. For a performance appraisal to be effective, all of the core components need to be included in the evaluation. With this in perspective, I expand in this chapter on what should be evaluated. I also discuss two other issues that need to be addressed in carrying out performance appraisals. First is the issue of when to conduct performance appraisals, and the second one relates to who should do such appraisals.

Both the administrative and developmental purposes of performance appraisal require that such performance appraisal distinguishes among employees' performances and that it is free of any systematic biases. I elaborate on the common errors in performance appraisal that lead to the violation of these two requirements.

Purposes of Performance Appraisal

One enduring human characteristic is to know how well one is doing in a task at hand. The first question a child asks after drawing a figure is, "How is this Mommy?" A student takes time to submit an assignment but wants to know as soon as possible (perhaps the next day) how well he or she has done in that assignment. Similarly, an employee of an athletic department is eager to know how well he or she performed in an assigned task (e.g., preparing a quarterly report for the department). The employee's concern is twofold. The first concern is the genuine concern with the quality of the work done. Does the director of the athletic department think that the assignment is as good as the employee thinks it is? Has the director identified and complimented the employee on the good elements of the work, pointed out the technical and conceptual errors in it, and made any suggestions for improvement in subsequent assignments? The second concern is the effect such an evaluation will have on subsequent pay or merit raises and on promotions. In addition, the employee may be concerned with a comparison of this evaluation with evaluations in other assignments or with the evaluations of other employees in similar assignments.

From the perspective of the athletic director, he or she has a twofold responsibility. The first responsibility is developmental; the director's feedback is aimed at developing the employee and at improving the employee's ability to conceive, organize, and articulate the thoughts in a coherent manner. The second responsibility is to evaluate the employee's performance in relation to that of others in the department for the purposes of personnel decision, such as merit raises or promotions. That is, the director needs to ensure that the evaluation is commensurate with the intellectual effort and energy that has gone into the work and that it is equitable compared with the evaluations of other employees and their effort and energy. Readers will recognize that the concept of equity of rewards discussed in chapter 7 is operative here.

These two thrusts are the essence of performance appraisal in the context of organizations and their management. **Performance appraisal** "refers to a formal structured system for measuring, evaluating, and influencing an employee's job-related at-tributes, behaviors, and outcomes, including absenteeism" (Schuler and Jackson 1996, 344). The two operative words in the definition are evaluating and influencing, which refer to the two main objectives of performance appraisal. That is, evaluating serves the organizational purpose of comparing an individual's performance with a set of standards or with performances of comparable others. Such comparisons facilitate personnel decisions, such as placements, promotions, salary increases, and training programs. These purposes of performance appraisal are properly labeled **administrative purposes** (Belcourt et al. 1996).

From a different perspective, such appraisals can be used as feedback to individuals in order to influence and enhance their subsequent performances. Here, the focus is on developing the employee's skills and abilities to perform the tasks associated with the current job and those that future, higher-level jobs will require. Thus, these purposes of performance appraisals are labeled **developmental purposes**. Table 11.1 shows these differing purposes of performance appraisal.

In Their View

> The strategic use of performance appraisals seeks to be sure that measures of performance reflect business objectives. This approach is gaining popularity as firms begin to understand how performance appraisals can be used to enhance organizational effectiveness. Employees tend to do what is expected and what they believe is valued by the "system," as generally defined by the performance appraisal system. (Schuler and Jackson 1996, 378)

Cleveland, Murphy, and Williams (1989) provided a more comprehensive classification of the uses of performance appraisal and the information thereof. These authors conceived of performance appraisal as

- between-person evaluation,
- within-person evaluation,
- systems maintenance, and
- documentation.

Figure 11.1 illustrates these four classes and the specific uses of performance appraisal. As noted before, the between-person evaluation uses of per-

Table 11.1   Purposes of Performance Appraisal

Administrative purposes	Developmental purposes
To give feedback to subordinates so that they know where they stand in terms of their performance relative to what was expected and to the performance of comparable others	To counsel and coach subordinates so that they will improve their performance and develop future potential
To develop valid data for pay (salary and bonus) and promotion decisions and to provide a means of communicating these decisions	To develop commitment to the larger organization through discussion of career opportunities and career planning
To help the manager in making discharge and retention decisions and to provide a means of warning subordinates about unsatisfactory performance	To motivate subordinates through recognition and support To strengthen supervisor-subordinate relations To diagnose individual and organizational problems

Adapted, by permission, from M. Beer, 1987, Performance appraisal. In *Handbook of organizational behavior,* edited by J.W. Lorsch (Englewood Cliffs, NJ: Prentice Hall), 286-290.

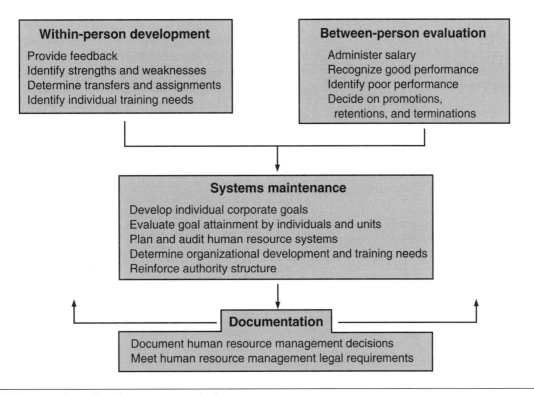

Figure 11.1   Functions of performance appraisal.

formance appraisal are largely concerned with human resource management decisions, such as salary increases, promotions, transfers, and terminations. The within-person uses focus on developing the individual by identifying strengths and weaknesses of the individual and assigning the individual to suitable positions and training programs. These two traditional functions of performance appraisal lead to a more general function of maintaining the organization as a whole. That is, the results of performance appraisal of all employees will provide some insights on the effectiveness of the human resource system, the developmental and training needs for the whole organization, and the setting and articulating of organizational goals for the employees. Finally, while performance appraisals are the foundation for human resource management decisions, they also provide the justification and documentation for such decisions. As noted in chapter 9, legal requirements govern the human resource management practices of organizations. When someone challenges the legality of any human resource management decision, the organization can defend itself based on the accurate and fair system of performance appraisals and their records. Clearly specifying what should be evaluated, when it should be evaluated, and who should do the evaluation enhances the fairness and accuracy of performance appraisals (Schuler and Jackson 1996).

In a Nutshell

Performance appraisal is a formal system of evaluating an employee's performance in terms of specified outcome and behaviors to achieve those outcomes. Performance appraisal may be used to develop an employee's skills and competencies and to make personnel decisions, such as salary increases, bonuses, promotions, or dismissals.

What Should Be Evaluated?

Perceptions of the fairness of performance evaluation depend on several factors. Perhaps the most critical of these factors is what is being evaluated, and many of the problems associated with performance appraisal stem from a confusion over the matter. Campbell's (1993) theory of performance outlines several domains of performance in an organizational context. His domains of performance are relevant to sport organizations, and they are described in the following sections.

Job-Specific Task Performance

Job-specific task performance refers to the content of the job description (see chapter 9). The elements of a job description describe the tasks that the job holder should complete. To the extent that the job description is specific and detailed, assessment of job-specific task performance appears to be an easy process. For example, when a fitness club employs a person for recruiting customers for the club and its various programs and sets a standard (e.g., 100 customers), the club easily can measure the performance of the employee against that standard. However, when the club is interested in the performance

of retaining those customers, appraisal of that performance becomes problematic because retention of customers is relatively more dependent on so many other factors including the performance of the fitness consultants, fitness leaders, maintenance of the facilities, and other supportive features. That is, several other individuals are involved in retaining customers. Two issues are present. First, the manager can judge the work of the fitness consultant (i.e., the human service) not only by the number of customers that he or she served but also by the quality of such services. Similarly, the exercise leader's performance is not only the number of classes conducted but also the motivational and instructional impact of that leader. In other words, the performance in human services (i.e., the work of fitness consultant and the exercise leader) are harder to measure. If performance evaluation in these instances is based on the criterion of number of clients served, then that evaluation has criterion deficiency (Saal and Knight 1995). By the same token, if such performance evaluation includes criteria that are irrelevant to performance (e.g., the age, gender, or marital status of the employees), then it has criterion contamination (Saal and Knight 1995).

The second issue is interdependence among tasks. That is, whenever the performance of one task is dependent on other tasks, isolating and assessing the performance in one specific job becomes difficult. In other words, when the attainment of an organizational objective is dependent on collective work, the manager cannot easily identify an individual's performance. Nevertheless, job descriptions do provide a basis for performance evaluation of job-specific task behaviors.

Written and Oral Communication

Several jobs may require extensive communication with co-workers, superiors, subordinates, or clients. For instance, the athletic director of a university has to articulate clearly and succinctly the mission, goals, and specific processes that the department adopted to university officials, students, athletes, coaches, and the media. The communication generally takes the form of oral presentations and interviews as well as written documents. If the communication is not clear, the athletic director may be misunderstood or misquoted. As another example, the event manager needs to communicate clearly to both the paid and volunteer workers all of the steps and procedures of staging the event. Any ambiguity or vagueness in communication may lead to serious difficulties. Similarly, the instructions of the fitness leader to the members in the class need to be clear and straight forward. In all of these cases, the written and oral communication becomes part of the performance domain and needs to be evaluated.

Supervision and Leadership

Some jobs also carry supervisory responsibilities. That is, the member may be expected to supervise and provide leadership to selected individuals. For example, a senior employee in a city recreation department may be required to supervise and provide coaching and guidance to selected junior employees. The extent to which the senior is able to influence positively the juniors and enhance their performance is critical to the organization. Campbell's (1993) contention was that the manager should recognize, evaluate, and suitably reward such leadership as part of an individual's performance domain.

Management and Administration

Another domain of performance that Campbell (1993) identified is the responsibility residing in some higher-level jobs to set and state the organizational mission, monitor the organizational activities toward the mission, and distribute the budget to various units or programs. This domain of performance and associated responsibilities are relevant mostly to positions in the upper echelons of an organization (e.g., director of a university athletic department, general manager of a professional sports club, director of a city recreation department, or the chief executive officer of a national sport governing body).

Non-Job-Specific Task Performance

This domain relates to all the activities outside of the job-specific domain articulated in a job description. This domain relates to those general activities of the workgroup, unit, or organization. For example, when an employee of the ticketing department of university athletics participates and contributes to group- or organization-wide meetings or committees, that person is performing in tasks that are critical to the organization and its effectiveness. In fact, committee membership is a significant component of the performance evaluation of university professors. Because these committee and leadership functions are critical to the survival and growth of the university, it is only appropriate that the manager adequately recognizes and rewards the individuals. One may question if membership on university or departmental committees can be considered non-job-specific behaviors in so far as they are officially declared to be part of the performance domain. However, the point is that a professor is not required to participate in those committees. Because these contributions are not specific to a job, they are not outlined clearly in a job description. However, that fact does not minimize the importance of the performance in that domain. In a similar manner, a fitness instructor's job description may not require specifically that he or she contribute to the overall management of the fitness club. Yet, the fitness instructor may pass on his or her insights for enhancing the overall performance of the club in meetings or other encounters with senior management. Such a contribution would be non-job-specific performance.

Effort

The familiar saying, "He or she gets an A for effort," implies that the extent to which an individual expends his or her effort in the performance of a job must also be taken into account. As noted earlier, the performance in a job may be contingent on other factors. Therefore, the evaluation of an employee's performance should not be restricted to the actual outcomes. Managers must consider the amount of effort an individual has put into the job as equally important as actual outcomes. For example, a person in charge of securing sponsorships for the athletic department of a small college in an urban center may not garner as much sponsorship as expected or desired despite extraordinary efforts. This could be a function of more attractive options available to the sponsors, such as major universities or professional teams. The point is that the employee's effort in this regard should not be overlooked in performance appraisal. When an individual puts forth considerable effort consistently, frequently, and even in adverse conditions, that individual needs to be evaluated positively in that domain of performance. Recall from chapter 7 that an individual's motivation can be inferred from the investments of time and effort in a job. More specifically, the direction, persistence, and intensity of effort is an indication of one's motivation to perform well in a job. According to Campbell (1993), such investments of effort also should be included in performance appraisal.

Personal Discipline

Chapter 1 emphasized that the self-care that volunteers exhibit may make them better able to serve the clients; that is, they become better volunteers. Such self-care needs to be included in evaluating the volunteer's contribution. The same concept extends to paid workers. Campbell (1993) offered the same notion when he suggested that a paid employee's personal discipline (which is similar to self-care) is part of the performance domain. Consider one example that Campbell (1993) offered—an employee's use of drugs. The obvious implication is that that employee is not likely to be operating at his or her best; therefore, the job-specific task performance is likely to suffer. From a different perspective, by using drugs employees tarnish the image of the organization. University athletic departments and even professional sport teams take several steps to discourage the use of drugs. If the concern is with just the athlete, the university quickly can alleviate the problem with the dismissal of the athlete. However, the problem is much more serious when the images of the department and the university are at stake. In several instances, personal discipline is a critical aspect of job performance. For example, the personal appearance of the employees when they report for work is a function of their personal discipline. If an employee stays up late at night and reports for work in a disheveled state regularly, this will affect not only his or her performance but also the image of the organization.

Facilitation of Peer and Team Performance

The manager also must consider as part of an individual's domain of performance the extent to which that person facilitates the performance of his or her peers and team or workgroup. Campbell (1993) suggested that just being a role model for other employees itself is an aspect of performance. The actions of an employee who carries out his or her job-specific task accurately and promptly serves as a model for other employees. For example, a playground supervisor in a city recreation department may set an example for other supervisors by doing his or her duties meticulously. In addition, the playground supervisor may assist other colleagues and superiors as the need arises and, thus, facilitate the effectiveness of the total program. Such activities do constitute a legitimate area of one's performance domain subject to evaluation.

Citizenship Behaviors

In addition to the above domains of performance that Campbell (1993) outlined, another form of behavior within an organization contributes to organizational effectiveness but is seldom noticed. This form is labeled pro-social behavior or organizational citizenship behavior. The latter term is more

In a Nutshell

An employee's domain of performance includes not only the job-specific task behaviors but also non-job-specific task behaviors, such as involvement in and facilitation of peer and workgroup tasks, effort, and personal discipline.

popular, and Organ (1988) introduced and defined it as "individual behavior that is discretionary, not directly or explicitly recognized by the formal reward system, and that in the aggregate promotes the effective functioning of the organization" (p. 4). The operative word here is discretionary, meaning that the behavior in question is not specified in the job description, required by other organizational rules, or expected by others. It refers to all of the little things that individuals in an organizational context do of their own volition and that contribute indirectly to organizational effectiveness. A fitness club employee may come to work before the scheduled time to "tidy up" the place, the accountant in the fitness club may step up to the reception desk to assist the receptionist at a time of heavy demand, and an experienced exercise leader may help the novice leader with settling in the job. A ticketing clerk in an athletic department may spend part of the lunch hour picking up trash in the stadium. These are the organizational citizenship behaviors that contribute to organizational growth and effectiveness.

Podsakoff, Ahearne, and MacKenzie (1997) suggested that "citizenship behaviors may enhance organizational performance because they 'lubricate' the social machinery of the organization, reduce friction, and increase efficiency" (p. 263). They outlined the specific benefits of citizenship behaviors as freeing up the resources devoted to maintenance functions for more productive uses, enhancing coworker performance, coordinating group activities, and making the workgroup and organization a more attractive place to work.

Organ (1988) classified the varying kinds of citizenship behaviors into altruism, conscientiousness, sportsmanship, courtesy, civic virtue, peacekeeping, and cheerleading. Table 11.2 describes these.

Managers acknowledge the importance of organizational citizenship behaviors; however, making the behaviors part of the formal performance appraisal process is difficult because they are so varied and not comparable to each other. Thus, such citizenship behaviors are not explicitly acknowledged and assessed as one component of task perfor-

Table 11.2   Categories of Citizenship Behaviors

Category	Description
Altruism	Extra-role behaviors to help another person (e.g., co-worker or supervisor) in an organizationally relevant task or problem
Conscientiousness	Behaviors beyond minimal requirements in aspects such as attendance, work efforts, and adherence to rules and regulations
Sportsmanship	Willingness to accept less-than-ideal circumstances without complaining about small things in working conditions
Courtesy	Behaviors facilitating smooth functioning of work in the group, such as informing others of any changes in one's own routine
Civic virtue	Behaviors indicating sincere concern about the workgroup and organization through participation and involvement in their affairs
Peacekeeping	Behaviors aimed at reducing conflicts among members or units and at resolving conflicts in a peaceful manner
Cheerleading	Behaviors geared to encouraging others (e.g., individuals and units) to perform well and to applauding their accomplishments

Adapted, by permission, from D.W. Organ, 1988, *Organizational citizenship behavior: The good soldier syndrome* (Lexington, MA: Lexington Books).

mance. However, evidence suggests that managers do use their perceptions of citizenship behaviors in evaluating the task performance of their subordinates (Podsakoff, MacKenzie, and Hui 1993). That is, managers tend to subjectively use an employee's citizenship behaviors in the appraisal of that person's task performance, which is purported to be objective. Podsakoff, MacKenzie, and Hui (1993) advanced several reasons why a person's citizenship behaviors influence managers in evaluating the task performance of that person. One reason is based on the norms of reciprocity or fairness. Insofar as the manager believes that an individual's extra-role behaviors contribute to his or her own performance as well as that of the organization, the manager is likely to evaluate more positively that person's task performance. Another reason for managers to use citizenship behaviors in their assessments is their belief that "good" employees engage in these citizenship behaviors in addition to the behaviors associated with their work roles. Another reason is that citizenship behaviors stand out as distinctive behaviors because all of the work-role behaviors are required of every employee. Perceptions of distinctive behaviors come to the forefront in performance appraisal and influence the process. Further, because citizenship behaviors are based on a person's internal and stable dispositions, such behaviors are given greater weight than actual task performance. Yet another reason for citizenship behaviors to play

an important part in performance appraisal is that managers may believe that task performance and citizenship behaviors are highly correlated.

In a Nutshell

Citizenship behaviors are behaviors that an individual voluntarily engages in to assist another employee, group, or organization. The role assigned to the individual does not specify them; therefore, they are seldom monitored. Yet, citizenship behaviors are critical to organizational health and image. Managers may favorably evaluate an employee's task performance based on his or her citizenship behavior for several reasons including a sense of reciprocity, a perception of a "good" employee, and the distinctiveness of such behavior.

Some of the reasons why managers use citizenship behaviors in performance appraisal are legitimate and functional, and some other reasons are inappropriate and dysfunctional. The reasons of reciprocity and fairness discussed earlier are quite legitimate insofar as the citizenship behaviors contribute to managerial and organizational effectiveness.

On the other hand, directly linking citizenship behaviors with task performance must be viewed with caution for three reasons. First, not all citizenship behaviors may be related to increased performance. In their study of workgroups in a paper mill, Podsakoff, Ahearne, and MacKenzie (1997) assessed three forms of citizenship behaviors: helping behavior (i.e., altruism), sportsmanship, and civic virtue. Their results showed that only helping behavior and sportsmanship had a significant effect on group performance, and civic virtue had no effect on performance.

Second, as both Organ (1988) and Podsakoff, Ahearne, and MacKenzie (1997) pointed out, the effects of citizenship behaviors on performance can be evaluated properly only if managers consider such behaviors of an individual over time or average such behaviors over all individuals in a group. That is, an individual's sporadic citizenship behaviors may not have much effect on group performance. The Podsakoff, Ahearne, and MacKenzie (1997) finding of a relationship between selected citizenship behaviors and group performance was based on measures of group citizenship behaviors and group performance indices.

The third issue is the distinction between citizenship behaviors and political influence tactics (Podsakoff, MacKenzie, and Hui 1993). That is, employees may engage in citizenship behaviors only to influence the decision makers. While citizenship behaviors are for the benefit of others in the organizations or of the organization itself, political influence tactics are for the benefit of the perpetrator. While managers can understand the distinction between the two intentions and are familiar with individuals with these two differing orientations, Podsakoff, MacKenzie, and Hui (1993) raised the question, Does it matter? They argue that

> if one is interested in the impact of the employee's behavior on organizational effectiveness, it is not clear that the intentions of the employee are as relevant. In this situation, does it really matter why an employee comes to work extra early or stays extra late? As long as the employee is really working, it should enhance the effectiveness of the organization. (p. 33)

Thus, managers must be careful in including an individual's citizenship behaviors in performance appraisal. One solution to the problem is to separate task performance from citizenship behavior and to reward them separately. For instance, if employees A and B perform equally well, they should be given equal performance rating. If, however, employee A engages in more constructive citizenship behaviors, employee A must be rewarded more in some tangible or intangible ways for such citizenship. By the same token, if employee C performs at a lower level but exhibits good citizenship, employee C must be evaluated lower on task performance and rewarded less. Before implementing this logic, however, managers must inform all employees that citizenship behaviors are important and that such behaviors are part of the performance appraisal and reward systems.

In sum, the **performance domain** includes all of the tasks specified in a job description as well as other nonspecified activities including citizenship behaviors as warranted. Table 11.3 gives a comprehensive list of the elements of performance domain.

Deficiency in and Contamination of Performance Measures

The foregoing clearly shows that managers must include in the domain of performance all pertinent activities associated with a job. Otherwise, as noted before, such performance measures would be deficient in so far as only segments of the performance domain are measured. On the other hand, managers must also ensure that what they have included in the measurement scheme does not contain any element that is not part of the job or any element that is dependent on external factors. If such extraneous elements are included in the performance measures, such measures are contaminated (Saal and Knight 1995). Courneya and Chelladurai (1991) illustrated this issue of **deficiency** in and **contamination** of performance measures with reference to baseball. They argued that random chance (e.g., bad bounce of the ball), the opponent's superior performance, choice of a particular performance strategy, or an official's wrong call could contaminate the most popular performance measures in sport (e.g., win-loss percentage). When evaluating a player's performance in games, such as baseball, they suggested that what others have done also can contaminate some of the common measures. For example, runs batted in, which is a common performance measure in baseball, depends on the ability of the batter to hit the ball as well as on how many preceding batters got on base. This issue is clearly illustrated in the difference between a solo home run and a grand-slam home run. The batter's performance is the same, but the performance or nonperformance of the preceding batters contaminates the measure of runs batted in. Based on this line of reasoning, Courneya and Chelladurai (1991) categorized the performance measures in baseball based on the validity of those measures into primary, secondary, and tertiary measures as shown in figure 11.2. Primary measures are the closest to actual

Table 11.3   Significant Domains of Performance

- Job-specific task performance
  - Exhibiting written and oral communications skills
  - Supervising and leading
  - Managing and administrating by articulating organizational goals, allocating resources, and monitoring goal attainment

- Non-job-specific task performance including group or unit activities
  - Maintaining consistent, frequent effort even in adverse conditions
  - Exhibiting personal discipline including following rules
  - Providing support, training, and guidance to facilitate group or unit performance

- Citizenship behaviors
  - Volunteering to carry out task activities that are not formally a part of the job
  - Persisting with extra enthusiasm or effort when necessary to successfully complete tasks
  - Helping and cooperating with others
  - Endorsing, supporting, and defending organizational objectives

Source: Campbell (1993), Organ (1988), Schuler and Jackson (1996).

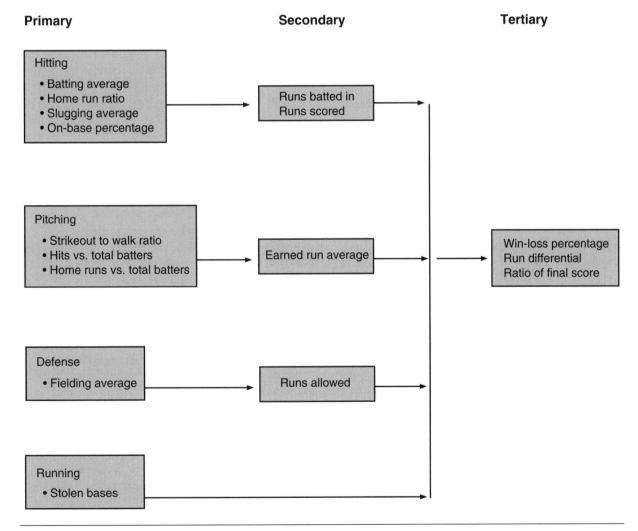

Figure 11.2   Categorization of performance measures in baseball.

Adapted, by permission, from K.S. Courneya and P. Chelladurai, 1991, A model of performance measures in baseball, *Journal of Sport and Exercise Psychology* 13: 16-25.

performance of the player while the tertiary measures are the most contaminated and most removed from the actual performance.

In a Nutshell

When a performance measure does not capture the total domain of performance, it is deficient. On the other hand, if a performance measure subsumes factors that are not related to an individual's performance, it is contaminated.

Outcome-Based Versus Behavior-Based Performance Criteria

Managers can apply the logic of Courneya and Chelladurai (1991) with reference to performance measures in baseball to performance measures in organizations. Stated otherwise, sport managers must consider the distinction between outcomes-based criteria and behavior-based criteria in evaluating performance. As noted earlier, performance appraisal is problematic when the jobs in an organization are interdependent on each other. That is, the performances of others in other jobs influences the performance (or the outcomes) in one job. Consider a student's involvement in group projects for various courses. Some of the projects might have turned out to be excellent ones because of the first-rate work that others in the project team did. In some other cases, the projects could have been failures due to the ineffective and substandard performance of other members of the groups. If a professor were to evaluate the student's personal performance only on the basis of the outcome (i.e., the quality of that project), his or her judgment would not be fair. In a similar manner, if the manager based his or her evaluation of the fitness instructor introduced earlier only on the retention rate of membership, the manager would not make a fair judgment. Therefore, researchers agree generally that choosing outcomes as the sole criteria for performance appraisal is not a good strategy (e.g., Saal and Knight 1995, Schuler and Jackson 1996).

The alternate strategy is to base performance evaluation on the behaviors in which an employee is supposed to engage for completing the job. The university expects a public relations person in the athletic department to be courteous to those who seek information, to collate all pertinent and correct information for distribution, to be regularly in contact with media people, and to be available at specified times. When that person engages in these be-

haviors consistently and effectively, the manager should evaluate that person's behavior as good without reference to the outcomes. The department or the team may get bad publicity in spite of the employee's optimal performance due to other reasons (e.g., the animosity between the press and the coaches). As noted earlier, the job description outlines what the employee should do.

In addition, the organization may have adopted the process of management by objectives. The emphasis of management by objectives is on the manager and the employee jointly setting objectives for the employee to attain in a given period (usually one year). Such discussions involve aligning the employee's objectives with the goals of the unit and the organization. The objectives set for the employee need to be consistent with the employee's capabilities and past achievements. The idea that setting challenging and achievable objectives is motivational is the central rationale for management by objectives (Saal and Knight 1995). These objectives serve as the criteria for evaluating the employee at the end of the specified period. While these objectives are good indicators of performance domain, they focus on what outcomes should be attained. Managers need to move beyond this frame of mind in performance appraisal and assess those behaviors that are most conducive to the attainment of those outcomes.

In a Nutshell

In assessing the performance of a person, focusing more on the behaviors that the person should engage in to achieve the desired outcome is more useful than focusing on the outcomes themselves because several other factors may influence the outcomes.

Following the discussion on what should be evaluated, MacLean and Chelladurai (1995) developed a scheme for the performance appraisal of coaches. In their scheme, the domain of coaching performance is defined as all behaviors and tasks associated with coaching and consists of six dimensions to reflect both the outcomes (or products as they called it) and the processes associated with coaching. That is, the results, as well as those activities that are purported to lead to those results, are included. The outcomes may accrue to the team as a whole or to the coach. The process factors consist of direct and indirect behaviors aimed at task achievement and behaviors oriented toward the maintenance of the system by supporting and maintaining the administration and public relations activities. MacLean and Chelladurai (1995) also noted that a coach's behaviors should also reflect the philosophy and values of the organization. The description of the dimensions of coaching performance are provided in table 11.4, and the relationships among these dimensions are illustrated in figure 11.3.

The scheme that MacLean and Chelladurai (1995) developed are applicable to positions in sport management. For example, an assistant director of a university recreation department in charge of intramural competitions can be evaluated on the basis of several factors including the performance of the unit in terms of number of sports and number of teams served and on the smooth operation of these competitions (i.e., the unit products); recognition by the university newspaper and student organizations (i.e., personal products); planning and organizing of the intramural competitions, effective deployment of personnel, interpersonal skills, and the nature of interactions with subordinates and participants (i.e., direct task behaviors); attendance of conferences and seminars to learn more about run-

ning the unit more effectively (i.e., indirect task behaviors); adherence to university and department policies and procedures and effective interaction with superiors and colleagues (i.e., administrative maintenance behaviors); and links with other similar operations inside and outside the university and promotion of the unit and its activities (i.e., public relations behaviors). Thus, the scheme generally is transferable to many other positions in sport management.

When to Conduct Performance Appraisal

The response to the question, When should I conduct performance appraisal? is based on the purpose of the evaluation. Is the purpose developmental or administrative? If it is developmental, it is most likely to be focused on an individual and, therefore, can be tailored to suit the individual's needs and experience. A novice employee may need more guidance and coaching; therefore, several appraisals can be carried out over a short period of

Table 11.4   Description of Dimensions of Coaching Performance

Behavioral product factors **Team products**	These products are the outcomes accruing to the team (or individual athlete) as reflected in the extent to which the team (or individual athlete) is successful in demonstrating excellence by winning competitions, improving from the previous year, or making the playoffs.
Personal products	These products are the outcomes that accrue only to the coach including the recognition and rewards that the coach receives from external agents, such as the media, the alumni, and other coaches. This dimension also includes the coach's publications, speaking engagements, and presentations at coaching clinics.
Behavioral process factors **Direct task behaviors**	These behaviors are the application of interpersonal skills and appropriate strategies and tactics used to enhance the performance of individual athletes and the team as a whole. More specifically, they are the quality of interaction with athletes, sound management of practice sessions, teaching of skills and techniques, application of appropriate strategies and tactics, proper use of available talent, and motivation of athletes.
Indirect task behaviors	These behaviors are behaviors of the court or field, such as recruiting quality athletes, scouting opponents, and applying statistics that contribute indirectly to the success of the program.
Administrative maintenance behaviors	These behaviors are the adherence to policies, procedures, and budget guidelines and to interpersonal relations with superiors and peers that strengthen the administration of the whole enterprise.
Public relations behaviors	These behaviors are liaison activities between one's program and the relevant community and peer groups that contribute to organizational welfare.

Adapted, by permission, from J.C. MacLean and P. Chelladurai, 1995, Dimensions of coaching performance: Development of a scale, *Journal of Sport Management* 9: 194-207.

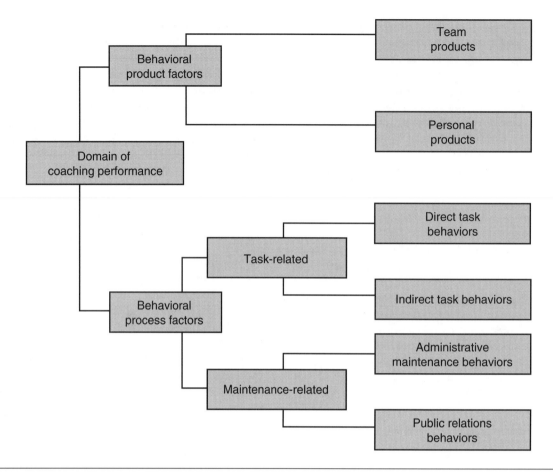

Figure 11.3   Relationships among performance measures.

Adapted from MacLean and Chelladurai 1995.

time. On the other hand, a senior employee who has worked with the organization for a long time may not need such guidance and coaching. Most often, performance appraisal is carried out for administrative or evaluative purposes to make judgments on salary, merit, bonuses, training programs, or promotions. In addition, managers can use these data to decide who to retain and who to release. Such purposes presuppose that the manager evaluates all employees during the same time period, which the manager specified in advance. Usually, organizations carry out such performance appraisals each year either at the end of the fiscal year or at the end of the calendar year. Some employees may be evaluated on their anniversary dates.

In some cases, a more elaborate and stringent performance appraisal may be employed after some years have elapsed. Two examples in a university setting are performance evaluation of professors for tenure purposes and the evaluation of coaches for extending or discontinuing the contract of their employment. In both cases, the professor and coach may be evaluated each year for the purposes of

In a Nutshell

If employee development is the focus of performance appraisal, managers should conduct such performance appraisals more frequently and scheduled to meet the developmental needs of the individual. If managers use performance evaluation to make personnel decisions, they should conduct the evaluations at prespecified intervals (usually annually) with a uniform protocol for all employees.

merit pay or bonus. In addition, the professor has to be appraised more rigorously after five to seven years of employment for tenure purposes. The assumption here is that it takes that long for a young university professor to carry out research and publish a few papers. Similarly, a coach may need from three to seven years to build a strong team and the traditions associated with it. Therefore, the contract is usually for an extended period of time at the end of which the university rigorously appraises his or her performance.

Who Should Do the Appraisal?

An equally important consideration in performance appraisal is who should be involved in the performance appraisal process. A basic assumption that managers must make in this regard is that no one person has the complete information on the performance of an employee. Even the employee may have an idea of how well he or she has done but may not know how that level of performance compares with the level of others. A supervisor may form a performance judgment based on his or her observation of several employees but may not fully recognize the reactions of customers to an individual employee. Thus, the quantity and quality of information on the performance of an individual is widely distributed among several sources. For instance, the information on the performance of a fitness instructor may reside in the minds of the supervisors, co-instructors, and even the locker-room attendant. More importantly, the customers perhaps have the best information on how well the instructor is performing. Hence, many organizations use all of these sources in evaluating the performance of the employee. The performance appraisal of university professors usually is based on student evaluation of teaching (i.e., information from clients), observer evaluation of teaching (i.e., information from professional colleagues from within the organization), number of publications in reputed journals (i.e., information from professional reviewers of the journals), and the dean's or director's evaluation of the candidate. Similarly, the performance of a coach can be evaluated from the data that the athletes, co-coaches, administrators, and external agents, such as the media and coaches in other universities, provide. Note that recently several scholars and practicing managers have emphasized the need to use customer satisfaction as a significant, if not the sole, indicator of individual or organizational performance. The issue of customer or client satisfaction is elaborated in chapter 14.

Errors in Rating

Whenever an individual's performance is evaluated, the appraiser or rater should guard against any type of error creeping into their evaluations. Some of the most common errors are discussed in this section.

Distributional Errors

Consider the various professors marking your assignments or examinations. One professor may mark the assignments strictly, but the second professor may mark them leniently. Note that the leniency on the part of the professor partly may be due to inflationary pressures to give high grades. These pressures, in turn, may be born out of the notions of equality or fear of retribution from students or subordinates. A third professor may be neither lenient nor strict but may tend to place all students in the central range of scores. These habits of different raters are errors reflecting strictness (i.e., hardness in rating all performances low), leniency (i.e., softness in rating all performances high), and central tendency (i.e., reluctance or inability to use either end of scores). Belcourt et al. (1996) viewed these as **distributional errors**.

In a Nutshell

To make the performance appraisal effective, managers need to compile comprehensive and accurate information from several sources including the individual, his or her co-workers, superiors, and clients or customers.

The ideal way to rate is for the professors to use a wider range of scores to contrast the better assignments with the poorer assignments. The habits of strictness, leniency, and central tendency are contrasted with the ideal way of rating in figure 11.4. An interesting issue here is that while the professors may vary in their rating tendencies, their appraisal of the students relative to each other may not differ much. For example, professor X gives the numerical grades of 81, 83, and 85 to students Jane, John, and June, respectively. Professor Y gives the numerical grades of 89, 91, and 93 to the same students in the same order. Professor Z gives the grades of 86, 87, and 88 to the same students in the same order. The numerical grades that the three professors give do not match at all, and they reflect the errors of strictness, leniency, and central tendency (see figure 11.4). However, the ranking of the three students is the same in all three cases. Because the relative ratings of the students remained the same in all three cases, one can say that all professors were fair in their evaluations. The problem arises when an external agent looks at these grades and concludes that student June did well in the course that professor Y taught and did poorly in the course that professor X taught. That conclusion may not reflect reality. Another issue is related to the fact that in the case of each professor, the ratings are lumped together. Thus, it becomes difficult to distinguish among the

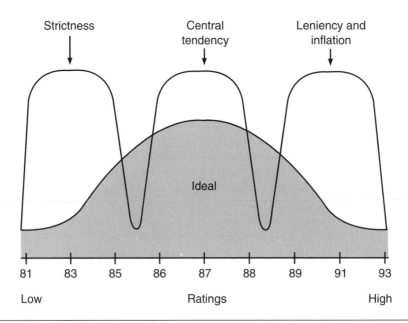

Figure 11.4   Comparisons among ideal and erroneous performance ratings.

three students. For instance, the three numerical grades of professor X are likely to be converted to a letter grade of C; all of the numerical grades of professor Y, to a letter grade of A; and those of professor Z, to a letter grade of B. As such, these practices do not discriminate between good and bad students and, therefore, are not fair to the students or to the educational system.

Similar errors can happen in other organizational contexts in which the errors among raters may result in unfair decisions relating to distribution of rewards or promotions. For example, two or more administrators in charge of different regions of a city recreation department may succumb to any of the above errors (i.e., leniency, strictness, or central tendency) in evaluating their respective subordinates. While their evaluations may be consistent with the relative performance of their own members, the errors do cause a problem when one attempts to employ these evaluations as the basis for merit raises or promotions across the entire department. For instance, when the director of the department makes the final decisions on salary increases or promotions, he or she is faced with evaluations from the different regions that are subject to the above errors; therefore, the decisions are not likely to be fair.

Temporal Errors

Belcourt et al. (1996) referred to another set of rating errors as **temporal errors**. These errors include recency error, which is the tendency to rate the annual performance of an employee based on the most recent behavior of that employee. For example, a playground supervisor may be evaluated based on his or her performance in the month of November or December, and the rating may be used to reflect his or her performance throughout the year. The supervisor's performance in the previous 10 months might not have been as good or as bad as the performance in the last two months.

Another temporal error is the contrast error, which refers to the tendency for a rater to compare or contrast a student or an employee with the person who has just been rated. Professors are most likely to succumb to this error. When they have to mark a stack of assignments or examinations, they are likely to rate a student based on how they rated a previous student. If the previous student was rated poorly, the next student looks good by contrast and is likely to receive a better grade. By the same token, a student may compare poorly with a previous student and, therefore, receive a poorer grade. In other words, a student's grade in an assignment depends not only on the quality of his or her work but also on the time that the professor marks the assignment. This contrast error can occur as easily when an athletic director is evaluating several coaches or when a city recreation director is evaluating a number of supervisors for administrative purposes. The director in either case should guard against being influenced by the ratings given to the preceding candidate (i.e., against the contrast error).

In a Nutshell

Managers who carry out performance appraisal should guard against being strict, lenient, or placing everyone in the center of the performance range (i.e., distributional errors). Further, they should not base their judgments only on one's recent performances or on how the previous individual was evaluated (i.e, temporal errors). Similarly, superior performance in one aspect of the job should not be transferred to other areas (i.e., halo effect).

Other Rater Errors

In some cases, good performance in one aspect of the job may be transferred to other aspects of the job. This tendency is called the halo error. For example, a school may use a teacher-coach's performance in coaching to evaluate his or her teaching. A university may evaluate a professor's teaching based on his or her reputation for research and publications. Similarly, a fitness club may use the activity level of an instructor during a class to evaluate him or her on the substance of his or her instruction. As noted earlier, a manager may evaluate an employee highly on task performance based on his or her citizenship behaviors.

Another form of error is for raters to judge the employees based on perceptions of themselves. That is, a supervisor may tend to view positively the performance of those employees who are perceived to be similar to the supervisor in some respects. For example, if the supervisor comes to the office very early in the morning, he or she may view all of those who come early quite positively. This view is not surprising because people tend to have a soft corner for those who are similar to themselves (e.g., having gone to the same schools, being the fan of the same teams, and having had a rough time in the past). However, if raters allow these feelings to influence their evaluation of performance, they commit the similarity error.

Finally, another form of error in performance evaluation is the use of inappropriate substitutes for performance. For instance, an individual's way of dressing or his or her congenial manner of interactions with others may be used wrongfully as a substitute for performance. Consider the receptionist in a tennis club. He or she may be quite polite and courteous to the customers and may exhibit a great sense of humor in interactions with the clients. While these are desirable qualities in a receptionist, they do not reflect how correctly he or she records customers' requests for tennis courts and informs them when and for how long they can use a court.

In Their View

Theoretically, as managers we should be interested in ends; that is, getting the job done! As one football coach remarked in approaching his ungraceful but effective field goal kicker: "It ain't pictures, it's numbers." Similarly, managers should be concerned with quality results. It's performance that counts! It may be difficult for some managers to accept, but they should not be appraising employees on how they look (means), but rather on whether they can score (end results). We propose, therefore, that organizations exist to "score," rather than to provide an environment for individuals to "look like players." Just like the football coach, managers must be concerned with evaluating their personnel on "numbers" and not on "pictures." (De Cenzo and Robbins 1994, 379)

Current Performance and Future Potential

Beer (1987) pointed out another problem in performance evaluation when managers use it for decisions on promotions. An employee may be performing well in the current job because he or she may possess the necessary abilities and experience. However, the current performance does not guarantee that that employee will perform well in another job if the new job requires different abilities. For example, an athletic trainer in a university athletic department may be performing extraordinarily well in working with the injured athletes and treating them effectively. Even though that particular individual may be performing at the highest level in that category of job, the university must be careful when promoting that individual to the position of supervisor of athletic trainers because the job requirements differ. Instead of working with injured athletes, the supervisor has to work with equally qualified athletic trainers and has to coordinate their activities. Thus, the successful performance as an athletic trainer does not guarantee effective performance as a supervisor.

Beer's (1987) solution to this problem was to separate the evaluation of current performance from the evaluation of potential for future performance.

The reasons for the errors in performance appraisal can be traced generally to individual differences among raters. That is, one rater may tend to be lenient in general, while another may tend to be strict. These are unintentional errors. In contrast, raters also may intentionally commit these errors for political reasons. Longenecker, Sims, and Gioia (1987) noted that managers intentionally may be lenient in their evaluations for several reasons. These include maximizing the merit raises for their subordinates, helping an individual who has personal problems, avoiding confrontations with employees, putting up a facade of good performance by the unit, and rewarding an employee who is showing improvement. Interestingly, Longenecker, Sims, and Gioia (1987) suggest that a supervisor may rate quite favorably an employee whom he or she dislikes in the hope that the organization will promote the employee out of the unit. By the same token, managers intentionally may deflate performance ratings of an employee to prod the employee to higher efforts, punish a rebellious employee, suggest that the employee should leave the organization, and build a record of poor performance so that the employee can be fired subsequently.

This is, in fact, the practice in many organizational contexts. Better performers at one level of the organization are targeted for training and evaluation for future promotions to the next higher level. Those individuals who do well in the training and in subsequent tests and examinations or other forms of evaluation are chosen for promotions. In sum, a manager should evaluate separately the current performance and future potential in a new job, and he or she should communicate the decisions regarding each to the employee (Beer 1987).

In Their View

Peter's (1972) famous Peter principle states that "In a hierarchy every employee tends to rise to his [or her] level of incompetence" (p. 4). He went on to explain that "for every job that exists in the world there is someone, somewhere, who cannot do it. Given sufficient time and enough promotions, he [or she] will eventually arrive at that job and there he [or she] will remain, habitually bungling the job, frustrating his [or her] coworkers, and eroding the efficiency of the organization" (pp. 4-5). Peter employs humor to drive home the point that competence in the current job does not guarantee good performance in a higher position.

Rater and Ratee Reactions

Personal reactions of the rater and the employee may create two significant problems in performance appraisal (Beer 1987). The first problem is the rater's ambivalence and avoidance. Some superiors are uncomfortable with their roles in making decisions

that might affect subordinate careers and progress. Thus, they are reluctant to perform a realistic appraisal because they fear the consequences to the ratee. In addition, they are not capable of managing the interpersonally difficult situations related to performance appraisal. In sum, they are uncertain about their subjective evaluations, and they are aversive of the need to let the subordinates know where they stand.

The second problem stems from the conflict between evaluation and developmental objectives of performance appraisal. This conflict places the superior as both the judge and helper. Therefore, the subordinate may become defensive about the process, blame others and circumstances, question the system of appraisal, or demean the sources of data. These reactions may lead to open hostility and denials. The worst case scenario is when the superior is ambivalent and the subordinate is defensive and resistant.

According to Beer (1987), one solution to the problem is to uncouple the evaluation and developmental aspects of performance appraisal. He suggests that two separate processes be instituted for the two different purposes. Further, appropriate, but different, performance data should be used for the two purposes. Behavioral data (e.g., specific performance-related behaviors that behavioral rating scales assess) are more appropriate when development is the purpose of performance appraisal. The emphasis here is on how they do their work and on the improvements they can make in how they do the work. Outcome data may be more appropriate when evaluation is the purpose. That is, the focus shifts to what the employee has done or achieved.

In a Nutshell

The interpersonal difficulties in performance appraisal relate to supervisors' lack of confidence in their judgments and reluctance to appraise correctly because of its effects on others' careers. Subordinates may become defensive and find fault with the system, the rater, or colleagues because of the developmental and administrative conflicts of the performance appraisal. Supervisors and subordinates may also be unwilling or incapable of managing the difficult interpersonal situation that performance appraisal poses.

In Their View

When performance has been good, when superiors and subordinates have an open relationship, when promotions and salary increases are abundant, when there is plenty of time for preparation and discussion—in short, whenever it's a pleasure—performance appraisal is easy to do. Most of the time, however, and particularly when it is most needed and most difficult (e.g., when performance is substandard), performance appraisal refuses to run properly. (Beer 1987, 286)

Summary

In summary, this chapter emphasizes the importance of performance appraisal. Performance appraisal serves the administrative purposes of monitoring and evaluating employee performance and making personnel decisions, such as salary increases and promotions. Performance appraisal also may be developmental in identifying employees' strengths and weaknesses, which forms the basis for further coaching, guidance, and training. The performance domain includes not only the job-specific task behaviors but also non-job-specific behaviors and citizenship behaviors. It also includes a person's effort in carrying out his or her assignments and his or her written and oral communications and leadership. Managers need to be cautious about possible errors in performance appraisal that may be distributional in nature, such as being too lenient or too strict or lumping every performance in the central range, or that may be temporal in nature, such as evaluating an individual's performance based on the most recent observation of the candidate or based on the evaluation of the preceding candidates. Performance appraisals may be more frequent and individualized if they are used for developmental purposes. If they are used for evaluative purposes, they must be carried out during specified time periods (e.g., quarterly or annually) with uniform processes for all employees. Performance evaluation also must be based on comprehensive information drawn from the candidate himself or herself, co-workers, supervisors, and clients or customers.

Key Terms

performance appraisal, administrative purposes, developmental purposes, performance domain, deficiency, contamination, distributional errors, temporal errors

Your Perspectives

- Quite often, universities admit students to graduate programs on the basis of their performance in the last year or last two years of their bachelor's degree. How does this practice relate to the recency error that was discussed in the chapter. Do you approve of this practice? Explain.

- Some sport managers may include participation in committee meetings as a component for purposes of performance evaluation. How would you categorize this performance? Discuss the pros and cons of this practice.

- Consider a commercial fitness club and the fitness unit of the university intramural department. Should the process of performance appraisal for the fitness instructors in these two settings be different? Why?

12 Reward Systems

Learning Objectives

After reading the chapter you should be able to

- explain the purposes of rewards in an organization,
- describe the various types of rewards in an organization,
- explain the various bases or criteria by which rewards can be distributed, and
- understand how various criteria and various rewards can be mixed to create a reward system to suit individual differences.

As noted in chapter 11, one of the purposes of performance appraisal is administrative in nature and facilitates personnel decisions including salary, wages, merit pay, promotion, and similar rewards. Volunteers work for the intrinsic rewards of volunteering (see chapter 1). Similarly, even paid workers may seek and receive intrinsic rewards of a job. At the same time, paid workers, by definition, work for the material resources they get from their jobs. Thus, it is critical to have a clear grasp of **reward systems** in organizations. Accordingly, this chapter describes the purposes, types, bases, and mix of rewards. In addition, it highlights some ways in which the rewards can be matched with individual preferences and how a work schedule itself can be used.

Although both intrinsic rewards and extrinsic rewards can be motivational, the distinction between the two forms of rewards must be noted. As noted in chapter 7, intrinsic rewards are largely a function of the job content. Organizations and their managers may follow the prescriptions of Hackman and Oldham and of Herzberg (see chapter 8) in redesigning jobs. However, the individual himself or herself derives and administers the intrinsic rewards. To the extent that intrinsic rewards reside in the job itself and that workers administer them, the organization does not have as much control over them as it has over extrinsic rewards, such as pay and bonus. Accordingly, this chapter focuses, for the most part, on extrinsic rewards.

Purposes of Reward Systems

Our discussion begins with a description of the **purposes of reward systems** in organizations. Several authors have described the purposes of reward systems from different perspectives (Belcourt et al. 1996, De Cenzo and Robbins 1994, Lawler 1987, Schuler and Jackson 1996). This section collates and describes these various perspectives.

Attracting and Retaining Good Employees

Every organization is in competition with other organizations in the same business or in other businesses for recruiting and retaining productive employees. For instance, two professional sport organizations may seek good candidates for front-office jobs. Two fitness clubs may require good accountants. Two university athletic departments may need to hire lawyers to direct the compliance units in their respective departments. The managers in these contexts must remember that the potential candidates are employable in different kinds of organizations. For instance, an accountant may find lucrative jobs with a construction company, a law firm, a hospital, or a university. Similarly, a lawyer can find employment in other universities or other kinds of organizations. Therefore, a sport organization must ensure that its reward structure matches at least the market rate if it wants to recruit and retain good employees. Thus, an effective rewards system is competitive with those of other similar or dissimilar firms seeking a particular kind of competency and talent and is more attractive to prospective candidates.

Reducing Absenteeism

An issue related to attracting and retaining good workers is absenteeism. According to Lawler (1987), organizations can design reward systems to reduce absenteeism by linking bonuses and other perks to levels of attendance. This strategy is particularly useful in compensating for low job content and poor working conditions that cannot be improved. For example, some of the jobs in facility management may be simple and routine and, therefore, may lack the motivational properties, as explained in chapter 7. Thus, individuals in those jobs are susceptible to absenteeism. The facility manager may attempt to reduce such absenteeism by linking certain rewards to attendance. For example, the manager may set a policy of giving a monetary bonus or extra days of paid leave for perfect or near perfect attendance.

Motivating Enhanced Performance

Organizational effectiveness is enhanced through employee performance that, in turn, an effective reward system can facilitate. Recall the Porter and Lawler (1968) model of motivation discussed in chapter 7. The model suggests that the linkage between performance and rewards (i.e., both intrinsic and extrinsic rewards) is a strong factor influencing subsequent performance. According to that model, a reward can motivate performance if

- the reward is attractive to the individual,
- the reward is tied to a certain level of performance, and
- the individual perceives that level of performance to be attainable.

An important point here is that although organizational rewards could be seen as rewards for past performance, they influence motivation for future performance. Accordingly, in designing a reward system for a sport organization, the manager must attempt to make the rewards attractive to individuals and offer the rewards to those who achieve realistic levels of performance.

Developing Employee Skills

A reward system can be used to enhance organizational effectiveness by using rewards to increase the skill level of employees. As noted in chapter 7, performance is a function of effort as well as ability. Based on that premise, an organization can design reward systems to reward individuals who develop their skills and, in turn, who contribute to higher productivity and organizational effectiveness. For instance, many school systems in the United States and Canada increase the base salary of their teachers after they have upgraded their training to a higher level. Similarly, an employee in a recreation center may be paid more for having passed a fitness certification course or a first-aid course. Note that the notion of skill development is not far removed from performance. Performance in a job is reflective of the skill that an individual possesses. Similarly, a promotion is presumably based on a person having acquired the skills necessary to perform the higher-level job.

Facilitating Organizational Culture and Strategic Objectives

Yet another way reward systems can influence organizational effectiveness is through cultivating and maintaining the organizational culture that fosters the specific goals and aims of the organization. Lawler (1987) noted that "reward systems can shape culture precisely because of their important influence on motivation, satisfaction, and membership. The behaviors they evoke become the dominant patterns of behavior in the organization and lead to perceptions of about what it stands for, believes in, and values" (p. 258). For example, Lawler (1987) suggested that high levels of pay may create a culture of elitism and that member participation in pay decisions may create a culture of participation. The relatively high salaries paid to athletes and coaches in professional sports do project an image of elitism and cultivate that sense among athletes and coaches. If a profit-oriented fitness or tennis club engages its employees in pay and bonus decisions, it facilitates a culture of participation and ownership among its employees.

Defining and Reinforcing Organizational Structure

Similar to this process, reward systems also can define and strengthen the organizational structure that embodies the status hierarchy. As Lawler (1987) noted,

> In general, a steeply hierarchical system [of rewards] makes the most sense when an organization needs relatively rigid bureaucratic behavior, strong top-down authority, and a strong motivation for people to move up the organizational hierarchy. A more egalitarian approach fits with a more participative management style and the desire to retain technical specialists and experts in nonmanagement or lower-level-management roles. It is not surprising, therefore, that many of the organizations that emphasize egalitarian perquisites are in high-technology and knowledge-based industries. (p. 265)

To extend Lawler's (1987) notions to the sporting context, directors and assistant directors of a university athletic department may be paid quite high salaries, and the lower-level managers and workers may be paid less than the market rate. Such a scheme would reinforce the top-down bureaucratic orientation. In contrast, a private sport-marketing firm may recruit and hire qualified professional marketers and pay them salaries commensurate with their qualifications, achievement, and the market rates. As Lawler (1987) noted, this egalitarian approach is consistence with the presence of technical specialists (i.e., sport marketers).

In a Nutshell

The purposes of reward systems include attracting and retaining good employees, motivating performance, encouraging skill development, cultivating organizational culture, and reinforcing the organizational structure.

Types of Rewards

The discussion in this section focuses on the **types of rewards** available in an organization. These can be described in terms of intrinsic and extrinsic rewards, financial and nonfinancial rewards, and performance-based and membership-based rewards (De Cenzo and Robbins 1994).

Intrinsic Versus Extrinsic Rewards

The discussion of individual motivation in chapter 7 distinguishes between intrinsic rewards and extrinsic rewards that accrue to an individual employee in his or her task performance. Herzberg's (1968) two-factor theory and Porter and Lawler's (1968) model of motivation both emphasize the significance of intrinsic motivation in employee

While reward systems reinforce the hierarchical structure of an organization, they also may delineate the critical areas of operation within an organization. For instance, a university athletic department may pay the marketing director more than it pays the heads of other departments to reflect the importance and status placed on the respective functions. A more familiar fact is that university athletic departments pay the football and basketball coaches more than they pay the coaches of other sports for the obvious reason that these sports are more popular and capable of generating revenue. A university may pay more for the basketball coach than for the football coach because basketball may be part of that university's history and tradition.

performance (see pages 103-104 and 97, respectively). The practice of job enrichment and the tenets of the job characteristics model are based on the proposition that the intrinsic rewards residing in the job itself are a potential source of motivation. Thus, management always must be attuned to the opportunities for enriching the jobs of their employees.

An equally potent source of motivation is the extrinsic rewards, such as pay, bonuses, and promotions, that the organization offers. As noted in chapter 7, the one difficulty with regard to extrinsic rewards is that employees may perceive them as inequitable because the distribution of such rewards is not based on clear, firm, and meaningful criteria; that is, rewards may not be linked properly to performance. The purpose of this section is to outline the basic features of a good reward system that an organization can implement.

Financial Versus Nonfinancial Rewards

The extrinsic rewards themselves can be categorized as financial and nonfinancial rewards. Financial rewards are rewards that enhance directly the financial well-being of the employee. For example, salaries, wages, and bonuses are financial rewards that the recipients can take home and use for any purpose. On the other hand, nonfinancial rewards do not increase the financial payoff to the employee: "Instead of making the employee's life better off the job [like financial rewards do], nonfinancial rewards emphasize making life on the job more attractive" (De Cenzo and Robbins 1994, 413). These types of rewards include things such as office furnishings, parking spaces, and top-line computers in the office. These examples show that nonfinancial rewards are motivational in their own right. They not only facilitate task performance but also create a sense of status and prestige and the associated positive feelings. Note that although these rewards do not provide any financial benefits to the employees, they do entail some financial cost to the organization.

Career Rewards Versus Social Rewards

From a different perspective, Schuler and Jackson (1996) classified nonmonetary (nonfinancial) rewards as career rewards or social rewards. As the name implies, career rewards are aimed at one's career in terms of job security and career growth. A commercial tennis club may offer job security instead of heavy increases in salary. Universities quite commonly offer free tuition to their employees if they are willing to upgrade their skills and qualifications. Note that the university is not incurring many expenses, but the benefit to the employees is great.

Social rewards relate to the good feelings that an employee has in social comparisons that may result from a title, a private office, and such other status symbols. Think of the significance of the key to the executives' washroom. Some organizations may have special and spacious washrooms for the exclusive use of their executives. Some consider getting access to the washroom a great privilege, and getting a key to that washroom may be a great reward to them.

In a Nutshell

Rewards can be intrinsic (i.e., residing in the job itself) or extrinsic (i.e., offered by the organization). Extrinsic rewards may be financial (e.g., salary or bonuses) or nonfinancial (e.g., office or computer). Nonfinancial rewards may relate to career progress (e.g., training at the company's cost) or to social status (e.g., titles or special privileges).

Direct and Indirect Compensation

Schuler and Jackson (1996) also noted that monetary (financial) compensation may be either direct or indirect. Direct compensation takes the form of things such as basic salary, wages, merit pay, and bonuses. Indirect compensation is divided into public protection, private protection, paid leave, and life cycle benefits (Schuler and Jackson 1996). Law requires organizations to provide public protection compensation, such as the contributions toward social security and premiums for unemployment and disability insurance. Private protection relates to the organization creating or contributing to a pension plan for the workers, life insurance, or savings. Paid leave refers to the organization allowing its employees to be absent with full pay for the purposes of further training, illness, vacation, and other legitimate reasons. Finally, life cycle benefits are aimed at enhancing the quality of life for employees by establishing things such as child care and elder care programs and park and playground facilities.

In a Nutshell

Typically, monetary rewards such as salary, wages, and bonuses are directly paid to the employees. However, some of the monetary rewards that an organization offers may take the form of indirect compensation. Such compensation may relate to public protection (i.e., legally required contributions, such as social security payments), private protection (i.e., contributions to organizationally sponsored pension and savings programs), and paid leave.

Performance-Based Versus Membership-Based Rewards

Organizations may offer performance-based or membership-based rewards. Performance-based rewards are linked directly to performance by the individual or the group. The essential point is that the organization evaluates the performances of the individual or the group and rewards the employee or employees based on those evaluations. When giving membership-based rewards, the organization allocates the rewards on the basis of an individual's membership in specified groups including membership in the organization. Such rewards normally take the form of increases, such as cost-of-living increases as a percentage of one's salary, seniority-based increases, and education-based increases. The focus is on specifying what membership in which group is critical to the organization and what member belongs to which group. For instance, several universities recently have allocated relatively more increases to female administrators and coaches to correct past inequalities in the salaries of men and women. The only criterion for distribution is whether one is a member of the female gender. Similarly, base salaries for directors, assistant directors, and lower-level employees of a city recreation department may be graded progressively higher, and every employee may be entitled to the base salary associated with the cadre of employment to which he or she belongs.

In a Nutshell

Rewards may be allocated based solely on organizationally relevant performance or based on membership in specific groups meaningful to the organization (e.g., seniority or rank).

Note that the categorizations of both De Cenzo and Robbins (1994) and Schuler and Jackson (1996) considerably overlap. Figure 12.1, which combines both of these categorizations, should assist the sport manager in understanding the various forms rewards can take. The manager should be able to identify from among the various forms of rewards those that are most relevant and feasible to his or her own context (i.e., the organization and its resources, the type of work done, and the type of employees).

As noted in chapter 1, other incentives may motivate volunteers as well. For example, a young person may volunteer to work in a sport organization to gain experience and skills to enhance his or her chances of securing a job. This is consistent with the career rewards offered to a paid worker. That is, the sport organization can help by exposing the student volunteer to more and more intricate and complex tasks so that the student can develop the necessary competencies. In addition, the organization also can motivate volunteers through social rewards, such as a title or other status symbols. For instance, volunteer members of a sport governing body may enjoy the special privileges that they have during competitions and other major events.

In summary, managers should recognize that altruistic motives do not preclude the effects of other incentives. As long as a sport organization needs the contribution of volunteers and as long as competition for volunteers exists among organizations, a sport manager must take the necessary steps to offer sufficient tangible and intangible rewards for the volunteers.

Work Schedules as Rewards

Although rewards may be strictly related to salary and wages, they can take several forms. As discussed, an organization can offer nonfinancial rewards to its employees. Benefits such as office space, office decor, and parking facilities are critical components of rewards. The term "nonfinancial rewards" means that the employees are not financially better off, but the organization may incur some costs. For example, if the organization improves an employee's office decor, the employee can enjoy working in that office but cannot take anything home; that is, the individual receives no financial benefit. In contrast, the organization did spend some money in improving the office decor.

An organization can undertake other strategies that employees may perceive as rewards and that may not cost the organization any additional expenditures. Three of these strategies—shorter work

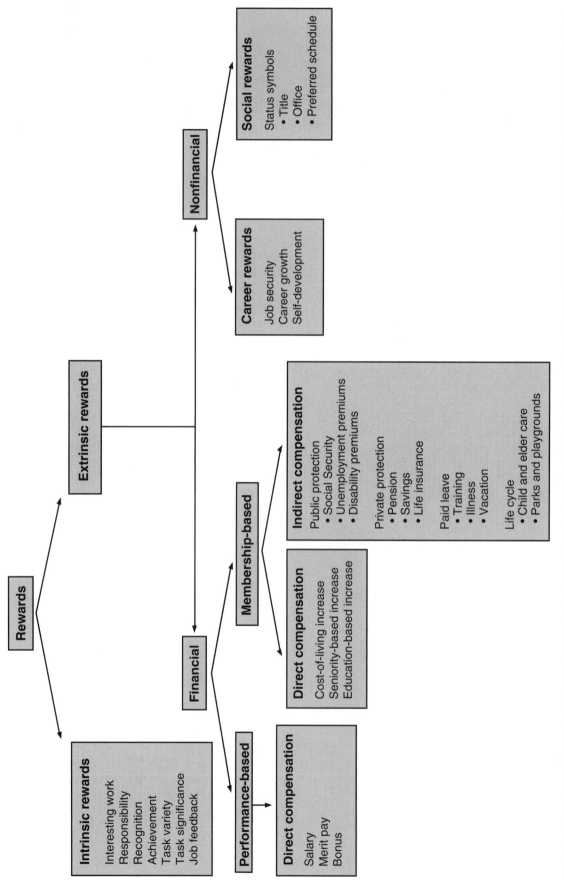

Figure 12.1 Classes of organizational rewards.

The description of various forms of rewards is more concerned with rewards for paid full-time workers than rewards for other types of workers. Insofar as many sport organizations capitalize on the services that volunteers provide, managers need to be concerned with rewards for volunteer workers. Obviously, the major form of rewards for the volunteers are the intrinsic rewards. While intrinsic rewards are generalizable to all workers, they are more critical to volunteer workers because the monetary rewards are not applicable to them. Intrinsic rewards for volunteers include the satisfaction derived from serving others. As noted in chapter 1, one reason that volunteers join a sport organization is their altruistic motive to serve others. To the extent that a sport organization's goals are oriented toward serving others, it is a forum for volunteers to satisfy their altruistic motive. However, managers cannot be satisfied with this assumption. Because many other organizations may offer the same opportunity to satisfy the altruistic motives, the volunteers are likely to choose one organization over another for other reasons than just the altruistic motive. Thus, a sport manager must be concerned with creating other incentives for the volunteer. For instance, the manager may enrich a volunteer's job by assigning progressively more challenging tasks with increasing responsibilities. If that volunteer desires such enriched jobs and is capable of adequately performing in those jobs, the sport manager would have gained two significant benefits for the organization. The organization would be successful in retaining an effective volunteer capable of performing in higher-level jobs. By the same token, the organization also would benefit in terms of cost reduction because the volunteer would be performing more challenging jobs without cost of salary and benefits.

The emphasis on intrinsic rewards and job enrichment should not minimize the importance of other rewards for the volunteers. For instance, as earlier noted, nonfinancial rewards, such as parking spaces, office settings, and office equipment, make life at work more enjoyable and attractive. This fact is equally relevant to both volunteer and paid workers. While volunteers forego their time and effort on behalf of the organization, they need not necessarily suffer from the lack of a suitable work environment. Thus, sport managers need to take efforts to make the workplace for the volunteers comfortable and attractive.

Further, while volunteers may be willing to extend their time and effort to a sport organization, some of them may not be able to incur any expenses on behalf of the organization. For example, when a volunteer has to drive to several locations in a city to carry out assigned tasks (e.g., a referee in youth sport leagues), he or she incurs the cost of transportation. In such a case, reimbursing the volunteer with money for the expenses is only appropriate.

week, staggered daily schedule, and flex-time—relate to work schedules.

Shorter Work Week

A sport organization may adopt a scheme in which the traditional five-day work week is shortened to a three- or four-day work week. However, the organization expects the employee to work the same total hours in a week. For example, if an employee in the ticketing department works 8 hours each day in a regular five-day work week, he or she would work a total of 40 hours (8 × 5). That employee needs to work 10 hours each day in a four-day week to make up the total of 40 hours for the week (10 × 4). In this scheme, the organization does not incur any additional expenses (i.e., it does not pay the employees anything more or less). However, it earns the good-will of the employees who are more satisfied with

work schedules and more motivated to perform well. Some studies have shown that absenteeism and requests for time off for personal reasons have been reduced in those organizations that have implemented shorter work weeks (Saal and Knight 1995, Schuler and Jackson 1996). From the employees' perspective, a shorter work week offers more leisure time and decreases commuting time.

On the down side, working longer hours each day may mean lower productivity at the end of the day. For example, an exercise leader is likely to be more tired and less effective in the last two hours of work in a four-day week schedule than in a five-day week schedule. Further, the scheme may not benefit everybody in the organization. For example, working mothers and fathers may find that the longer hours each day may hinder their child-rearing and child-minding activities. Another problem is that the good feelings about the shorter work week may not last for long as one gets used to the routine of it. Note also that the employees may have some reservations about a shorter work week if the employer fixes and dictates the number of days and number of hours of work. Sport managers may consider allowing their employees to choose the work week that best suits them.

Staggered Daily Schedule

Staggered daily schedule refers to the variations in the times that employees report to work and leave from work. With the requirement that every worker will work for a certain number of hours each day, those number of hours can be staggered through the day. That is, some workers may be allowed to report to work earlier (e.g., one hour earlier) and leave from work earlier, and others may come to work later and leave from work later. The employees also may be rotated every week (or any fixed period of time) through the various schedules. The staggered daily schedule creates variety for the workers. Workers may enjoy changing schedules instead of sticking to a permanent daily schedule. Another benefit of the staggered daily schedule is that the manager can tailor the schedule to suit the needs and preferences of individual workers. If possible, the manager may give the employees a choice of the daily schedule. Reporting early and leaving early may be attractive to some employees, and reporting late and leaving late may be attractive to others. Hence, the manager may offer the employees a choice in the matter. However, the approach creates more work for management because management has to keep track of the schedules for individual workers and monitor their adherence to the schedule.

Flex-Time

Flex-time is a scheme originating from Germany where it is called Gleitzeit, meaning gliding time (French 1990). In the system, the manager expects an individual to work a given number of hours each week but permits him or her to choose the hours of work within certain limits. Usually, the plan includes a given number of core hours (i.e., from four to six hours, such as from 10 A.M. to 4 P.M.) with a flexibility band surrounding the core. In some cases, one can accumulate extra hours and take a day off at the end of the month. One is expected to finish the given jobs, and the scheme emphasizes paying for productivity rather than for attendance. Some research has shown that the scheme reduces employee tardiness, decreases absenteeism, reduces job fatigue, and increases loyalty (Saal and Knight 1988). The scheme would be helpful to individuals who have to manage both career and family roles. From the perspective of an employee, he or she has complete control over scheduling the work hours on a daily basis outside of the specified core hours. While employees would enjoy such flexibility in their work schedule, managers must note that they cannot effectively direct their employees outside of the core time. Even evaluating their performances outside of the core may become difficult.

In a Nutshell

Variations in the work schedule itself may prove to be a reward for employees. A shorter work week permits employees to work longer hours each day for fewer days in the week. A staggered daily schedule permits workers to come to and to leave from work at different times during the day. Flex-time permits the employee to vary the number of hours worked in a day subject to a total number of hours in a given period and a daily core period.

Bases of Rewards

The foregoing sections described the purposes of rewards and the types of rewards. The more critical

One of the difficulties that employees in large urban centers encounter is the traffic jams during office hours. The problem is more pronounced at the beginning of the work day when everybody wants to get to the office and at the end of the office day when everybody is in a hurry to get home. One way to alleviate this problem is to schedule the work day to begin at different times in the morning (e.g., 7:30 A.M., 8:00 A.M., and 8:30 A.M.) and to end correspondingly at different times (e.g., 3:30 P.M., 4:00 P.M., and 4:30 P.M.). This practice is known as *staggered start time* (Gottlieb, Kelloway, and Barham 1998; Pierce, Newstrom, Dunham, and Barber 1989). Hypothetically speaking, if all organizations in an urban center would have three different start times, then the traffic jam would be cut by 67% because at any one time only one-third of the workforce will be driving to work.

concern is with the bases on which the rewards are distributed to organizational members. The following section outlines some general themes regarding what criteria are used to decide who gets what and how much of it. Note that some of the concepts in this section necessarily parallel those discussed earlier because the purposes and types of rewards are intertwined with the **bases of rewards**.

Job as the Base

A traditional approach in distributing rewards is based solely on the type of job that a person performs. That is, the manager evaluates the job in relation to other jobs then bases the rewards on such evaluations. Thus, a locker-room attendant may be paid less than the coach, and a caretaker may be paid less than the exercise specialist in a fitness club. According to Lawler (1987): "This approach is based on the assumption that job worth can be determined, and that the person doing the job is worth only as much to the organization as the job itself is worth" (p. 260). This assumption is valid in most circumstances, and it provides an objective basis for allocation of rewards.

Note that the notion of job worth parallels the notion of intrinsic rewards of a job. Generally speaking, jobs of higher worth entail relatively more responsibilities, greater autonomy, and greater opportunities for achievement. These are the ingredients of job enrichment. As noted in chapter 8, one difficulty that a manager faces in enriching the jobs is that the workers (and their labor unions) may expect more salary for the work. In their view, job enrichment increases job worth; therefore, the pay should be commensurate with that worth.

Skill as the Base

Another approach is to reward employees on the basis of the skills they possess. The assumption here is that the skills under consideration are those that can be used within the organization. Thus, one's skills in gardening may not have much relevance in a fitness and recreation club or in the public relations unit of an athletic department. However, the skills related to first aid or accounting may be meaningful in either of these two organizational contexts. The first advantage of a skill-based scheme is that employees believe that the organization values their personal growth: "This policy can create a climate of concern for personal growth and development and produce a highly talented work force" (Lawler 1987, 260). It is an important consideration because such feelings lead to greater com-

mitment to the organization and increased motivation in job performance.

From a different perspective, the organization gains in enhancing its human capital. That is, the workers become more knowledgeable and capable of handling many other additional duties. It means that the organization has a flexible workforce at its disposal and uses it as necessary. For instance, if an exercise leader in a fitness club increases his or her accounting skills, the club can use this expertise also when the demand for exercise classes is low.

The negative aspect of a skill-based reward system is that it is more expensive than a job-based scheme. That is, a job incumbent may acquire more skills than necessary to execute that job effectively. If all job incumbents have more skills than necessary for their respective jobs and if the organization implements the skill-based scheme, the organization would be spending more money than if it implemented the job-based scheme. Take our previous example of an exercise leader acquiring accounting skills. Imagine the situation in which all of the exercise leaders in the fitness club acquire accounting skills, and the accountants qualify as exercise leaders. If the fitness club adopts the skill-based reward scheme, it would be paying for the skills of all its employees although those skills would be redundant for the most part. Another difficulty is deciding what skills are relevant to a particular organizational context.

Given these concerns, many organizations prefer to base the reward schemes on the jobs themselves. The rationale for such an approach is that different jobs require different skills that the organization identifies in the respective job descriptions. That is, job-based schemes take into account the skills needed for specific jobs, so they are, in fact, skill-based schemes. However, if an organization desires a flexible workforce, it should adopt the skill-based scheme. This is particularly true of smaller organizations that can afford only a few employees. If the fitness club in our example employs one or two exercise leaders, it may find that paying those leaders for enhancing their accounting skills is more advantageous than hiring an accountant.

Seniority as the Base

A common practice for many organizations, particularly government agencies, is to base their reward systems on seniority. That is, the organization uses the number of years that a person has been in a job as the basis for salary increases or bonuses. Compared with the bases of rewards discussed earlier, years of experience in a job is an easily measured and objective base. Therefore, many organizations adopt this approach. The organization could justify using this approach by linking seniority to skills and mastery of the job. That is, the organization can expect a person performing a job for a number of years to have mastered the skills associated with that job, so he or she is entitled to higher pay than a newcomer to that job.

The notion that seniority-based reward schemes subsume the advantages of both job-based and skill-based schemes may not be valid in all contexts. The fast and vast changes in technology have changed the nature of many of the jobs. For instance, an older accountant in a university athletic department may not be familiar with or skilled in the use of computers in accounting; however, the younger person is more likely to have mastered that aspect of the job and, therefore, is more likely to be more proficient than the older accountant. Further, seniority may not have any bearing on certain kinds of jobs. For instance, being effective as an exercise leader is based more on the mastery of current knowledge, energy, and enthusiasm. These attributes do not have any association with seniority. Thus, seniority-based reward schemes would not have any motivational effect on young exercise leaders; in fact, such a scheme would have a negative effect on motivation.

Performance as the Base

Another form of reward scheme bases the rewards on the performance of employees. A simple example is that of piece-rate adopted in many manufacturing organizations. An employee producing 110 units in a factory will get a bigger reward than the person producing 100 units. On first sight, it seems to be a reliable, valid, and objective measure for a reward scheme. This may be true in some circumstances but unrealistic in other circumstances. Consider, for example, an athletic trainer. While the number of injured clients served is critical, he or she must consider the quality of the service provided. Further, the severity and complications of an injury may prohibit an athletic trainer from attending to and serving many more clients.

As noted in chapter 11, performance in a job may comprise several components of which the number of units produced may be just one component. More specifically, the domains of performance would include several non-job-specific aspects, such as citizenship behaviors (see chapter 11, table 11.3). The athletic trainer, in our example, can contribute to the training and development of junior trainers,

facilitate the performance of other trainers, and suggest ways of improving the total operation. As noted in chapter 11, performance appraisal should include all of these behaviors.

In Their View

The decision of whether to relate pay to performance is a crucial one in any organization. It can be a serious error to assume automatically that they should be related. A sound linkage can contribute greatly to organizational effectiveness. But a poor job can be harmful. Specifically, if performance is difficult to measure and/or rewards are difficult to distribute on the basis of performance, a pay-for-performance system can motivate counterproductive behaviors, invite lawsuits charging discrimination, and create a climate of mistrust, low credibility, and managerial incompetence. (Lawler 1987, 263)

Given the fundamental notion that organizational effectiveness depends on individual performances, the emphasis on individual performances is legitimate and logical. Accordingly, performance-based reward schemes facilitate individual performances and, thus, organizational effectiveness. However, as noted in chapter 11, two issues in performance appraisal exist. The first issue concerns what should constitute performance, which the previous section discussed. The second issue is how to measure different aspects of performance. To the extent that performance appraisal is deficient and contaminated, the performance-based reward schemes also would suffer. Lawler (1987) summarized the difficulties associated with performance-based schemes: "A true merit pay or promotion system is often more easily aspired to than done, however. . . . It is difficult to specify what kind of performance is desired and often equally difficult to determine whether that performance has been demonstrated" (pp. 260-261).

In a Nutshell

Rewards can be distributed on the basis of the relative worth of the jobs themselves, skills and competencies of the employees, seniority among employees, or performance of the employees.

One important consideration for sport managers is to ensure that the reward systems within their organizations do not violate any of the legal requirements. For instance, laws relating to minimum wage, overtime pay, equal pay (i.e., discouraging discrimination on the basis of things such as gender, race, religion), and comparable worth (i.e., ensuring pay equity on the basis of comparable worth of jobs that different groups of people hold) provide clear guidelines for organizations to follow.

Mix of Rewards

The advantages of employing various bases for the distribution of rewards were discussed earlier. An organization can use more than one criterion or base to structure its reward system (i.e., **mix of rewards**). For example, a university campus recreation department may base their annual salary increases on a given percentage of one's salary as cost-of-living increases, a given dollar amount for performing the same or similar jobs, and variable amounts as merit increases. Percentage increases to cover the rising cost of living tend to yield more dollar amounts to senior employees who already earn more money than junior employees. On the other hand, an equal amount of dollars for all employees irrespective of their seniority is a job-based reward; that is, everyone is given the same amount for performing the same or similar jobs. Note that this equal dollar amount translates into a higher percentage increase for junior employees. Merit pay is allotted on the basis of performance as judged through regular performance appraisal however that performance is appraised. Thus, the hypothetical reward system in this campus recreation example is a mixture of job-based, skill-based, seniority-based, and performance-based criteria. Sport managers must consider the flexibility that such a perspective offers in instituting a reward system in their organizations. Instead of attempting to choose one best base for rewards, they must look at a mix of bases that are meaningful to their employees and feasible in their organizational context.

In a Nutshell

Sport managers may employ a mix of bases for distributions of the rewards. One portion may be based on the job category, another portion to cover cost of living, and another portion on merit.

Reward Systems and Member Preferences

One element in the structure of rewards systems is that of member preferences. In the discussion of various forms of rewards and the various bases on which those rewards are distributed, the implicit assumption was that the reward system in place would influence all employees the same way and in the same direction. However, this is not always the case. As noted, the shorter work week may not be acceptable to working mothers and fathers. Take the case of group-based benefits, such as group insurance and dental care. Group insurance plans and medical schemes are less costly for the members than individually organized plans are. Thus, these organizationally arranged group benefits constitute significant indirect rewards. Yet, they may not have the desired effect on all employees. For instance, if a person's spouse has extensive medical coverage for the whole family from his or her employer, whatever coverage that person's employer gives is redundant to that person. Therefore, it loses its motivating potential. For another example, some educational institutions convert part of the total package of rewards into free tuition to employees' children. This benefit would lose its motivating potential on employees who had to pay heavily to educate their children in the past.

Cafeteria-Style Benefits

One recent way of alleviating the problem is labeled the cafeteria-style benefit program. In such a scheme, an individual is allowed to choose from among a set of differentially priced perks and benefits for a given total amount. For instance, employees of a sport-marketing firm may be allowed to choose from among several benefits (e.g., medical coverage, pension contribution, paid leave, and straight cash) for the total of the bonus allotted in a year, for example $1,000. Such an approach would satisfy the varying preferences of the employees. Older employees may opt for more medical coverage, and younger employees may prefer straight cash to pay for children's expenses. However, in each case, the total cannot exceed the limit of $1,000. According to Lawler (1987): "The theory is that if individuals are allowed to tailor their own reward packages to fit their particular needs, the organization will get the best value for its money, because it will give people only those things that they desire" (p. 265).

Lump-Sum Payments

The term "lump-sum payments" is used in conjunction with bonuses as well as salary raises. Bonuses are lump-sum payments to employees in recognition of their performance during a specified period (e.g., quarterly, semi-annual, or annual bonuses). A bonus is not added to one's base salary as is the case with salary increases or merit increases. It implies that a worker has to be performing above a certain level each year to receive the bonus. In the case of salary or merit increases, the increases are added to the base salary, which implies that the increase given in one year would be given each year even though the worker might not be performing at the same level in subsequent years. Sport managers may consider bonuses as an option because they can be tied to organizational performance in each year. For example, a commercial fitness club may offer larger bonuses when it makes huge profits and lesser amounts when its profits are lowered. Further, the fitness club is not committed to a huge salary account in the coming years because bonuses are not added to base salaries. The idea that bonuses are tied to profit levels makes clear that bonuses may not be appropriate to nonprofit organizations.

Lump-sum payments may also be made when salary or merit increases are announced. The traditional practice is to include the increase in the base salary and to distribute the increase over the next 12 months. Thus, a person in the ticket office who gets a $2,400 annual increase will see his or her monthly paycheck increase by $200 for the next 12 months. Suppose that the athletic department offers to pay the $2,400 as a lump-sum payment at the beginning of the year. What effect would such a proposal have? Although the lump-sum payment of $2,400 is the same as the $200 over 12 months, psychologically it looks like a much larger amount. Further, lump-sum payments tend to accentuate the salary or merit increases between high and low performers. A $2,400 increase relative to a $1,200 increase sounds more impressive than the $200 per month increase relative to a $100 increase.

Apart from the psychological boost that lump-sum payments offer, these payments may be more attractive to workers because they can use the lump sum for some kind of investment. For example, a young member of the event management office can use the amount as a down payment for a car or a house or even as a loan payoff. Note that how the employees view the lump-sum payments is a function of personal habits, orientations, and needs. Some employees are careful in financial matters, and some are spendthrifts who cannot hold on to the money they get. Some may have an immediate need for a lump-sum amount, and others (e.g., a mother or father with a newborn baby) may need a steady income over the next 12 months. Due to these different uses for the money, a sport organization may leave the choice of a lump-sum payment or monthly increases to its employees. The good feelings and the sense of control that the employees have over the choice is motivational by itself. Further, the organization would have achieved the objective of tailoring its rewards scheme to individual needs and preferences.

In a Nutshell

In designing a reward system, managers must consider the preferences of the employees. The cafeteria-style benefit package permits the employees to choose the mix of benefits that they like without any additional cost to the organization. Managers can extend similar logic to all forms of rewards.

Creativity in Reward Systems

The foregoing description of how different rewards can be distributed shows that ample room exists for creativity in designing the reward systems. Sport managers can conceive of several configurations of types of rewards, bases for those rewards, member choices, and timing of the rewards. Although the reward system is subject to the legal requirements, ample room exists to mix these elements to create a unique system meaningful to a particular organizational context. Employee choices may be an important ingredient in the mix of rewards, and their participation in designing the reward system itself is equally important. When managers engage their employees in designing the reward system, such participation is a reward in itself to the employees. Second, they bring their unique needs and preferences that the reward system could target. Third, as noted earlier, creativity and ingenuity is widely distributed among organizational members. Thus, the members generate more creative and meaningful options for the group to discuss and approve. Finally, when employees are involved in designing the reward scheme, they develop a sense of ownership over the scheme and, thus, are likely to see it as fair and equitable.

In Their View

Reward systems should be assessed from a cost-benefit perspective. The cost can be managed and controlled and the benefits planned for. The key is to identify the outcomes needed for the organization to be successful and then to design the reward system in such a way that these outcomes will be realized. (Lawler 1987, 258)

Summary

The reward system should be aimed at attracting and retaining good employees, motivating them toward higher performance, developing the human capital (i.e., skill and competency development), cultivating and maintaining organizational culture, and strengthening the organizational structure. Further, the reward system must abide by the letter and spirit of all legal requirements. While rewards can be either intrinsic or extrinsic, this chapter focused on extrinsic rewards. These extrinsic rewards can be financial, such as salary increases, or nonfinancial, such as office furnishings or parking spaces. The nonfinancial rewards can be oriented toward employee career progress, such as training that the organization pays for, or toward one's social status, such as titles and other symbols of status. In addition, the compensation can be indirect in the form of publicly sanctioned protection of the employees, such as payment of premiums for social security and unemployment insurance. Indirect compensations also can be in the form of organizationally sanctioned pension and savings plans and in the form of health insurance. Rewards can be distributed on the basis of the job itself, the skills one possesses, the number of years in service (i.e., seniority), and performance. Rewards also can take the form of varying work schedules, such as a shorter work week and flex-time. Finally, managers need to be creative in mixing the types and bases of rewards to suit member needs and preferences. Involving members in this process brings forth not only their unique needs and preferences but also their ingenuity in developing an effective reward system for the organization.

Key Terms

reward systems, purposes of reward systems, types of rewards, bases of rewards, mix of rewards

Your Perspectives

- Consider your own experience as a volunteer or paid worker in a sport organization. Describe its reward system and its components. What were your reactions to each one of those components?

- What mix of rewards would you like if you were working in a university athletic department, professional sport club, or commercial tennis club? Weigh the relative importance of your own preferences and the organizational characteristics in your choice of the rewards.

- If you were the owner or manager of one of the organizations in the previous question, what system of rewards would you institute? Would that be different from your preferences as a worker? Explain.

13 Organizational Justice

Learning Objectives

After reading this chapter you will be able to

- gain an insight into justice in organizations and the components of distributive, procedural, and interactional justice;

- understand the principles of equity, equality, and need underlying distributive justice;

- distinguish among various forms of contributions that members or units bring to the distributive situation;

- learn the rules that facilitate procedural justice; and

- understand the notion of interactional justice.

While the notion of justice has been part of every civilization, the discussion of **organizational justice** and the significance attached to it are of recent origin. The governments of various countries have instituted several laws, rules, and regulations to ensure just and fair practices in business and educational institutions. These government regulations are designed from a macro perspective to force and monitor fair practices across all organizations. However, they do not cover all managerial practices within an organization and the circumstances surrounding those practices. Thus, while it is necessary for all managers to adhere to government regulations, managers should realize that they themselves are the guardians of justice within their organizations. Therefore, sport managers must understand the various perspectives and interpretations of organizational justice so that they can do everything in their power to ensure that their actions are just and fair. This chapter defines organizational justice and discusses three forms of organizational justice—distributive justice, procedural justice, and interactional justice—and the interrelationships among them. In addition, the chapter outlines the principles or rules associated with each form of justice.

Perspectives on Organizational Justice

The importance of the concept of justice to organizations and their managers can be highlighted from three perspectives—ethical, business, and legal (Gilliland 1993). First, the ethical perspective. In so far as society sanctions and supports organizations, the organizations need to abide by the same conceptions and standards of justice as those that society adopts in general. This overall view emphasizes that all of an organization's activities should be just and fair whether such actions are directed at the community at large, the customers, or the employees. That is, while an organization's efforts to maximize profits for the owners are legitimate in themselves, the justice expectation is that nobody else should be harmed in the process. Thus, for example, society expects organizations not to contribute to air or water pollution and expects customers not to be charged differentially for a good or service based on their gender or race.

The business perspective emphasizes the losses that may accrue to an organization because of its unjust and unfair practices. First, society in general, and customers in particular, may boycott the organization and its products if they perceive that the organization is unjust or unfair. The employees also may withhold their full efforts and cooperation if they perceive any injustices in organizational activities directed at the community or employees as a group or at themselves as individuals. Their dissatisfaction and alienation would result in lower productivity, and the organization would suffer for it.

The third perspective is the legal one. As noted in chapter 2, the rising educational level of society in general (its workforce in particular) and the sophistication of training have made the distinction between professional and nonprofessional cadres of an occupation sufficiently narrow. The same line of reasoning can be advanced here in the legal aspect of organizational justice. That is, increasing customer and employee awareness of what constitutes just practices leads to the expectation for more justice in the workplace. Further, as society moves toward more litigation, organizations are confronted with all kinds of lawsuits. Justice in the workplace is fast becoming an arena for such legal actions.

Forms of Organizational Justice

While the foregoing notions of justice in the organizational context covers the community, customers, and employees, the focus of this chapter is on organizational justice from the employees' perspective. Although almost every organizational activity and managerial decision is subject to the norms of justice, the areas in which justice concerns are more pronounced relate to personnel decisions (e.g., recruitment, placement, performance evaluation, promotion, salary, wage, bonus, and fringe benefits), resource allocation to units, and leadership or supervision.

In a Nutshell

Managers should be concerned seriously with organizational justice because it is morally expected of them as custodians of socially sanctioned enterprises, because organizational justice is the foundation of good employee and customer relations that ensure organizational effectiveness, and because legal ramifications of being unjust in managerial practices exist.

In each of the areas of organizational activity, organizational justice can be analyzed in terms of the outcomes accruing to individuals or units, the decision processes by which the outcomes to different parties were determined, and the way the processes and outcomes were communicated to individuals or groups. These three analytical approaches are called

- distributive justice (which addresses outcomes),
- procedural justice (which addresses the decision procedures), and
- interactional justice (which addresses the manner in which the decisions are communicated).

Figure 13.1 illustrates the relationships among these three forms of organizational justice.

Figure 13.1 shows that distributive justice is more critical of the three components in the sense that it addresses the actual outcomes (e.g., salary, fringe benefits, and office space) accruing to individuals. Such outcomes tend to be concrete. On the other hand, procedural justice is concerned with the procedures for determining the outcomes to various individuals and units. The solid line flowing from procedural justice to distributive justice illustrates this relationship. Finally, interactional justice addresses outcomes after the fact. That is, it relates to explaining the outcomes after management has decided them and the procedures by which management determined the outcomes. Thus, dotted

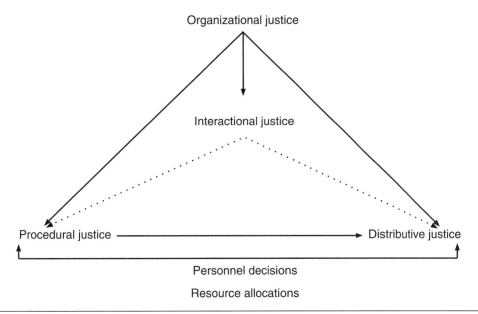

Figure 13.1   Relationships among procedural, distributive, and interactional forms of organizational justice.

lines show its connection to procedural and distributive justice. The following sections outline these three forms of justice in greater detail.

Distributive Justice

The primary focus in the discussion and determination of organizational justice has been on the outcomes that individuals or groups receive relative to other individuals or groups (i.e., **distributive justice**). (Cohen 1987). That is, the major thrust has been and still is with the distribution of resources to individuals or groups. For example, employees may perceive salary increases to different individuals or groups as just or unjust. Similarly, they may perceive the budget allotment to different units of a sport organization (e.g., a city recreation department) as just or unjust. From a different perspective, they may make a justice judgment regarding the office rooms allotted to different volunteers.

While the amount of resources received is the immediate catalyst of justice judgments, the arguments on the topic invariably turn to the principles underlying the distribution of the resources. For instance, an employee of a professional sport franchise may be disappointed if he or she receives a $500 raise when he or she expected a $1,000 raise. The immediate feelings of disappointment and frustration will either be relieved or aggravated when that employee realizes that this allocation was based on fair criteria or principles. If the employee realizes that the franchise had suffered a loss in the previous year and had to cope with the loss by holding back on salary increases for all individuals, he or she may

accept the lower increase. The organization may have based the salary increases on relative performance. If the employee accepts that performance should be the basis of salary distribution and that other employees performed better, then he or she may not be so disturbed over the lower increase. In the first scenario, everybody received an equal amount, and in the second, everybody received an amount equitable to their performance. That is, two different principles of distribution were involved. The major distributive principles are

- equity,
- equality, and
- need.

These principles and their subrules are described in table 13.1. The following sections explore these principles in greater detail.

Principle of Equity

Chapter 7 presented Adams' theory of inequity. The thrust of the theory is that individuals perceive **equity** when their rewards or outcomes are comparable with those of other persons. The chapter also noted that, in the evaluation of equity, individuals should not only consider the actual rewards received but also the contributions that the other persons make. In essence, the comparison is based on what one receives relative to his or her own contribution versus what the other receives in return for his or her contribution. The same line of reasoning applies to the question of justice. That is, the equity principle of justice specifies that the

Table 13.1   Distributive Principles and Their Subrules

Principle	Subrule	Description
Equity		Distribution of resources is based on contributions that members make to a group or organization.
	Effort	The amount of effort that the member expends is considered a significant contribution.
	Ability	Members receive resources on the basis of their relative abilities.
	Performance	The absolute performance is the criterion for distribution of resources.
Equality		Resources are distributed equally to all members.
	Treatment	Equality is maintained at a particular time of resource distribution.
	Results	Equality is maintained over a period of time and a number of distribution situations.
	Opportunity	Equality is maintained by ensuring the same opportunity for every individual to receive the resources.
Need		Resources are distributed on the basis of the needs of individuals or units.

Source: Törnblom & Jonsson (1985).

resources and rewards of an organization should be distributed to individuals or groups on the basis of their contributions to the organization and its efforts. Thus, a university coach who has a consistent record of winning championships and who generates publicity, prestige, and donations for the university is likely to be rewarded more than another coach who lags behind in these respects. Similarly, a volunteer who raises funds for a sport organization is likely to be regarded more highly than another volunteer who assists in the routine affairs of the organization.

Most employees will agree to the principle of equity as a basis for organizational justice; that is, organizational resources and rewards should be distributed on the basis of the contributions that individuals or groups make. This consensus is shattered quickly in the determination of what constitutes "contributions." In the example of coaches, some would argue that quality of coaching, and not the win-loss record, should be the only or the major contribution that the organization should consider in the distribution of rewards. Similarly, a volunteer sport organization exists to provide a service to community, and it can be argued, therefore, that the contributions of those who are directly involved in the production of that service should be regarded more highly than those contributions made behind the scene.

In discussing the inputs or contributions that organization members may bring to an equity-based distributive situation, Törnblom and Jonsson (1985,

In Their View

Distributive justice is viewed as "being concerned not only simply with the distribution of economic goods, but with the distribution of conditions and goods that affect well-being, which includes psychological, physiological, economic, and social aspects. Distributive justice, although not the only source of conflict in organizations, is a general theme that permeates many aspects of organizational behavior . . . . Distributive justice issues and principles are considered as deep structures or currents within organizations which, even though they may not be dominant issues within a specific conflict situation, play an important role in shaping an overall pattern of both conflict sources and people's cognitions about conflict. Therefore, the importance of distributive justice as a source of conflict in organizations not only stems in part from its status as a fundamental human issue, but it also stems from the fact that organizations use different and even competing distributive rules" (Kabanoff 1991, 417).

1987) proposed three subrules of equity. According to these authors, a member's contributions may be formulated in terms of

- effort that a member expends,
- innate or achieved ability of the member, or
- performance of the member.

In the sport context, for example, an athletic director may evaluate how frequent and intense the practice sessions are for various teams and may distribute the budget for the next year on that basis. The athletic director also may look at the ability level of the athletes themselves and provide more funds for those teams that have athletes of high ability. Finally, the win-loss record of the various teams may be used as the basis for distribution of resources. While all of these contributions may be used as the basis for distribution of rewards, difficulty arises when different individuals emphasize different contributions in their justice judgments. Thus, most of the discussion and disputes over the equity principle of distribution centers around what should be considered as one's contribution and not on the idea that contribution should be the basis for distribution of resources. The discussion of procedural justice will touch on this issue.

In a Nutshell

The principle of equity suggests that justice is maintained if resources are distributed in proportion to the contributions of members (or units). Such contributions may relate to their effort, ability, or performance.

Principle of Equality

While equity has been the distributive principle most often used in organizations, organizations also use the principle of **equality** according to which organizational resources and rewards should be distributed equally among all who are entitled to such rewards. Labor unions widely support equality as a distributive principle. In their bargaining with management over wage increases, they are most likely to emphasize that all workers should be given an equal raise in wages or salaries. They can justify the claim of equality in the types of jobs in which all workers perform similar routine jobs. For example, all workers in an assembly line perform similar jobs, and the pace of the machine controls all of them. Under those circumstances, the organization should reward equally everybody in the assembly line. This line of reasoning can be extended to all workers in an industry who are involved in similar jobs. For instance, pay raises in government bureaucracies tend to be equal for members of a particular rank.

From a different perspective, the principle of equality may be justified, and even necessary, under some circumstances. For instance, the principle of equity can be employed meaningfully only if the organization is clear about what contributions should be considered in allocating rewards, if the organization can isolate one's contribution from those of others, and if the organization can measure objectively such a contribution. Consider coaches of university athletic teams. Winning competitions is considered a measure of a coach's contribution to the athletic program. Accordingly, the university may reward coaches on the basis of their winning percentages. If more than one coach, such as defensive coaches in football, was involved, the organization would have more difficulty identifying the individual contributions toward winning; therefore, the coaches of that unit may be given equal salary increases. From a different perspective, instead of being so categorical about winning, some universities may prefer to evaluate their coaches on the basis of their contribution in terms of developing leadership and citizenship qualities among the athletes. While this is a noble contribution, the university cannot easily measure it. Therefore, such universities may give equal pay raises to all coaches.

Törnblom and Jonsson (1985, 1987) proposed three subrules of the principles of equality:

- Treatment
- Results
- Opportunity

If one applies the equality of treatment principle, then every individual or unit will receive the same amount of resources. For example, each employee of a fitness club may get the same salary increase as every other comparable employee. By the same token, the organization may allot each unit of the fitness club (e.g., aerobics and weight training) the same amount for operating expenses.

In the principle of results, everyone has the same results in the long run although inequalities may occur in the short run. In applying this principle, the director of a recreation department may decide to give a larger budget for equipment to one of three units in the first year, to another unit in the second year, and to the third unit in the third year. In this instance, inequality occurs each year, but the results at the end of the third year are similar. That is, every unit received similar amounts in the long run. In the case of equality of opportunity, everyone has the same possibility or chance to receive a certain amount of resources. For example, if a fitness club receives an all-paid invitation for one individual to attend a national convention of fitness leaders, how would the club owner or manager decide which of the fitness leaders would go? The principle of treatment is not applicable because the trip cannot be divided among the employees. Similarly, the principle of results is not relevant because such a trip will not be available in subsequent years. One meaningful option for the club owner is to draw lots among the fitness leaders. This option ensures that each fitness leader has the same opportunity as every other leader to win the lottery. This method is labeled equality of opportunity.

In a Nutshell

Organizational justice can be based on the principle of equality in which every member or unit receives the same amount of resources at a particular point in time (i.e., equality of treatment), receives the same amount over a period of time (i.e., equality of results), or has the same opportunity to receive the resource as everybody else (i.e., equality of opportunity).

Principle of Need

The third significant principle of distributive justice is that the resources and rewards should be distributed according to the needs of different individuals or units. An extreme example of the application of the **need** principle is an organization offering pay increases on the basis of the number of children each employee has to support. The argument is simple; an employee with a greater number of children needs more money to support them. In fact, the income tax codes of many countries apply this principle wherein an individual taxpayer can claim additional exemptions for every dependent he or she supports. Along similar lines, Rawls (1971) outlined a "difference principle" according to which a society's resources should be redistributed in order to improve the relative conditions of the people who are disadvantaged. In such redistribution, it is acknowledged and accepted that the conditions of those who are advantaged may be worsened.

In an organizational context, however, personal needs cannot be used indiscriminately as criteria for distribution of resources. Personal needs may be accommodated in such things as fringe benefits (e.g., health insurance covering families of varying sizes). In general, the needs of an individual or unit should be perceived from a performance perspective. That is, certain individuals or units may need certain resources for performing their assigned duties. For example, a hockey team requires a larger budget than a volleyball team to pay for the broken hockey sticks and for renting an arena. Even though both teams are seen as equally significant enterprises, the distribution of resources (i.e., budgets) is differential because of the varying needs of the two teams. Similarly, the long distance telephone budget for the marketing department tends to be higher than that for facility management because the employees in the marketing department need to make relatively more long distance calls to perform their duties.

Some authors have debated whether the equity and equality principles (including all of the subrules) are indeed different from each other. One set of authors claims that all of the principles are derivatives of the equity rule (e.g., Deutsch 1975). They differ only in the types of contributions considered for determining equity. For example, when somebody distributes the rewards equally to all members of a unit, they may be using the equity principle insofar as membership in the unit is itself viewed as the contribution. Take the example of uniforms for all members of a team. The design and cost of the uniforms is the same for all members who deserve them just on the basis of membership. Similarly, when resources are distributed on the basis of need, the degree of need (or conversely, the degree of affluence) is what members bring to the situation (i.e., their contribution). In the case of an athletic team, the coach may decide to spend a little more time with the freshman athletes because they need such attention. The relative abilities and experience that different players bring to the situation is the contribution on which the coach's allocation of his or her time is based. Therefore, the differential allocation of a coach's time is equitable. On the other hand, Reis (1986) noted that empirical research supports the distinctions between equity, equality, and need principles. According to the author: "Each justice rule predicts specifically how much of what kind of input is to be associated in what way with how much of what kind of outcome" (p. 39). It is better for a practicing manager to disengage himself or herself from these arguments and consider the circumstances under which each distributive principle will be most appropriate.

In a Nutshell

The principle of need simply implies that the needs of individuals or units should be the criterion for distribution of resources. The need principle may be meaningful in organizational contexts if the needs are seen as basic to performance.

Organizational Values and Task Type

In deciding on what principle should be applied in a particular distributive situation, one needs to take into account the organizational values and the task type in which the members are engaged.

Organizational Values

Meindl (1989) suggested that various organizational values may be subsumed under productivity or solidarity. Productivity and profitability may be the central concern in some organizations and in some situations. This was, and still is, the case with some of the American organizations that face intense competition from more efficient foreign firms. Under those circumstances, the administrators, as well as workers, may opt for distributive justice based on productivity as contribution. For instance, a sport-marketing company may distribute its rewards based on productivity of individual employees (e.g., signing up new sponsors). This type of distribution is reasonable because the company competes with other such companies for clients and their business. The success of the company is based largely on the productivity of individual employees.

In contrast, inter-individual and inter-group friction among members of an organization may engender disruptions in the work flow of the organization that, in turn, may result in productivity losses. In such cases, solidarity and the good will among members or units may be the goal of the organization; therefore, the organization may prefer to distribute the rewards on the basis of equality. For instance, a fitness club manager may believe that its fitness leaders must collaborate with each other to provide quality service to its clients. Any conflicts among them may translate into disruptions in the operation of the club that, in turn, may tarnish the image of the club. The concern with this issue may prompt the owner of the club to focus on solidarity among the employees and use the principle of equality. Members and units may also consider such distribution as just.

Task Type

Chapter 8 presented the nature of tasks and their attributes and noted that variations in the interdependence among tasks entail different forms of coordination. Such variations in interdependence among jobs within an organization also call for different principles of distribution. For instance, a sport-marketing firm may employ different marketing experts to take care of business in different regions and may design their tasks to be sufficiently independent of each other. Under those circumstances, the productivity of individual employees may be used as the basis for distribution of rewards (i.e., the principle of equity). In contrast, the sport-marketing firm may organize its marketing experts into project teams. Because the combined contributions of members of a team determine the success of the project, the members of the team share equally the rewards accruing to the team. In general, administrators tend to prefer the principle of equity based on performance in independent tasks and tend to lean more toward the principle of equality as the task becomes progressively more interdependent.

In a Nutshell

The principle that promotes organizational justice in a particular context is dependent on the relative emphasis placed on productivity compared with solidarity. It also depends on the degree of interdependence among the tasks that members perform.

Törnblom and Jonsson (1985) and Hums and Chelladurai (1994a, 1994b) used the term "retribution" to refer to withdrawal of resources from members or units. However, note here that the term "retribution" normally is used to refer to some form of punishment levied against someone for having committed a crime or a prohibited behavior. In this sense, our criminal justice system is largely concerned with meeting out retributive justice. A $100 fine for speeding ensures retributive justice. Similarly, retributive justice is established when the accused person is proven guilty of committing a crime and when an appropriate penalty is assessed against that person. Such punishments are expected to deter further acts of those crimes.

From a different perspective, retributive justice also can mean an award of some resource to the aggrieved party. For example, when a copyright infringement occurs, the guilty party must pay a certain amount of money to the aggrieved party as

One of the issues that scholars and practitioners alike often overlook is the applicability of the justice principles to both the situations in which certain resources are available for distribution and the situations in which certain resources need to be withdrawn from members or units. The modern phenomenon of cutbacks is a case in point. When organizations are constrained to cut back on their expenditures, the principles (i.e., principles of equity, equality, or need) they apply in withdrawing resources take center stage. For instance, when an athletic department has to cut down its budget by 5%, it could decide to apply the equality principle and cut each team's budget by the same 5%. It could also apply the equity principle and take out a higher percentage from some teams and a lower percentage from other teams based on their relative contributions to the department's overall objectives. The department could also decide not to cut the budget of a team based on the "needs" principle because that particular team needs all of its present budget to operate at all.

a restitution for lost revenues. In the context of sports, retributive justice is implemented when the referee awards two free throws to a basketball player who was fouled in the act of shooting. That is, the player and the team have the opportunity to make up for the two points that the player might have made if he or she was not fouled. Recognize also that the offending player and his or her team also are penalized because the foul counts against the total allowed.

Justice Among Athletic Teams

Researchers have investigated the notion of justice in the context of intercollegiate athletic departments. Hums and Chelladurai (1994b) examined the principles of distributive justice that male and female coaches and athletic administrators from all three divisions of the NCAA hold in allocating resources within athletic departments. Briefly, the instrument consisted of 2 scenarios (or 12 total scenarios) to depict each of the instances of distribution and retribution or withdrawal of money, facilities, and support services. Following each scenario, they listed eight rules of distributive justice. The first three of the eight allocation principles listed under each scenario reflected equality: equality of treatment, equality of results, and equality of opportunity. The next four reflected equity based on contributions of productivity, spectator appeal, effort, and ability. The last principle was need. Note that seven of the eight principles were suggested as subrules of equality (i.e., treatment, results, and opportunity), equity (i.e., productivity, effort, and ability), and need (see table 13.1). Hums and Chelladurai (1994a) added the principle of spectator appeal as one more factor of contribution in determining equity. Some of the sports attract a large number of spectators, but others are not so popular with sport fans. Sports that

have greater spectator appeal also draw the attention of and coverage by the media. This coverage, in turn, generates a great amount of publicity and prestige for the university. The spectator events also bring together the students, the faculty, and the community who take pride in their team. In addition, these sports generate revenue through ticket sales, sponsorships, and media coverage. Given these extraordinary contributions stemming from spectator appeal, using it as a subrule of contributions was only legitimate.

In each distributive situation, the researchers asked the subjects to rate the justness of each of eight allocation principles and to choose one of the eight principles for implementation (see figure 13.2). The results showed that all subgroups (i.e., male and female administrators and coaches) rated equality of treatment, need, and equality of results as the most just and the other principles as relatively unjust. These principles were also the principles that the subjects most frequently chose for implementation. Note that these results only suggest what ought to be the principles applied in different distributive situations. They do not reflect the actual principles that decision makers use. Take, for example, spectator appeal. The coaches and administrators of Hums and Chelladurai's (1994b) study did not endorse this principle in any of the distributive situations. However, the annual budgets of many university athletic departments allocate larger amounts of money per capita to some sports than to other sports. Further scrutiny may show that this unequal distribution of resources may parallel the degree of spectator appeal that different sports engender. That is, sports that draw more spectators are likely to get more resources. Other factors, such as pressure from media and alumni, might create this difference between perceptions of what ought to be and what actually happens.

The board of governors has asked the athletic department to trim its budget. How should the budget cuts be shared among teams? Listed below are several options open to athletic departments. Please indicate the extent to which each option is just or unjust by marking the appropriate number on the seven-point scale provided.

	Very unjust					Very just	
1. Equal amounts should be withheld from all teams.	1	2	3	4	5	6	7
2. The teams that have received less money in the past should have the least amount cut.	1	2	3	4	5	6	7
3. The teams should be randomly selected to receive cuts.	1	2	3	4	5	6	7
4. The teams that have the best records should have the least amount cut.	1	2	3	4	5	6	7
5. The teams that draw the most spectators should have the least amount cut.	1	2	3	4	5	6	7
6. The teams that work the hardest should have the least amount cut.	1	2	3	4	5	6	7
7. The teams that have the best players should have the least amount cut.	1	2	3	4	5	6	7
8. The teams that need the money the most should have the least amount cut.	1	2	3	4	5	6	7

Figure 13.2   Sample case to evaluate distributive justice.

Adapted, by permission, from M. A. Hums and P. Chelladurai, 1994a, Distributive justice in intercollegiate athletics, *Journal of Sport Management* 8(3): 194, 206.

Justice in Community Recreation

The notion of justice is also relevant from the perspective of clients and groups of clients. Take the case of community recreation that local governments offer. These agencies must consider the justice implications of their decisions in allocating their resources to various programs and localities. This issue was the focus of studies by Wicks and Crompton (1987, 1990). These authors were concerned with assessing the preferences of citizen groups, elected officials, and paid administrators for one or more principles in budgeting for outdoor swimming pools, neighborhood parks, and organized athletic programs. Wicks and Crompton (1987) used the term "equity" to refer to justice and defined it as

1. equity as equality wherein the resources are distributed equally to every individual or unit of analysis,

2. equity as need where the resources are allocated on the basis of the needs of those disadvantaged (i.e., lower socio-economic level) or where fewest services now exist,

3. equity as demand where the allocations are based on the rates of consumption of the services or on the strength of claims or advocacy of citizen groups,

4. equity as market equity where allotments are based on the user fee or tax revenues that clients pay or on contributions to government through general taxation, and

5. equity as efficiency reflecting the least cost of providing a service.

The results of their studies showed that the most preferred options were equal allocation to all and were where fewest services now exist. In creating neighborhood parks, the residents (i.e., the clients) preferred the "leveling up" option for neighborhood parks (i.e., distribute the resources to areas where fewest services existed). They also preferred the "fees covering costs" for athletic programs. Equally significant was that the market equity models (i.e., allocations on the basis of amount of taxes paid) received little support from the residents. These results imply that the three groups of respondents (i.e., citizen groups, elected officials, and paid administrators) share both the egalitarian perspective (which is derived from equality principle) and the compensatory perspective (which is derived from the need principle).

In a follow-up study, Wicks and Crompton (1990) investigated the relationship of individual difference factors, such as age, gender, race, education, and political preference (i.e., liberal compared with conservative) with perceptions of distributive justice. The general finding was that the political preferences of the residents had an effect in most of the allocation situations. The liberals disliked the perspective of market equity (i.e., where fees covered the cost) and opted for the need perspective (i.e., areas where fewest services exist and allocations to the disadvantaged). The conservatives preferred allocating resources in accordance with the amount of taxes paid (i.e., market equity). Note that the pattern of preferences mirror the respective values that different groups of people hold.

In Their View

Folger and Greenberg (1985) alerted their readers to a distinction between process control and decision control. Process control is centered in the development and selection of information and criteria for resolving a dispute. For instance, the manager of a sport organization may outline the criteria for a performance evaluation of the subordinates and may outline the information on the performance of individual employees on those criteria. Decision control refers to the extent to which a committee may control the outcome (i.e., decide on the outcome for each employee). These authors cited Sheppard's (1984) following analogy to emphasize the distinction between process control and decision control:

> A football referee, who may influence the flow of the game but not its outcome, has process control; but a diving judge, who assesses the performer's quality and does not influence the process of the dive itself, has decision control. (Folger and Greenberg 1985, 145)

Procedural Justice

As noted earlier, distribution of rewards and resources has been the primary focus of any discussion of organizational justice. In recent years, a new thrust has emerged that addresses the procedures employed in determining the outcomes for individuals and groups (Folger 1987). **Procedural justice**, as it is called, refers to the degree to which individuals, whom allocations of resources or rewards affect, perceive that the organization made the allocations according to fair methods and guidelines (Niehoff and Moorman 1993). That is, the individuals may perceive as fair or unfair the procedures and guidelines that the organization used in such decisions. As Folger and Greenberg (1985)

noted, procedural justice refers to the means whereby the organization attains the various ends or the content or consequences (i.e., distributive justice).

The earlier conceptions of procedural justice rested on the control or voice that an individual has over the processes (Thibaut and Walker 1975). That is, to the extent that an individual has some control or input into the procedures adopted for the distribution of rewards, an individual is likely to perceive the procedures to be fair. Because of the negative connotations of the word "control," theorists tend to use the word "voice." In many organizations, individual employees may have some influence (i.e., voice) in the determination of the procedures for allocating resources. However, such participation, or voice, is not a necessary condition for one to perceive procedural justice. For example, individual citizens may not have exercised their influence in writing the tax laws. Yet, these citizens may consider the tax laws and the procedures associated with them as just and may abide by them.

The foregoing description of procedural justice implies that procedures are instrumental to the attainment of distributive justice, which is the end that all participants seek. That is, procedural justice is only an intermediary stage, and distributive justice is the end or bottom line. However, "reactions to a given procedure may also at times reflect an assessment of that procedure as an end-in-itself" (Folger and Greenberg 1985, 158). In other words, procedures may have equal, if not more, weight than the actual outcomes in perceptions of justice. For example, employees of a university campus recreation department may perceive organizational justice when the criteria for evaluating their performance and the processes of such evaluation are clear and just even though the actual salary increases they received were less than what they expected.

In Their View

Folger and Greenberg (1985) distinguished between choice and voice as the two significant features of procedural justice. Choice is present when the procedures allow members to choose one outcome over another as in the case of cafeteria-style benefits discussed in chapter 12. This element of choice is distinguished from voice (or process control) in which the members have a say in what procedures the organization will employ in distributing the resources.

A manager can take steps to ensure procedural justice. Several authors have provided some guidelines in this regard (Folger and Greenberg 1985, Leventhal 1980). Leventhal suggested that the following six rules underlie procedural justice:

- Consistency specifies that allocation procedures should be consistent across persons and over time.

- Bias suppression implies that decision makers should prevent personal self-interest or biases in the allocation process.

- Accuracy means that all allocation decisions must be based on accurate information.

- Representativeness implies that the allocation process is representative of the concerns of all recipients.

- Ethicality implies that allocations must adhere to prevailing ethical and moral standards of the community.

- Correctibility envisages that decision makers unintentionally may violate one or more of the rules and err in making allocations. According to this rule, managers can modify allocation decisions and correct errors.

Interactional Justice

The notion of **interactional justice**, the third component of organizational justice, refers to the type and manner of the explanations for the distribution of outcomes and the procedures thereof (Bies and Moag 1986, Bies and Shapiro 1987, Greenberg 1990,

In a Nutshell

Procedural justice refers to the perceived fairness of the procedures employed to allocate resources to individuals or units. If procedures are consistent, free of biases, accurate, representative of all concerned, ethical, and correctable, individuals will perceive them as just.

Tyler and Bies 1990). That is, individuals or groups may evaluate what is being communicated about the outcomes and procedures and how it is being communicated as just or unjust. The members of an organization appreciate any explanation of the decisions even when the decision is negative to the individuals or groups. First, the substance of such explanations is quite critical to the perceptions of interactional justice. If the explanation is meager or faulty, members are not likely to perceive justice in the process. The second component of interactional justice is the manner in which the explanation is presented to an individual. Some of the questions that underlie perceptions of interactional justice include the following: Was there respect and concern for the individual? Was there pleasantness and warmth in the encounter? For instance, when the coach yells at an athlete or the team and says, "It is my way or the highway," he or she is violating both aspects of interactional justice. First, the coach gives no explanation at all in that statement for whatever decision he or she might have made. Second, the coach gives no respect in that statement for the individual or the team.

The rules of procedural justice are very similar to the attributes of a good performance appraisal system, which was discussed in chapter 11. Not surprisingly, substantive overlaps exist between performance appraisal systems and the concept of procedural justice. After all, performance appraisal is a procedure by which the organization assesses the contributions of individual employees for allocations of rewards. At the same time, major differences exist between the concepts of performance appraisal and procedural justice. While organizations use performance appraisal to assess only the performances of individuals, they use procedural justice to assess the procedures of both performance appraisal and distribution of rewards. Further, they use procedural justice to assess the evaluation of departmental units or groups and the allocation of resources to those units. For instance, when the director of the city recreation department evaluates the performance of the leader of a youth sport program or the manager of a park or facility, the evaluation is properly labeled performance appraisal. However, if the director of the city council evaluates the contributions or usefulness of the various sport and recreation programs or the facilities and decides on the budget allocations for each, he or she is addressing distributive issues. The question of whether such budget decisions were based on quality information, were consistent, and were without biases falls in the domain of procedural justice.

In a Nutshell

Interactional justice refers to the extent to which the manager gives a clear and correct explanation regarding the distribution of resources and the procedures employed to arrive at such distribution. The manner in which the manager presents such explanations (including warmth and respect for recipients) are also part of interactional justice.

Summary

In summary, this chapter outlined the concept of organizational justice and its components and associated rules. Insofar as the notion of justice pervades all organizational and managerial activities, managerial effectiveness ultimately depends on how well managers respect and implement organizational justice. Thus, organizational justice should be a foundational theme for all managerial practices. Figure 13.3 summarizes most of the material presented in this chapter as a set of rules of procedural, interactional, and distributive justice.

As noted earlier, in performance-oriented organizations, the principle of equity is dominant. In such organizations, managers are justified in distributing rewards and resources in proportion to member contributions. This view is simplistic because two fundamental issues are present. The first issue is the priority among various contributions that different members of the organization make.

Rules of justice

Procedural justice	Interactional justice	Distributive justice
Consistency	Explanation	Equity based on effort
Bias suppression	Respect	Equity based on ability
Accuracy	Warmth	Equity based on productivity
Representativeness	Concern	Equality of treatment
Ethicality		Equality of opportunity
Correctibility		Equality of results
		Need

Process stage　　　　　　　　　　　　　　　　　　　Decision stage

Communication stage

Figure 13.3　Guidelines for organizational justice.

That is, different contributions must be ranked in terms of how critical those contributions are for the survival and growth of a specific organization.

The second issue relates to how the manager evaluates an individual on the contributions that the organization has prioritized. For example, how members of an event management unit in a university are evaluated, and who (e.g., superiors, subordinates, or visiting teams) evaluates them are critical questions the athletic director needs to address.

Further, several sport organizations are oriented toward providing services to participants in sport and recreation (e.g., city and university recreation departments and youth sport leagues) in which the principles of equality and need are likely to be more relevant. Even when the application of the principle of equality may be straight forward, the question of which of the three rules of equality (i.e., treatment, results, or opportunity) should be applied under what circumstances still remains. If the principle of need is applied, how is "need" determined and who makes that decision? These issues plague management, and the effective managers understand these issues and engage their members in resolving them.

Key Terms

organizational justice, distributive justice, equity, equality, need, procedural justice, interactional justice

Your Perspectives

- Recall one occasion when you thought that your parents were not being fair in distributing weekly allowances. Were you concerned with the actual amount you received or with the procedure employed to reach that decision?

- Were there occasions during your days in secondary school when you believed that the administrators were not just in distributing the school resources? What principles of organizational justice were violated? Explain.

- Focusing on your university, explain the contexts in which you would prefer that the principles of equity, equality, or need would be applied.

- Consider three or four different types of sport organizations. Which of the principles of distributive justice is appropriate to which type of sport organization? Why?

- Do you have a preference for one principle of distribution over another? Is that preference reflective of your value system?

Part IV

Attitudinal Outcomes

The outcomes in any organizational context are of two kinds: productivity and member reactions. Productivity refers to the extent to which the organization achieves its purpose. For profit-oriented organizations, such productivity often, and more easily, is measured by the actual profits made. The absolute dollar amount of profits made is the yardstick in this approach.

Alternately, organizations also may be concerned with the rate of return on the capital. The issue here is the profits as a percentage of capital outlay. When an enterprise makes $100,000 more than a competitor, it could be satisfied with the outcome. However, that $100,000 profit may represent only 10% return on its capital outlay, whereas the competitor may get a 15% return. Similarly, a fitness firm may aim to make a profit of $10,000 or to get a 15% return on its capital outlay. Likewise, a professional sport franchise may focus on absolute dollar profit or a rate of return.

A closely related outcome is productivity or efficiency, which refers to the maximization of the output relative to a given input. While all organizations are concerned with efficiency, it becomes a singular concern in times of crises. For example, dwindling financial resources have forced educational institutions to consider efficiency in their operations. The notions of down-sizing and right-sizing are all aimed at increasing the efficiency of the operations to counter the reduction in financial resources. Many university athletic departments also are currently involved in efficiency drives to make up for the extra demands placed on their resources by Title IX requirements and gender equity movements. Similar concerns with efficiency can result in a fitness club or a city recreation department dropping those programs that do not have a demand. They also may reduce their staff by firing or through attrition.

Some organizations also may emphasize their share of the market. For instance, General Motors has been and is the dominant enterprise in the automobile industry, holding the largest share of that market. Although stiff competition from Ford, Chrysler, and foreign corporations have eroded, to some extent, the share that General Motors has, the corporation cherishes its continuing status as the major player in the market. Even universities tend to have as an objective the recruitment of a percentage of the total student population in their respective regions. Businesses providing fitness and sport services also compete for a larger percentage of the market in their geographical area. One of the concerns of professional sport franchises in any large metropolitan area (e.g., New York or Chicago) is to compete with other entertainment agencies for the share of the dollars that the citizens of the locality are willing to spend on entertainment.

Another indicator of productivity is the growth of the organization, i.e., growth in terms of profits, total revenue, market share, number of employees, or the number of products or activities. The growth concept is equally relevant to both profit and nonprofit organizations. For instance, a department of sport management may seek to increase its number of faculty members and the number of courses that it offers. Because size is often equated with status, it is not uncommon for nonprofit organizations to emphasize growth as their primary objective. Many athletic departments tout the number of men's and women's sports that they support. Similarly, a city recreation department may emphasize the number of playgrounds and arenas it operates or the number of participants in its programs.

Organizations may also endeavor to be leaders in the market in terms of the products they produce or the methods of production. For example, Bill Gates' Microsoft makes billions of dollars in profit every year. However, an equally impressive achievement is that it continues to be the leader in the market by introducing new and innovative products. In addition, sporting goods manufacturers (e.g., Nike) compete with each other to introduce new and improved products, such as footwear and protective equipment. Universities (and departments of sport management) also take pride in offering new and more relevant courses or programs.

Because the content and thrust of this text has been on management of human resources, the focus of this section is on human resource-related outcomes. It is granted that if an organization does not achieve the productivity outcomes, the concern with human resource outcomes becomes mute because the organization itself may cease to exist. However, the productivity outcomes themselves may depend on the human resource-related outcomes. Therefore, focusing on the outcomes as related to human resources of the organization is important.

Accordingly, chapter 14 describes and discusses the concept of satisfaction. The traditional practice in organizational and industrial psychology has been to focus on job satisfaction of paid employees of an organization. In this text, however, the focus is on the satisfaction of paid workers as well as volunteer workers and clients. As noted earlier, these three sets of human resources are critical for the success of most sport organizations. Volunteers, by definition, are not concerned with pay and such other organizationally sanctioned monetary benefits; therefore, the chapter outlines the meaning and significance of other aspects of their work. Equally important is the notion of client satisfaction. The modern thrusts in management, such as total quality management, emphasize the customer-focused operations; management stresses these operations particularly in service operations. Quality practices, such as keeping the premises and equipment clean, providing quick responses to clients' requests, and establishing a congenial atmosphere, are all aimed at satisfying customers. In the case of sport and recreation, the customer-focused operations are even more important because the clients not only consume the services but also help produce those services. Thus, this chapter delves into satisfaction of participants in leisure and athletic services.

Chapter 15 addresses organizational commitment. Commitment of members, such as paid and volunteer workers and clients, to the organization is a clear indication of the effectiveness of the organization. Such commitment reflects members' attachment not only to the organization but also to the organization's goals and processes. In other words, organizational commitment may be seen as an endorsement of the management practices described in part III.

14 Satisfaction

Learning Objectives

After reading this chapter you will be able to

- define the concept of job satisfaction,
- explain how dissatisfaction stems from a discrepancy between what is expected and what is received,
- describe job satisfaction as a function of need satisfaction,
- describe various facets of satisfaction and their relationships to needs, and
- explain the critical aspects of satisfaction of participants in sport and physical activity.

I have provided in part I a description of the human resources at the disposal of a sport manager (volunteers, professional workers, and clients). This was followed in part II by a discussion of individual differences among these sets of human resources (i.e., individual differences in ability, personality, values, and motivation). In part III, I outlined some of the critical processes in managing human resources including job design, staffing, performance appraisal, reward systems, leadership, and organizational justice. These managerial processes are undertaken in order to achieve certain critical outcomes. As noted in the opener to this part IV, the focus in this text is on human resource-related outcomes rather than on productivity outcomes. One of these human resource outcomes is job satisfaction, the content of this chapter.

In the following sections, I describe various theories of job satisfaction and their relevance to sport management. I follow this by a discussion of satisfaction of volunteers as a distinct class of workers. The chapter also includes a description of satisfaction of our clients. Relating job satisfaction to sport and recreation clients is somewhat unorthodox because the description and discussion of customer or client satisfaction normally relates to a product that a customer or client has purchased or consumed. However, as noted earlier, sport and recreation clients also are involved in the production of services. Therefore, consideration of their satisfaction with the organizational and interpersonal processes that are used in the production of a service and the quality of such a service is only appropriate. With the client in perspective, I introduce the topics of participant satisfaction, satisfaction with services, leisure satisfaction, and athlete satisfaction. I conclude the chapter with the topic of measurement of satisfaction, and a description of two of the more popular instruments measuring job satisfaction.

Definitions of Job Satisfaction

Researchers have made several attempts to define and describe **job satisfaction**. The essence of all these definitions, as Dawis and Lofquist (1984) pointed out, is that job satisfaction is "a pleasurable affective condition resulting from one's appraisal of the way in which the experienced job situation meets one's needs, values, and expectations" (p. 72). In a similar vein, Rice, McFarlin, and Bennett (1989) believed that

> satisfaction is determined, in part, by the discrepancies resulting from a psychological comparison process involving the appraisal of current job experiences against some personal *standards of comparison* (e.g., what workers want, feel entitled to, see others getting, have experienced in the past, etc.). (p. 591)

Balzer et al. (1990) defined job satisfaction slightly differently as "the feelings a worker has about his or her job or job experiences in relation to previous experiences, current expectations, or available alternatives" (p. 6).

Job satisfaction is an attitude people have about their jobs. Attitudes, in turn, are "relatively stable affective, or evaluative, dispositions toward a specific person, situation, or other entity" (Saal and Knight 1988, 296). An attitude comprises a cognitive component (i.e., a belief about the target entity), an emotional component (i.e., a degree of like or dislike for the target entity), and a behavioral component (i.e., the tendency to act in specific ways toward the target entity).

Job satisfaction is perhaps the most often studied topic in management and industrial psychology. At the same time, these research efforts have been frustrating and futile because they have not found a strong relationship between job satisfaction and any other organizationally relevant factors. Any evidence of a relationship between job satisfaction and other organizationally relevant outcome variables, such as performance, absenteeism, or turnover, has been weak (Saal and Knight 1995, Schermerhorn et al. 1997). This confusing state of affairs may lead some managers to be indifferent to

the notion of job satisfaction and to be more concerned with the "bottom line" issue of productivity.

The position taken in this text is that of Balzer et al. (1990), who argued that job satisfaction is of great significance at three different levels: humanitarian, economic, and theoretical. At the humanitarian level, most managers are concerned with the welfare of their workers: "Furthermore, since job satisfaction has been found to be related to life satisfaction and mental and physical health, improved satisfaction has become an important outcome in its own right" (p. 6).

In Their View

"Given that most people must work, and that most people will spend the majority of their adult lives at work, it can be argued that employers have a *moral obligation* to make the experience personally rewarding (or, at minimum, not painful or dehumanizing)" (Vecchio 1988, 117).

At the economic level, management should be interested in job satisfaction because "increased satisfaction with aspects of the job may prove to be a bonus to the organization in many areas including reduced absenteeism, decreased turnover, and fewer work-related accidents" (Balzer et al. 1990, 6). Finally, at the theoretical level, many theories of work motivation and work behavior incorporate the concept of job satisfaction. Theoretical concerns relate to satisfaction as a direct cause of increased work performance and cooperation or as a consequence of such behavior leading to organizational rewards.

In addition, the lack of a relationship between job satisfaction and other productivity related variables may be due to measurement problems. That is, although a strong relationship may exist between job satisfaction and productivity, researchers have failed to measure adequately either of these concepts and, therefore, have been unable to identify the strong link between them. For instance, Fisher and Locke (1992) pointed out that the problem may be in measuring job behavior as a single type of act over a limited time by a single method, and job satisfaction is a general attitude. However, "a strong attitude-behavior correlation will only occur when there is correspondence between the levels of aggregation represented in the attitude and behavior measures" (Fisher and Locke 1992, 166). Further, as Ostroff (1992) noted, most of the research linking satisfaction and other outcomes were conducted on an individual level. Ostroff suggests that "it is likely that a study of satisfaction-performance at the organizational level would show that organizations that have more satisfied employees are more productive and profitable than organizations whose employees are less satisfied" (p. 963).

Another concern is that other factors may constrain and control one's performance. For example, the lackluster performance of other dissatisfied workers may counterbalance the significant contribution to a group task that a satisfied worker makes. Further, some of the commonly accepted measures of performance may indeed be invalid. Take, for example, the measure of runs batted in in baseball. As noted in chapter 11, the measure of runs batted in is contaminated by the order of batting and the performance of the previous batters. Thus, a home run by a batter may yield anywhere from four to one run batted in (Courneya and Chelladurai 1991).

Another important reason for the interest in job satisfaction exists. The description of the services in sport and recreation suggests that most of the clients engage in sport and physical activity for their own enjoyment, fun, and well-being. They are partial employees of the sport and recreation enterprise. Therefore, their positive feelings about their involvement and the organizational processes facilitating their involvement are critical measures of the effectiveness of the enterprise.

In a Nutshell

Job satisfaction is a critical outcome by itself from an economic, as well as from a humanistic and moralistic, perspective. Because the human resources in sport and recreation include both paid and volunteer workers and because the sport and recreation clients are the partial employees, the concept of satisfaction should be extended to all three components of human resource.

Finally, measures of wins and losses solely cannot judge the activities in pursuit of excellence because these contests are zero-sum games. That is, for every winner, there must be a loser. One or two points decide many games in the NBA in which the two teams jointly score more than 200 points. Yet, one team is declared a winner; the other, a loser. While the losers might have been disappointed with the loss, they might have been satisfied fully with their efforts, the teamwork, the practice sessions, and the coaching that they had received. These feelings of satisfaction are important in their own right. Therefore, for all of the reasons cited, job satisfaction should be considered an outcome independent of other organizational factors and valued for its own sake.

Theories of Job Satisfaction

Because of the importance that both theorists and practitioners attach to job satisfaction, researchers have made several attempts to define and describe job satisfaction and to identify the sources of such satisfaction (i.e., **facets of satisfaction**). This section discusses a few of the better-known theories.

Herzberg's Two-Factor Theory

As noted in chapter 7, Herzberg and his associates found in their study of engineers and accountants that one set of factors was associated with their subjects' satisfaction and that another set of factors was associated with their dissatisfaction (Herzberg 1966; Herzberg, Mausner, and Snyderman 1959). According to their theory, the presence of the first set of factors, which are termed "motivators," in a job is directly related to satisfaction, and the absence of them leads to a neutral state. On the other hand, absence of the second set of factors, which are termed "hygienes," leads to dissatisfaction; their presence, to the neutral state. Because these authors postulated that satisfaction and dissatisfaction are two different continuums that two different sets of factors affect, the theory is called a two-factor, or dual-factor, theory.

The motivators relate to the content of the job, such as the challenge, achievement, recognition, and autonomy, that one experiences in performing one's task. Note that these satisfactions are mediated personally, and other external agents do not control them. On the other hand, the hygiene factors relate to the context in which the job is performed and includes elements such as company policy and procedures, working conditions, supervision, and the interpersonal relations within the workgroup. These aspects of a job are largely out of the individual's control.

Authors (e.g., Evans 1986, Kanfer 1990, King 1970, Schneider and Locke 1971, Soliman 1970) have criticized Herzberg's two-factor theory from several perspectives; however, the most serious problem is that the theory predicts the same level of satisfaction for all members performing the same or similar jobs (i.e., jobs possessing the same level of motivators and hygiene factors). The theory overlooks the fact that people react to their jobs in different ways and that people in the same or similar jobs are satisfied differently with their jobs.

Therefore, focusing on the processes within the individual to get a grasp of the concept of satisfaction is necessary.

Discrepancy Theories

Recall that the Rice, McFarlin, and Bennett (1989) definition of satisfaction included the notion of **discrepancy** arising out of a psychological comparison between what one receives and a standard of comparison. The extent of discrepancy is related to the level of job satisfaction. This idea of discrepancy permeates most other theories of job satisfaction. Of course, they do differ in specifying what the standards of comparison are. Some of these theories and the standards of comparison contained therein are explained in this section.

Lawler's Facet Model of Satisfaction

Lawler (1973) provided a good example of a discrepancy theory of job satisfaction (see figure 14.1) and suggested that job satisfaction is a function of the extent to which what one receives from a job (box b) matches what one thinks he or she should receive from that job (box a). This simple compari-

son becomes more complex when several other factors come into play to determine one's perceptions of what one ought to receive and perceptions of what one actually receives. As illustrated in figure 14.1, an individual's skill, experience, knowledge, and such other assets that one brings to the job situation (i.e., perceived personal job inputs) and the difficulty and responsibility of the job (i.e., perceived job characteristics) are critical determinants of what one ought to receive. In addition, the person also considers what comparable others bring to the situation and what they get (i.e., perceived inputs and outcomes of referent others) as another factor in estimating what the person should get. As for the perceived amount received (box b), the actual outcome received is compared with the perceived outcome of referent others. For example, an employee in a sport-marketing firm would be satisfied if he or she perceives that the rewards (e.g., merit pay) are consistent with the time and effort he or she has put into the job effort and his or her performance (e.g., business generated). At the same time, this person also would compare the rewards relative to personal job inputs and performance to the rewards that comparable others receive relative to their job

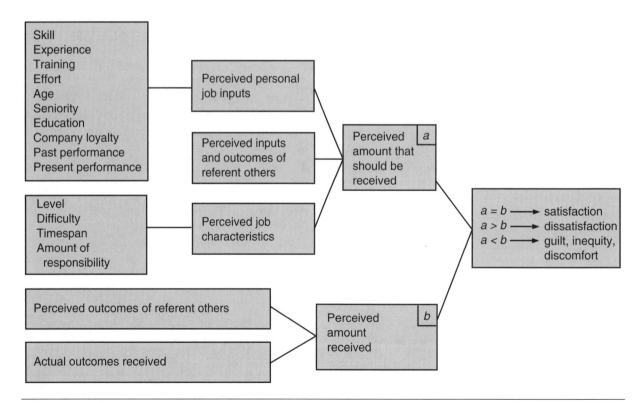

Figure 14.1   Lawler's model of facet satisfaction.

Reprinted, by permission, from E.E. Lawler, III, 1973, *Motivation in work organizations* (Pacific Grove, CA: Brooks/Cole).

inputs and performance. If the comparison is not favorable, the person would be dissatisfied. Lawler's (1973) approach is based, to some extent, on Adams' (1963) theory of inequity, which is discussed in chapter 7. Such comparisons, judgments about fairness of distribution of rewards, and subsequent satisfaction or dissatisfaction also relate to the concepts of performance appraisal and distributive justice, which were discussed in chapters 11 and 13, respectively.

In a Nutshell

Job dissatisfaction can stem from a discrepancy between what one perceives his or her inputs and job requirements are and what one perceives he or she should receive from that experience. What one perceives he or she should receive from a job may be intrinsic factors, such as challenge and achievement, or may be extrinsic factors, such as salary and wages, working conditions, and supervision. What others receive would also affect one's perception of what one receives.

Need-Based Satisfaction Theories

Some theorists have suggested that job satisfaction is a function of the extent to which one's **needs** are satisfied in a job (i.e., **need satisfaction**) (McClelland 1961, Murray 1938). These need theories, which are discussed in chapter 7, suggest that need deprivation leads to a state of tension and unhappiness. To the extent that a job can fulfill several of the needs that are important to a person, the job can be a source of satisfaction for the individual. Accordingly, a person who has a high level of need for achievement may be satisfied with a challenging job, but a person who has a low level of that need, in fact, may be dissatisfied with the same job. By the same token, two different individuals may have different needs that the same job satisfies. For example, one fitness instructor may have a high level of need for achievement that the challenge in making the clients fit and healthy can satisfy. Another fitness instructor who has a high level of need for affiliation may have that need satisfied through the positive task and social interactions with the clients.

Minnesota Model of Job Satisfaction. Researchers at the University of Minnesota have been working on the concept of job satisfaction for a long time (Dawis, England, and Lofquist 1964; Dawis and Lofquist 1984). Their approach also emphasizes the notion of needs, which was discussed in chapter 7. From among several needs, these authors identified 20 needs relevant to the job context and categorized them into six dimensions. These six dimensions and the associated needs are presented in table 14.1. The measurement of the extent to which these needs are satisfied in a job is carried out through the Minnesota Satisfaction Questionnaire, which is described later in this chapter.

Locke's Value-Based Theory of Satisfaction. From a different perspective, Locke (1976) argued that individuals place more or less **value** on each of all possible outcomes from their jobs. The outcomes, for example, may be salary, prestige, or working conditions. Some individuals may value salary more than others value it (i.e., they want or desire more salary), and some others may value the prestige associated with their jobs. According to Locke (1976), the extent to which what is present in a job matches what an individual values (or desires) influences the level of job satisfaction. For example, several students graduating from sport management degree programs may prefer to work in a university athletic department for the sake of the prestige and status associated with the department even though the salary rate may be lower than in other organizations.

Smith's Facets of Job Satisfaction. Smith and her associates have been researching the topic of job satisfaction for more than two decades (Balzer et al. 1990; Smith, Kendall, and Hulin 1969). These authors demonstrated that the essence of job satisfaction can be captured by measuring five facets of a job—work itself, pay, promotions, co-workers, and supervision. Table 14.2 provides the definitions of these facets. In addition to measuring satisfaction with these five facets of a job, these authors suggested that the overall satisfaction with the job in general can also be measured. The specific instrument used to measure these five facets and the job in general is known as the Job Descriptive Index, which is described later in this chapter.

In a Nutshell

Facets of job satisfaction are derived from specific needs of job holders. That is, as scholars and researchers define it, each facet satisfies a need or cluster of needs that people bring to the job situation.

Table 14.1 Description of Needs in the Minnesota Model of Job Satisfaction

Dimension	Need	Description
Achievement		The extent to which the job environment encourages accomplishments
	Ability use	The extent to which one's abilities are used
	Achievement	The feeling of accomplishment that the job provides (being able to see the results of the work I do)
Comfort		The job environment that is comfortable and not stressful
	Activity	The extent to which the worker is busy in the job
	Independence	The opportunity to work alone on the job
	Variety	Being able to do something different every day
	Compensation	The extent to which one's pay compares well with that of other workers (the amount of pay for the work I do)
	Security	The extent to which the job provides for steady employment
	Working conditions	Good working conditions of the job (e.g., heating, lighting, and ventilation)
Status		The extent to which the job environment provides recognition and prestige
	Advancement	The extent to which the job provides opportunities for advancement
	Recognition	The extent to which one can get recognition for the work done
	Authority	The extent to which one can tell other people what to do (the chance to have other workers look to me for direction)
	Social status	The extent to which the job makes one a "somebody" in the community (the social position in the community that goes with the job)
Altruism		The extent to which the job environment fosters harmony with and service to others
	Co-workers	The ease of making friends with co-workers (the spirit of cooperation among my co-workers)
	Moral values	The extent to which one can do the work without feeling it is morally wrong
	Social service	The extent to which one can do things for other people
Safety		The extent to which the job environment is predictable and stable
	Company policies	The extent to which the company administers, and practices, its policies and procedures fairly (the policies and procedures toward employees of this company)
	Supervision— human relations	The extent to which the supervisor backs up the workers (with top management) (the way my supervisor and I understand each other)
	Supervision— technical	The extent to which the supervisor trains the workers well (the technical "know-how" of my supervisor)
Autonomy		The extent to which the job environment stimulates initiative
	Creativity	The extent to which one can try out some of one's own ideas
	Responsibility	The extent to which one can make decisions on his or her own (the chance to be responsible for planning my work)

Adapted, by permission, from R.V. Dawis and L.H. Lofquist, 1984, *A psychological theory of work adjustment: An individual-differences model and its applications* (Minneapolis, MN: University of Minnesota Press).

Table 14.2   Facets That the Job Descriptive Index Measures

Facet	Description
Work	Satisfaction with work and its attributes includes the opportunities for creativity and task variety and the ability to increase his or her knowledge, responsibility, work amount, autonomy, and complexity. Satisfying work appears to be work that can be accomplished and is intrinsically challenging (routine work).
Pay	Satisfaction with work is based on the perceived difference between actual pay and expected pay that, in turn, is based on perceived inputs and outputs of the job and the pay of other comparable employees. The personal financial situation of the employee, the economy, and the amount of pay an employee has received previously also influences satisfaction (income adequate for normal expenses).
Promotions	Satisfaction with promotion is based on the employee's satisfaction with the company's promotion policy and the administration of that policy. It is thought to be a function of frequency of promotions, the importance of promotions, and the desirability of promotions (good opportunities for promotion).
Supervision	Satisfaction with the supervision is based on an employee's satisfaction with his or her supervisor's knowledge and competence and his or her supervisor's knowledge and competence and his or her warm, interpersonal orientation (hard to please).
People on the job	Satisfaction with people on the job, which is often called the co-worker facet, refers to the satisfaction with one's fellow employees or clients. Separate facets may be created using the same items to measure satisfaction with people, such as staff, and satisfaction with clients (helpfulness).
Job in general	Satisfaction with the job in general reflects the employee's global, long-term evaluation of his or her job. It subsumes the evaluation of the above five facets and their interactions as well as the employee's evaluation of other long-term situational and individual factors (better than most).

Adapted, by permission, from W.K. Balzer, P.C. Smith, D.A. Kravitz, S.E. Lovell, K.B. Paul, B.A. Reilly, and C.E. Reilly, 1990, *User's manual for the Job Descriptive Index (JDI) and the Job In General (JIG) scales* (Bowling Green, OH: Bowling Green State University), 44-45.

In Their View

General job satisfaction is an important part of a system of interrelated satisfactions, analogous to a river with small tributaries converging into ever-larger branches and eventually into a lake or sea. Satisfactions with specific aspects of a job situation cause satisfactions with facets of the job, with the job in general, and eventually with life. (Smith 1992, 5)

Satisfaction With Volunteer Work

The foregoing discussion of job satisfaction was based on theories and research pertaining to paid work. Because the focus is on three types of human resource (i.e., paid workers, volunteer workers, and clients or participants), the discussion must move beyond the satisfaction theories related to paid work to the unique facets of satisfaction relevant to volunteer workers and clients.

The study of satisfaction in volunteer work has been sparse and sporadic because, until recently, researchers believed that volunteer work was solely based on altruism, implying that volunteers had no expectation of any kind of return. In the absence of such expectations, studying satisfaction in volunteering has no point. However, as noted in chapter 1, volunteer work is "the result of multiple causation, with altruism being a very minor factor in most organized volunteerism" (Smith 1981, 25). Volunteer work, then, is an exchange of one's time and effort for satisfactions and psychic rewards in that work (Gidron 1983). Therefore, volunteer satisfaction needs to be studied and understood. Such an understanding would assist the sport manager in recruiting and retaining the volunteers in their organizations.

In discussing volunteer satisfaction, the first thing to remember is that volunteerism involves some work. That is, as Gidron (1983) wrote,

> it involves a situation where there is a job to be done, the job can utilize one's skills and creativity, one's efforts can bear fruit in the form of results or achievements, and one can be recognized for it. (p. 21)

Thus, volunteer work is quite similar to paid work in some respects; therefore, some of the facets of satisfaction relating to paid work may also be relevant to volunteer work (see table 14.2). For instance, satisfaction with supervision or co-workers should be equally meaningful in both paid and volunteer work. Similarly, the interactions with clients should be the source of the same kind of satisfactions or frustrations to both the paid and volunteer worker. Obviously, satisfactions relating to pay, fringe benefits, or promotions may not be relevant to the volunteer worker. For example, paid and volunteer workers involved in Special Olympics derive the same kinds of satisfaction in serving their clients and have similar reactions to the supervision that they receive.

From a different perspective, volunteer work is unique in several respects. Gidron (1983) pointed out that because volunteer work is undertaken freely, one may engage in it or discontinue at will, whereas paid work is necessary for livelihood for most people. This critical distinction establishes different kinds of relationships (and different forms of compliance) with the organization for the paid worker and volunteer worker. In most organizations, the level of pay to paid workers can be equated with recognition of good work. Such concrete forms of recognition are not available in the case of volunteer workers. In addition, as Gidron (1983) stated: "In many cases volunteer work is an addition to and not a substitute for the major activity in which one engages such as salaried work, study, or homemaking" (p. 21). It is evident from the foregoing that the volunteer worker may bring to the situation different needs or expectations. Fulfillment of those needs and expectations is critical for the involvement of volunteers in sport and recreation organizations.

In his study of volunteer work, Gidron (1983) identified 12 different factors that could be sources of satisfaction for the volunteer (see table 14.3). As the table shows, several of these facets of satisfaction parallel those in the context of paid work. More

specifically, work itself, task achievement, task convenience, stress factors, supervisor (both instrumental and expressive), and client are equally relevant and important to both volunteers and paid workers. On the other hand, family, social acceptance, recognition (as Gidron defines), and other volunteers are sources of satisfaction that are unique to volunteering. Gidron (1983) also found that work itself, task achievement, task convenience, and lack of stressors contributed the most to volunteer satisfaction. In his words,

> in order to be satisfied, a volunteer needs, above all, a task in which self-expression is possible—a task which is seen as a challenge, a task where achievements can be seen. . . . The volunteer should not have to waste time getting to work, looking for tools, or arguing with officials about what to do and how to do it. (p. 32)

A note of caution is in order here about work itself. The foregoing conclusion of Gidron (1983) suggests that managers strive to enrich the job for all volunteers. (The notion of job enrichment was discussed in chapter 8). As noted earlier, not all individuals have the same degree of need for growth in the workplace or possess the necessary skills and traits to be successful in enriched jobs. From a different perspective, a volunteer may be involved in a highly enriched job in his or her full-time paid work (e.g., a medical doctor, an architect, or a university professor). To such a volunteer, the need for growth and achievement can be fulfilled in paid work rather than in volunteer work. In fact, that kind of a volunteer may indeed seek a "mindless" job in volunteer work. This view is consistent with Kabanoff and O'Brien (1980) who identified three possible relationships between work and nonwork—compensatory hypothesis (i.e., nonwork activities compensate for the deficiencies in the workplace and vice versa), generalization or spill-over hypothesis (i.e., work and nonwork satisfactions will correlate positively or parallel each other), and the segmentation hypothesis (i.e., work and nonwork activities have an independent effect on individuals). By extending the notions of compensation and segmentation, one could suggest that those who have enriched jobs in paid work may be content with routine jobs in their volunteer work and that routine work has different effects in the context of paid and volunteer work. By the same token, some volunteers may be involved in highly routine jobs in paid work although they may have the skills and inclination to be involved in enriched jobs in volunteer

Table 14.3   Facets of Job Satisfaction Among Volunteers

Facet	Description
Work itself	A challenging, interesting, and responsible job that uses one's skills and knowledge and allows for independence
Task achievement	The progress that the clients make
Task convenience	Convenient hours and location of volunteer work
Stress factors	Insufficient knowledge and experience, lack of essential materials, and ambiguity about the job (Note that the absence of the stress factors would increase satisfaction.)
Family	Encouragement from the family for volunteer activity
Supervisor—instrumental	Supervision that provides clear directions for work and teaches new things
Professionals	Acceptance by and appreciation and assistance from professional workers
Social acceptance	Acceptance of volunteer work as worthwhile by people inside and outside of the organization
Client	Compliance, cooperation, and appreciation from clients
Recognition	Recognition in the form of letters of thanks, special events and trips, and publication of names
Supervisor—expressive	Encouragement, appreciation, and acceptance from supervisor
Other volunteers	Teamwork and friendship among volunteers

Adapted, by permission, from B. Gidron, 1983, "Sources of job satisfaction among service volunteers," *Journal of Voluntary Action Research* 12: 20-35.

work. Therefore, such volunteers may indeed seek challenging jobs in their volunteer work.

In a Nutshell

A job is a job whether a paid or volunteer worker does it. Therefore, the same factors in and around a job may affect both paid and volunteer workers. In addition, volunteer workers may bring additional needs and expectations to be fulfilled.

Participant Satisfaction

A discussion of participant satisfaction is more complicated because participation takes several forms. As noted in chapter 3, people participate for different reasons; therefore, participant services can be classified into pursuits of pleasure, skills, excellence, and health. Participants in each of these activities have differing orientations, needs, and expectations. Therefore, considering satisfaction separately for each of these categories is appropri-

ate. Unfortunately, few researchers have made the effort to understand the dynamics of satisfactions in these contexts. However, the findings from other similar contexts can be extrapolated to participation in sport and recreation.

Satisfaction With Services

Berry and Parasuraman (1991) suggested that consumers of a service use five dimensions to evaluate that service (see table 14.4).

Berry and Parasuraman's (1991) five dimensions of evaluation can be perceived as sources of satisfaction of the consumers of sport and recreation services. In fact, the descriptions of the five dimensions appear to be more germane to some of the services in our field, such as those that a commercial fitness club offers. For instance, overweight and unfit clients have to persevere and work hard to alleviate their problems. The motivation toward such a tremendous amount of effort can be enhanced if the fitness instructor is empathetic toward the clients and responsive to their needs and frustrations. These are two of Berry and Parasuraman's (1991)

Table 14.4   Dimensions of Evaluation of Services

Dimension	Description
Reliability	The ability to perform the promised service dependably and accurately
Tangibles	The appearance of physical facilities, equipment, personnel, and communications materials
Responsiveness	The willingness to help customers and to provide prompt service
Assurance	The knowledge and courtesy of employees and their ability to convey trust and confidence
Empathy	The provision of caring, individualized attention to customers

Source: Berry and Parasuraman (1991).

evaluative dimensions of service. For another example, consider the services that athletic trainers provide. Clients expect these services to be reliable (i.e., dependable and accurate); responsive (i.e., being prompt in helping); assured (i.e., creating trust through knowledge and courtesy); and empathetic (i.e., providing individualized attention). Of course, the tangibles (i.e., the setting including the facilities and equipment) must be adequate.

Leisure Satisfaction

In a similar manner, the definition and description of satisfaction in leisure should yield some concepts relevant to sport and recreation. Because most of the participants under consideration participate in sport and physical activity as leisure activities, the discussion begins with **leisure satisfaction** and a definition of leisure activities.

> Leisure activities (representing participation) were defined as non-obligatory and non-work activities which individuals choose to do in their free time, excluding activities that meet biological needs such as eating and sleeping. Activities can be active or inactive, such as sports, outdoor activities, social activities, or hobbies. (Ragheb and Tate 1993, 62)

This broad definition includes all the activities in which our clients participate and it also subsumes the notion that volunteer work is also a leisure activity. Therefore, a discussion of leisure satisfaction has great implications for sport and recreation managers.

Beard and Ragheb (1980) did the seminal work on leisure satisfaction. They argued that an understanding of the subjective meaning that people at-

tach to their leisure participation is fundamental to leisure management and that the measurement of leisure satisfaction captures such meanings. They define leisure satisfaction as

> the positive perceptions or feelings an individual forms, elicits, or gains as result of engaging in leisure activities and choices. It is the degree to which one is presently content or pleased with his/her general leisure experiences and situations. This positive feeling of contentment results from the satisfaction of felt or unfelt needs of the individual. (p. 22)

Beard and Ragheb (1980) proposed a six-dimensional scheme of leisure satisfaction that was confirmed through statistical procedures in subsequent research. Their six facets of leisure satisfaction are described in table 14.5.

All of these six dimensions or facets of leisure satisfaction are applicable to sport and recreation clients as well as to volunteer workers. In fact, most, if not all, of them are equally relevant to paid workers also. Note the close correspondence between some of the six dimensions of leisure satisfaction and several of the facets of job satisfaction discussed earlier. For instance, the psychological and educational dimensions of leisure satisfaction parallel the facet of satisfaction with work in the Job Descriptive Index of Balzer et al. (1990) and the facets of achievement and autonomy in the Minnesota Model of Job Satisfaction. Similarly, the social dimension of leisure satisfaction is similar to the facets of supervision and people on the job in the Job Descriptive Index. Finally, the aesthetic dimension contains elements included in working conditions of the Minnesota model. However, the relaxation and physiological dimensions of leisure satisfaction are unique

Table 14.5 Dimensions of Leisure Satisfaction

Dimension	Description
Psychological	Psychological benefits, such as a sense of freedom, enjoyment, involvement, and intellectual challenge
Education and intellectual	Intellectual stimulation and opportunities to learn about oneself and one's surroundings
Social	Rewarding relationships with other people
Relaxation	Relief from the stress and strain
Physiological	Physical fitness, health, weight control, and overall well-being
Aesthetic and environmental	Aesthetic rewards from pleasing, interesting, beautiful, and generally well-designed activities

Source: Beard and Ragheb (1980).

to leisure participation, and they do not have corresponding facets in the job satisfaction literature. Obviously, these two are significant components as far as sport and recreation clients are concerned. These two dimensions are germane to volunteer work too. Several of sport and recreation volunteers may engage in sport and recreation activities as a means of relief from the stress and strain of paid work or household chores. Similarly, when a volunteer offers to coach a juvenile soccer team, that individual actually may see it as an opportunity to improve personal physical fitness.

In a Nutshell

Client satisfaction is critical in sport management because clients are part of the human resource and because the operations depend on their approval. The literature on service and leisure satisfaction suggests that the facets of satisfaction in sport participation generally reflect those in other forms of services and work settings.

Note that Berry and Parasuraman's (1991) dimensions of service focus on the processes of delivering a service including employee behavior, and Beard and Ragheb's (1980) scheme emphasizes the outcomes that the clients experienced. One can argue that desired outcomes can be related logically to appropriate processes; therefore, emphasis on either the processes or outcomes yields the same results. However, in reality, processes are not perfectly related to desired outcomes. The matter is further confounded when the outcomes have meaning only as perceived by clients. Therefore, sport managers need to focus on both the processes and outcomes that their clients experience.

Athlete Satisfaction

The need to discuss separately **athlete satisfaction** stems from two unique features of athletics (Chelladurai and Riemer 1997). First, athletes are the prime beneficiaries of intercollegiate athletics; that is, intercollegiate athletics exist for the student athletes (Knight Foundation 1991). The second perspective is that when intercollegiate athletics are perceived as entertainment, the athletes become the prime producers of such entertainment (Chelladurai and Riemer 1997). Further, athletes spend an inordinate amount of time training relative to the time spent in a competition (i.e., the actual time of performance). For example, a high school basketball team may spend two hours each day for four days for a game on Friday that lasts less than two hours. Therefore, the satisfaction of an athlete over what happens during the training sessions is equally as important for our purposes as what happens in the game situation. As mentioned in the NBA example given earlier, a related uniqueness of athletics is that the contests are zero-sum games (i.e., for every winner, there is a loser). To illustrate, two profit-oriented fitness clubs competing with each other can make profits and, therefore, can be winners. In contrast, only one team can be champion in any given sport league or competition. Therefore, managers of athletic programs need to go beyond the mere win-loss records to assess the effectiveness of their programs. According to Chelladurai and Riemer (1997): "Athlete satisfaction may indeed prove to be the ultimate measure of organizational effectiveness of an athletic program" (p. 135). Thus, the satisfaction of athletes gains a significant role from the perspective of management. Based on this line of reasoning, Chelladurai and Riemer (1997) presented a classification of facets of athlete satisfaction, which is shown in table 14.6.

Note the resemblance of some of these facets to those that other authors identified in the context of paid and volunteer work and of leisure. Some other

Table 14.6   Facets of Athlete Satisfaction

Broad category	Specific facet	Description
Performance	Team	Team's performance in competitions
	Individual	An individual's personal performance
Improvement	Team	The extent to which the team has improved its performance over time
	Individual	The extent to which one has improved his or her personal performance
Leadership	Practice	The training methods employed, the severity of workouts, and the orderliness of practice sessions
	Ability use	The extent to which the coach uses the abilities of all athletes efficiently and effectively
	Strategy selection	The appropriateness of the strategies that the coach selects
	Equity in playing time	The amount of time an athlete is used in competitions based on abilities, talents, or efforts
	Equitable rewards	The extent to which the coach rewards and recognizes all athletes equitably
	Loyalty to athletes	The loyalty and support from the coach
	Attitude regarding winning	The positive and balanced attitude toward winning
	Ethics	The extent to which the coach rewards and recognizes all athletes equitably
Teammates	Task	The extent to which teammates contribute to and facilitate one's task learning and performance
	Social	The extent to which the interactions within the team are warm, friendly, and cohesive
Support staff		The help and assistance received from support staff, such as academic counselors, trainers, and managers
Administration	Facilities and equipment	The quality and availability of facilities and equipment for practices and games
	Scholarships	The number and amount of scholarships awarded to the team
	Budget	The budget allotted to the team relative to other teams (particularly items relating to things such as travel and uniforms)
Community support		The support from the university community, alumni, local public, and media

Source: Chelladurai and Reimer (1997).

facets are unique to the athletic context (e.g., playing time, strategy selection, loyalty to athletes, and scholarships). A first impression is that because participation in athletics is voluntary and because the specific sport has the same rules and performance requirements for both the athletes and other recreation participants, the satisfaction facets should be similar across athletes, recreation participants, and volunteer workers. However, as noted in chapter 3, athletics is pursuit of excellence that has its own bottom line requirements, particularly the exclusive focus on the job at hand. In every other context, such exclusivity is not imposed. Because of the total involvement of the athlete both in the physical and psychological sense, measuring athlete satisfaction from perspectives different from those in other contexts is necessary.

In a Nutshell

Athletes are prime beneficiaries of athletic departments and the prime producers of the associated entertainment. Thus, their satisfaction with their involvement in athletics is a major responsibility of managers of those operations. Further, athlete satisfaction should be used in the evaluation of athletic programs.

Measurement of Satisfaction

So far, the focus has been on identifying and describing various facets of satisfaction relevant to paid workers, volunteer workers, and clients. While such descriptions are important in their own right, their usefulness is realized fully only when they are validly and reliably measured. However, before proceeding with the description of the various methods of measuring satisfaction, consider the issue of global versus facet satisfaction.

Global Versus Facet Satisfaction

Job satisfaction may be viewed either as a global index of the feelings one has about a job as a whole or as a collection of feelings about different aspects of a job. Viewing job satisfaction as a global concept may be useful in some respects; however, from a managerial perspective, viewing job satisfaction as comprising satisfactions with different facets of a job is more appropriate. This dominant view has led to the development of several schemes to describe and measure the facets of a job, some of which were described earlier. After having measured a worker's

satisfaction with different facets of a job, researchers sum or average these scores to derive a measure of overall satisfaction. Smith and her associates recently have questioned this practice (Balzer et al. 1990). In their most recent work on their five-facet model of job satisfaction (which was described earlier in the chapter), they argued that while measures of the facets of a job may help managers identify and rectify problems in the job situation, "they do *not* indicate whether employees are satisfied with their job *overall*" (p. 8). A composite index of the sum (or mean) of the facets fails to represent overall feelings because it is not clear if satisfaction in one aspect compensates for dissatisfaction in another, if such computations give equal weight to each facet that denies individual differences in the importance attached to these facets, if the time frames associated with the facets may be short term whereas overall satisfaction is a long-term effect, and if simply adding the scores on a specified number of facets overlooks other aspects not included in the measurement scheme but important to the worker. For these reasons, Balzer et al. (1990) suggested that one should measure overall satisfaction separately. In fact, their measure of satisfaction contains subscales to measure five facets of a job and a separate scale to measure overall job satisfaction. These are described in the following section.

The Minnesota Satisfaction Questionnaire

The Minnesota studies have been quite comprehensive. The researchers (Dawis et al. 1964; Dawis and Lofquist 1984; Weiss, Dawis, England, and Lofquist 1967) have developed a questionnaire to assess the importance attached by individuals to 20 aspects of the job. This scale is known as Minnesota Importance Questionnaire. Similarly, they have developed another scale named Minnesota Job Description Questionnaire to measure a worker's perception of his or her work situation. All of these measures are used in counseling for work adjustment.

Of more relevance to the present context is the **measurement** of job satisfaction. The Minnesota Model of Job Satisfaction includes 20 work-related needs (see table 14.1). Based on the model, the same group of scholars (Dawis, England, and Lofquist 1964; Dawis and Lofquist 1984) developed the **Minnesota Satisfaction Questionnaire** that contains 100 items to measure 20 different aspects of a job that correspond to the 20 work-related needs. The respondent must indicate the level of satisfaction with each aspect on a five-point scale, ranging from very dissatisfied to very satisfied. In addition to the measurement of the 20 facets, the short form of the Minnesota Satisfaction Questionnaire, which contains 20 items (i.e., one critical item from each of the 20 facets), measures overall satisfaction with the job.

One example of research employing this questionnaire in our context is that of Koehler (1988). She administered the questionnaire to 23 female and 7 male corporate fitness managers and found that her subjects were least satisfied with advancement and compensation (i.e., the mean was less than 16 on a 25-point scale). Koehler (1988) suggested that the lower satisfaction with advancement and compensation was a reflection of the lack of opportunities available in the recently emergent field of corporate fitness. Further, this finding could be an artifact of most of her subjects being women who traditionally have been paid less than the male counterparts. On the other hand, she found that the subjects were most satisfied with social service and moral values (i.e., the mean was more than 22 on a 25-point scale). She argued that

> at first glance, the results of this study seem consistent with the nature of corporate fitness at this time. First to consider is the value of improved health and fitness for employees within the workplace. With this purpose in mind, it should not be surprising that the factors of social service and moral values would provide a great deal of satisfaction for corporate fitness managers. Moreover, given that the backgrounds of the subjects included such emphases as physical education, recreation, health, nursing, and nutrition, it is understandable that the subjects would have a social-service and moral value orientation. (p. 104)

Job Descriptive Index

The **Job Descriptive Index** is perhaps the most popular scale for measuring job satisfaction (Balzer et al. 1990; Smith, Kendall, and Hulin 1969). It measures Smith's five facets of a job that were described earlier (i.e., work itself, pay, promotions, co-workers, and supervision) and the job in general. Table 14.2 provides the definitions of these facets and a sample item for measuring each one them.

The job descriptive index contains 72 items (i.e., words or phrases) to measure these five facets (i.e., 18 work, 9 pay, 9 promotion, 18 supervision, 18 people items). The measure of satisfaction with the job in general contains 18 items. Typically, workers (or research subjects) are asked to indicate whether the word or phrase about a particular facet describes (or does not describe) that aspect of his or her job. For example, one responds "Y" for yes if the item describes the facet in question, "N" for no if it does not describe the facet, or "?" if one cannot decide. For example

Pay   —   Bad
      —   Well paid
      —   Less than I deserve

The scoring scheme is three points for a "Y" response, zero points for an "N" response, and one point for a "?" response. The scoring is reversed for negatively worded items. In the example, a "Y" response to "Well paid" receives three points, and an "N" response to "Bad" receives three points. Finally, the sum (or mean) of the items in each facet is used as the score for that facet. The scores in those facets that have only 9 items (i.e., pay and promotion) are doubled to be comparable with the other facets that have 18 items.

Some of the studies that have used the Job Descriptive Index and job-in-general scale are described in this section. Pastore (1994) employed both the Job Descriptive Index and the job-in-general scale in her study of satisfaction among NCAA coaches. She found that female coaches expressed greater satisfaction than male coaches in pay, promotion, supervision, and job in general; Division III coaches were more satisfied with pay, promotion, and co-workers than coaches in the other two divisions; and coaches of different sports varied in their satisfaction with different facets.

Using the Job Descriptive Index, Snyder (1990) found that there were no gender differences in satisfaction with work, supervision, pay, promotions, and co-workers among full-time and part-time coaches in four-year institutions in California. However, the leader behavior of athletic directors had differential effects on satisfaction of male and female coaches. Although athletic directors' consideration behavior (i.e., behavior expressing concern for members' well-being and for warm and friendly group atmosphere) had a significant effect on satisfaction with supervision for both genders, the leaders' structuring behavior (i.e. behavior reflecting a concern for clarity of roles and task performance) affected satisfaction with co-workers only among female coaches. Snyder (1990) argued that perceptions of structuring behavior extended uniformly to all members could have led to the women's satisfaction with co-workers.

Wallace and Weese (1995) in their study of the effects of transformational leadership on job satisfaction of employees of Canadian YMCA organizations employed the job-in-general scale of Balzer et al. (1990) to measure overall satisfaction with the job. They found that transformational leadership did not have any significant effects on employee satisfaction with the job in general. This result was contrary to previous research and the authors' expectations. They explained that

An explanation for this finding of nonsupport might rest with the type of employee attracted to the YMCA organizations. There were uniformly high levels of employee satisfaction in every YMCA organization, regardless of the transformational leadership situation in each respective setting. The YMCA organizations are altruistic organizations that attract staff members with similar orientations. . . . YMCA organizations are staffed by volunteers and paid employees who work together

to design and implement programs and services to help their clients and/or enrich their lives. (Balzer et al. 1990, 189)

Job Diagnostic Survey

Recall the job characteristics model of Hackman and Oldham (1980) described in chapter 8. These authors developed a scale called the Job Diagnostic Survey to measure each one of the variables of their model. Several items of the Job Diagnostic Survey measure employee satisfaction with job security, pay, co-workers, and supervision. In addition, items measure growth satisfaction and general satisfaction. These are collated and presented in table 14.7. Respondents express their satisfaction with the aspect of the job described by each item on a seven-point scale, ranging from extremely dissatisfied to extremely satisfied. While several authors have used the entire job diagnostic survey to test the

Table 14.7   Satisfaction Items From the Job Diagnostic Survey

Facet	Item
Job security[a]	The amount of job security I have
	How secure things look for me in the future in this organization
Pay[a]	The amount of pay and fringe benefits I receive
	The degree to which I am fairly paid for what I contribute to this organization
Co-worker[a]	The people to whom I talk and with whom I work
	The chance to get to know other people while on the job
	The chance to help other people while at work
Supervision[a]	The degree of respect and fair treatment I receive from my supervisor
	The amount of support and guidance I receive from my supervisor
	The overall quality of the supervision I receive in my work
General[b]	How satisfied I am with my job
	The kind of work I do in this job
	The frequency with which I think of quitting my job (reverse scored)
	How satisfied most of my co-workers are with their job
	The frequency with which my co-workers think of quitting their job (reverse scored)
Growth[a]	The amount of personal growth and development I get in doing my job
	The feeling of worthwhile accomplishment I get from doing my job
	The amount of independent thought and action I can exercise in my job
	The amount of challenge in my job

[a]The response format for the items in these facets is a seven-point scale ranging from extremely dissatisfied to extremely satisfied.

[b]The response format for the items in these facets is a seven-point scale ranging from disagree strongly to agree strongly.

J. Hackman/G. Oldham, *Work redesign*, © 1980 by Addison-Wesley Publishing Co., Inc. Adapted and reprinted by permission of Addison Wesley Longman.

propositions of the job characteristics model, others have used just the satisfaction component in other research.

In our context, Cleave (1993) studied the effects of job characteristics as described in Hackman and Oldham's (1980) model on job satisfaction of administrators of physical education, recreational sport, and intercollegiate athletics in Canada and Illinois. She employed the scales that Hackman and Oldham (1980) developed and Idaszak and Drasgow (1987) subsequently refined. She found that job characteristics partially influenced the psychological states that, in turn, enhanced general satisfaction and internal work motivation. In addition, job characteristics had a direct positive effect on growth satisfaction.

Choosing a Measure of Satisfaction

The Job Descriptive Index, the Job Diagnostic Survey, and the Minnesota Satisfaction Questionnaire are just three examples of measurement of satisfaction in the workplace. Managers in sport and recreation may use any of these methods or any alternative method. What is more critical is the selection of

the facets or components that are relevant to the job at hand, the paid and volunteer workers in the organization, and the clients of one's organization. In this context, the characteristics of a good scheme for the measurement of job satisfaction that Balzer et al. (1990) outlined should serve as very useful guidelines for us all. They include the following:

1. Satisfaction measures should include the principal aspects of job satisfaction.

2. Satisfaction measures should be easy to administer and complete.

3. Satisfaction measures should be easy to score and interpret.

4. Satisfaction measures should apply to all jobs in all organizations.

5. Satisfaction measures should show evidence that they are measuring what they are supposed to measure in a consistent fashion.

6. Satisfaction measures should be useful for identifying problems, choosing solutions, and evaluating changes.

Note that the fourth characteristic is meaningful only if one is interested in studying job satisfaction

While the purpose of the present section is to describe the means of measuring satisfaction with different facets of a job, the measurement instruments themselves are copyrighted, so researchers must secure permission to use these questionnaires from appropriate individuals or agencies. The addresses are as follows:

Minnesota Satisfaction Questionnaire

Vocational Psychology Research
N657 Elliot Hall
University of Minnesota
Minneapolis, MN 55455-0344
Phone: 612-625-1367, FAX: 612-626-0345

Job Descriptive Index

Department of Psychology
Bowling Green State University
Bowling Green, OH 43403
Phone: 419-372-8247, FAX: 419-372-6013

Job Diagnostic Survey
    The Job Diagnostic Survey is not copyrighted, so it may be used without the author's permission (Hackman and Oldham 1990). However, interested individuals may confer with the publishers of the book to confirm this or to secure the book itself.

Addison-Wesley Publishing Company
1 Jacob Way
Reading, MA 01867
Phone: 800-447-2226, FAX: 800-367-7198

across different organizations. A manager interested in studying satisfaction within one organization to identify problem areas would disregard that specific guideline and focus on including the aspects that are more critical and relevant to his or her own organizational context.

Given the uniqueness of certain organizational contexts or occupation characteristics, one may develop a special satisfaction scale applicable to that context. For instance, Li (1993) investigated the job satisfaction and performance of coaches in the Chinese specialized sport schools wherein talented youngsters were trained and groomed to be elite athletes. He designed a nine-item scale of job satisfaction applicable to that specific organizational context. He found that his subjects were relatively well satisfied with their jobs (i.e., mean was higher than four on a seven-point scale). Interestingly, he also found that the leadership that the school administrator provided had a significant effect on coaches' job satisfaction but did not have an effect on their performance.

With reference to facets of athlete satisfaction, Riemer and Chelladurai (1998) developed a scale to measure most of the facets described in table 14.6. Similarly, Ogasawara and Chelladurai (1998) developed a scale to measure satisfaction among athletic coaches. Although these efforts are undergoing refinement and publication, they do suggest that sport and recreation managers may develop their own satisfaction scales to suit our purposes.

In a Nutshell

While several instruments are available to measure job satisfaction, the sport manager should judiciously choose the one that best suits his or her organizational contexts. It is also possible for managers to create their own scales to measure satisfaction with specific aspects of the jobs in their organization.

Summary

Job satisfaction is the affective reaction that individuals have toward their jobs and their experiences in them. It is multifaceted and subsumes factors such as salary, security, achievement, and challenge. These various facets of job satisfaction may be related to one's needs and values. The concept of job satisfaction also can be extended to volunteers whose work experiences are quite similar to paid work in many respects. In a similar manner, sport and recreation managers also can conceive of their clients as partial employees of their organizations and can view the clients' satisfaction as most critical to their operations. Accordingly, some of the dimensions of service proposed elsewhere are quite relevant to sport and recreation managers. Similarly the facets of satisfaction developed in the context of leisure experiences also are germane to sport and recreation operations because most of the services are leisure activities for the clients.

Key Terms

job satisfaction, facets of satisfaction, discrepancy, needs, need satisfaction, value, leisure satisfaction, athlete satisfaction, measurement, Minnesota Satisfaction Questionnaire, Job Descriptive Index

Your Perspectives

- Consider the various work experiences you have had in your life including delivering papers, babysitting, mowing a neighbor's lawn, and working in other regular organizations, such as a fast-food restaurant, grocery store, or lumberyard. Which of these work experiences was most satisfying? Explain the factors contributing to such good feelings.

- Which of the work experiences considered in the previous scenario was least satisfying? Why?

- Now consider your own experiences as a participant in sport and physical activity. In thinking about these experiences, include the service providers, other participants, and the settings of such participation. Which of these experiences was most satisfying? Why? Your answer should touch upon all relevant factors, such as the activity itself, your performance in it, the service provider (e.g., leader, teacher, or coach), and other participants (e.g., teammates or opponents).

- Which of the experiences of participation considered in the previous scenario was least satisfying? What factors contributed to such dissatisfaction?

15 Commitment

Learning Objectives

After reading this chapter you should be able to

- define and describe organizational commitment;
- understand the bases or motives underlying organizational commitment;
- distinguish among affective, continuance, and normative forms of commitment;
- distinguish among the different foci (or targets) of organizational commitment;
- explain the antecedents and consequences of organizational commitment;
- distinguish among organizational commitment, occupational commitment, job satisfaction, and job involvement; and
- explain how an organization's supportiveness and member's sense of personal importance contribute to organizational commitment.

Chapter 14 was devoted to a discussion of satisfying the three forms of human resources (i.e., professional workers, volunteer workers, and clients). The focus was on their reactions to and sense of satisfaction with their experiences with their jobs and organizational practices. Satisfaction of our human resources is an important outcome variable, particularly in the case of sport and recreation organizations. An equally important outcome variable is called the **organizational commitment**. One meaning of the words "commit" and "commitment" refers to "the act of pledging or engaging oneself to something or somebody" (*Webster's New Twentieth Century Dictionary* 1976). Thus, friends commit to each other, athletes commit to pursuit of excellence, health-seeking individuals commit to a training or dieting regimen, and volunteers commit to a cause. It is this latter meaning (i.e., someone committing himself or herself to something) that is applied to the concept of organizational commitment.

Our interest in organizational commitment stems from the fact that unless members of an organization are committed to the organization and to its goals and processes, they are not likely to wholeheartedly participate in organizational activities and to discharge their duties to the best of their abilities. An organization may have all the resources it requires including human resources, but it cannot reach its potential unless the members are committed to the organization. It is the members of the organization who need to expend their efforts in ways meaningful to the organization and to exploit the other material resources to maximal advantage.

From a different perspective, organizational commitment creates a sense of belonging among members and contributes to their well-being. In the absence of organizational commitment, members operate in an alienated environment that may cause undue stress and unhappiness. Therefore, organizations and their managers must focus on cultivating organizational commitment for the benefit of both the organization and its members.

This chapter discusses the important concept of organizational commitment, i.e., the extent to which workers in an organization are committed to the organization, its goals and values, and its processes. The chapter begins with defining organizational commitment and describes various forms of such commitment in terms of the bases of commitment (i.e., the reasons or rationale for such commitment) and the foci of commitment (i.e., the specific targets of attachment). The chapter also describes the antecedents and consequences of organizational commitment and compares organizational commitment with occupational commitment, job involvement, and job satisfaction. The chapter concludes with a discussion of commitment of volunteers and clients.

In a Nutshell

Organizational commitment is a critical outcome variable because it underscores a worker's wholehearted participation in organizational activities, exertion of his or her efforts, and performance in those activities. The collective commitment of workers contributes to organizational success.

Definitions of Organizational Commitment

Like many other topics in organizational psychology, organizational commitment has been conceptualized and defined in different ways. For instance, Buchanan (1974) defined organizational commitment as "a partisan affective attachment to the goals and values of an organization, to one's role in relation to these goals and values, and to the organization for its own sake, apart from its purely instru-

mental worth" (p. 553). The emphasis here is on the goals and values of the organization and the individual's role in relation to those goals and values. These two elements contribute to the development of a psychological attachment to the organization.

Mowday, Porter, and Steers (1982) defined organizational commitment as

> the relative strength of an individual's identification with and involvement in a particular organization. Conceptually, it can be categorized by at least three factors: (a) a strong belief in and acceptance of the organization's goals and values; (b) a willingness to exert considerable effort on behalf of the organization; and (c) a strong desire to maintain membership in the organization. (p. 27)

In expanding the meaning of organizational commitment from a mere attachment to a willingness to work on behalf of the organization and a desire to continue membership in the organization, Mowday, Porter, and Steers (1982) provided a greater impetus to the study of organizational commitment.

The given definitions refer to the attitudinal and affective elements of an organization. With the development of a positive attitude toward and liking for the organization and its goals, individuals are likely to continue membership in the organization and to exert effort on its behalf. For example, an employee of a city recreation department may accept the organizational goals and values to provide quality recreation opportunities for the members of the community and also may perceive the department's processes as purposeful and effective in providing those services. Further, the individual also may perceive his or her role in the total operation as quite meaningful. These perceptions and feelings may lead the individual to develop a sense of commitment to the organization.

In contrast to this view of organizational commitment, Becker (1960) suggested that "commitment comes into being when a person, by making a side-bet, links extraneous interest with a consistent line of activity" (p. 32). Becker's (1960) position is that an individual may get locked into a line of activity (e.g., continuing membership in the organization) because of his or her past investments in the activity or the costs associated with discontinuing that activity. In this view, organizational commitment is based on the material cost of withdrawing from an organization. In the example of the city recreation department employee, the person may evaluate the investments he or she has made in terms of time and effort, friendships, and development of skills specific to that organization that are not transferable to other organizations. In addition, the individual also may consider the cost of leaving the organization in terms of loss of those investments and other accrued benefits, such as pension and benefits. Along with the effort and time needed to move to another organization, the individual may evaluate the existing opportunities for such movement. When the perceived benefits and ease of moving to another organization are less than the sunken costs in the present organization, the individual is likely to continue membership in the current organization. In these calculations, the focus is on the individual and his or her courses of action (i.e., continuing or discontinuing membership in the organization) rather than on the organization itself.

As another example, consider the case of a university athlete. Although he or she may be disenchanted with the coach, the team, or the department, the athlete may not leave the team to join another team because of the costs associated with it. For example, the NCAA regulations stipulate that the athlete must sit out one year. The perceived cost of sitting out for one year may be greater than the discomfort experienced at the moment, and, therefore, the athlete may decide to continue membership with the present team.

In Their View

In addressing whether organizational commitment is still a useful concept when organizations are rapidly changing, Meyer and Allen (1997) argued that commitment matters even though organizations may become leaner and flatter. First, the remaining members constitute the "heart, brain, and muscle" of the organization. Thus, their loyalty and commitment are critical. Further, jobs are changing from a collection of tasks to broader roles with a variety of skills. Therefore, skilled or trained employees' commitment is critical. In addition, as machines and computers assume routine jobs, people are left with more challenging and more responsible jobs. Their trustworthiness becomes critical to organizational welfare; commitment would make them loyal and true to the organization. Finally, all people are prone to be committed to something (e.g., profession, occupation, or union); it is better for the organization to cultivate that tendency in its favor.

Multidimensionality of Organizational Commitment

The two contrasting perspectives on organizational commitment described (i.e., liking for the organization and cost of leaving the organization) suggest that an individual can commit to the organization for more than one reason. That is, a person may be both committed to his or her organization and constrained from leaving that organization because of the heavy cost of moving to another organization. As Becker (1992) and Becker et al. (1996) noted, distinguishing the bases of organizational commitment (i.e., the motives or reasons engendering commitment) from the foci of commitment (i.e., the individuals, groups, or units to whom an employee is attached) is useful. The following section elaborates on the bases and foci of commitment.

Bases of Commitment

In their most recent work on organizational commitment, Meyer and Allen (1997) described organizational commitment in terms of the three distinct components of

- affective commitment,
- continuance commitment, and
- normative commitment.

In their words,

Affective commitment refers to the employee's emotional attachment to, identification with, and involvement in the organization. Employees with a strong affective commitment continue employment with the organization because they *want* to. Continuance commitment refers to an awareness of the costs associated with leaving the organization. Employees whose primary link to the organization is based on continuance commitment remain because they *need* to. Finally, normative commitment reflects a feeling of obligation to continue employment. Employees with a high level of normative commitment feel that they *ought* to remain with the organization. (Meyer and Allen 1991, 67)

Note that the three components are indeed based on three different reasons for individuals to be committed to the organization. Figure 15.1 illustrates these three components of organizational commitment and their content.

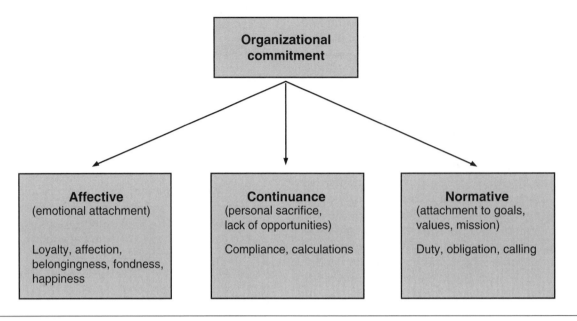

Figure 15.1 Components of organizational commitment.

Affective Commitment

Affective commitment, also referred to as identification commitment (O'Reilly and Chatman 1986), reflects "the degree to which an individual is psychologically attached to an employing organization through feelings, such as loyalty, affection, warmth, belongingness, fondness, happiness, pleasure, and so on" (Jaros et al. 1993, 954). That is, an employee approves and likes the organization and its processes, and the extent of liking impels him or her to be committed to and to work hard on behalf of the organization. The supervisor's leadership and the social and task relations within the workgroup facilitate this emotional attachment.

Continuance Commitment

Continuance commitment is a derivative of Becker's (1960) side-bet theory, and it refers to one's attachment to an employing organization based on "the degree to which an individual experiences a sense of being locked in place because of the high costs of leaving" (Jaros et al. 1993, 953). As noted earlier, continuance commitment is based on cost-benefit analysis of remaining with or leaving the organization. O'Reilly and Chatman (1986) labeled this component as compliance commitment. Some authors call it the calculative commitment (Mathieu and Zajac 1990, 172).

Note that the emphasis in this form of commitment is on whether the individual will continue his or her membership in the organization. It does not reflect an individual's concern with organizational goals or their achievement. That is, even after the individual decides to continue with the organization, that individual may not put forth any extra effort for the benefit of the organization. Instead, he or she may work up to the minimum that is expected. In other words, the person may simply comply with the minimal requirements of the organization (hence the name compliance commitment).

As noted earlier, one factor underlying continuance commitment is the cost of leaving the organization, and the other factor is the lack of opportunities to move to another organization. Because these two factors are separate and distinct, considering continuance commitment to consist of lack of alternatives and personal sacrifice would be fruitful. Evidence suggests that continuance commitment is composed of these two distinct, but related, dimensions (Meyer, Allen, and Gellatly 1990; McGee and Ford 1987). For example, a manager in a city recreation department may find that other cities do not have openings, so he or she may continue to work in the present department. In contrast, even if other cities had job openings, the manager may decide to continue to work in the present job because of the sacrifices involved in such a move, such as losing pension benefits, leaving friends and family, and disrupting children's education. The notion of perceived sacrifices is what Becker (1960) implied in his exposition of side-bets, or sunken costs.

Normative Commitment

The third component of organizational commitment, **normative commitment**,

> is the degree to which an individual is psychologically attached through an internalization of its goals, values, and missions. This form of commitment differs from affective commitment because it reflects a sense of duty, an obligation, or calling, to work in the organization, but not necessarily emotional attachment. It differs from continuance commitment because it does not necessarily fluctuate with personal calculation of inducements or sunk costs. (Jaros et al. 1993, 955)

A worker may identify with the organizational goals and take it as a duty or obligation to work in that organization and facilitate the achievement of those goals. Normative commitment is distinguished from affective commitment because the latter reflects an emotional attachment to the organization and from continuance motivation because normative commitment does not involve calculation of inducements and costs (Jaros et al. 1993). An employee of a sport organization serving the youth in the community may be committed to the organiza-

tion not because of any affective and emotional component but because the organization serves the youth in sport, which is consistent with the focal employee's strong belief in both youth and sport.

In a Nutshell

The three components of organizational commitment are affective, continuance, and normative commitments. Affective commitment is based on emotional attachment to organizational practices and characteristics of the workgroup. Continuance commitment arises out of the costs of discontinuing membership in the organization. Normative commitment is derived from an individual's acceptance of organizational goals and values and a conviction that one ought to strive to achieve those goals.

Meyer and Allen (1997) suggested that these three components are not mutually exclusive; that is, all three components may bear upon an individual in his or her decision to continue membership in an organization and to work toward organizational goals. For instance, the recreation employee in the previous example may continue to work for the department because the organizational environment including leadership and workgroup processes is acceptable (i.e., affective commitment), the cost of leaving the organization is prohibitive (i.e., continuance commitment), and he or she has a

---

O'Reilly and Chatman (1986) proposed a somewhat different scheme to describe three bases of organizational commitment: compliance, identification, and internalization. According to them,

> Compliance occurs when attitudes and behaviors are adopted not because of shared beliefs but simply to gain specific rewards. . . . Identification occurs when an individual accepts influence to establish or maintain a satisfying relationship; that is, an individual may feel proud to be part of a group, respecting its values and accomplishments without adopting them as his or her own. Internalization occurs when influence is accepted because the induced attitudes and behavior are congruent with one's own values; that is, the values of the individual and the group or organization are the same. (p. 493)

While O'Reilly and Chatman's (1986) scheme is similar to that of Meyer and Allen (1991, 1997) to some extent, note the significant difference between the compliance commitment of O'Reilly and Chatman (1986) and the continuance commitment of Meyer and Allen (1991, 1997). While continuance commitment refers to an employee continuing membership in the organization, it does not specify anything about that employee's behavior and performance. In contrast, compliance commitment does reflect an employee's decision to continue membership in the organization. In addition, it suggests that the employee will do whatever it takes to gain his or her personal rewards.

conviction to be involved in providing recreation services for the community (i.e., normative commitment).

In Their View

Taken together, considerable evidence across a wide variety of samples and performance indicators suggests that employees with strong affective commitment to the organization will be more valuable employees than those with weak commitment. Similar, albeit weaker, effects are reported for normative commitment. The picture that emerges from the existing research involving continuance commitment, however, is rather disappointing. As with affective and normative commitment, employees who believe that strong costs are associated with leaving their organization are unlikely to do so. At the same time, however, they are also less likely to make positive contributions to the organization. Indeed, evidence suggests that employees with strong continuance commitment might be poorer performers, engage in fewer citizenship behaviors, and exhibit more dysfunctional behaviors than those with weak continuance commitment. (Meyer and Allen 1997, 38)

Which Component of Organizational Commitment?

In summary, the three components of organizational commitment (i.e., affective, continuance, and normative) stem from three different bases: emotional attachment, cost-benefit analysis, and internalization and acceptance of organizational goals. The natural question now is, Which one of these forms of commitment is more critical to the organization?

From an organization's perspective, the most desirable situation is when an employee is committed to the organization based on one's pride and desire for membership (i.e., affective component) and sharing a sense of duty and obligation to achieve organizational goals (i.e., normative component). An organization can expect such an employee to remain in and work hard for the organization. Commitment based on emotional attachment alone increases the possibility that the employee will remain with the organization but does not guarantee maximal effort

to the achievement of organizational goals. However, internalization of organizational goals without emotional attachment leads to the expectation that the worker will do his or her best to achieve organizational goals but does not exclude the possibility that the worker may leave for another organization with similar goals. Regarding continuance commitment, the member may remain with the organization, but he or she may not put forth the best efforts on behalf of the organization. Any extra effort put forth at all would be based on calculations of personal benefits only.

Foci Commitment

In the discussion of the components of organizational commitment, the focus was on an employee's commitment to the organization as a whole. In fact, the label of organizational commitment does strengthen that assumption. However, because an organization itself may have different goals and is made up of several units and constituencies, an employee may be committed differentially to these aspects of an organization (Becker 1992, Becker et al. 1996, Reichers 1985). For example, an athletic department in a university is made up of several units, such as facility management, event management, marketing department, ticketing department, and personnel department. From a different perspective, the athletic department also has different constituencies, such as the athletes themselves, the general student body, alumni, university administrators, the general public, the media, the donors, suppliers, and the NCAA. From yet another perspective, hierarchical levels (e.g., athletic director, assistant directors, and supervisors of various units) and workgroups within each unit also characterize the athletic department. An employee of the athletic department may be attached to one or more of these elements in varying degrees. For example, an employee in the ticketing unit may be more committed to that unit and to the supervisor and co-workers in the unit and may be less committed to the unit concerned with facility management. As another example, a coach may be committed to varying degrees to the coaching occupation, the president and athletic director of the university, other coaches in the department, and the athletes themselves. An individual's commitment possibly may not extend beyond his or her particular unit at all. For example, an academic counselor may be quite committed to the unit and the athletes it serves. However, such strong commitment may not extend to other units or to the athletic department as a whole.

While the global concept of organizational commitment is pertinent to both paid and volunteer workers, the three components of organizational commitment (i.e., affective, continuance, and normative) are likely to have different implications for volunteer and paid workers. As noted in chapter 1, an individual may volunteer for altruistic reasons, and his or her choice of one organization over another may be a function of the extent to which the organizational processes and workgroup characteristics are congruent with the individual's needs and preferences. Thus, a volunteer's continued participation in a particular organization reflects both normative commitment born out of altruistic motives and affective commitment born out of the liking for organizational process and interpersonal interactions. The implication for sport managers is that, although one can expect a volunteer to carry out the assigned tasks adequately based on normative commitment (i.e., altruistic reasons), one can expect greater motivation and performance if affective commitment also can be cultivated. Sport managers should note that the volunteer's normative commitment could be extended to other organizations with similar goals. That is, the volunteer may switch allegiance to another organization if he or she does not develop an affective commitment to the present organization. In other words, continuance commitment may be less relevant to volunteer workers because no monetary sacrifice is involved. However, a volunteer may consider his or her costs, in terms of efforts expended on behalf of the organization and the status and prestige gained in an organization, as sunken costs. For example, a volunteer member of the national governing body of a sport may be reluctant to leave that sport organization for another similar organization. To this volunteer, the time and effort that he or she has spent building up the organization, the recognition that he or she receives from followers of the sport, and the network that he or she has built would all be considered sunken costs. A concern with these costs moderates any thought of leaving the organization.

Once again, note that these different foci are not mutually exclusive. That is, an individual may be attached to the goals, management, co-workers, clients, and owners of an organization simultaneously, but the strength of such attachment may vary among the different targets. Note also that organizational commitment is best viewed as a collection of multiple commitments to various constituencies of the organization (Reichers 1985). Further, commitment to all of these foci would cumulatively indicate the commitment to the organization as a whole as shown in figure 15.2.

In a Nutshell

The foci, or targets, of a worker's commitment include several elements, such as organizational goals, units, hierarchical levels, co-workers, and clients. Individuals may be committed differentially to one or more of these aspects of an organization. Thus, it is useful to consider organizational commitment as a collection of commitments to different foci.

Profiles of Organizational Commitment

The foregoing sections outlined the various bases or components of organizational commitment as well as the various foci, or targets, of such commitment. Figure 15.3 is a grid based on these distinctions, and it illustrates the differing profiles of two individuals, Jane and John, of the same work unit (e.g., marketing unit of a university athletic department), based on their bases and foci of commitment. Jane and John are shown to differ in the extent to which they are committed to various foci and also in the bases of such commitment. Jane is more committed to co-workers than John is, and John is more committed to the supervisor than Jane is. Further, Jane and John are committed equally to the work unit, but the bases of commitment are different for them; that is, Jane's base of commitment is normative, John's base of commitment is affective. Such differences also can be found in commitment to other aspects of the department.

The placement of Jane and John in different cells of figure 15.3 is to illustrate only the possibility that Jane (or John) may have a higher level of one or more

Commitment to

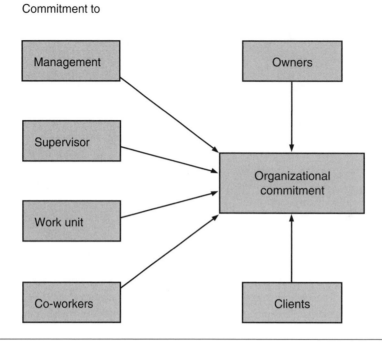

Figure 15.2   Organizational commitment as a collection of commitments.

Foci	Bases		
	Affective (emotional attachment)	Continuance (cost-benefit analysis)	Normative (acceptance of organizational goals)
Organization	Jane	John	
Management			
Supervisor	John		
Work unit	John		Jane
Co-workers			Jane

Figure 15.3   Grid of bases and foci of commitment.

aspects of organizational commitment than the other has. It does not show the absolute strength of commitment in any one cell. For example, even though Jane is shown to have a higher level of affective commitment to the organization than John has, Jane's level in this form of commitment may be lower than that of other members. The level could be lower than her commitment to other aspects.

Occupational Commitment

The conclusion that commitment can be to the organization, leadership, workgroup, co-workers, or

organizational goals raises the possibility of such psychological attachment to other entities in the organizational context. Indeed, organizational commitment has been contrasted with occupational commitment (Blau, Paul, and St. John 1993; Meyer and Allen 1997; Vandenberg and Scarpello 1994). Occupational commitment refers to a person's belief in and acceptance of the values of his or her chosen occupation or line of work and to a willingness to maintain membership in that occupation (Vandenberg and Scarpello 1994). That is, an employee in a sport organization may be committed differentially to the organization and his or her

In Their View

According to Ilsley (1990): "commitment is central to the volunteer experience. We may define commitment as a state of being in which one is bound morally, emotionally, and/or intellectually to some entity or idea (or to other people or to an ideology, for example)" (p. 33). In emphasizing that commitment is a more central foundation for volunteer motivation and performance, Ilsley (1990) likened motivation to the ripples and commitment to water that runs deep. He also noted that motivation can be inferred from actions while commitment cannot. Although he did not specifically address the bases and **foci of commitment** as discussed in this chapter, he did suggest that individuals may commit to targets, such as clients, social causes, other volunteers, community organizations, God, and their country. In our context, volunteers may be committed differentially to foci, such as the sport itself, the clients, and the community. Ilsley (1990) also noted that volunteer commitment is rooted in one's values, such as peace, learning, literacy, health, justice, and leisure. The values (e.g., health, justice, leisure, competition, and success) of volunteers in sport and recreation may guide them. Chapter 6 discussed some of the dominant American values as related to sport. Ilsley (1990) made the telling point: "Commitment cannot be imposed from the outside, any more than motivation can. The depth of commitment that makes a volunteer willing to face isolation or physical danger and give up leisure, prosperity, or even life itself must come from deep within the individual. Volunteer managers, however, can try to understand volunteer commitment" (p. 55).

control, autonomy, and loyalty to clients, are juxtaposed against organizational value systems of organizational or managerial control, discipline, and loyalty to the organization. Vandenberg and Scarpello (1994) also pointed out that the occupational values system is learned over a period of time before entry into any one organization, but the organizational value system is learned only after entry into an organization. Given these contradictory value systems, managers can expect that as occupational commitment increases, organizational commitment decreases and vice versa.

While an individual's commitment to the occupation and the organization may be at odds in some circumstances, commitment to these two foci possibly may be congruent. Consider, for example, a private sport-marketing firm that employs three marketing professionals. The firm may permit its employees considerable independence, autonomy, and initiative to identify and implement profitable projects. Fewer rules and procedures are present to constrain a member's activities. Such an approach is consistent with the entrepreneurial nature of the firm. In this case, the values and goals of the marketing occupation and those of the firm are likely to be congruent; therefore, an individual's commitment to these two entities may not be conflicting. In contrast, the same marketing professional in a university athletic department may find that adherence to occupational values may be at odds with organizational values and processes. Greater emphasis on education values and bureaucratic rules and regulations in a university athletic department are, to some extent, inconsistent with the occupational values of marketing. Thus, the possibility of conflict between organizational and occupational commitment exists.

Development and Effects of Organizational Commitment

So far, the chapter has described organizational commitment from the perspectives of motives behind one's psychological attachment to an organization (i.e., bases of commitment) and the targets of such attachment (i.e., foci of commitment). In addition to understanding the meaning of commitment in its various manifestations, it also is necessary to gain some insight into the development of organizational commitment and its effects on other organizationally relevant factors. The following sections describe these issues as **antecedents and consequences of organizational commitment**.

occupation. As suggested in chapter 2, a sense of loyalty to their profession characterizes professionals. Such loyalty is independent of the commitment to the employing organizations. This view can be extended to all occupations. For example, a marketing specialist and an athletic trainer in an athletic department may be committed as much to their respective occupations as to the athletic department itself.

Occupational commitment and organizational commitment conceivably can be contradictory to each other. As Vandenberg and Scarpello (1994) noted, the occupational value system may stress that values, such as collegial control and self-

Antecedents of Organizational Commitment

Researchers have made several attempts to relate specific personal, organizational, and workgroup variables to commitment. A recent analysis of previous studies (Mathieu and Zajac 1990) showed a positive relationship between organizational commitment and personal characteristics of age and perceived competence; job characteristics of skill variety, challenge, and job scope; and leader characteristics of initiating structure, consideration, communication, and participative leadership. In contrast, perceived role ambiguity, role conflict, and role overload were related negatively to organizational commitment.

While most of the relationships were moderate, perceived personal competence, job challenge, job scope, leader's communication, and participative leadership were correlated more strongly with organizational commitment. The implication of these findings for management is that variables that were more strongly correlated are under the control of management. That is, management can manipulate these variables to facilitate the development of organizational commitment. For example, job scope can be enhanced to include greater skill variety and challenge. Chapter 8 discussed this issue of job design and job enrichment in greater detail. Similarly, a manager may consciously modify his or her leadership to be more communicative and participative (see chapter 10 for an in-depth review of leadership). In sum, organizations also can provide an environment for individuals to grow and develop their competence.

Meyer and Allen (1997) derived two significant themes underlying several research studies showing a relationship between organizational commitment and several antecedent factors. In their view, work experiences of employees give the impression that "the organization is supportive of its employees, treats them fairly, and enhances their sense of personal importance, and competence by appearing to value their contributions to the organization" (p. 46). The two themes embedded in their statement are **supportiveness and fairness** and **personal importance and competence**. While supportiveness and fairness are reflected in the general policies and procedures of the organization, they also are demonstrated in the face-to-face and day-to-day interactions of the manager with the subordinates. As discussed in chapter 10, managers need to clarify a worker's role and how it relates to organizational goals and processes, to provide the necessary coaching and guidance to enhance the competence, and to impress on the worker how significant his or her contributions are. In doing so, the manager is likely to demonstrate supportiveness as well as to enhance the sense of personal importance and competence. Recall the discussion of organizational justice in chapter 13. As perceived fairness is critical for the development of organizational commitment, the notions of procedural, distributive, and interactional justice must be maintained if workers are to develop organizational commitment.

Consequences of Organizational Commitment

The most critical outcomes that researchers have studied as consequences of commitment are performance and turnover. By definition, committed workers stay with the organization (i.e., absence

Researchers have found some indication that age, experience in the current job, and position in the organization also are correlated with organizational commitment (Mathieu and Zajonc 1990). As one gets older, one becomes more experienced and rises to a higher position. However, how these three variables are related to organizational commitment is not clear. One view is that older people have fewer opportunities to move from one organization to another, so they stick with the current organization. Further, because their sunken costs with that organization are relatively higher, older people are likely to stay with the organization. These factors reflect continuance commitment discussed earlier. From a different perspective, organizational commitment preceded one's experience and position in the organization. That is, because a person was committed to the organization in the first place, he or she continued with that organization, and because of the person's commitment, he or she rose to higher levels in the organization. This latter view is suggestive of affective commitment. However, as noted earlier, age, experience, and position are not related as strongly to organizational commitment as the variables of job and leader characteristics.

of turnover) and work toward the attainment of organizational goals (i.e., performance). From a practical perspective, sport managers need to be concerned with both outcomes. That is, their interest is in retaining good performers.

In a Nutshell

While the relationships between organizational commitment and the background characteristics of age, experience, and tenure are weaker, such relationships are stronger in the case of perceived personal competence, job scope, and leadership. By being supportive and fair and by enhancing members' competence and their sense of importance, the organization facilitates the development of organizational commitment.

Performance

Unfortunately, the relationship between organizational commitment and **performance** is not strong. This low commitment-performance relationship can be attributed to several factors, such as the ability of the individual, the resources made available to the individual, and the degree to which the task is dependent on other people or tasks. Further, as Mathieu and Zajac (1990) noted, organizational policies themselves may strengthen or weaken the commitment-performance relationship.

> The relationship between organizational commitment and performance is likely to be moderated by such factors as pay policies. One would expect that calculated commitment [continuance commitment] would exhibit high positive correlation with performance in instances where pay is tied closely to performance (e.g., piece-rate system), and less so where there is little connection (e.g., straight salary systems). Alternately, attitudinal commitment [affective commitment] could be expected to correlate more positively with performance when role expectations are clearly defined than when they are ambiguous. (Mathieu and Zajac 1990, 185)

Becker et al. (1996) raised another issue affecting the commitment-performance relationship. As noted earlier, an employee may be committed differentially to different foci, such as the workgroup, supervisor, and organization. In this scenario, the workgroup and the supervisor are closer to the focal employee than to the wider organization in terms of task and social interactions.

> It seems to us that norms regarding in-role behaviors are often established by such local foci as supervisors and work groups. If so, their commitment to local foci should lead to an acceptance of performance norms. . . . We suspect that, for most employees, local foci are psychologically more proximal than are global foci [e.g., organizational commitment]. . . . Further, because of their proximity and regular interaction with employees, local foci are probably more effective than global foci in monitoring, rewarding, and influencing employee behaviors. Proximity and regular interactions also make it easier for employees to seek and receive feedback on actions consistent with the values and goals of local foci. (Becker et al. 1996, 467)

The foregoing comment of Becker et al. (1996) points to the pivotal role of the workgroup and the supervisor in cultivating organizational commitment in an individual employee. That is, the group norms are reflected in the extent to which the workgroup and the supervisor themselves share the organizational goals and values and work toward achieving them; that is, a high degree of organizational commitment characterizes the workgroup itself. To the extent that the employee is committed to the workgroup or supervisor, he or she is most likely to abide by the group norms and, in turn, exhibit organizational commitment.

In a Nutshell

The weaker relationship between organizational commitment and performance is attributable to poor linkage between pay and performance, lack of ability or other needed resources, and interdependence among tasks. Organizational commitment is more strongly correlated with intention to leave and turnover, which is a costly proposition for the organization.

Turnover

In contrast to the commitment-performance relationship, the relationships of organizational commitment with intention to leave and actual **turnover** are stronger. This is a critical finding because turnover can be costly to an organization in terms of recruiting new candidates and training them. In addition, employee turnover may tarnish the image of the organization to the extent that it triggers the perception that the organization is a bad place to work. Thus, sport managers must be concerned with organizational commitment as a critical outcome variable in itself despite the fact that it is not correlated strongly with performance.

In Their View

With regard to the low correlation between organizational commitment and outcomes of interest, Meyer and Allen (1997) pointed out that even small changes in employee performance attributed to organizational commitment may have a great impact on the bottom line for an organization. Performance is a function of many factors including one's ability, experience, resources available to the individual, and one's motivation. A manager can expect commitment to enhance an employee's motivation, which is fundamental to increased performance. Task design may control and constrain performance, such as in the case an assembly line. Performance may differ according to the foci of commitment. Thus, small increments in organizationally relevant outcomes would make an organization competitive.

Correlates of Organizational Commitment

One of the difficulties that both researchers and practitioners face is the concept that organizational commitment is closely related to several other work attitudes. The two work attitudes more closely related to organizational commitment are job satisfaction and job involvement. Although the relationships among these work attitudes are strong, they are distinct enough to be considered separately, particularly because these three attitudes (i.e., organizational commitment, job satisfaction, and job involvement) are critical to organizational success. These three attitudes are compared and contrasted in the next section.

Organizational Commitment and Job Satisfaction

Meyer and Allen (1997) noted that recent research permits the conclusion that organizational commitment is distinguishable from **job satisfaction**. Mowday, Porter, and Steers (1982) distinguished commitment from satisfaction by stating that commitment is a global affective response to the whole organization and that job satisfaction is an immediate and limited reaction to job experiences. Conceivably, an individual may be attached to the organization because his or her values may be consistent with the goals of the organization or because of the status of the organization. However, the specific job that the individual performs may not be satisfying to the extent that it does not meet individual needs and desires. For example, an employee of an intercollegiate athletic department may be committed to the department because it pursues excellence in athletics, helps aspiring young individuals reach their potential in athletics, and has a high profile in the community. However, that person may be assigned to a routine job that does not offer much challenge and variety in the tasks. If that person has a high level of need for growth, he or she may find the job less satisfying. Thus, organizational commitment is more global, encompassing all the attributes of the organization; job satisfaction is confined to one's job.

In Their View

While organizational commitment may facilitate retention of employees and increase their efforts, this commitment can have a downside. As Saal and Knight (1995) noted,

> Extremely high commitment may limit individual growth, reduce opportunity for mobility, and stifle creativity. Over commitment might also bring on stress in family and personal relationships, and "role overload." The organization may also suffer from overcommitted employees, a situation that may reduce organizational flexibility, lead employees to accept company goals and procedures unquestioningly, and even increase levels of illegal and unethical behavior. (pp. 296-297)

Mowday, Porter, and Steers (1982) noted two other distinctions between organizational commitment and job satisfaction. First, organizational commitment takes time to develop, and job satisfaction is often an immediate reaction to the job. This distinction probably occurs because the individual is exposed to the job on a daily basis and because the exposure to processes and practices of the organization to achieve its goals takes time to affect the individual. Consider, for example, the distribution of organizational rewards, such as salary increases. The process is normally an annual process, and the evaluation of the equitability of distribution of rewards is rather subjective. Any judgments that an individual makes about the reward system likely result from the experiences over a period of time. Thus, cultivation of organizational commitment takes time.

The second attribute contrasting organizational commitment and job satisfaction is the variability of the feelings. While organizational commitment takes time to develop, it is also less variable in the sense that individuals do not change easily their liking for and allegiance to the organization. In contrast, job satisfaction can vary rapidly with any changes in the job attributes. For example, the individual in the athletic department who is dissatisfied with his or her job at the moment may become satisfied if the job is altered to include some challenge and autonomy.

In a Nutshell

Organizational commitment is more global, takes more time to develop, and is less variable than job satisfaction. On the other hand, job satisfaction is an immediate reaction to job experience that varies with changes in the job situation.

Organizational Commitment and Job Involvement

Blau (1986) and Blau and Boal (1987, 1989) highlighted the distinction between **job involvement** and organizational commitment. They defined job involvement as "the extent to which an individual identifies psychologically with his/her job," and they defined organizational commitment as "the extent to which an employee identifies with the nature and goals of a particular organization and wishes to maintain membership in that organization" (Blau and Boal 1989, 116). Thus, "job involvement and organizational commitment represent two related but distinct types of work-related attitudes because of their different referents" (p. 578). The referents are, of course, the job and the organization. To some, the job is an important source of their self-image, so they do care about the job and tend to identify psychologically with the job. As noted before, organizational commitment reflects a positive orientation toward one's organization and its goals.

Blau and Boal (1987) also suggested that the job

may satisfy one's intrinsic growth needs while the organization may meet the social and other extrinsic rewards. This idea that the job and the organization may satisfy different sets of needs is the essence of Herzberg's two-factor theory discussed in chapter 7 and Hackman and Oldham's job characteristics model described in chapter 8. Another point to note is that by definition job involvement implies that individuals who have a high level of job involvement spend their time and effort on the tasks associated with the job, and individuals who have a high level of organizational commitment help to facilitate group maintenance and goal accomplishment. Thus, both job involvement and organizational commitment are functional. More importantly, they are not antithetical to each other.

While both job involvement and organizational commitment are desirable from the perspective of the organization, individuals may differ in the relative emphasis they place on these two psychological attachments. That is, individuals can have a high level of both job involvement and organizational commitment, a low level of both aspects, and a high level of one and a low level of another. Blau and Boal (1987) categorized people in an organization into four classes based on high and low combinations of job involvement and organizational commitment as shown in figure 15.4.

The first class, labeled institutionalized stars, comprises individuals who have a high level of both job involvement and organizational commitment. These institutionalized stars would be the ideal employees. Although the organization benefits from such individuals, it also suffers great costs when these high performers leave the organization in terms of replacing them, immediate productivity loss, and disruption of communication flow. The second class, labeled lone wolves, comprises individuals who are involved in the job but are not as committed to the organization or its goals as the institutionalized stars. Because lone wolves are not attached to the organization, they are likely to move on to another organization if it provides better task-related opportunities. The third class, labeled corporate citizens, consists of people who do not see their work as personally important but are attached to the organization and its goals. Blau and Boal (1987) suggested that corporate citizens are not as valuable as institutionalized stars or even as lone wolves. Yet, their role in the organization is significant to the extent that they contribute to workgroup cohesiveness and inter-unit cooperation. The fourth category, labeled apathetic employees, consists of individuals who have a low level of both job

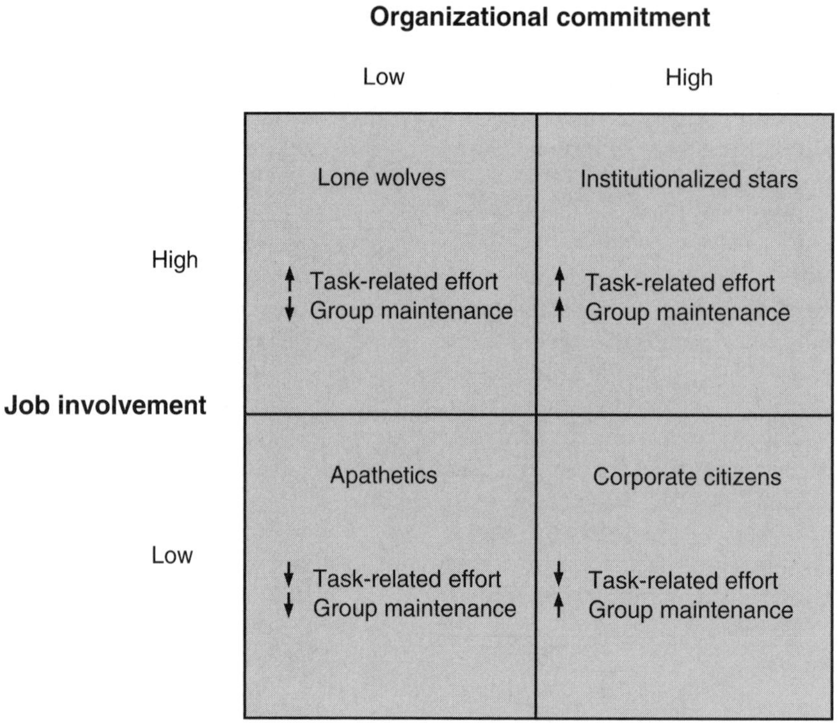

Organizational commitment

Low   High

High

Lone wolves	Institutionalized stars
↑ Task-related effort	↑ Task-related effort
↓ Group maintenance	↑ Group maintenance

Job involvement

Low

Apathetics	Corporate citizens
↓ Task-related effort	↓ Task-related effort
↓ Group maintenance	↑ Group maintenance

Figure 15.4   Interaction of organizational commitment and job involvement.

Adapted, by permission, from G.J. Blau and K.B. Boal, 1987, "Conceptualizing how job involvement and organizational commitment affect turnover and absenteeism," *Academy of Management Review* 12: 288-300.

involvement and organizational commitment. To them the work is not important personally, and the organization and its goals are not appealing. They tend to exert the minimal effort. "Therefore, the individuals in this cell represent the least valued members to an organization, that is *apathetic employees*" (Blau and Boal 1987, 296). Departure of any member falling into this final category may benefit the organization in the sense that somebody who could fall into any of the other three functional categories can replace the departing person.

In a Nutshell

Job involvement is different from organizational commitment because the focus of attachment is the job and the organization, respectively. Job involvement is based on intrinsic rewards, and organizational commitment is fostered by extrinsic rewards of the organization. Based on the relative strengths of job involvement and organizational commitment, employees can be categorized as institutional stars, lone wolves, corporate citizens, and apathetic employees.

Summary

In summary, this chapter defined and described both organizational commitment from a global perspective and its specific components. The specific components of affective, continuance, and normative commitment were described from an emotional attachment, calculations of cost of leaving the organization, and sense of duty, respectively. In addition, commitment might be targeted toward the organization as a whole, top management, supervisors, workgroup, co-workers, clients, and such other constituencies of the organization. Thus, the multidimensionality of organizational commitment is derived from both the bases and foci of commitment.

Managers can facilitate the development of organizational commitment through organizational practices that provide support to members, create a sense of fairness among members, enhance members' competence, and foster feelings of personal importance among members. Organizational commitment is related, albeit weakly, to performance. Even small increments in performance are significant in gaining a competitive edge. Note that the relationship between organizational commitment is stronger. Because turnover is costly in terms of replacing and training newcomers, managers need to be concerned with developing organizational commitment among their members.

The chapter also outlined the relationships among organizational and occupational commitment, job satisfaction, and job involvement. Organizational commitment and occupational commitment (i.e., identification with the values of the occupation) might be incongruent in some organizational con-

texts and congruent in other contexts. Job satisfaction is an immediate reaction to the job experiences and is variable as the job situation changes. Organizational commitment is a global attitude that takes time to develop and is stable over time. Finally, although job involvement contributes to higher and quality performance, the ideal worker is one who has a high level of both job involvement and organizational commitment. The least desirable worker is one who has a low level of both attributes.

Key Terms

organizational commitment, affective commitment, continuance commitment, normative commitment, foci of commitment, antecedents and consequences of organizational commitment, supportiveness and fairness, personal importance and competence, performance, turnover, job satisfaction, job involvement

Your Perspectives

- Considering your own experience with a sport or recreation organization, identify a person to whom or a unit to which you are committed. Describe your relationship with that person or unit. Explain the reasons or motives behind your commitment to that person or unit.

- Referring to that experience, what effect has such commitment had on your performance or satisfaction?

- Explain your commitment to other units or managers relative to your commitment to the focal person or unit.

- How would you describe your job involvement? How did it relate to your organizational commitment?

Conclusion: Founding and Guiding Themes

Learning Objectives

After reading this chapter you should be able to

- understand the general themes that should guide human resource practices in sport and recreation,
- relate the themes of this conclusion to the content of the previous chapters,
- describe the concept of person-organization fit, and
- explain the contingency view of human resource management in terms of production-line approach and empowerment approach.

As a conclusion to the book, this chapter brings together the salient principles on which effective management of human resources is founded and guided. In addition, the chapter places specific managerial practices described earlier under general themes that should drive and underlie all of those practices. These themes highlight human resource management practices from both humanistic perspectives and performance imperatives. Before beginning the discussion of the themes, this section reiterates the significance of human resource management itself. The increasing focus on human resource management should be viewed from several perspectives. One perspective is derived from financial imperatives of business enterprises. The growing realization is that all innovations in production technologies and processes basically are reliant on people who implement the policies and procedures of the organization. Managers expect any attention to human resource management to yield greater returns through greater productivity of the workers and their commitment to the organization. A careful reading of the literature on total quality management clearly shows that human resources at a manager's disposal are the ultimate source of quality and profits (Chelladurai 1995, Goetsch 1994).

While the financial and quality concerns are probably the immediate catalysts of any changes among organizations, they also constitute a transitory force. That is, such concerns may recede in good economic times, so the emphasis on human resource management also may fade away. Two other, rather permanent, forces are acting here. The first force is the increasing sophistication of both employees and consumers. As they become more and more educated and informed, their perceptions of what constitute good human resource management practices and their expectations for such practices increase. The cumulative effects of modern **worker-client awareness**, alertness, influence, and altered values have refocused management attention to human resources.

The second force is that organizations are agencies of society at large, and society sustains them. Because almost all adults within a society are workers of one organization or another, it is a societal duty for every organization to cater to the welfare of its workers and to enhance the quality of their life. Thus, management of human resources merits extreme care not only from the economic, efficiency, and quality perspectives, but also from the social responsibility perspective.

In a Nutshell

Effective human resource management practices should address the financial imperatives of the organization by making it more productive (profitable) and efficient. In addition, human resource management practices should also reflect the social responsibility of the organization by caring for, and addressing the needs of, its employees and clients.

Human Resource Management in Human Services

As noted in the introduction, human resources gain greater significance in service organizations because their products are intangible rather than tangible, customer involvement is necessary for the production of services, and the consumption of services occurs simultaneously with their production (Jackson and Schuler 1992, Schneider and Bowen 1992).

These fundamental differences cast the service providers, or the front-line workers, in a different, but more significant, role compared with the workers in conventional organizations. As Schneider and Bowen (1992, 1995) noted, frequent contacts of service providers with both the clients and the organization make them both a part of the organization and a part of the consumers' world. Thus, the service employees serve as **boundary spanners**. These

service providers then become the vital link between the organization and its critical markets. This view of service providers as boundary spanners has led to the suggestion that the service firm should be viewed as an inverted triangle (see figure 1). The front-line workers are at the top, and all other units including management should be viewed as support units (Fitzsimmons and Fitzsimmons 1994; Grönroos 1990; Schneider, Wheeler, and Cox 1992). For example, the tennis professional in a tennis club (or a fitness instructor in a fitness club) is the person who delivers the service directly to the club's clients. Therefore, the tennis professional gains a prominent place in the organizational structure of the club. Other units, such as facility and equipment maintenance, reception, and accounting, provide the support services to facilitate the core service that the tennis professional provides. Finally, management coordinates the activities of all units and creates an environment to enhance the quality of the service that the tennis professional provides. The idea of an inverted triangle is only to contrast it from the traditional bureaucratic hierarchy in which management sits at the top and issues orders to those below including the service providers.

The role of service providers as boundary spanners is much more pronounced in the case of human services. Human services are unique because the inputs are humans. The input is variable in terms of age, gender, and fitness, for example. Because the input is variable, the processes cannot be standardized. Although client expectations are legitimate, only professional experts decide on the service to be

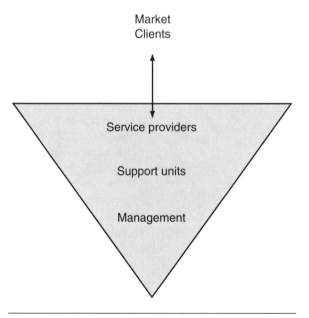

Figure 1   Service providers as boundary spanners.

provided. Finally, sport and recreation clients who are the input get involved actively in the process (Williamson 1991).

As noted, the last factor (i.e., the active involvement of sport and recreation clients in the production of participant services) is problematic in two different ways. First, the client's active involvement may hinder the employee's activities and judgment. The other problem is that the client may not be compliant to expert directions (Hasenfeld 1983). These two issues are accentuated in the sport and recreation context because production of some of the services requires the clients to engage in quite agonistic and prolonged activities. For instance, the provision of fitness and health-oriented services depends on the extent to which the clients adhere to the guidance of the service provider and participate in vigorous activities. Similarly, pursuit of excellence in a sport requires the client to be involved in strenuous practice sessions and to forego other more pleasurable activities. These unique characteristics of human services in sport and recreation highlight the significance of human resource management in ensuring that the service providers are professionally competent and, at the same time, are skilled in social interactions. In addition, the human resource management practices are fundamental to the delivery of quality services in the sport and recreation field.

In a Nutshell

Human resource management practices take on added significance in human services because the workers have to address human inputs who are variable and whose involvement is critical to the production of those services.

Human Resource Management and Strategic Management

As the significance of human resource management gains increasing recognition, researchers have suggested that it should be part of the strategic management, particularly in the service industry (Grönroos 1990, Schneider and Bowen 1995). **Strategic management** refers to identification of goals for an organization, the delineation of its market, and the specification of necessary processes to achieve the organizational goals. In essence, strategic management defines the business in which the organization is and the market in which it serves. From this perspective, consideration of human resource management practices must be consonant with the business of an organization and its market. In accordance with the foregoing, the following sections present themes that should serve as foundations of formulating and implementing an effective program of human resource management.

Theme One: Products

The introduction discussed the notion that every organization or industry exists to exchange a product or products with its environment and that the production and marketing of those products define the industry and the organizations within it. Accordingly, the introduction presented the classes of services that sport and recreation organizations produce and presented the differences among them. The three major classes of sport products or services are **participant services**, **spectator services**, and **sponsorship services**. The participant services include

- consumer-pleasure or consumer-health services (i.e., scheduling facilities or equipment and organizing and conducting tournaments) for clients who may engage in the activity for pleasure or for health reasons;
- human-skills or human-excellence services (i.e., expert application of teaching technology and leadership) to develop clients skills and excellence; and
- human-sustenance or human-curative services (e.g., organizing and conducting exercise and fitness programs) to sustain the present status or to cure any deficiency in fitness, health, or physical appearance.

In a Nutshell

The type of services that the organization produces has an impact on human resource management practices. Participant services, spectator services, and sponsorship services are broad classifications of these services. Spectator and sponsorship services are offshoots of human excellence services that are one form of participant services.

A clear understanding of the products of a sport and recreation organization is essential for instituting human resource practices. For instance, the type of employees hired, their training, and their performance evaluation in a consumer services operation are different from those in a human services operation. Thus, a sport organization needs to define its own business (i.e., its products) before instituting specific human resource management programs.

Theme Two: People

Another consideration in instituting human resource management practices is to understand the types of people or the human resources available to a sport organization. Generally, three forms of human resources are involved in the production and marketing of sport services—volunteer workers, paid professional workers, and clients. From the perspective of strategic management, these three forms of human resources constitute the internal and external markets. Chapters 1, 2, and 3 discussed the attributes of these three forms of human resources. The following sections summarize those chapters.

Volunteers

As noted in chapter 1, approximately 10% of the American population extend their time and efforts in promoting and organizing sport and recreation, and their services exceed in quantity those that the professional sport organizations render. In fact, the estimated $15 billion value of volunteer work in sport and recreation is an impressive figure indeed compared with the total worth of $10 billion of all major league professional sports in North America (Howard and Crompton 1995). In addition to the economic value, **volunteers** bring credibility and legitimacy to an organization, objectivity and open mindedness in evaluating organizational activities, creativity in designing organizational activities and processes, and conductivity for connecting with the community. Thus, sport and recreation managers must be cognizant of these benefits and make every effort to recruit and retain volunteers.

One significant area to which managers should be tuned is the incentives that motivate volunteers. Knoke and Prensky (1984) presented three broad categories of incentives. The utilitarian incentives may take the form of extending the household work of child-rearing and child-minding functions or enhancing one's abilities, expertise, and experience through volunteer work. The affective incentives reflect one's desire for interpersonal relations, sense of belonging to a group, and the prestige and status associated with such membership. Finally, the normative incentives reflect one's sense of doing what is right and what is good for the community that, in turn, may be embedded in organizational goals and programs. In an effort to make the best use of

available volunteers, sport and recreation managers need to gain an insight into what incentives are critical for the volunteers within the organization and how organizational activities can provide these incentives.

Professionals

Chapter 2 provided an elaborate description of what a profession is and how an occupation attains the **professional** status. A critical issue for sport managers is that the professionally oriented individuals are likely to prefer considerable autonomy in their jobs and that the principles and guidelines that external professional associates establish are likely to influence these individuals. These professional orientations are points of friction between an organization (including its managers) and the professionally oriented worker. An astute manager balances these individual orientations and organizational requirements.

From a different perspective, it is not critical that workers in the sport and recreation field (including managers) be considered as professionals. Striving to be professional rather than to be a profession is more important. Being professional emphasizes the application of technical skills based on advanced education and training by competent personnel who follow codes of conduct or ethics and who are committed to their calling and serving the public.

Professionalism and Volunteerism

While conflicts between volunteer and professional workers in an organization may occur, such conflicts are likely to be transitory. Fundamentally, the desires to learn and know, to act or do something effectively, and to serve and help others impel both volunteer and professional workers. Thus, sport and recreation managers need to minimize the differences between the two sets of workers and highlight the underlying common core values that motivate them both.

Clients

The third set of human resource are the **clients** themselves. Chapter 3 discussed the reasons for including them and their attributes. The significance of clients as a set of human resources hinges on two factors. First, the only sustainable evaluation of services is based on the perceptions of the clients regarding how well a service provider performs (Zeithaml, Parasuraman, and Berry 1990). Second, as noted earlier, sport and physical activity services require the active physical exertion of the client or customer (Chelladurai 1992). Therefore, securing their compliance is necessary to ensure the production of the services. Thus, the clients constitute a significant set of human resources in the sport and recreation context.

Human resource management practices aimed at the clients must consider their motives for participation. Pursuit of pleasure, pursuit of skill, pursuit of excellence, or pursuit of health or fitness summarize these motives (Chelladurai 1992). Recall that the classification of sport services or products partly was based on client motives. People may participate in physical activity because they enjoy the kinesthetic sensations experienced in a physical activity or the competition that certain activities pose (e.g., a game of squash). Only during participation can they enjoy the pleasures that they seek. The desire to acquire physical skills is innate to the human species. This desire may impel people to participate in physical activity. That is, individuals may focus on perfecting their skills through continued vigorous physical activity. People possibly may participate in some form of physical activity to excel in that activity or in another activity. A weight lifter, a basketball player, and a discus thrower may train with weights in order to enhance their performance capability in their respective sports. Some others may participate in vigorous physical activity mainly for those health-related benefits, such as fitness, stress reduction, and relaxation, that accrue as a consequence of participation.

Although these motives are distinct from each other, the activities that are selected to satisfy any one of these motives may result in other outcomes. However, from the human resource management perspective, the primary purpose for participation in a program of physical activity must be established so that its development and implementation are smooth and coordinated. Further, the service providers (i.e., the paid and volunteer workers) have to be more attuned to client motives than the managers themselves are.

In a Nutshell

The human resources available to sport and recreation managers include volunteer and paid workers and the clients themselves. These sets of human resources have their own orientations, incentives, and motives. Effective human resource management practices cater to these varying needs and, at the same, forge them toward a common end.

A note of caution is in order. The view of clients as partial employees of the organization is restricted only to participant services. The clients or customers in spectator and sponsorship services do not participate in the production of the service, so they do not constitute our human resources.

Theme Three: Purposes of Human Resource Management

The chapters in part II detailed individual differences in ability, personality, values, and motivation. The chapters in part III were concerned with job design, staffing, leadership, performance appraisal, reward systems, and organizational justice. Collectively, they underscore the **purposes of human resource management**. This section expands on that theme and explicates further the purposes of human resource management from two perspectives—the organization and its members.

Organizational Perspective

When human resource management is viewed from the perspective of the organization, it needs to accomplish two important functions. According to Jackson and Schuler (1992), human resource management should ensure both the technical and control aspects of organizations. The concern in the technical perspective is to ensure that a person in a job has the right skills to effectively perform that job. Accordingly, the emphasis is placed on hiring the people with the right technical skills, training them further in those skills, appraising their performance, and compensating them on the basis of skill-related performance (Jackson and Schuler 1992). Because the delivery of consumer services requires simple skills, hiring and training the employees are also simple and straightforward. Replacement of employees also is easier (e.g., locker-room attendants or caretakers). Human services, however, require that the employees are well educated and highly trained in their specialties to be able to process the information flow and make optimal decisions. Further, replacing the human services employees (e.g., a tennis professional or an exercise physiologist) is difficult. Therefore, managers must handle with great care the recruiting, selecting, and hiring of these employees.

The control aspect (which this text labels citizenship) refers to the predictability and reliability of social interactions to ensure behavior according to organizationally approved norms and values. That is, social performance and job performance are the desired ends. In sum, the organization should design human resource management to develop technical, as well as citizenship, skills and behaviors.

Another useful scheme in the development of training programs is that of Humphrey and Ashforth (1994) who pointed out that two types of knowledge structures are necessary for effective service encounters. A script structure refers to a service worker's expectation for a series of coherently organized events in a successful service encounter and the alternative courses of action available for every event. Categorical knowledge refers to an understanding of the different types of clients with specific needs, wants, and personal characteristics. Such knowledge results in the development of prototypes of clients. According to Humphrey and Ashforth (1994): "Agents must have both categorical and script knowledge. Categorical knowledge helps them understand customers, whereas scripts help them understand the service options available to meet customers' varying needs" (p. 176). In the sport and recreation context, the training on categorical knowledge emphasizes the distinction among various classes of customers (e.g., youth, women, and the elderly) and their motives for participation (e.g., pleasure, excellence, or health). The script knowledge entails training in the technical skills needed to provide the service (e.g., techniques and strategies of coaching) and the various stages of providing that service (e.g., progressive training regimen during practice sessions).

Member Perspective

Schneider and Bowen (1992, 1993) suggested that human resource management should be designed to foster two kinds of climates within an organization—employee well-being and service. Creating a climate for employee well-being involves redesigning jobs to create more challenge and autonomy, ensuring the safety and security of employees, reducing their stress, and having superiors treat them warmly and considerately. The essential thrust of their argument is that "the culture employees experience will be the culture customers experience" (Schneider and Bowen 1995, 240). This is a form of osmosis whereby the effects of human resource management practices filter through to the clients. Schneider and Bowen (1992) noted that the climate for employee well-being is a necessary precondition for the service climate, but it does not presuppose such a service climate.

The climate for service entails, in addition to enriched jobs, the promotion of creativity and quality in service. Schneider, Wheeler, and Cox (1992)

called it the climate of passion for service. Along similar lines, Grönroos (1990) proposed that "[Human resource management] practices should be geared to foster a service culture where there is an appreciation for good service . . . [and which] is considered a natural way of life at work" (p. 244). Employee perceptions of passion for service result in greater responsiveness to customer opinion, efficient procedures for the delivery of service, and greater emphasis on service to external customers. In addition, passion for service is reflected in the human resource management practices of hiring, performance feedback, internal equity of compensation, and training. In summary, human resource management practices need to foster climate for employee well-being and a passion for service. Note also that the climate for service in the sport and recreation context does necessarily subsume the welfare of the clients.

Person-Organization Fit

The foregoing discussion of creating and maintaining both employee-oriented and service-oriented climates (Schneider and Bowen 1992) and the concerns with technical and control aspects (Jackson and Schuler 1992) clearly show: "The focus of HRM [human resource management] practices must be the *organization*, rather than the *job*. . . . Entry, training, and reward issues need to be reconceptualized so they address the organizational imperative of service" (Schneider and Bowen 1992, 8). That is, human resource management practices should be aimed at **person-organization fit** instead of the traditional person-job fit. Organizations must attempt to attract people with requisite personality and ability to participate and to promote the organizational climate for service and, at the same time, to perform effectively the tasks of a particular job. Figure 2 shows that the person-organization fit consists of the fit between one's knowledge, skills, and abilities and the task demands and consists of the fit between overall personality (i.e., traits, interests, and values) and the climate of the organization. In other words, the person must fit both the content and the context of the job.

The training programs of human resource management also should focus on "developing a *holistic view* of the service organization; developing *skills* concerning how various tasks are to be performed; and developing *communication and service skills*" (Grönroos 1990, 253). Similarly, Schneider and Bowen (1992) divided the content of training into technical job skills, interpersonal or customer relationships skills, and cultural values and norms.

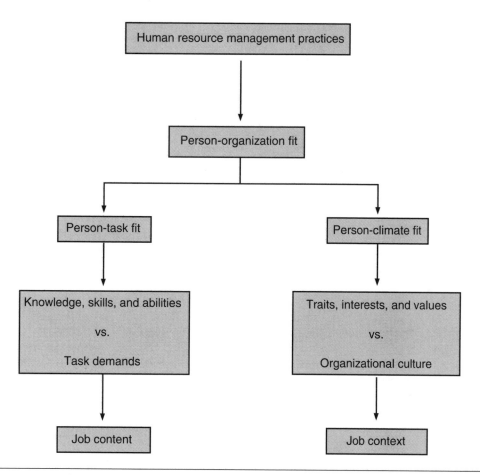

Figure 2   Components of person-organization fit.

Once the organization has recruited and trained the workers (i.e., both volunteer and paid workers), the next major task in human resource management is to institute structural and procedural mechanisms to motivate the employees. In this context, two emergent approaches or concepts are present—empowerment and organizational justice.

Theme Four: Empowerment

The dictionary meaning for the word "empower" is "to give power or authority to; to authorize; and to give ability to; to enable."

The two components of **empowerment** (i.e., having authority or power and having the ability to exercise that authority) are derived from organizational processes that include

1. designing jobs to ensure that individuals enjoy challenge, responsibility, and autonomy in jobs;
2. sharing power throughout the organization so that individuals are able to exercise appropriate authority in execution of their jobs;

3. sharing information about the organization, its units, and their performance so that individuals can make intelligent and effective decisions in carrying out their assignments;
4. sharing knowledge to perform various tasks of the organization to enhance the expertise and information base of members; and
5. sharing rewards based on organizational and individual performance (Schneider and Bowen 1995).

In a Nutshell

The major purposes of human resource management are to create a fit between the individual and the organization including the match between the abilities and orientations of the person with the requirements of the job and the convergence of a person's value and culture systems with those of the organization, and to cultivate a climate of employee well-being and a climate of service.

Recognize that empowerment strategy implies that managers have to let go of their authority and control and adjust to the new environment of empowerment. Another basic assumption is that members of an organization are willing and able to take on more authority and make good decisions and that they have the ability to effectively execute those decisions. Further, empowerment can be too expensive for low-cost, high-volume operations. Despite these limitations, the process of empowerment may prove to be beneficial and, at times, necessary. The best approach to take is to consider empowerment as a philosophy of management and to attempt to progressively institute the processes of empowerment.

A manager can better begin the process of empowerment with the content of a job. For example, a sport-marketing director may allow his or her employees autonomy in selecting would-be sponsors and in the manner in which they would present their case to the sponsors. This step is similar to job enrichment discussed in chapter 8. Allowing such discretion also empowers the marketing employee to the extent that he or she gets the authority or power to decide on the courses of action. Despite this move, the employee still may not be empowered fully because the goals of the organization, its organizational structure, the performance appraisal, and the reward systems may not support this empowerment initiative. To the extent that these contextual factors inhibit the realization of empowerment, they also must be modified to enhance the empowerment of employees. Because these factors span the whole organization, changing them takes considerable time and effort (Ford and Fottler 1995).

In a Nutshell

Empowerment is the passing of decision making authority and responsibility from managers to employees. Fundamentally, it is the process of encouraging and rewarding employee initiative and imagination.

What may prove to be problematic for the sport manager is the distinction between management practices toward empowerment (e.g., sharing of power and information) and the psychological empowerment that members actually feel. The notion of empowerment loses all its potency if members do not feel empowered. A member's feeling of being empowered is labeled psychological empowerment: "A motivational construct manifested in four cognitions: meaning, competence, self-determination, and impact. Together, these four cognitions reflect an active, rather than a passive, orientation to the work role" (Spreitzer 1995, 1444). These four cognitions, described in table 1, combine additively and lead to intrinsic task motivation.

Theme Five: Reward Systems

Chapter 12 presented a discussion of reward systems in greater detail. One concern with a reward system is whether it serves the purpose for which the manager created it in the first place. Note Kerr's (1975, 1995) consistent caution against a persistent folly of most reward systems. In his view, the conventional reward systems tend to reward noncritical behaviors and hope for more critical behaviors.

Table 1   Dimensions of Psychological Empowerment

Dimension	Description
Meaning	Meaning refers to the value of a work goal. It is a fit between the requirements of a work role and beliefs, values, and behaviors.
Competence	Competence refers to an individual's belief in his or her capability to perform activities with skill. The focus is on efficacy to a specific work role (not global efficacy).
Self-determination	Self-determination refers to an individual's sense of having choice in initiating and regulating actions. It reflects autonomy in the initiation and continuation of work behaviors and processes.
Impact	Impact refers to the degree to which an individual can influence strategic, administrative, or operating outcomes at work.

Adapted from Spreitzer 1995.

Most businesses and government agencies reward their employees for regular attendance or punish them for absence and tardiness. For instance, a city recreation department may reward its employees for reporting as scheduled for work and special assignments. The department hopes that the employees in attendance will carry out the assignments adequately. In sports, the manager or coach emphasizes teamwork but rewards star performers more so than other team members. Kerr (1995) suggested that this folly of rewarding A and hoping for B persists because managers

- are fascinated with objective criteria, such as attendance or the number of points scored in a game;
- overemphasize highly visible behaviors; and
- emphasize morality or equality rather than efficiency.

Because services are intangible, the associated critical employee behaviors cannot be assessed easily. Therefore, managers may take the easy way out and may reward their employees on the basis of their attendance or the number of clients that they serve. The issue is accentuated in the case of human services. From a different perspective, reward systems in service operations may fail if they rely solely on monetary rewards that can satisfy only the needs for security (Schneider and Bowen 1995). Sport and recreation managers must understand the dynamics of intrinsic rewards inherent in delivering a service and must foster such rewards because they satisfy the needs for achievement and self-esteem.

In a Nutshell

Managers should focus reward systems, which are one element of human resource management, more on the specific goals set for individuals and reward attainment of goals (i.e., outcomes) and should reduce the emphasis on the associated processes (e.g., attendance).

Theme Six: Organizational Justice

Chapter 13 outlined the concept of **organizational justice** as an emerging area of concern in human resource management. A manager's responsibility to uphold organizational justice is relatively more critical in the areas of personnel and budgetary

decisions, policies and procedures associated with those decisions, and management's and leadership's treatment of the workers in dispensing the decisions. These respectively are called

- distributive justice (which refers to the outcomes to individuals or groups),
- procedural justice (which refers to the procedures used to come to decisions), and
- interactional justice (which refers to the manner in which a decision is communicated to individuals).

As also noted, the chosen principle for distribution of resources (i.e., equity, equality, or need) should be consistent with organizational values and purposes. In a solidarity-oriented organization, the principle of equality may be more relevant, but in a productivity-oriented organization the principle of equity may be more appropriate. Procedural justice can be maintained if managers

- consistently apply the procedures over time and across individuals,
- suppress personal and built-in biases,
- represent the concerns of all parties,
- conform to community standards of ethics and morality,
- allow for correcting any wrong decisions that have been made, and
- make public all procedures in advance of acting on those procedures.

Finally, interactional justice largely is based on how managers and supervisors interact with their subordinates. Although positive supervisor-subordinate interactions are important in general, they are more critical when managers have to announce personnel and budgetary decisions to the concerned parties. Even though the actual decisions and associated processes would have been fair, the perceptions of such fairness would be diminished if the recipients believe that the communication of such decisions was not straightforward or that the interaction was not warm.

Theme Seven: Contingency View of Human Resource Management

This section presents one final note on human resource management practices in sport and recreation. Bowen and Lawler's (1992) **contingency view**

In a Nutshell

A significant component of effective human resource management is the maintenance of organizational justice. Organizational justice consists of the fairness of the distribution of a given resource, fairness of the procedures employed to distribute the resource, and fairness and warmth with which employees are treated when communicating the distribution of resources.

of human resource management suggests that managers can overemphasize good human resource management practices. The point is that service employees must deliver according to the different expectations that different markets and customers hold. Figure 3 illustrates the two approaches to delivery of service. The first approach is the production-line approach that standardized and procedurally driven operations, task specialization, and low employee discretion characterize. The second approach is the empowerment approach, and it offers the employees autonomy and freedom from policies and procedures to enable them to present a flexible, spontaneous, problem-solving phase for customers.

The extent to which organizations may adopt either the production-line approach or one of the empowerment approaches depends on the costs and benefits of empowerment and the strategy of the firm. A high-volume, low-cost strategy entails the production-line approach. This strategy is characteristic of consumer services, such as renting of sport facilities, wherein low-skilled workers who can be trained or replaced with relative ease carry out the simple and routinized activities (Chelladurai 1985, 1992). In contrast, when an organization offers customized and personalized services, such as in human services, empowering service employees is warranted because they face nonroutine and complex encounters; they have to make independent decisions on the service they provide. The continuum at the bottom of figure 3 illustrates this contingency approach to human service practices.

Summary

In conclusion, human resource management as a component of strategic management must be tailored to be consistent with the type of business that a sport organization undertakes and the types of human resources at its disposal. Several themes serve as the foundation for effective human resource management. These themes describe the purposes of human resource management from the perspective of the organization as well as the individual, stress the need to create a fit between the person and organization, describe the notion of empowerment, and describe the three forms of organizational justice (i.e., distributive, procedural, and interactional). Finally, as noted, managers view human resource management from a contingent

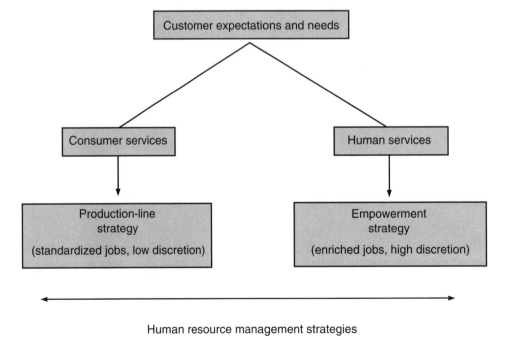

Figure 3   Contingency approach to human resource management.

In a Nutshell

Whether an organization adopts the production-line approach or the empowerment approach depends on the type of products it produces. The production-line approach is more appropriate with consumer services, and the empowerment approach is more appropriate with human services.

perspective, meaning that the appropriateness or effectiveness of specific human resource management practices depend on the type of organization, its goals, its products, the technologies associated with those products, and the markets it serves. These themes are powerful tools that sport and recreation managers may use in enhancing the human capital and securing member commitment and productivity.

Key Terms

worker-client awareness, boundary spanners, strategic management, participant services, spectator services, sponsorship services, volunteers, professional, clients, purposes of human resource management, person-organization fit, empowerment, organizational justice, contingency view

Your Perspectives

In responding to the following, keep the material from all chapters of the text in perspective.

- Recall your experiences in a specific paid or volunteer job. Identify a particular human resource management practice that you enjoyed and appreciated most. Explain.

- Based on your past experiences, what aspects of human resource management are addressed adequately in sport and recreation management? What aspects are not carried out well?

- From your perspective, what aspects of human resource management are more critical? Why?

- The chapter suggested a contingency approach to human resource management. Explain the concept. Have you had any experience with the production-line approach to human resource management? What were your reactions to that experience?

- Have you had any experience with the empowerment approach to human resource management? What were your reactions to that experience?

- Suggest examples of contexts in which the production-line approach would be more appropriate and in which the empowerment approach would be more meaningful.

References

Adams, J.S. (1963). Toward an understanding of inequity. *Journal of Abnormal Social Psychology, 67*, 422-436.

Adams, J.S. (1965). Inequity in social exchange. In L. Berkowitz (Ed.), *Advances in experimental social psychology* (Vol. 2, pp. 267-299). Santa Monica, CA: Goodyear.

Adams, J.S. (1977). Inequity in social exchange. In B.M. Staw (Ed.), *Psychological foundations of organizational behavior*. Santa Monica, CA: Goodyear.

Adler, N.J. (1990). *International dimensions of organizational behavior*. Boston: Kent.

Adorno, T., Frenkel-Brunswick, E., Levinson, D., & Sanford, R.N. (1950). *The authoritarian personality*. New York: Harper & Row.

Allport, G.W. (1937). *Personality*. New York: Holt, Rinehart & Winston.

Allport, G.W., & Odbert, H.S. (1936). Trait names: A psychological study. *Psychological Monographs, No. 47*.

Amis, J., & Slack, T. (1996). The size-structure relationship in voluntary sport organizations. *Journal of Sport Management, 10*, 76-86.

Anderson, J.C., & Moore, L.F. (1978). The motivation to volunteer. *Journal of Voluntary Action Research, 7*(3-4), 120-125.

Backman, S.J., & Crompton, J.L. (1991). The usefulness of selected variables for predicting activity loyalty. *Leisure Sciences, 13*, 205-220.

Ball, D.W. (1973). Ascription and position: A comparative analysis of "stacking" in professional football. *Canadian Review of Sociology and Anthropology, 10*(2), 97-113.

Balzer, W.K., Smith, P.C., Kravitz, D.A., Lovell, S.E., Paul, K.B., Reilly, B.A., & Reilly, C.E. (1990). *User's manual for the Job Descriptive Index (JDI) and the Job In General (JIG) scales*. Bowling Green, OH: Bowling Green State University.

Bandura, A. (1986). *Social foundations of thought and action: A social cognitive theory*. Englewood Cliffs, NJ: Prentice Hall.

Barney, J.B. (1986). Organizational culture: Can it be a source of sustained competitive advantage? *Academy of Management Review, 11*, 656-665.

Barrick, M.R., & Mount, M.K. (1991). The big five personality dimensions and job performance: A meta-analysis. *Personnel Psychology, 44*, 1-26.

Bass, B. (1982). Individual capability, team performance, and team productivity. In M.D. Dunnette & E.A. Fleishman (Eds.), *Human performance and productivity*. Hillsdale, NJ: Erlbaum.

Bass, B.M. (1985). *Leadership and performance beyond expectations*. New York: Free Press.

Bass, B.M. (1990, Winter). From transactional to transformational leadership: Learning to share the vision. *Organizational Dynamics*, 19-31.

Batson, C.D. (1991). *The altruism question: Toward a social-psychological answer*. Hillsdale, NJ: Erlbaum.

Beamish, R. (1985). Sport executives and voluntary associations: A review of the literature and introduction to some theoretical issues. *Sociology of Sport Journal, 2*, 218-232.

Beard, J.G., & Ragheb, M.G. (1980). Measuring leisure satisfaction. *Journal of Leisure Research, 12*(1), 20-33.

Becker, B., & Gerhart, B. (1996). The impact of human resource management on organizational performance. *Academy of Management Journal, 39*, 779-801.

Becker, H.S. (1960). Notes on the concept of commitment. *American Journal of Sociology, 66*, 32-42.

Becker, T.E. (1992). Foci and bases of commitment: Are they distinctions worth making? *Academy of Management Journal, 35*, 232-244.

Becker, T.E., Billings, R.S., Eveleth, D.M., & Gilbert, N.L. (1996). Foci and bases of employee commitment: Implications for job performance. *Academy of Management Journal, 30*, 464-482.

Beer, M. (1987). Performance appraisal. In J.W. Lorsch (Ed.), *Handbook of organizational behavior* (pp. 286-290). Englewood Cliffs, NJ: Prentice Hall.

Beer, M., & Spector, B. (1985). Corporatewide transformations in human resource management. In R.E. Walton & P.R. Lawrence (Eds.), *Human resource management HRM: Trends and challenges*. Boston: Harvard Business School Press.

Belcourt, M., Sherman, A.W., Bohlander, G.W., & Snell, S.A. (1996). *Managing human resources: Canadian edition*. Toronto: Nelson Canada.

Berry, L.L., & Parasuraman, A. (1991). *Marketing services: Competing through quality*. New York: Free Press.

Bies, R.J., & Moag, J.S. (1986). Interactional justice: Communication criteria of fairness. In R.J. Lewicki, B.H. Sheppard, & M.H. Bazerman (Eds.), *Research on negotiations in organizations* (Vol. 1, pp. 43-55). Greenwich, CT: JAI Press.

Bies, R.J., & Shapiro, D.L. (1987). Interactional fairness judgements: The influence of causal accounts. *Social Justice Research, 1*, 199-218.

Bitner, M.J. (1990). Evaluating service encounters: The effects of physical surroundings and employee responses. *Journal of Marketing, 54*, 69-82.

Blakley, B.R., Quintones, M.A., Crawford, M.S., & Jago, I.A. (1994). The validity of isometric strength tests. *Personnel Psychology, 47*, 247-274.

Blau, G., & Boal, K. (1989). Using job involvement and organizational commitment interactively to predict turnover. *Journal of Management, 15*, 115-127.

Blau, G., Paul, A., & St. John, N. (1993). On developing a general index of work commitment. *Journal of Vocational Behavior, 42*, 298-314.

Blau, G.J. (1986). Job involvement and organizational commitment as interactive predictors of tardiness and absenteeism. *Journal of Management, 12*, 577-584.

Blau, G.J., & Boal, K.B. (1987). Conceptualizing how job involvement and organizational commitment affect turnover and absenteeism. *Academy of Management Review, 12*, 288-300.

Bowen, D.E., & Lawler, E.E. III (1992). The empowerment of service workers: What, why, how, and when? *Sloan Management Review, 33*, 31-39.

Broekhoff, J. (1979). Physical education as a profession. *Quest, 31*(2), 244-254.

Brown, M.A. (1976). Values—A necessary but neglected ingredient of motivation on the job. *Academy of Management Review, 1*(4), 15-23.

Brunkan, R.J. (1991). Psychological assessment in career development. In C.P. Hansen & K.A. Conrad (Eds.), *A handbook of psychological assessment in business* (pp. 237-257). New York: Quorum Books.

Bryant, J.E. (1993). Sport management and the interdependence with sport sociology: Sport as a social product. *Journal of Sport Management, 7*, 194-198.

Buchanan, B. (1974). Building organizational commitment: The socialization of managers in work organizations. *Administrative Science Quarterly, 19*, 533-546.

Burke, R.J. (1984). Mentors in organizations. *Group and Organizational Studies, 9*, 253-272.

Buskirk, R.H. (1974). *Modern management & Machiavelli.* New York: New American Library.

Byars, L.L., & Rue, L.W. (1994). *Human resource management* (4th ed.). Burr Ridge, IL: Irwin.

Campbell, J.P. (1993). A theory of performance. In Schmitt et al. (Eds.), *Personnel selection in organizations* (pp. 35-70). San Francisco: Jossey-Bass.

Campion, M.A., & Thayer, P.W. (1985). Development and field evaluation of an interdisciplinary measure of job design. *Journal of Applied Psychology, 70*(1), 29-43.

Canadian Olympic Association. (1986). *The state of the volunteer-professional relationship in amateur sport in Canada.* Montreal: Canadian Olympic Association.

Carron, A.V., & Chelladurai, P. (1981). Cohesiveness as a factor in sport performance. *International Review of Sport Sociology, 2*(16), 21-41.

Carter, N. (1983). Collaboration and combat in networking. In M.S. Moyer (Ed.), *Managing voluntary organizations: Proceedings of a conference* (pp. 63-76). Toronto: Faculty of Administrative Studies, York University.

Cattell, R.B. (1957). *Personality and motivation, structure and measurement.* Yonkers-on-Hudson, NY: World Book.

Certo, S.C. (1992). *Modern management: Quality, ethics, and the global environment* (5th ed.). Boston: Allyn & Bacon.

Chatman, J.A. (1989). Improving interactional organizational research: A model of person-organization fit. *Academy of Management Review, 14*, 333-349.

Chelladurai, P. (1976). Manifestations of agility. *CAHPER Journal, 42*(3), 36-41.

Chelladurai, P. (1978). *A contingency model of leadership in athletics.* Unpublished doctoral dissertation, University of Waterloo, Waterloo, ON.

Chelladurai, P. (1981). The coach as motivator and chameleon of leadership styles. *Science Periodical on Research and Technology in Sport.* Ottawa, ON: Coaching Association of Canada.

Chelladurai, P. (1984). Discrepancy between preferences and perceptions of leadership behavior and satisfaction of athletes in varying sports. *Journal of Sport Psychology, 6*, 27-41.

Chelladurai, P. (1985). *Sport management: Macro perspectives.* London, ON: Sports Dynamics Publishers.

Chelladurai, P. (1987). The design of sport governing bodies: A Parsonian perspective. In T. Slack & C.R. Hinings (Eds.), *The organization and administration of sport* (pp. 37-57). London, ON: Sports Dynamics Publishers.

Chelladurai, P. (1992). A classification of sport and physical activity services: Implications for sport management. *Journal of Sport Management, 6*, 38-51.

Chelladurai, P. (1993a). Leadership. In R.N. Singer, M. Murphey, & L.K. Tennant (Eds.), *Handbook of research on sport psychology* (pp. 647-671). New York: Macmillan.

Chelladurai, P. (1993b). Styles of decision making in coaching. In J.M. Williams (Ed.), *Applied sport psychology: Personal growth to peak performance* (2nd ed., pp. 99-109). Palo Alto, CA: Mayfield.

Chelladurai, P. (1994). Sport management: Defining the field. *European Journal for Sport Management, 1,* 7-21.

Chelladurai, P. (1995a). Total quality management in sport industry. *Journal of Japan Society of Sports Industry, 5*(1), 23-39.

Chelladurai, P. (1995b, September). *Human resource management in sport and recreation.* Keynote address presented at the Third European Congress on Sport Management, Budapest, Hungary.

Chelladurai, P. (1996, October). *Quality in sport services.* Paper presented at the plenary session of the Fourth European Congress on Sport Management, Montpelier, France.

Chelladurai, P., & Arnott, M. (1985). Decision styles in coaching: Preferences of basketball players. *Research Quarterly for Exercise & Sport, 56,* 15-24.

Chelladurai, P., & Carron, A.V. (1982, May). *Individual and task differences, and preferred leadership.* Paper presented at the annual conference of the North American Society for the Psychology of Sport and Physical Activity, College Park, MD.

Chelladurai, P., & Doherty, A. (1998). Styles of decision making in coaching. In J.M. Williams (Ed.), *Applied sport psychology: Personal growth to peak performance* (3rd ed.). (pp. 115-126) Mountain View, CA: Mayfield Publishing Company.

Chelladurai, P., & Haggerty, T.R. (1978). A normative model of decision styles in coaching. *Athletic Administrator, 13,* 6-9.

Chelladurai, P., Haggerty, T.R., & Baxter, P.R. (1989). Decision style choices of university basketball coaches and players. *Journal of Sport and Exercise Psychology, 11,* 201-215.

Chelladurai, P., Imamura, H., Yamaguchi, Y., Oinuma, Y., and Miyauchi, T. (1988). Sport leadership in a cross-national setting: The case of Japanese and Canadian university athletes. *Journal of Sport and Exercise Psychology, 10,* 374-389.

Chelladurai, P., & Kuga, D.J. (1996). Teaching and coaching group and task differences. *Quest, 48,* 470-485.

Chelladurai, P., Kuga, D.J., & O'Bryant, C.P. (in press). Individual differences, perceived task characteristics and preferences for teaching and coaching. *Research Quarterly for Exercise and Sport.*

Chelladurai, P., & Quek, C.B. (1995). Decision style choices of high school basketball coaches: The effects of situational and coach characteristics. *Journal of Sport Behavior, 17,* 276-293.

Chelladurai, P., & Riemer, H.A. (1997). A classification of facets of athlete satisfaction. *Journal of Sport Management, 11,* 133-159.

Chelladurai, P., & Saleh, S.D. (1980). Dimensions of leader behavior in sports: Development of a leadership scale. *Journal of Sport Psychology, 2,* 34-45.

Christie, R., & Geis, F. (1970). *Studies in Machiavellianism.* New York: Academic Press.

Cialdini, R.B., Schaller, M., Houlihan, D., Arps, K., Fultz, J., & Beamna, A.L. (1987). Empathy-based helping: Is it selflessly or selfishly motivated? *Journal of Personality and Social Psychology, 52,* 749-758.

Cleave, S. (1993). A test of the Job Characteristics Model with administrative positions in physical education and sport. *Journal of Sport Management, 7,* 228-242.

Cleveland, J.N., Murphy, K.R., & Williams, R.E. (1989). Multiple uses of performance appraisal: Prevalence and correlates. *Journal of Applied Psychology, 74,* 130-135.

Cohen, R.L. (1987). Distributive justice: Theory and research. *Social Justice Research, 1,* 19-40.

Conger, J.A., & Kanungo, R.N. (1987). Toward a behavioral theory of charismatic leadership in organizational settings. *Academy of Management Review, 12,* 637-647.

Conger, J.A., & Kanungo, R.N. (Eds.). (1988). *Charismatic leadership.* San Fransisco: Jossey-Bass.

Connor, P.E., & Becker, B.W. (1975). Values and the organization: Suggestions for research. *Academy of Management Journal, 18*(3), 550-561.

Courneya, K.S., & Chelladurai, P. (1991). A model of performance measures in baseball. *Journal of Sport and Exercise Psychology, 13,* 16-25.

Cox, T.H., Jr. (1991). The multicultural organization. *The Academy of Management Executive, 5,* 34-47.

Cox, T.H., Jr. (1993). *Cultural diversity in organizations.* San Francisco: Berrett-Koehler.

Cratty, B.J. (1989). *Psychology in contemporary sport.* Englewood, NJ: Prentice Hall.

Davis H.J., & Rasool, S.A. (1988). Values research and managerial behavior: Implications for devising culturally consistent managerial styles. *Management International Review, 28,* 11-20.

Dawis, R.V., England, G.W., & Lofquist, L.H. (1964). A psychological theory of work adjustment. In *Minnesota Studies in Vocational Rehabilitation, XV.* Minneapolis: University of Minnesota Industrial Relations Center, Work Adjustment Project.

Dawis, R.V., & Lofquist, L.H. (1984). *A psychological theory of work adjustment: An individual-differences model and its applications.* Minneapolis: University of Minnesota Press.

De Cenzo, D.A., & Robbins, S.P. (1994). *Human resource management: Concepts and practices* (4th ed.). New York: Wiley.

Deutsch, M. (1975). Equity, equality, and need: What determines which value will be used as the basis of distributive justice? *Journal of Social Issues, 31*(3), 137-149.

Dishman, R.K. (1993). Exercise adherence. In R.N. Singer, M. Murphey, & L.K. Tennant (Eds.), *Handbook of research on sport psychology* (pp. 779-798). New York: Macmillan.

Doherty, A.J. (1997). The effect of leader characteristics on the perceived transformational/transactional leadership and impact of interuniversity athletic administrators. *Journal of Sport Management, 11*, 275-285.

Doherty, A.J., & Danylchuk, K.E. (1996). Transformational and transactional leadership in interuniversity athletic management. *Journal of Sport Management, 10*, 292-309.

Dovidio, J.F. (1995). With a little help from my friends. In G.G. Brannigan & M.R. Merrens (Eds.), *The social psychologists: Research adventures* (pp. 98-113). New York: McGraw-Hill.

Dreher, G.F., & Ash, R.A. (1990). A comparative study of mentoring among men and women in managerial, professional, and technical positions. *Journal of Applied Psychology, 75*(5), 539-546.

Drucker, P.F. (1992). *Managing for the future: The 1990s and beyond.* New York: Truman Talley Books/Dutton.

Edvardsson, B., & Olsson, J. (1996). Key concepts for new service development. *The Service Industries Journal, 16*, 140-164.

Edwards, J.N., & White, R.P. (1980). Predictors of social participation: Apparent or real? *Journal of Voluntary Action Research, 9*, 60-73.

Eitzen, D.S., & Sage, G.H. (1986). *Sociology of North American sport* (3rd ed.). Dubuque, IA: Brown.

Ellis, S.J., & Noyes, K.H. (1990). *By the people: A history of Americans as volunteers.* San Francisco: Jossey-Bass.

Etzioni, A. (1969). *The semi-professions and their organization.* New York: Macmillan.

Etzioni, A. (1973). The third sector and domestic missions. *Public Administration Review, 33*, 314-327.

Evans, M.G. (1986). Organizational behavior: The central role of motivation. *Journal of Management, 12*, 203-222.

Fagenson, E.A. (1989). The mentor advantage: Perceived career/job experiences of proteges versus non-proteges. *Journal of Organizational Behavior, 10*, 309-320.

Fiedler, F.E. (1954). Assumed similarity measures as predictors of team effectiveness. *Journal of Abnormal and Social Psychology, 49*, 381-388.

Fiedler, F.E. (1967). *A theory of leadership effectiveness.* New York: McGraw-Hill.

Fiedler, F.E. (1973). Personality and situational determinants of leader behavior. In E.A. Fleishman & J.G. Hunt (Eds.), *Current developments in the study of leadership* (pp. 41-60). Carbondale, IL: Southern Illinois University Press.

Fielding, L.W., Pitts, B.G., & Miller, L.K. (1991). Defining quality: Should educators in sport management programs be concerned with accreditation? *Journal of Sport Management, 5*, 1-17.

Fisher, C.D., & Locke, E.A. (1992). The new look in job satisfaction research and theory. In C.J. Cranny, P.C. Smith, & E.F. Stone (Eds.), *Job satisfaction: How people feel about their jobs and how it affects their performance* (pp. 165-194). New York: Lexington Books.

Fitt, L.W., & Newton, D.A. (1981). When the mentor is a man and the protege a woman. *Harvard Business Review, 59*(2), 56-60.

Fitzsimmons, J.A., & Fitzsimmons, M.J. (1994). *Service management for competitive advantage.* New York: McGraw-Hill.

Flashman, R., & Quick, S. (1985). Altruism is not dead: A specific analysis of volunteer motivation. In L.F. Moore (Ed.), *Motivating volunteers: How the rewards of unpaid work can meet people's needs.* Vancouver, BC: Vancouver Volunteer Center.

Fleishman, E.A. (1964). *The structure and measurement of physical fitness.* Englewood Cliffs, NJ: Prentice Hall.

Fleishman, E.A. (1972). Structure and measurement of psychomotor abilities. In R.N. Singer (Ed.), *The psychomotor domain: Movement behavior.* Philadelphia, PA: Lea and Febiger.

Fleishman, E.A. (1975). Toward a taxonomy of human performance. *American Psychologist, 30*, 1127-1149.

Fleishman, E.A. (1979). Evaluating physical abilities required by jobs. *Personnel Administrator, 21*(6), 82-90.

Fleishman, E.A. (1988). Some new frontiers in personnel selection research. *Personnel Psychology, 41*(4), 679-701.

Fleishman, E.A. (1992). *Fleishman Job Analysis Survey.* Bethesda, MD: Management Research Institute, Inc.

Fleishman, E.A., & Hempel, W.E., Jr. (1954). Changes in factor structure of a complex psychomotor test as a function of practice. *Psychometrika, 19*, 239-252.

Fleishman, E.A., & Quaintance, E.A. (1984). *Taxonomies of human performance.* Orlando, Florida: Academic Press, Inc.

Fleishman, E.A., & Reilly, M.E. (1992). *Handbook of human abilities: Definitions, measurement, and job task requirements.* Bethesda, MD: Management Research Institute, Inc.

Fleishman, E.A., & Rich, S. (1963). Role of kinesthetic and spatial-visual abilities in perceptual-motor learning. *Journal of Experimental Psychology, 66*, 6-11.

Folger, R. (1987). Distributive and procedural justice in the work place. *Social Justice Research, 3*, 141-183.

Folger, R., & Greenberg, J. (1985). Procedural justice: An interpretive analysis of personnel systems. In K.M. Rowland & G.R. Ferris (Eds.), *Research in personnel and human resource management* (Vol. 3, pp. 141-183). Greenwich, CT: JAI Press.

Ford, R.C., & Fottler, M.D. (1995). Empowerment: A matter of degree. *Academy of Management Executive, 9*, 21-31.

Forsyth, P., & Danisiewicz, T.J. (1985). Toward a theory of professionalism. *Work and Occupations, 12*(1), 59-76.

French, W.L. (1990). *Human Resources Management* (2nd ed.). Boston: Houghton Mifflin Boston.

Friedson, E. (1973). Professions and the occupational principle. In E. Friedson (Ed.), *Professions and their prospects* (pp. 19-38). Beverly Hills, CA: Sage.

Frisby, W., & Kikulis, L. (1996). Human resource management in sport. In B.L. Parkhouse (Ed.), *The management of sport: Its foundation and application* (2nd ed., pp. 102-118). St. Louis, MO: Mosby.

Gaskill, L.R. (1991). Same-sex and cross-sex mentoring of female proteges: A comparative analysis. *The Career Development Quarterly, 40*, 48-63.

Gelfand, M.J., Kuhn, K.M., & Radhakrishnan, P. (1996). The effect of value differences on social interaction processes and job outcomes: Implications for managing diversity. In M.N. Ruderman, M.W. Hughes-James, & S.E. Jackson (Eds.), *Selected research on work team diversity* (pp. 53-71). Washington, DC: American Psychological Association.

George, J.M. (1992). The role of personality in organizational life: Issues and evidence. *Journal of Management, 18*(2), 185-213.

Gidron, B. (1983). Sources of job satisfaction among service volunteers. *Journal of Voluntary Action Research, 12,* 20-35.

Gilbert L.A., & Rossman, K.M. (1992). Gender and the mentoring process for women: Implications for professional development. *Professional Psychology: Research and Practice, 23*(3), 233-238.

Gill, D.L., Gross, J.B., & Huddleston, S. (1983). Participation motives in youth sports. *International Journal of Sport Psychology, 14*, 1-14.

Gilliland, S.W. (1993). The perceived fairness of selection systems: An organizational justice perspective. *Academy of Management Review, 18,* 694-734.

Goetsch, D.L. (1994). *Introduction to total quality: Quality, productivity, competitiveness.* New York: Macmillan.

Goldberg, L.R. (1990). An alternative "description of personality": The Big-Five factor structure. *Journal of personality and social psychology, 59,* 1216-1229.

Goldthwait, J.T. (1996). *Values: What they are & how we know them.* Amherst, NY: Prometheus Books.

Goode, W. J. (1969). The theoretical limits of professionalization. In A. Etzioni (Ed.), *The semi-professions and their organization* (pp. 266-313). New York: Free Press.

Gordon, C.W., & Babchuk, N. (1959). A typology of volunteer organizations. *American Sociological Review, 24,* 22-29.

Gordon, L.V. (1970). Measurement of bureaucratic orientation. *Personnel Psychology, 23,* 1-11.

Gottlieb, B.H., Kelloway, E.K., & Barham, E.J. (1998). *Flexible work arrangements: Managing the work-family boundary.* Chichester, West Sussex, England: John Wiley & Sons.

Gough, H.G. (1969). *California Psychological Inventory* (Rev. ed.). Palo Alto, CA: Consulting Psychologists Press.

Gough, H.G. (1984). A managerial potential scale for the California Psychological Inventory. *Journal of Applied Psychology, 69,* 233-240.

Government of Canada (1992). *Sport: The way ahead.* The report of the Minister's Task Force on Federal Sport Policy (H93-104/1992E). Ottawa, ON: Fitness and Amateur Sport, Government of Canada.

Graves, C.W. (1970). Levels of existence: An open system theory of values. *Journal of Humanistic Psychology, X*(2), 131-155.

Greenberg, J. (1990). Organizational justice: Yesterday, today, and tomorrow. *Journal of Management, 16,* 399-432.

Greenberg, J., Mark, M.M., & Lehman, D.R. (1985). Justice in sports and games. *Journal of Sport Behavior, 8*(1), 18-33.

Greer, D.L., & Stewart, M.J. (1989). Children's attitude toward play: An investigation of their context specificity and relationship to organized sport experiences. *Journal of Sport and Exercise Psychology, 11,* 336-342.

Grönroos, C. (1990). *Services marketing and management.* Lexington, MA: Lexington Books.

Grove, S.J., & Dodder, R.A. (1982). Constructing measures to assess perceptions of sport functions: An exploratory investigation. *International Journal of Sport Psychology, 13,* 96-106.

Guilford, J.P. (1967). *The nature of human intelligence.* New York: McGraw-Hill.

Hackman, J.R., & Lawler, E.E. (1971). Employee reactions to job characteristics. *Journal of Applied Psychology Monograph, 55,* 259-286.

Hackman, J.R., & Oldham, G.R. (1976). Motivation through the design of work: Test of a theory. *Organizational Behavior and Human Performance, 16,* 250-279.

Hackman, J.R., & Oldham, G.R. (1980). *Work design.* Reading, MA: Addison-Wesley.

Hackman, J.R., Oldham, G., Janson, R., & Purdy, K. (1975). A new strategy for job enrichment. *California Management Review, 17*(4), 57-71.

Hall, D.T. (1976). *Careers in organizations.* Pacific Palisades, CA: Goodyear.

Halpin, A.W., & Winer, B.J. (1957). A factorial study of the leader behavior description. In R.M. Stogdill & A.E. Coons (Eds.), *Leader behavior: Its description & measurement.* Columbus, OH: The Ohio State University.

Handy, C. (1992). Types of voluntary organizations. In J. Batsleer, C. Cornforth, & R. Paton (Eds.), *Issues in voluntary and non-profit management* (pp. 13-17). Reading, MA: Addison-Wesley.

Hansen, H., & Gauthier, R. (1989). Factors affecting attendance at professional sport events. *Journal of Sport Management, 3,* 15-32.

Hasenfeld, Y. (1983). *Human service organizations.* Englewood Cliffs, NJ: Prentice Hall.

Hasenfeld, Y., & English, R.A. (1974). Human service organizations: A conceptual overview. In Y. Hasenfeld & R.A. English (Eds.), *Human service organizations: A book of readings* (pp. 1-23). Ann Arbor, MI: The University of Michigan Press.

Hathaway, S.R., & McKinley, J.C. (1967). *Minnesota Multiphasic Inventory* (Rev. ed.). New York: Psychological Corporation.

Haug, M. (1975). The deprofessionalization of everyone? *Sociological Focus, 8,* 197-213.

Hay, R., & Gray, E. (1974). Social responsibilities of business managers. *Academy of Management Journal, 17,* 135-143.

Hellriegel, D., Slocum, J.W., & Woodman, R.W. (1992). *Organizational behavior* (6th ed.). St. Paul, MN: West Publishing Company.

Henderson, K.A. (1981). Motivations and perceptions of volunteerism as a leisure activity. *Journal of Leisure Research, 13*(3), 208-218.

Henderson, K.A. (1985). Issues and trends in volunteerism. *Journal of Physical Education, Recreation and Dance, 56*(1), 30-32.

Hendry, L.B. (1968). The assessment of personality traits in the coach-swimmer relationship and a preliminary examination of the "father-figure" stereotype. *Research Quarterly, 39,* 543-551.

Hendry, L.B. (1969). A personality study of highly successful and "ideal" swimming coaches. *Research Quarterly, 40,* 299-305.

Heneman, H.G., Schwab, D.P., Fossum, J.A., & Dyer, L.D. (1983). *Personnel/human resource management.* Homewood, IL: Richard D. Irwin, Inc.

Henry, F.M. (1960). Increased response latency for complicated movements and "memory drum" theory of neuromotor reaction. *Research Quarterly, 31,* 448-458.

Herzberg, F. (1966). *Work and the nature of man.* Cleveland: World.

Herzberg, F. (1968). One more time: How do you motivate people? *Harvard Business Review, 46,* 53-62.

Herzberg, F. (1987). One more time: How do you motivate people? *Harvard Business Review* [Exhibit I].

Herzberg, F., Mausner, B., & Snyderman, B. (1959). *The motivation to work.* New York: Wiley.

Hill, S.E., Bahniuk, M.H., & Dobos, J. (1989). The impact of mentoring and collegial support on faculty success: An analysis of support behavior, information adequacy, and communication apprehension. *Communication Education, 38*(1), 15-33.

Hilliard, S. (1990). Smashing the glass ceiling. *Black Enterprise, 21*(1), 99-108.

Hinings, C.R., & Slack, T. (1987). The dynamics of quadrennial plan implementation in national sport organizations. In T. Slack & C.R. Hinings (Eds.), *The organization and administration of sport* (pp. 127-151). London, ON: Sports Dynamics Publishers.

Hogan, J.C. (1991). Structure of physical performance in occupational tasks. *Journal of Applied Psychology, 76,* 495-507.

Hogan, J., Hogan, R., & Busch, C.M. (1984). How to measure service orientation. *Journal of Applied Psychology, 69,* 167-173.

House, R.J. (1971). A path-goal theory of leader effectiveness. *Administrative Science Quarterly, 16,* 321-338.

House, R.J., & Dessler, G. (1974). The path-goal theory of leadership: Some post hoc and a priori tests. In J.G. Hunt & L.L. Larson (Eds.), *Contingency approaches to leadership.* Carbondale, IL: Southern Illinois University Press.

House, R.J., & Mitchell, T.R. (1974). Path-goal theory of leadership. *Journal of Contemporary Business, 3,* 81-97.

House, R.J., & Podsakoff, P.M. (1994). Leadership effectiveness: Past perspectives and future directions for research. In J. Greenberg (Ed.), *Organizational behavior: The state of the science.* Hillsdale, NJ: Lawrence Erlbaum Associates.

Howard, D.R., & Crompton, J.L. (1995). *Financing sport.* Morgantown, WV: Fitness Information Technology, Inc.

Hoy, W.K., & Miskel, C.G. (1982). *Educational administration: Theory, research, and practice.* New York: Random House.

Hughes, C.L., & Flowers, V.S. (1975). Toward existentialism in management. *The Conference Board Record, 12,* 60-64.

Humphrey, R.H., & Ashforth, B.E. (1994). Cognitive scripts and prototypes in service encounters. *Advances in Services Marketing and Management, 3,* 175-199.

Hums, M.A., & Chelladurai, P. (1994a). Distributive justice in intercollegiate athletics: Development of an instrument. *Journal of Sport Management, 8,* 190-199.

Hums, M.A., & Chelladurai, P. (1994b). Distributive justice in intercollegiate athletics: The views of NCAA coaches and administrators. *Journal of Sport Management, 8,* 200-217.

Hunt, D., & Michael, C. (1983). Mentorship: A career training and development tool. *Academy of Management Review, 8,* 475-480.

Idaszak, J.R., & Drasgow, F. (1987). A revision of the Job Diagnostic Survey: Elimination of a measurement artifact. *Journal of Applied Psychology, 72,* 69-74.

Ilsley, P.J. (1990). *Enhancing the volunteer experience: New insights on strengthening volunteer participation, learning, and commitment.* San Francisco: Jossey-Bass.

Inglis, S. (1997). Roles of board in amateur sport organizations. *Journal of Sport Management, 11,* 160-176.

Inglis, S., Danylchuk, K.E., & Pastore, D. (1996). Understanding retention factors in coaching and athletic management positions. *Journal of Sport Management, 10,* 237-249.

Jackson, D.N. (1984). *Personality Research Form Manual.* Port Huron, MI: Sigma Assessment Systems, Inc.

Jackson, J. A. (1970). Professions and professionalization: Editorial introduction. In J.A. Jackson (Ed.), *Professions and professionalization* (pp. 3-15). Cambridge, MA: Cambridge University Press.

Jackson, S.E. (Ed.). (1992). *Diversity in the workplace: Human resources initiatives.* New York: Guilford Press.

Jackson, S.E., & Schuler, R.S. (1992). Human resource management practices in service-based organizations: A role theory perspective. *Advances in Services Marketing and Management, 1,* 123-157.

Jamieson, L.M. (1987). Competency-based approaches to sport management. *Journal of Sport Management, 1,* 48-56.

James, K., Chen, D., & Cropanzano, R. (1996). Culture and leadership among Taiwanese and U.S. workers: Do values influence leadership ideals? In M.N. Ruderman, M.W. Hughes-James, & S.E. Jackson (Eds.), *Selected research on work team diversity* (pp. 33-52). Washington, DC: American Psychological Association.

Jaros, S.J., Jermier, J.M., Koehler, J.W., & Sincich, T. (1993). Effects of continuance, affective, and moral commitment on the withdrawal process: An evaluation of eight structural equation models. *Academy of Management Journal, 36,* 951-995.

Jennings, E.E. (1967). *The mobile manager: A study of the new generation of top executives.* Unpublished doctoral dissertation, University of Michigan.

Johns, G. (1988). *Organizational behavior: Understanding life at work.* Glenview, IL: Scott, Foresman.

Jurkus, A.F. (1978). Professionalism in management. In L.R. Bittel & M.A. Bittel (Eds.), *Encyclopedia of professional management* (pp. 983-985). New York: McGraw-Hill.

Kabanoff, B. (1991). Equity, equality, power, and conflict. *Academy of Management Review, 16,* 416-441.

Kabanoff, B., and O'Brien, G.E. (1980). Work and leisure: A task attributes analysis. *Journal of Applied Psychology, 65,* 596-609.

Kanfer, R.L. (1990). Motivation theory and industrial/organizational psychology. In D.M. Dunnette (Ed.), *Handbook of industrial and organizational psychology* (pp. 75-170). Palo Alto, CA: Consulting Psychologists Press.

Kanter, R.M. (1977). *Men and women of the corporation.* New York: Basic Books.

Katz, D., Maccoby, N., Gurin, G., & Floor, L. (1951). *Productivity, supervision, and morale among railroad workers.* Ann Arbor, MI: University of Michigan.

Katz, D., Maccoby, N., & Morse, N. (1950). *Productivity, supervision & morale in an office situation.* Ann Arbor, MI: University of Michigan.

Katz, R.L. (1972). Skills of an effective administrator. *Harvard Business Review, 52,* 90-102.

Keeley, M. (1983). Values in organization theory and management education. *Academy of Management Review, 8,* 376-386.

Kerr, S. (1975). On the folly of rewarding A, while hoping for B. *Academy of Management Journal, 18,* 769-783.

Kerr, S. (1995). On the folly of rewarding A, while hoping for B. *Academy of Management Executive, 9,* 7-14.

Kerr, S., & Jermier, J.M. (1978). Substitutes for leadership: Their meaning and measurement. *Organizational Behavior and Human Performance, 22,* 375-403.

Killian, R.A. (1976). *Human resource management.* New York: AMACOM Press.

King, N. (1970). Clarification and evaluation of the two-factor theory of job satisfaction. *Psychological Bulletin, 74,* 18-31.

Klemp, G.O., Jr., & McClelland, D.C. (1986). What characterizes intelligent functioning among senior managers? In R.J. Sternberg & R.K. Wagner (Eds.), *Practical intelligence: Nature and origins of competence in the everyday world* (pp. 31-50). New York: Cambridge University Press.

Knight Foundation (1991). *Keeping faith with the student athlete: A new model for intercollegiate athletics.* Charlotte, NC: Knight Foundation.

Knoke, D. (1986). Associations and interest groups. *Annual Review of Sociology, 12,* 1-21.

Knoke, D., & Prensky, D. (1984). What relevance do organization theories have for voluntary associations? *Social Science Quarterly, 65*(1), 3-20.

Koehler, L.S. (1988). Job satisfaction and corporate fitness managers: An organizational behavior approach to sport management. *Journal of Sport Management, 2,* 100-105.

Korman, A.K. (1977). *Organizational behavior.* Englewood Cliffs, NJ: Prentice Hall.

Kouri, M.K. (1990). *Volunteerism and older adults.* Santa Barbara, CA: ABC-CLIO, Inc.

Kram, K.E. (1980). *Mentoring process at work: Developmental relationships in managerial careers.* Unpublished doctoral dissertation, Yale University.

Kram, K.E. (1983). Phases of the mentor relationship. *Academy of Management Journal, 26,* 608-625.

Kram, K.E. (1985). *Mentoring at work.* Glenview, IL: Scott, Foresman.

Landy, F.J., & Becker, W.S. (1987). Motivation theory reconsidered. In L.L. Cummings & B.M. Staw (Eds.), *Research in organizational behavior* (Vol. 9, pp. 1-38). Greenwich, CT: JAI Press.

Lawler, E.E. III. (1973). *Motivation in work organizations.* Pacific Grove, CA: Brooks/Cole.

Lawler, E.E. III (1987). The design of effective reward systems. In J.W. Lorsch (Ed.), *Handbook of organizational behavior* (pp. 255-271). Englewood Cliffs, NJ: Prentice Hall.

Lawrence, P.R., & Lorsch, J.W. (1967). *Organization and environment: Managing differentiation and integration.* Boston: Harvard University Press.

Lawson, H.A. (1979). Paths toward professionalization. *Quest, 31*(2), 231-243.

Lawson, H.A. (1985). Knowledge for work in the physical education profession. *Sociology of Sport Journal, 2,* 9-24.

Lefton, L.A. (1991). *Psychology.* Boston: Allyn & Bacon.

Legge, K. (1995). HRM: Rhetoric, reality and hidden agendas. In J. Storey (Ed.), *Human resource management* (pp. 33-59). London: Routledge.

Lengnick-Hall, C.A. (1995). The patient as the pivot point for quality in health care delivery. *Hospital and Health Services Administration, 38*(3), 45-56.

Lengnick-Hall, C.A. (1996). Customer contributions to quality: A different view of the customer-oriented firm. *Academy of Management Review, 21,* 791-824.

Leventhal, G.S. (1980). What should be done with equity theory? New approaches to the study of fairness in social relationships. In K.J. Gergen, M.S. Greenberg, & R.H. Willis (Eds.), *Social exchange: Advances in theory and research* (pp. 27-55). New York: Plenum Press.

Levinson, D.J. (1978). *The seasons of a man's life.* New York: Knopf.

Levitt, T. (1973). *The third sector: New tactics for a responsive society.* New York: AMACOM Press.

Lewin, K. (1935). *A dynamic theory of personality.* New York: McGraw-Hill.

Li, M. (1993). Job satisfaction and performance of coaches of the spare-time sports schools in China. *Journal of Sport Management, 7,* 132-140.

Lillibridge, J.R., & Williams, K.J. (1992). Another look at personality and managerial potential: Application of the five factor model. In K. Kelley (Ed.), *Issues, theory, and research in industrial organizational psychology* (pp. 91-113). Amsterdam: Elsevier Science.

Local Government Management Board (1993). Managing tomorrow. In *Panel of Inquiry Report* (p. 8). London, England: Local Government Management Board.

Locke, E.A. (1976). The nature and causes of job satisfaction. In M.M. Dunnette (Ed.), *Handbook of industrial and organizational psychology.* Chicago: Rand McNally.

London, M. (1991). Career development. In K.N. Wexley (Ed.), *Developing human resources* (pp. 5.152-5.184). Washington, DC: The Bureau of National Affairs, Inc.

Longenecker, C.O., Sims, H.P., & Gioia, D.A. (1987). Behind the mask: The politics of employee appraisal. *The Academy of Management Executive, 1,* 183-193.

Lorsch, J.W., & Morse, J.J. (1974). *Organizations and their members: A contingency approach.* New York: Harper & Row.

Lovelock, C.H. (1996). *Service Marketing* (3rd ed.). Englewood Cliffs, NJ: Prentice Hall.

Luthans, F. (1985). *Organizational behavior* (4th ed.). New York: McGraw-Hill.

MacLean, J.C., & Chelladurai, P. (1995). Dimensions of coaching performance: Development of a scale. *Journal of Sport Management, 9,* 194-207.

Maddi, S.R. (1980). *Personality theories: A comparative analysis* (4th ed.). Homewood, IL: Dorsey.

Maehr, M.L., & Braskamp, L.A. (1986). *The motivation factor: A theory of personal investment.* Lexington, MA: Lexington Books.

Mark, M.M., & Greenberg, J. (1987). Evening the score. *Psychology Today, 21*(1), 44-50.

Martin, C.L. (1990). The employee/customer interface: An empirical investigation of employee behaviors and customer perceptions. *Journal of Sport Management, 4,* 1-20.

Maslow, A.H. (1943). A theory of human motivation. *Psychological Review, 50,* 370-396.

Mason, D.E. (1984). *Voluntary nonprofit enterprise management.* New York: Plenum Press.

Mathieu, J.E., & Zajac, D.M. (1990). A review and meta-analysis of the antecedents, correlates, and consequences of organizational commitment. *Psychological Bulletin, 108,* 171-194.

McClelland, D. (1996). Foreword. In N. Boulter, M. Dalziel, & J. Hill (Eds.), People and competencies: *The route to competitive advantage* (2nd ed., pp. 15-19). London: Kogan Page.

McClelland, D.C. (1961). *The achieving society.* New York: Van Nostrand.

McClelland, D.C. (1975). *Power: The inner experience.* New York: Irvington.

McClelland, D.C., & Burnham, D.H. (1976). Power is the great motivator. *Harvard Business Review, 54,* 100-110.

McClelland, D.C., & Winter, D.G. (1969). *Motivating economic achievement.* New York: Free Press.

McCrae, R.R., & Costa, P.T. (1987). Validation of the five-factor model of personality across instruments and observers. *Journal of Personality and Social Psychology, 52,* 81-90.

McGee, G.W., & Ford, R.C. (1987). Two (or more?) dimensions of organizational commitment: Reexamination of the affective and continuance commitment scales. *Journal of Applied Psychology, 72,* 638-642.

McKechnie, J.L. (Ed.). (1976). *Webster's new twentieth century dictionary of the English language* (2nd ed.). Cleveland: Collins-World.

McPherson, B.D. (1975). Past, present and future perspectives for research in sport sociology. *International Review of Sport Sociology, 10*(1), 55-72.

McPherson, J.M., & Smith-Lovin, L. (1986). Sex segregation in voluntary organizations. *American Sociological Review, 51,* 61-79.

Meglino, B.M., Ravlin, E.C., & Adkins, C.L. (1989). A work values approach to corporate culture: A filed test of the value congruence process and its relationship to individual outcomes. *Journal of Applied Psychology, 74,* 424-432.

Meglino, B.M., Ravlin, E.C., & Adkins, C.L. (1992). The measurement of work value congruence: A field study comparison. *Journal of Management, 18,* 33-43.

Meindl, J.R. (1989). Managing to be fair: An exploration of values, motives, and leadership. *Administrative Science Quarterly, 34,* 252-276.

Merton, R.K. (1982). *Social research and the practicing professions.* Cambridge, MA: ABT Books.

Meyer, J.P., & Allen, N.J. (1991). A three-component conceptualization of organizational commitment. *Human Resource Management Review, I,* 61-89.

Meyer, J.P., & Allen, N.J. (1997). *Commitment in the workplace: Theory, research, and application.* Thousand Oaks, CA: Sage Publications Inc.

Meyer, J.P., Allen, N.J., & Gellatly, I.R. (1990). Affective and continuance commitment to the organization: Evaluation of measures and analysis of concurrent and time-lagged relations. *Journal of Applied Psychology, 75,* 710-720.

Miller, H.B. (1982). Altruism, volunteers and sociology. In J.D. Harman (Ed.), *Volunteerism in the eighties.* Washington, DC: University Press of America.

Mills, P.K., & Margulies, N. (1980). Toward a core typology of service organizations. *Academy of Management Review, 5,* 255-265.

Mills, P.K., & Morris, J.H. (1986). Clients as "partial" employees of service organizations: Role development in client participation. *Academy of Management Review, 11*(4), 726-735.

Mischel, W. (1973). Toward a cognitive social learning reconceptualization of personality. *Psychological Review, 80,* 252-283.

Mish, F.C. (Ed.). *Webster's ninth new collegiate dictionary.* (1986). Springfield, MA: Merriam-Webster.

Mitchelson & Slack. (1983). *The volunteer sport administrator.* Ottawa, ON: Canadian Association for Health, Physical Education, and Recreation.

Mondy, R.W., & Noe, R.M. (1993). *Human resource management* (5th ed.). Boston: Allyn & Bacon.

Morford, W.R. (1972). Toward a profession, not a craft. *Quest, 18,* 88-93.

Morrison, I. (1986). A new era for volunteerism: An overview. In *A new era for volunteerism.* Proceedings of a Conference. Toronto, ON, June 1-3, 1986. Toronto, ON: United Way of Greater Toronto.

Morrow, P.C., & Goetz, J.F. (1988). Professionalism as a form of work commitment. *Journal of Vocational Behavior, 32,* 92-111.

Morse, J.J. (1976). Person-task congruence and individual adjustment and development. *Human Relations, 28,* 841-861.

Morse, J.J., & Young, D.F. (1973). Personality development and task choices: A systems view. *Human Relations, 26*(3), 307-324.

Mount, M.K., & Barrick, M.R. (1995). The big-five personality dimensions: Implications for research and practice in human resources management. *Research in Personnel and Human Resources Management, 13,* 153-200. Greenwich, CT: JAI Press.

Mowday, R.T., Porter, L.W., & Steers, R.M. (1982). *Employee-organization linkages: The psychology of commitment, absenteeism, and turnover.* New York: Academic Press.

Moyer, M.S. (1985). Voluntary action research: A view from Canada. *Journal of Voluntary Action Research, 14*(2-3), 15-16.

Mullin, B.J., Hardy, S., & Sutton, W.A. (1993). *Sport marketing.* Champaign, IL: Human Kinetics.

Murray, H.A. (1938). *Explorations in personality.* New York: Oxford University Press.

Murrell, A.J. & Dietz, B. (1992). Fan support of sport teams: The effect of a common group identity. *Journal of Sport and Exercise Psychology, 14,* 28-39.

Mussen, P.H. (1963). *The psychological development of the child.* Englewood Cliffs, NJ: Prentice Hall.

Myers, D.C., Gebhardt, D.L., Crump, C.E., & Fleishman, E.A. (1993). The dimensions of human physical performance: Factor analysis of strength, stamina, flexibility, and body composition measures. *Human Performance, 6*(4), 309-344.

Myers, I. (1987). *Introduction to type: A description of the theory and application for the Myers-Briggs Type Indicator.* Palo Alto, CA: Consulting Psychologists Press.

Nadler, D.A., Hackman, J.R., & Lawler, E.E. III. (1979). *Managing organizational behavior.* Boston: Little, Brown.

NASPE-NASSM Joint Task Force. (1993). Standards for curriculum and voluntary accreditation of sport management education programs. *Journal of Sport Management, 7,* 159-170.

Newby, T.J., & Heide, A. (1992). The value of mentoring. *Performance Improvement Quarterly, 5*(4), 2-15.

Niehoff, B.P., & Moorman, R.H. (1993). Justice as a mediator of the relationship between methods of monitoring and organizational citizenship behavior. *Academy of Management Journal, 36,* 527-556.

Nieva, V.F., & Gutek, B.A. (1981). *Women and work.* New York: Praeger.

Noe, R.A. (1988). Women and mentoring: A review and research agenda. *Academy of Management Review, 13,* 65-78.

Odiorne, G.S. (1984). *Strategic management of human resources.* San Francisco: Jossey-Bass.

Ogasawara, E., & Chelladurai, P. (1998, May). *Gender differences in job satisfaction and commitment among NCAA coaches.* Paper presented at the annual conference of the North American Society for Sport Management. Buffalo.

Ogilvie, B.C., & Tutko, T.A. (1966). *Problem athletes and how to handle them.* London: Pelham Books.

O'Reilly, C.A., & Chatman, J. (1986). Organizational commitment and psychological attachment: The effects of compliance, identification, and internalization of prosocial behavior. *Journal of Applied Psychology, 71,* 492-499.

Organ, D.W. (1988). *Organizational citizenship behavior: The good soldier syndrome.* Lexington, MA: Lexington Books.

Osborn, R.N., & Hunt, J.G. (1975). An adaptive-reactive theory of leadership: The role of macro variables in leadership research. In J.G. Hunt & L.L. Larson (Eds.), *Leadership frontiers.* Kent, OH: Kent State University.

Ostroff, C. (1992). The relationship between satisfaction, attitudes, and performance: An organizational level analysis. *Journal of Applied Psychology, 77,* 963-974.

Palisi, B.J., & Jacobson, P.E. (1977). Dominant statues and involvement in types of instrumental and expressive voluntary associations. *Journal of Voluntary Action Research, 6,* 80-88.

Parasuraman, A., Zeithaml, V.A., & Berry, L.L. (1990). Perceived service quality as a customer-based performance measure: An empirical examination of organizational barriers using an extended service quality model. *Human Resource Management, 30*(3), 335-364.

Parsons, F. (1909). *Choosing a vocation.* Boston: Houghton Mifflin.

Pastore, D.L. (1994). Job satisfaction and female college coaches. *Physical Educator, 50*(4), 216-221.

Peter, L.J. (1972). *The Peter prescription: How to make things go right.* New York: Bantam Books.

Peters, R. (1987). *Practical intelligence: Working smarter in business and everyday life.* New York: Harper & Row.

Peterson, N.G., & Bownas, D.A. (1982). Skill, task structure, and performance acquisition. In M.D. Dunnette & E.A. Fleishman (Eds.), *Human performance and productivity.* Hillsdale, NJ: Erlbaum.

Pettinger, R. (1997). *Introduction to management.* (2nd ed.). London: Macmillan.

Phillips, M. (1982). Motivation and expectation in successful volunteerism. *Journal of Voluntary Action Research, 11*(2), 118-125.

Pierce, J.L., Newstrom, J.W., Dunham, R.B., & Barber, A.E. (1989). *Alternative work schedules.* Boston: Allyn & Bacon.

Pincus, C.S., & Hermann-Keeling, E. (1982). Self-help systems and the professional as volunteer: Threat or solution? *Journal of Voluntary Action Research, 11*(2-3), 85-96.

Pinder, C.C. (1984). *Work motivation.* Glenview, IL: Scott, Foresman.

Podsakoff, P.M., Ahearne, M., & MacKenzie, S.B. (1997). Organizational citizenship behavior and the quality and quantity of work group performance. *Journal of Applied Psychology, 82,* 262-270.

Podsakoff, P.M., MacKenzie, S.B., & Hui, C. (1993). Organizational citizenship behaviors and managerial evaluation of employee performance: A review and suggestions for future research. In G.R. Ferris (Ed.), *Research in personnel and human resource management* (Vol. 11, pp. 1-40). Greenwich, CT: JAI Press.

Porter, L.W., & Lawler, E.E. (1968). *Managerial attitudes and performance.* Homewood, IL: Irwin.

Poulton, E.C. (1957). On prediction in skilled movement. *Psychological Bulletin, 54,* 467-478.

Raelin, J.A. (1987). The professional as the executive's ethical aide-de-camp. *The Academy of Management Executive, 1*(3), 171-182.

Ragheb, M.G., & Tate, R.L. (1993). A behavioral model of leisure participation, based on leisure attitude, motivation and satisfaction. *Leisure Studies, 12,* 61-70.

Raghuraman, S., & Garud, R. (1996). The vicious and virtuous facets of workforce diversity. In M.N. Ruderman, M.W. Hughes-James, & S.E. Jackson (Eds.), *Selected research on work team diversity* (pp. 155-180). Washington, DC: American Psychological Association.

Ragins, B.R. (1989). Barriers to mentoring: The female manager's dilemma. *Human Relations, 42*(1), 1-22.

Ragins, B.R., & Cotton, J.L. (1991). Easier said than done: Gender differences in perceived barriers to gaining a mentor. *Academy of Management Journal, 34,* 939-951.

Rawls, J. (1971). *A theory of justice.* Cambridge, MA: Belknap Press.

Rees, W.D. (1996). *The skills of management* (4th ed.). London: International Thomson Business Press.

Reichers, A.E. (1985). A review and reconceptualization of organizational commitment. *Academy of Management Review, 10,* 465-476.

Reis, H.T. (1986). The multidimensionality of justice. In R. Folger (Ed.), *The sense of injustice* (pp. 25-61). New York: Plenum Press.

Rice, R.W., McFarlin, D.B., & Bennett, D.E. (1989). Standards of comparison and job satisfaction. *Journal of Applied Psychology, 74,* 591-598.

Riemer, H.A., & Chelladurai, P. (1998). Development of Athlete Satisfaction Questionnaire (ASQ). *Journal of Sport and Exercise Psychology, 20,* 127-156.

Riley, S., & Wrench, D. (1985). Mentoring among women lawyers. *Journal of Applied Social Psychology, 15,* 374-386.

Robbins, S.P. (1976). *The administrative process: Integrating theory and practice.* Englewood Cliffs, NJ: Prentice Hall.

Robbins, S.P. (1997a). *Essentials of organizational behavior* (5th ed.). Upper Saddle River, NJ: Prentice Hall.

Robbins, S.P. (1997b). *Managing today!* Upper Saddle River, NJ: Prentice Hall.

Rokeach, M. (1973). *The nature of human values.* New York: Free Press.

Rotter, J. (1966). Generalized expectancies for internal vs. external control of reinforcement. *Psychological Monographs, 80,* No. 1 (whole no. 609).

Saal, F.E., & Knight, P.A. (1988). *Industrial/organizational psychology: Science and practice.* Pacific Grove, CA: Brooks/Cole.

Saal, F.E., & Knight, P.A. (1995). *Industrial/organizational psychology: Science and practice* (2nd ed.). Pacific Grove, CA: Brooks/Cole.

Samson, E.E. (1969). Studies in status congruence. In L. Berkowitz (Ed.), *Advances in experimental social psychology, 4* (pp. 225-270). New York: Academic Press.

Sasser, W.E., Olsen, R.P., & Wyckoff, D.D. (1978). *Management of service operations.* Rockleigh, NJ: Allyn & Bacon.

Scandura, T.A., & Ragins, B.R. (1993). The effects of sex and gender role orientation on mentorship in male-dominated occupations. *Journal of Vocational Behavior, 43,* 251-265.

Schein, E.H. (1978). *Career dynamics.* Reading, MA: Addison-Wesley.

Schermerhorn, J.R., Hunt, J.G., & Osborn, R.N. (1985). *Managing organizational behavior* (2nd ed.). New York: Wiley.

Schermerhorn, J.R., Hunt, J.G., & Osborn, R.N. (1991). *Managing organizational behavior* (4th ed.). New York: Wiley.

Schermerhorn, J.R., Hunt, J.G., & Osborn, R.N. (1997). *Organizational behavior* (6th ed.). New York: Wiley.

Schindler-Rainman, E., & Lippit, R. (1975). *The volunteer community: A creative use of human resources* (2nd ed.). Fairfax, VA: NTL Learning Resources Corporation.

Schmenner, R.W. (1995). *Service operations management.* Englewood Cliffs, NJ: Prentice Hall.

Schneider, B., & Bowen, D.E. (1992). Personnel/human resource management in the service sector. *Research in Personnel and Human Resources Management, 10,* 1-30.

Schneider, B., & Bowen, D.E. (1993). The service organization: Human resources management is crucial. *Organizational Dynamics, 21*(4), 39-52.

Schneider, B., & Bowen, D.E. (1995). *Winning the service game.* Boston: Harvard Business School Press.

Schneider, B., Wheeler, J.K., & Cox, J.F. (1992). A passion for service: Using content analysis to explicate service climate themes. *Journal of Applied Psychology, 77,* 705-716.

Schneider, J., & Locke, E.A. (1971). A critique of Herzberg's classification system and a suggested revision. *Organizational Behavior and Human Performance, 12,* 441-458.

Schuler, R.S., & Jackson, S.E. (1996). *Human resource management: Positioning for the 21st century* (6th ed.). Minneapolis: West.

Schutz, R.W., Smoll, F.L., Carre, F.A., & Mosher, R.E. (1985). Inventories and norms for children's attitudes toward physical activity. *Research Quarterly for Exercise and Sport, 56,* 256-265.

Schwartz, S.H. (1992). Universals in the content and structure of values. In M. Zanna (Ed.), *Advances in experimental social psychology* (Vol. 25, pp. 1-65). New York: Academic Press.

Shapiro, G.L., & Farrow, D.L. (1988). Mentors and others in career development. In S. Rose & L. Larwood (Eds.), *Women's careers: Pathways and pitfalls.* New York: Praeger.

Sheldon, W.H. (1954). *Atlas of men: A guide to somatotyping the adult male at all ages.* New York: Harper & Row.

Sheppard, B.H. (1984). Third party conflict intervention: A procedural framework. In B.N. Staw & L.L. Cummings (Eds.), *Research in organizational behavior, 6* (pp. 141-190). Greenwich, CT: JAI Press.

Sills, D.L. (1972). Voluntary associations: Sociological aspects. In D.L. Sills (Ed.), *International encyclopedia of the social sciences* (Vol. 16). New York: Cromwell, Collier and MacMillan.

Singer, M.R. (1987). *Intercultural communication: A perceptual approach.* Englewood Cliffs, NJ: Prentice Hall.

Singer, R.N. (1972). *Coaching, athletics, and psychology.* New York: McGraw-Hill.

Slack, T.S. (1985). The bureaucratization of a voluntary sport organization. *The International Review for the Sociology of Sport, 20*(3), 145-165.

Smith, D.H. (1981). Altruism, volunteers, and volunteerism. *Journal of Voluntary Action Research, 10*(1), 21-36.

Smith, P.C. (1992). In pursuit of happiness: Why study general job satisfaction. In C.J. Cranny, P.C. Smith, & E.F. Stone (Eds.), *Job satisfaction: How people feel about their jobs and how it affects their performance* (pp. 5-19). New York: Lexington Books.

Smith, P.C., Kendall, L.M., & Hulin, C.C. (1969). *The measurement of satisfaction in work and retirement.* Chicago: Rand McNally.

Smith, S. (1986). Technology and its impact on the voluntary sector. In *A new era for volunteerism.* Proceedings of a conference. Toronto, ON, June 1-3, 1986. (pp. 82-89). Toronto, ON: United Way of Greater Toronto.

Snyder, C.J. (1990). The effects of leader behavior and organizational climate on intercollegiate coaches' job satisfaction. *Journal of Sport Management, 4,* 59-70.

Soliman, H.M. (1970). Motivation-hygiene theory of job attitudes. *Journal of Applied Psychology, 55,* 452-461.

Sonnenfeld, J.A., & Peiperl, M.A. (1988). Staffing policy as a strategic response: A typology of career systems. *Academy of Management Review, 13,* 588-600.

Spreitzer, G.M. (1995). Psychological empowerment in the workplace: Dimensions, measurement, and validation. *Academy of Management Journal, 38,* 1442-1465.

Sproull, L.S. (1984). Beliefs in organizations. In P.C. Nystrom & W.H. Starbuck (Eds.), *Handbook of organizational design: Vol. 2. Remodeling organizations and their environments* (pp. 203-224). New York: Oxford University Press.

Steckel, R., & Simons, R. (1992). *Doing best by doing good.* New York: Penguin Books.

Stephens, W.N. (1991). *Altruists and volunteers: Life histories.* Walla Walla, WA: MBA.

Stevenson, C.L. (1989). Perceptions of justice in the selection of national teams. *Sociology of Sport Journal, 6,* 371-379.

Stewart, R. (1982). The relevance of some studies of managerial work and behavior to leadership research. In J.G. Hunt, U. Sekaran, & C. Schriesheim (Eds.), *Leadership: Beyond establishment views* (pp. 11-30). Carbondale, IL: Southern Illinois University Press.

Stogdill, R.M. (1963). *Manual for the Leader Behavior Description Questionnaire-form XII.* Columbus, OH: The Ohio State University.

Stone, E.F., & Gueutal, H.G. (1985). An empirical derivation of the dimensions along which characteristics of jobs are perceived. *Academy of Management Journal, 28,* 376-396.

Storey, J. (1995). Human resource management: Still marching on, or marching out? In J. Storey (Ed.), *Human resource management* (pp. 3-32). London: Routledge.

Sullivan, W. (1997). *Entrepreneur Magazine: Human resources for small businesses.* New York: John Wiley & Sons, Inc.

Taylor, J.C., & Bowers, D.G. (1972). *Survey of organizations: A machine-scored standardized questionnaire instrument.* Ann Arbor, MI: Institute for Social Research, The University of Michigan.

Tedrick, T., & Henderson, K. (1989). *Volunteers in leisure.* Reston, VA: American Alliance for Health, Physical Education, Recreation, and Dance.

Tett, R.P., Jackson, D.N., & Rothstein, M. (1991). Personality measures as predictors of job performance: A meta-analytic review. *Personnel Psychology, 44,* 703-742.

Thibault, L., Slack, T., & Hinings, B. (1991). Professionalism, structures and systems: The impact of professional staff on voluntary sport organizations. *International Review for Sociology of Sport, 26*(2), 83-97.

Thibaut, J., & Walker, L. (1975). *Procedural justice: A psychological analysis.* Hillsdale, NJ: Erlbaum.

Thompson, J.D. (1967). *Organizations in action.* New York: McGraw-Hill.

Tocqueville, A. (1961). *Democracy in America.* Garden City, NJ: Doubleday.

Toren, N. (1975). Deprofessionalization and its sources. *Sociology of Work and Occupations, 2,* 323-337.

Törnblom, K.Y., & Jonsson, D.S. (1985). Subrules of the equality and contribution principles: Their perceived fairness in distribution and retribution. *Social Psychology Quarterly, 48,* 249-261.

Törnblom, K.Y., & Jonsson, D.S. (1987). Distribution vs. retribution: The perceived justice of the contribution and equality principles for cooperative and competitive relationships. *Acta Sociologica, 30,* 25-52.

Tosi, H.L., Rizzo, J.R., & Carroll, S.J. (1986). *Managing organizational behavior.* Marshfield, MA: Pitman.

Trail, G.T. (1997). *Intercollegiate athletics: Organizational goals, processes, and personal values.* Unpublished doctoral dissertation, The Ohio State University.

Turner, A.N., & Lawrence, P.R. (1965). *Industrial jobs and the worker: An investigation of response to task attributes.* Boston: Harvard Graduate School of Business Administration.

Tyler, T.R., & Bies, R.J. (1990). Beyond formal procedures: The interpersonal context of procedural justice. In J.S. Carroll (Ed.), *Applied social psychology and organizational settings* (pp. 77-88). Hillsdale, NJ: Erlbaum.

Ulrich, D. (1997). *Human resource champions: The next agenda for adding value and delivering results.* Boston: Harvard Business School Press.

U.S. Bureau of the Census. (1996). *Statistical Abstracts of the United States.* (116th ed.). Washington, DC: U.S. Bureau of the Census.

Vaillancourt, F., & Payette, M. (1986). The supply of volunteer work: The case of Canada. *Journal of Voluntary Action Research, 15*(4), 45-56.

Van de Ven, A.H., & Delbecq, A.L. (1974). A task contingent model of work-unit structure. *Administrative Science Quarterly, 19,* 183-198.

Vandenberg, R.J., & Scarpello, V. (1994). A longitudinal assessment of the determinant relationship between employee commitments to the occupation and organization. *Journal of Organizational Behavior, 15,* 535-547.

Vecchio, R.P. (1988). *Organizational behavior.* Chicago: Dryden Press.

Vroom, V.H. (1959). Some personality determinants of the effects of participation. *Journal of Abnormal and Social Psychology, 59,* 322-327.

Vroom, V.H. (1964). *Work and motivation.* New York: Wiley.

Vroom, V.H., & Jago, A.G. (1978). On the validity of the Vroom-Yetton model. *Journal of Applied Psychology, 63,* 151-162.

Vroom, V.H., & Jago, A.G. (1988). *The new leadership: Managing participation in organizations.* Englewood Cliffs, NJ: Prentice Hall.

Vroom, V.H., & Yetton, R.N. (1973). *Leadership and decision-making.* Pittsburgh: University of Pittsburgh Press.

Wallace, M., & Weese, W.J. (1995). Leadership, organizational culture, and job satisfaction in Canadian YMCA organizations. *Journal of Sport Management, 9,* 182-193.

Wann, D.L., & Branscombe, N.R. (1993). Sports fans: Measuring degree of identification with their team. *International Journal of Sport Psychology, 24,* 1-17.

Warriner, C.K., & Prather, J.E. (1965). Four types of voluntary associations. *Sociological Inquiry, 35,* 138-148.

Watson, D., & Clark, L.A. (1984). Negative affectivity: The disposition to experience aversive emotional states. *Psychological Bulletin, 96,* 465-490.

Watson, D., Clark, L.A., & Tellegen, A. (1988). Development and validation of brief measures of positive and negative affect: The PANAS scale. *Journal of Personality and Social Psychology, 54,* 1063-1070.

Weaver, M.A., & Chelladurai, P. (in press). A model of mentoring: Implications for sport and physical education. *Quest.*

Weber, M. (1947). *The theory of social and economic organization* (A.M. Henderson & T. Parsons, Trans.). New York: Oxford University Press. (Original work published 1922)

Weese, W.J. (1995). Leadership and organizational culture: An investigation of Big Ten and Mid-American Conference campus recreation administrators. *Journal of Sport Management, 9,* 119-134.

Weese, W.J. (1996). Do leadership and organizational culture really matter? *Journal of Sport Management, 10,* 197-206.

Weiss, D.J., Dawis, R.V., England, G.W. & Lofquist, L.H. (1967). *Manual for the Minnesota Satisfaction Questionnaire* (Minnesota Studies on Vocational Rehabilitation, vol. 22). Minneapolis, MN: Industrial Relations Center, Work Adjustment Project, University of Minnesota.

Werther, W.B., Davis, K., Schwind, H.F., Das, H., & Miner, F.C. (1985). *Canadian personnel management and human resources* (2nd ed.). Toronto, ON: McGraw-Hill Ryerson.

Whittal, N.R., & Orlick, T.D. (1978). The sport satisfaction inventory. In G.C. Roberts & K.M. Newell (Eds.), *Psychology of motor behavior and sport* (pp. 144-155). Champaign, IL: Human Kinetics.

Wicks, B.E., & Crompton, J.L. (1987). An analysis of the relationship between equity choice preferences, service type and decision making groups in a U.S. city. *Journal of Leisure Research, 19,* 189-204.

Wicks, B.E., & Crompton, J.L. (1990). Predicting the equity preferences of park and recreation department employees and residents of Austin, Texas. *Journal of Leisure Research, 22,* 18-35.

Wiener, Y. (1988). Forms of value systems: A focus on organizational effectiveness and cultural change and maintenance. *Academy of Management Review, 13,* 534-545.

Wilensky, H.L. (1964). The professionalization of every-one? *American Journal of Sociology, 70,* 137-158.

Williams, J.A., & Ortega, S.T. (1986). The multidimensionality of joining. *Journal of Voluntary Action Research, 15*(4), 35-44.

Williamson, J. (1991). Providing quality care. *Human Services Management, 87*(1), 18-27.

Wolensky, R.P. (1980). Toward a broader conception of volunteerism in disasters. *Journal of Voluntary Action Research, 8,* 43-50.

Wynne, B.E., & Hunsaker, P.L. (1975). A human information-processing approach to the study of leadership. In J.G. Hunt & L.L. Larson (Eds.), *Leadership frontiers.* Kent, OH: Kent State University.

Yiannakis, A. (1989). Some contributions of sport sociology to the marketing of sport and leisure organizations. *Journal of Sport Management, 3,* 103-115.

Young, D. (1990). Mentoring and networking: Perceptions of athletic administrators. *Journal of Sport Management, 4,* 71-79.

Yukl, G.A. (1981). *Leadership in organizations.* Englewood Cliffs, NJ: Prentice Hall.

Yukl, G.A. (1989). *Leadership in organizations* (2nd ed.). Englewood Cliffs, NJ: Prentice Hall.

Yukl, G.A., & Van Fleet, D.D. (1992). Theory and research on leadership in organizations. In M.D. Dunnette & L.M. Hough (Eds.), *Handbook of industrial and organizational psychology* (2nd ed., pp. 147-197). Chicago: Rand McNally.

Zeigler, E.F. (1989). Proposed creed and code of professional ethics for the North American Society for Sport Management. *Journal of Sport Management, 3,* 2-4.

Zeithaml, V.A., Parasuraman, A., & Berry, L.L. (1990). *Delivering quality service: Balancing customer perceptions and expectations.* New York: Free Press.

Zey, M. (1985). Mentor programs: Making the right moves. *Personnel Journal, 64*(2), 53-57.

Zey, M.G. (1984). *The mentor connection.* Homewood, IL: Dow Jones-Irwin.

Index

Tables are denoted by an italicized t following the page number; figures by an italicized f.

facets of 233, 235*t*
and organizational commitment 258-259
theories of 231-235
among volunteers 237*t*
job simplification 116
job specification 138
job-specific task performance 184-185, 189*t*
job termination 147
Johns, G. 149
Jonsson, D.S. 216, 217, 219
Journal of Sport Management 38
Jurkus, A.F. 34-35
justice. *See also* organizational justice
among athletic teams 220, 221*f*
in community recreation 221-222
distributive 214, 215-222
interactional 214, 223, 224*f*
procedural 214, 222-223, 224*f*
retributive 219-220

K
Kabanoff, B. 216, 236
Kanter, R.M. 156
Katz, D. 161
Katz, R.L. 167
Keeley, M. 93
Kerr, S. 171, 270
Killian, R.A. 13
Klemp, G.O., Jr. 57-59
Knight, P.A. 116, 137, 258
Knight Foundation 1991 239
Knoke, D. 19, 23, 266
knowledge, explosion of 34
Koehler, L.S. 242
Korman, A.K. 57
Kouri, M.K. 140, 149
Kram, K.E. 154, 155, 156
Kuga, D.J. 120, 124, 126-127, 150

L
labor unions 217
Landy, F.J. 107
late career stage 150-151
Lawler, E.E., III 95-100, 106-107, 164, 207-208, 210, 232-233, 271
Lawrence, P.R. 121
Lawson, H.A. 34
leader behavior
actual 167
descriptions of 160-161
dimensions of, in sports 163*t*
preferred 165-167
required 164-165
leadership
appraisal of 185
contingency model of 168-169

and decision making 174-176
definitions of 160
modified multidimensional model of 173*f*
multidimensional model of 161, 163*f*, 164-167, 169-170
and values 91
leadership style 168
Lefton, L.A. 66
Legge, K. 14
leisure satisfaction 238-239
leisure time 93
Lengnick-Hall, C.A. 44
Leventhal, G.S. 223
Levinson, D.J. 154, 156
Levitt, T. 16
Lewin, K. 67
Li, M. 245
life cycle benefits 202
life satisfaction 110
limb movement speed 61*t*
litigatory society 214
Locke, E.A. 230, 233
locus of control 74, 75*t*
Lofquist, L.H. 230
Lombardi, Vince 175
London, M. 150
lone wolves 259
Longenecker, C.O. 196
Lopiano, Donna 173, 174
Lorsch, J.W. 119, 167
love, and social needs 101
Lovelock, C.H. 2
loyalty. *See* commitment
lump-sum payments 210
Luthans, F. 66

M
Machiavelli, Niccolò 75-76
Machiavellianism 75-76
MacKenzie, S.B. 186, 187, 188
MacLean, J.C. 190-191
Maddi, S.R. 66
Maehr, M.L. 96, 107-110
management
appraisal of 185
as profession 34-35
skills for 57-59
management by objectives 190
management values 91
managerial competence career anchor 151*t*
managerial competencies 57*t*, 58*t*
managerial motivation, theory of 170
managerial potential 78
Managerial Practices Survey 162*t*
Managing for the Future (Drucker, 1992) 160

Mandela, Nelson 173
manual dexterity 61*t*
Margulies, N. 4-5
market, defined 43-44
market share 227
Martin, C.L. 146
Maslow, A.H. 89, 95, 96, 100, 101-102
Mason, D.H. 16
mass media, influence of 93
Mathieu, J.E. 250, 256, 257
Mausner, B. 102, 107
McClelland, D. 53
McClelland, D.C. 57-59, 166, 167, 170, 233
McCrae, R.R. 69
McFarlin, D.B. 230, 232
McGee, G.W. 250
McKinley, J.C. 69
McPherson, B.D. 18
McPherson, J.M. 22
meaningfulness, as task attribute 122-123
mechanistic job design 128*t*, 129
Meglino, B.M. 90, 91
Meindl, J.R. 219
member benefit organizations 20
member characteristics
and preferred behavior 166-167
and required behavior 165
member perspective 268
membership-based rewards 203
mentoring
about 153-154
functions of 154, 155*t*
intervening variables 156-157
organizational model 154*f*
outcomes of 154
mentor-protégé compatibility 156
merit performance appraisal 192
Merlton, R.K. 39
mesomorphy 68*t*
Meyer, J.P. 249, 250, 251-252, 254, 256, 258
Michigan, University of 160-161
Microsoft 228
Miller, H.B. 25
Mills, P.K. 2, 4-5, 9, 30
mimic professions 33-34
Minnesota, University of 233
Minnesota Job Description Questionnaire 241-242, 244
Minnesota model of job satisfaction 233, 234*t*, 238
Minnesota Multiphasic Personality Inventory 69
Mischel, W. 66, 67
Miskel, C.G. 96
Mondy, R.W. 147

About the Author

Packianathan Chelladurai is a professor in the School of Physical Activity and Educational Services at The Ohio State University. Widely recognized as a leader in the field of sport management, Chelladurai has taught human resource management in sport and recreation for the past 25 years, in both Canada and the U.S. He is the author of three books, including *Sport Management: Macro Perspectives*, which was the first book to apply organizational theory to sport management. He has also written more than 60 journal articles and 14 book chapters. His writings on leadership and decision making are particularly well known; perhaps best known is his Leadership Scale for Sports (LSS), which has been translated into more than 10 languages. In 1991 he served as editor of the *Journal of Sport Management*. He is a member of the North American Society for Sport Management (NASSM); the European Association of Sport Management; the American Alliance for Health, Physical Education, Recreation and Dance; and the Academy of Management.

Chelladurai received an MASc and a PhD in management science from the University of Waterloo. In 1990 the American Academy of Kinesiology and Physical Education elected him as a Corresponding Fellow of the Academy. In 1991 he was the first recipient of NASSM's prestigious Earle F. Zeigler Award. Chelladurai's favorite leisure activities include playing tennis and playing bridge.

Related Books from Human Kinetics

Recreational Sport Management
(Third Edition)
Richard F. Mull, MS, Kathryn G. Bayless, MS, Craig M. Ross, ReD, and Lynn M. Jamieson, ReD
1997 • Hardback • 344 pp • Item BMUL0808
ISBN 0-87322-808-1 • $38.00 ($56.95 Canadian)

Written from a programmer's point of view, this classic text explains how to initiate, develop, and maintain an effective recreational sports program in a variety of settings.

Effective Leadership in Adventure Programming
Simon Priest, PhD, and Michael A. Gass, PhD
1997 • Hardback • 336 pp • Item BPRI0637
ISBN 0-87322-637-2 • $38.00 ($56.95 Canadian)

Authored by two of the world's leading authorities in the field of adventure programming, this comprehensive text goes beyond the technical skills of outdoor leadership to address facilitation skills and metaskills.

Contemporary Sport Management
Janet B. Parks, DA, Beverly R.K. Zanger, MEd, and Jerome Quarterman, PhD, Editors
1998 • Hardback • 360 pp • Item BPAR0836
ISBN 0-87322-836-7 • $45.00 ($67.50 Canadian)

Incorporating the perspectives of 26 contributors, this popular text provides a comprehensive introduction to the sport management field.

Understanding Sport Organizations
The Application of Organization Theory
Trevor Slack, PhD
1997 • Hardback • 360 pp • Item BSLA0948
ISBN 0-87322-948-7 • $38.00 ($56.95 Canadian)

Weaving together the research, ideas, and real-life examples that shape organization studies, this in-depth text examines the structures and processes of sport organizations.

Sport Marketing
Bernard J. Mullin, PhD, Stephen Hardy, PhD, and William A. Sutton, EdD
1993 • Hardback • 312 pp • Item BMUL0449
ISBN 0-87322-449-3 • $44.00 ($65.95 Canadian)

This popular text covers the basic principles of this emerging discipline and provides a balance of theoretical models and case studies from today's world of sport.

To request more information or to order, U.S. customers call 1-800-747-4457, e-mail us at humank@hkusa.com, or visit our Web site at www.humankinetics.com. Persons outside the U.S. can contact us via our Web site or use the appropriate telephone number, postal address, or e-mail address shown in the front of this book.

 HUMAN KINETICS
The Information Leader in Physical Activity